SSSP

Springer
Series in
Social
Psychology

SSSP

Public Self
and
Private Self

Edited by
Roy F. Baumeister

Springer-Verlag New York Berlin Heidelberg
London Paris Tokyo

Roy F. Baumeister
Department of Psychology
Case Western Reserve University
Cleveland, Ohio 44106
U.S.A.

With 4 Figures

Library of Congress Cataloging in Publication Data
Public self and private self.
  (Springer series in social psychology)
  Bibliography: p.
  Includes index.
  1. Self-presentation. 2. Self. I. Baumeister,
Roy F. II. Series.
BF697.5.S44P82   1986   155.2   86-1905

Typeset by Publishers Service, Bozeman, Montana.
Printed and bound by R.R. Donnelley & Sons, Harrisonburg, Virginia.
Printed in the United States of America.

9 8 7 6 5 4 3 2 1

ISBN 0-387-96303-0 Springer-Verlag New York Berlin Heidelberg
ISBN 3-540-96303-0 Springer-Verlag Berlin Heidelberg New York

Preface

Psychology has worked hard to explore the inner self. Modern psychology was born in Wundt's laboratory and Freud's consulting room, where the inner self was pressed to reveal some of its secrets. Freud, in particular, devoted most of his life to exploring the hidden recesses inside the self—hidden even from the conscious mind, he said. From Freud's work right down to the latest journal article on self-schemata or self-esteem, psychologists have continued to tell us about the inner self.

More recently, psychology has turned some of its attention to the outer self, that is, the self that is seen and known by other people. Various psychologists have studied how the outer self is formed (impression formation), how people control their outer selves (impression management), and so forth.

But how is the outer self related to the inner self?

There is an easy answer, but it is wrong. The easy answer is that the outer self is mostly the same as the inner self. Put another way, it is that people reveal their true selves to others in a honest and straightforward fashion, and that others accurately perceive the individual as he or she really is. Sometimes it works out that way, but often it does not. The issue is far too complex for the easy answer.

The terms "inner self" and "outer self" have several misleading meanings. They seem to imply that the psyche is layered like an onion, and that all visible action goes with the outer self while the inner self can never be glimpsed in action. Both implications are probably quite wrong. As a result, the inner–outer metaphor has fallen into disuse among most psychologists interested in the self. For this book, the terms "public self" and "private self" were preferred. The public self is the self that is manifested in the presence of others, that is formed when other people attribute traits and qualities to the individual, and that is communicated to other people in the process of self-presentation. The private self is the way the person understands himself or herself and is the way the person really is—even if other people fail to recognize it.

So: How is the public self related to the private self?

For this book I have invited leading theorists and researchers to answer that question. I told them we needed some new answers, some new ideas. Their responses fill this book. Obviously, what's "new" is defined partly on the basis of what's "old," so let me take a moment here at the start to review what is old. There are two main sets of old ideas that concern us. This book is an attempt to break out of the tiresome stalemate of these two sets.

The first set of old ideas is psychology's effort to interpret everything in terms of inner processes, motivations, and goals, oblivious to the communicative aspect of the self. This set of ideas simply ignores self-presentation. For example, consider someone's reaction to a humiliating failure in front of three other people. A psychologist using this set of ideas would interpret the reaction in terms of the threat to the individual's self-esteem. The fact that the presence of the three others probably made a huge difference would not be considered. For another example, consider someone who denies that a persuasive magazine essay has changed his opinion. This denial would simply be interpreted as a failure of persuasion—ignoring the possibility that the person was trying to avoid *seeming* like a gullible, easily swayed person.

The second set of old ideas comprises most of the history of research on self-presentation. In it, people's behavior was seen as often guided by attempts to make a good impression on whoever happened to be there. Researchers in this tradition challenged the work done using the first set of ideas. They would choose some pattern of behavior that had been shown and discussed in terms of inner processes and motivations and show that that behavior changed or disappeared depending on whether the subject was alone or with other people. The implication was that if behavior changed depending on the presence or absence of others, then it was shaped by the desire to impress the others. This sort of result was obtained over and over.

Needless to say, these research findings of differences between private (alone) and public (with others) behavior were not universally popular. Many psychologists had spent their lives and staked their careers on theories about inner motives. They were less than delighted to be told that their theories were egregiously mistaken, that they had overlooked a (or even *the*) main cause. They could not dismiss self-presentation, but they did not have to like it. Self-presentation grew up as an all-purpose alternative explanation for many other theories. It was greeted and treated like a rude bastard relative at a family gathering.

Self-presentation was slow to develop its own body of theory, which is why this book is appearing in 1986 rather than 1976 or 1966. One reason for this slowness is that self-presentation researchers launched their careers by taking on other people's theories, such as dissonance (Tedeschi, Schlenker, & Bonoma, 1971), defensive attributions (Weary Bradley, 1978), self-esteem (Baumeister & Jones, 1978), or reactance (Baer, Hinkle, Smith, & Fenton, 1980). Self-presentation researchers were too busy attacking other theories to erect one of their own. Self-presentation was the perennial challenger, rarely or never the codified theory in its own right. But I think there are three other reasons for the slow development of self-presentation theory.

One reason concerns the conceptual organization of social psychology. Social psychology is a field dominated by dependent variables. Ask a social psychologist what he or she studies, and the answer will tend to be a dependent variable, such as attitude change, aggression, attraction, helping, impression formation, and so forth. Self-presentation, however, is usually studied as an independent variable, as a comparison between public and private situations. Many people were surprised when in 1982 I published a review of research on self-presentation. They hadn't realized that there was so much. One reason for that is that social psychologists group things according to dependent variables, but my review was based on an independent variable. Thus, the area of self-presentation is out of step with the way social psychologists tend to think. Like those few other research areas that are defined by an independent variable (e.g., self-awareness), it has tended to remain outside the mainstream.

A second reason for the slow development of self-presentation theory concerns its status in personality research. Unlike social psychology, personality tends to feature independent variables. A personality researcher will describe his or her work in terms of independent variables such as self-esteem, locus of control, depression, and self-monitoring. Self-presentation might have fit in well in personality, and indeed some of the chapters in this book explore self-presentation in relation to personality. But this has been slow to happen due to the unfortunate way self-presentation got started. The first major book on self-presentation, at least in the modern period, was E. Goffman's *The Presentation of Self in Everyday Life* (1959). Goffman was a sociologist, and like most sociologists he was dubious and skeptical of personality. In Goffman's world, people were actors who might change masks but could never really remove them. The idea of self-presentation became associated with Goffman, and the antipathy between his ideas and personality theory precluded any substantial personality-oriented work in self-presentation.

The third reason for the slow development of self-presentation theory is that it is out of step with the current academic fashions. There are two main aspects to human behavior, motivation and cognition. Fashions in psychological theory have shifted emphasis between these two. In the 1940s, for example, motivation was dominant. Drive theory attempted to synthesize psychoanalytic theory and animal research, both of which were heavily motivational. Only the "New Look" in perception provided some exciting ideas regarding human cognition. In the past decade, however, the pendulum has swung far the other way. Social psychology and even personality are full of cognitive processes and models, while motivation is downplayed. Self-presentation, however, is basically a neo-drive theory, emphasizing motivation over cognition. The reason people behave differently in public than in private is they *care* about how others regard them: They are motivated to make a good impression. This motivational basis is not easily disguised by focusing on their cognitive processes. For example, one might look at what thoughts the self-presenter wants the other person to think about him or her, but these are rarely surprising. The self-presenter wants others to think him competent, likable, and perhaps virtuous. In short, self-presentation is a motivational construct in a field that is dominated by cognitive constructs. In this respect, too, it is out of step.

Once again, then: How is the public self related to the private self?

The field is overdue for some good answers to this question. There are the old, easy answers, and there is ample evidence that those answers are inadequate.

Research has now established (to nearly everyone's satisfaction, I presume) that there is a difference between purely inner processes and self-presentational motives. The public self is no longer mistaken for the private self, but, in severing the old, false links between public self and private self, researchers have begun to act as if the two selves are completely unrelated. We have divested ourselves of many wrong ideas about how public self and private self are related, and so we are ready to examine that relationship with a newly open mind. To work, then . . .

References

Baer, R., Hinkle, S., Smith, K., & Fenton, M. (1980). Reactance as a function of actual versus projected autonomy. *Journal of Personality and Social Psychology, 38*, 416–422.

Baumeister, R. F. (1982). A self-presentational view of social phenomena. *Psychological Bulletin, 91*, 3–26.

Baumeister, R. F., & Jones, E. E. (1978). When self-presentation is constrained by the target's knowledge: Consistency and compensation. *Journal of Personality and Social Psychology, 36*, 608–618.

Goffman, E. (1959). *The presentation of self in everyday life.* Garden City, NY: Doubleday, Anchor Books.

Tedeschi, J. T., Schlenker, B. R., & Bonoma, T. V. (1971). Cognitive dissonance: Private ratiocination or public spectacle? *American Psychologist, 26*, 685–695.

Weary Bradley, G. (1978). Self-serving biases in the attribution process: A re-examination of the fact or fiction question. *Journal of Personality and Social Psychology, 36*, 56–71.

Contents

Contributors

Robert M. Arkin, Department of Psychology, University of Missouri-Columbia, Columbia, Missouri 65211, U.S.A.

Roy F. Baumeister, Department of Psychology, Case Western Reserve University, Cleveland, Ohio 44106, U.S.A.

Ann H. Baumgardner, Department of Psychology, Virginia Polytechnic Institute and State University, Blacksburg, Virginia 24061, U.S.A.

Stephen R. Briggs, Department of Psychology, University of Tulsa, Tulsa, Oklahoma 74104, U.S.A.

Peter M. Gollwitzer, Max-Planck-Institut für Psychologische Forschung, 8000 München 40, West Germany.

Jeff Greenberg, Department of Psychology, University of Arizona, Tucson, Arizona 85721, U.S.A.

Martha G. Hill, Department of Psychology, Ohio State University, Columbus, Ohio 43210, U.S.A.

Robert Hogan, Department of Psychology, University of Tulsa, Tulsa, Oklahoma 74104, U.S.A.

Janet Moore, Department of Psychology, University of Georgia, Athens, Georgia 30602, U.S.A.

Tom Pyszczynski, Department of Psychology, University of North Carolina, Chapel Hill, North Carolina 27514, U.S.A.

Frederick T. Rhodewalt, Department of Psychology, University of Utah, Salt Lake City, Utah 84112, U.S.A.

Barry R. Schlenker, Department of Psychology, University of Florida, Gainesville, Florida 32601, U.S.A.

Stephanie H. Smith, Department of Psychology, Indiana University Northwest, Gary, Indiana 46408, U.S.A.

Sheldon Solomon, Department of Psychology, Skidmore College, Saratoga Springs, New York 12866, U.S.A.

James T. Tedeschi, Department of Psychology, State University of New York at Albany, Albany, New York 12222, U.S.A.

Abraham Tesser, Department of Psychology, University of Georgia, Athens, Georgia 30602, U.S.A.

Dianne M. Tice, Department of Psychology, Princeton University, Princeton, New Jersey 08544, U.S.A.

Gifford Weary, Department of Psychology, Ohio State University, Columbus, Ohio 43210, U.S.A.

George I. Whitehead, III, Department of Psychology, Salisbury State University, Salisbury, Maryland 21801, U.S.A.

Joan Williams, Department of Psychology, Ohio State University, Columbus, Ohio 43210, U.S.A.

Chapter 1
Private and Public Experiences and the Self

James T. Tedeschi

A concern about the relationship of private and public events has been a central one for social psychology. One of the earliest experiments in social psychology affirmed that the performance of children was different when an audience was present than when they were alone (Triplett, 1897). The entire problem of social conformity revolves around an assumed discrepancy between what people "really" believe or want to do and what they say they believe or what they actually do when they experience pressure from others to make judgments, express attitudes, or engage in behaviors that are opposed to such private preferences. Indeed, a distinction between what is said and done in public and what is inside the individual's mind (and hence private) has been central to the interpretation of many other phenomena in social psychology, including social facilitation, group polarization effects, social conformity, anticipatory attitude change, attitude change in the forced compliance situation, psychological reactance, and trangression-compliance.

A distinction between what is external and open to observation and that which is private and available only to self-observation has also been a dominating concern for personality theory. According to Hogan and Cheek (1982), such a concern is revealed by notions of introversion and extraversion, inner- and other-direction, internal and external control orientation, and private and public self-consciousness.

What seems to be missing from the theoretical literature is a careful examination of the terms "public" and "private." These terms are almost never explicated. Rather, it is assumed that the vernacular, everyday meanings will suffice for scientific purposes. One purpose of this chapter is to carefully examine the concepts of private and public.

In the past decade there has been a great resurgence of interest, theory, and research on the topic of the "self." Ever since William James provided the classic view of the self, it has been generally accepted that there are public and private aspects to the self. Consideration of the dynamics between the public and private selves has led to interesting new theories, such as the socioanalytic development of personality (Hogan, 1982), social identity (Schlenker, 1982), self-verification

(Swann, 1984), self-consciousness and control (Carver & Scheier, 1985), and the self as audience for self-presentations (Greenwald & Breckler, 1985).

The above theories postulate that the self is formed, organized, and maintained in social interactions, and that in the mature individual the self takes on the function of controlling behavior. The relationship of public behavior to the development of the self, and the function of the private self as a controller of behavior are discussed here as separate aspects of the relationship between private and public realms of experience.

Public and Private Psychological Events: Definitions

Social scientists have given very different definitions to the concepts of "private" and "public." An understanding of these differences helps to clarify questions of interest to scientists who study the self. The definition of "private" prevalent among social psychologists refers to mental events in one person that are inherently unobservable by another person. The actor is viewed as having a choice of whether or not to reveal these private events to others, that is, to make them public. A related question is whether there are cognitive events that cannot be "observed" by the person within whom they occur (Nisbett & Wilson, 1977). Psychoanalysts have long held that most of mental life is unconscious (e.g., Freud, 1938).

While the tendency of social psychologists is to equate "private" with phenomenological experience, other social scientists have given quite a different meaning to the concept. A public/private distinction based on the status of agents is a major concern of political scientists. A person acting to enhance his or her own interests is said to be acting privately, but officials of public institutions, such as cities, states, or nations, are legally obligated to act in the interests of the people they represent.

Similarly, in economics the public/private dimension focuses on whose interests are served by financial decisions. A private business acts to benefit those who are financially tied to the enterprise, while a public institution focuses on services to members of the community. A somewhat different view is associated with ownership. Owners have a right to limit access to or use of their things. Such control over accessibility may be considered an aspect of privacy or private goods. In contrast, a public beach, for example, is a place that may be used by anyone.

The Greek word for private is *idios* and means "one's own" or "pertaining to oneself" (Moore, 1984, p. 82). *Demios* is the word for public and literally means "having to do with people." Among the aristocracy of ancient Greece it was expected that a citizen would fully participate in the affairs of the community, and hence privacy carried a negative connotation (e.g., "idiot" is an English word derived from *idios*).

A definition of "public" somewhat closer to the usage by social psychologists is that public behavior is open to the observations of anyone. Privacy entails the ability (or right) to control who can view one's behavior (Sennett, 1978). The stodgy private clubs of 18th-century London were agreeable to members because the members could choose to be surrounded by particular audiences. Intimate relationships may be considered private because the interactants choose to be with each other, but can exclude other people. Intimate others are given access to observations of behavior and information about the self that are not freely given to strangers or mere acquaintances. For example, in Western cultures the family is typically a backstage area where public performances can be discussed. These distinctions are consistent with the view of Confucius (1938), who identified public events with governmental affairs and considered privacy as referring to family life.

Benn and Gaus (1983) proposed three dimensions of publicness and privateness: agency, access, and interest. They noted that cultures vary considerably in what they choose to control access to and what behaviors constitute invasion or trespass. There are societies in which little privacy exists. For example, small face-to-face groups, such as those among the nomadic Siriono Indians of the rain forests of South America, provide almost no privacy for individuals (Moore, 1984). Aries (1962) claimed that in Europe before the 17th century no one was ever alone. Totalitarian governments deliberately reduce the amount of privacy among individuals so as to extend public control over conduct. One of the concerns of Libertarians nowadays is the ability of electronic surveillance techniques to intrude into our daily lives and hence reduce the degree of privacy people maintain.

Table 1-1 summarizes the meanings that have been given to public and private experiences. Most relevant for understanding the self are the dimensions of phenomenology-behavior and control or lack of control over access to information. Of particular importance for this paper is the linkage of access to information within intimate relationships. Intimate self-disclosures are clearly limited to a small number of others and access is not ordinarily given to those with whom relationships remain impersonal. Of course there are exceptions to the rule, as when a person reveals very intimate information to a total stranger in a bar or while sharing adjacent seats in a public form of transportation. It is instructive to examine some of the relationships, questions, and problems that result from adopting different definitions of public and private experiences and from distinguishing between intimate and impersonal relationships.

The Self as Object: The Impact of Public Behavior on Self-Theory

For a considerable period of the 20th century psychologists attempted to construct a science of behavior based on the evolutionary design of and/or the physical events surrounding organisms. Various approaches were taken, including S-R (stimulus-response), S-S, and R-R theories of behavior (Guthrie, 1952; Hull, 1952; Skinner, 1953). Unfortunately, it has become clear that human (and probably animal) behavior is too complex to be explained with such simple theories. An alternative strategy has been to develop theories of intentional systems, ascribing to the person values and beliefs that, in the context of some postulates about constraints, serve as a basis for predictions.

The perception that there is considerable continuity and organization of behavior over time has suggested to some theorists that there is a system of beliefs, referred

Table 1-1. Summary of the Various Uses of the Terms "Private" and "Public"

Private	Public
Phenomenological experience	Observable behavior
Acting only for self	Acting as agent for others
Actor controls access to information regarding self	Information about self not controlled by actor
Acting in the interest of a limited number of people	Acting in the interest of the community

to as the self, that actively appropriates experiences and guides the behavior of the individual. Thus, the self has been given ontological status as an active agent as well as an object of experience, guiding the behavior of the individual.

A major focus of research on the self has been on the development of self-conceptions. It has been suggested that beliefs about the self are organized into a self-theory, which may then filter information, store information, motivate behavior, and affect decisions the person makes (see Epstein, 1973; Schlenker, 1982). Self-theories do not have the logical consistency of scientific theories and they are evaluated by nonsystematic methods; hence, self-schemata are only loosely referred to as theories. However, the self largely consists of a person's explanations of his or her own behaviors. Such explanations are themselves anticipatory of the need to provide accounts to others in social interactions (Scott & Lyman, 1968). The development of a self-theory has occupied the attention of major theorists in social psychology throughout the 20th century (e.g., Cooley, 1902; Festinger, 1954; Mead, 1934).

Most of the theory and research on the development of the individual's theory of self has centered on processes of social comparison. A fundamental distinction implicitly made in this literature is between the private cognitions of the individual and his or her observable (public) behavior. Almost entirely ignored in scholarly work on the development of the individual's self-theory is the distinction between private behavior that occurs in intimate relationships and the kind of public behavior that occurs in impersonal relationships. It is ironic that sociologists (e.g., Sennett, 1978) consider the home and family as the epitome of private life, while social psychologists tend to view any behavior carried out in the presence of highly significant others as extremely public. One may ask whether the presence of intimate and impersonal audiences has differential effects on the development of self-theories. I next examine the role of self-presentation in the context of social comparison and in intimate and impersonal relationships.

Social Comparisons, Self-Presentations, and the Development of Self-Theory

It is not necessary to examine each and every theory of the self to focus on the relationship of private to public self (and vice versa). In the literature on the development of the self (Cooley, 1902; Festinger, 1954) it has been emphasized that self-conceptions are typically composed of inferences made through social comparisons and reflective appraisals (i.e., the social mirror). There is a feedback loop cycling from one's own behavior to observations by others, to perceptions by others, to perceptions by oneself of the perceptions of others, to an inference about oneself. In other words, public behavior has consequences for one's private concept of self. In this analysis "private" refers to the individual's phenomenological experience, to which no one else has direct access, and "public" refers to the behaviors that others observe whether or not the individual is aware of being observed. Actors may be affected by what others observe only in terms of how these others respond to them. In sum, the individual must make attributions about the kinds of attributions others are making about him or her.

Of course there is a good deal of room for error in so amorphous an intellectual task as reflective appraisals. Self-presentations insofar as they are deliberate and planned behaviors may have been designed to project or bolster a particular identity. Because norms make it impolite and disruptive to reject the identities put forth by actors, audiences are likely to affirm or at least publicly accept the identities presented at face value even though privately they do not accept them. It is for this reason that reflective appraisals may not always mirror the impressions that others have of the actor (Felson, 1981).

There has been considerable acceptance of the notion that self-presentations, whether forthcoming and sincere or offered as trial balloons or outright deceptions, can significantly affect the self-theory of an actor. Whatever else the self is, it is developed in the context of relationships with others during which self-presentational behavior is performed. Indeed, if one removed the identities of the individual as a parent, sibling, offspring, productive worker, and so on, it is doubtful there would be anything left to refer to as the self. Other aspects of the self, such as competence, moral qualities, and character traits, also have meaning only in the context of social interactions.

Intimate and Impersonal Relationships and the Development of Self-Theory

Historical accounts clearly indicate that self-theories naively constructed by people depend upon cultural elements (Lyons, 1978). Before the development of nation-states and industrialization, there was little sense in a person having an inner or private self that was separate from and governed an external or public self. Religion dominated the lives of people, and an all-seeing, omniscient God was an inescapable audience of all thoughts, desires, and actions.

During the Enlightenment people were considered to have natural character. Although there was variability of behavior, an inner character was a common thread of all humanity. Character was revealed in certain critical situations, but it was not something that could be controlled, learned, or changed. As the conditions of life changed, and particularly as a result of the development of large cities, people increasingly came into contact with strangers and immediate impressions became important indicators of what others were like. With the growing concern for controlling the impressions one projected to others, self-presentations became self-conscious.[1] However, because impressions signified personality, self-observations of behavior change led to change in one's theory of self. As Sennett (1978, p. 153) stated, "appearances made in the world are not veils but guides to the authentic self of the wearer." The person is to a large degree a prisoner of momentary appearances, and each mask is a face, not a disguise.

People began to view their impersonal relationships, consisting of acquaintances and strangers, as somehow detached from their true selves, which were revealed in intimate relationships. Behavior in public was viewed as more controlled by circumstances than by the needs and values of the self. Acting at a distance from the self required a control over emotions. Whereas it had been characteristic of European audiences in the 17th century to become emotionally involved in the theater, crying openly or giving boisterous demonstrations of approval and disapproval, modern audiences are taught to control their emotions in public. Clint Eastwood (and in an earlier time Gary Cooper) is an ideal representation of a person who perfectly controls his or her emotions in public.

Some theories of emotion imply that it is not easy to veil one's emotions. The Darwinian theory of emotions focused on the organizations of muscles, organs, and reactions that were given emotional labels (Darwin, 1872). Similarly, a facial theory of emotions (Ekman & Friesen, 1975) postulated that the distribution of muscle responses in the face provide the basis for identifying specific emotions. Hence, it is not the emotion that produces the facial expression, but rather the other way around. These evolutionary theories of emotion explicitly postulate that physiological factors automatically give rise to various emotional experiences. Emotional expression precedes conscious experience. As a consequence, when it comes to emotions, appearance is reality.

Goffman (1961) developed the notion of role distance to describe one tactic actors use in public to maintain privacy in the sense of controlling information about the self. People often go to great lengths to make it clear that their behavior is strictly role-related, obligatory, and not representative of what they would choose to do. Thus, a parent accompanying a child at an amusement park may, on meeting a friend, indicate that he or she is there in the role of parent and not because of a frivolous desire to ride the roller coaster.

Sincerity and Authenticity

In a thoughtful analysis of literature as a struggle to understand the self and the self's relationship with others, Trilling (1973) distinguished between sincerity and authenticity. The Latin word *sincerus* means "clean," "sound," or "pure." In Shakespeare's time sincere meant the absence of feigning or pretence. Iago said "I am not

---

[1]Self-presentational behavior has probably always been a factor in social interactions. However, it is likely that people in tribal and traditional agricultural societies associated self-presentations with rituals and status hierarchies rather than with personality or motivation. The importance of self-presentation in everyday life has grown with the individuation of people in modern developed societies.

what I am," and of course this was the era of Machiavelli. In the 17th century in Europe people for the first time imagined themselves in more than one role and as looking at their own personalities from outside themselves. The feeling of inner and outer selves gave birth to the impulse to reveal oneself to others, and to do so in a believable manner. Sincerity refers to the exposure in public of what one feels privately. Thus, in self-portraits and autobiography great artists engaged in psychic strip teases for newly sensed audiences.

"Sincerity," incorporating notions of credibility, trustworthiness, and truthfulness, refers to the relationship between words, intentions, and deeds. Communication depends upon a norm of sincerity. Grice's (1969) influential theory of meaning asserts that utterances have meaning because a speaker intends that a listener respond in a particular way and because the listener recognizes what the speaker intends. If communications were not basically trustworthy, they would fail in their purpose of transmitting meanings from one person to another; the intentions of the speaker would not be recognized by the listener. Occasional lies and mistakes can be tolerated without causing serious communication problems, but if everyone constantly engaged in trying to deceive everyone else, no one would be able to understand what anyone else meant by any remark. Thus, self-presentations in the form of linguistic communications are usually faithful to the private (cognitive or experiential) events they represent.

The term "authenticity" is used in museums for tests of art objects by experts to ascertain whether they are what they appear to be and hence worth the admiration or price we give to them. In reference to a person we might ask whether he or she is what he or she appears to be. This is not a question of sincerity, because the actor may not be feigning an identity but may be suffering a delusion, such a belief that he is Napoleon. For Heidegger (1962) and Sartre (1957) a key element in authenticity was freedom of action. Mindless behavior consisting of habits or obedience to social rules out of fear and anxiety over how others would react is interpreted as neither free or responsible. An authentic person is one who takes responsibility for freely chosen actions that represent some internal standards—of self, potentialities, or principles. The importance of authenticity in modern life was noted by Oscar Wilde (1969) when he reminded us that the old maxim "know thyself" has been changed in the modern world to "be thyself."

The Role of Perceived Freedom and Emotions
in Development of Self-theories

Among the reasons for the relative importance of intimate as compared to impersonal relationships in the development of a self-concept are perceived freedom and emotional arousal. Perceived freedom, as Bem (1972) alerted us, is a necessary condition for self-attributions. A person can hardly appropriate as part of his or her self an action that is perceived as coerced by external circumstances. Without emotional arousal, the individual would not perceive actions as significant for self-definition or evaluation, an insight incorporated in attribution theory by the notion of hedonic relevance (Jones & Davis, 1965).

It is suggested here that the arousal of emotions during public self-presentations leads to a self-attribution that the identity presented was authentic. Cooley (1902) suggested that the emotions of fear, pride, and shame were essential in the development of the self. Pride might be experienced when an audience indicates acceptance of a preferred and positive identity and shame might be experienced if it is believed an audience perceives one in a negative way. As Sennett (1978) has said, "dramatic displays of feeling become signals to others that you are 'for real', and also by whipping you up to fever pitch, convince you yourself that you are 'for real' " (p. 309).

Displays of emotion in public are perceived as lapses in self-control and hence as revealing the "true" personality, values, or self of the individual. The normative structure of intimate relationships allows, encourages, and even requires expressions of emotions. Intimacy assumes authenticity, and authentic self-presentations are incorporated into the actor's theory of self. A person is more likely to introject self-presentational behaviors as part of a theory of the self when they occur in the context of intimate relationships or when emotional displays are made in public. Rosenberg (1979) reported data showing that young children's self-concepts are largely dependent upon their parents' views of them. For adolescents the "truth" about the self is most strongly affected by best friends.

Emotional displays in impersonal relationships are typically confined to anger or a congenial interpersonal style. Displays of other emotions may, however, be required as part of a person's work role. Hochschild (1983) referred to the requirement for expressive behavior as "emotional labor." She found that airline flight attendants and bill collectors attempted to withdraw from the work role, were alienated from their own emotions, or took on insincere interpersonal styles. Hochschild attributed these reactions by people in the two work roles studied to the requirement to perform emotional labor.

Expressing emotions to others may induce a corresponding feeling state in the actor. Baumeister and Tice (1986) have reviewed research indicating that at least some of the time subjective feelings are derivative from the expressive aspects of emotions. Feelings are amplified by emotional expression and dampened when expression is inhibited (Lanzetta, Cartwright-Smith, & Kleck, 1976; Lanzetta & Orr, 1980). Laird and his associates asked subjects to arrange facial muscle groups until happy or angry expressions were achieved (e.g., Laird, 1974; Laird, Wagener, & Szegda, 1982). Such subjects rated themselves as happier or angrier than control subjects.

If these results can be generalized to the relation of self-presentations to self-theories, it might be argued that insincere self-presentations involving emotional expressions might be incorporated into self-theory, since the individual cannot stave off the residue of actual feeling such expressions induce. Confirmation of this hypothesis would constitute indirect evidence that emotions play an important role in the social comparison process.

As an aside it is interesting to note the possibility that the so-called impostor effect may be related to problems of authenticity in impersonal relationships. People who are successful in making money in American society sometimes feel that they have no special abilities, that their fortunate circumstances are due to hard work and luck, and that others will discover they are impostors (i.e., inauthentic). Such people may lack intense intimate relationships because of working very hard, and hence most of their feedback about themselves comes from impersonal relationships. On the other hand, intimate others often do not observe the behaviors that lead to success and hence cannot provide the appraisals affirming special abilities or talent. The success in earning money is therefore divorced from the intimate relationships that provide the source of information used to develop a self-theory. The trappings of success are disconnected from the "true" self, and one way to interpret the success is as a function of luck and hard work.

Self-Presentation and Self-Deception

When do self-presentations get incorporated into the individual's self-theory in the absence of feedback from audiences? Frequently the actor is not certain about performances and may ask others "How did I do?" When such feedback is not available the individual must attempt to evaluate performances in light of past experience. Even if feedback from others is available, the actor may reject it because of conclusions reached through self-analysis. Schlenker (1980) suggested that an insincere self-presentation might be introjected as part of the actor's self-theory if the actor believes in retrospect that he or she had been sincere or had not been lying. Development of the self is in part, therefore, a function of self-deception.

While the idea of self-deception is an intriguing one, there is no compelling empirical demonstration for such a process. Gur and Sackheim (1979) attempted to develop a method for testing the three basic components of self-deception: (a) a conscious belief (X), (b) an unconscious counterbelief (not-X), and (c) some motivational state keeping the counterbelief in the unconscious (see Gergen, 1985). None of these three components is directly observable and hence it is difficult to develop a methodology that allows for strong inferences to them. It should not be surprising, therefore, that the methodology used by Gur and Sackheim has been shown to be inadequate (Douglas & Gibbins, 1983).

The metatheoretical problems associated with a postulated process of self-deception are formidable. Martin (1985) summarized a number of paradoxes that scholars have associated with the concept of self-deception. For example, the idea of deceiving oneself implies a duplicitous actor and a deceived audience. The mitosis of the self into two produces an undesirable dualism. To avoid a dualism and the logical problem of believing both X and not-X at the same time, there is a need to invent the unconscious, a place where ideas can be held apart from those contained in consciousness. So, in place of dividing the self, we divide consciousness, bringing on ontological questions too complex to review here (see Martin, 1985).

Self-Presentation to Self as Audience

Social psychological theories that view the self as a more or less integrated but naive theory run into conceptual difficulty in converting the structural aspects of the self into an agent of behavior. There is an implication of additional processes between the self-theory and subsequent behavior (Gergen, 1984). These additional processes tend to include a decision-making mechanism and a motive system (i.e., need for positive self-esteem). It is a small theoretical step to make the further assertion that the self is an audience for one's own behavior that can be pleased or dissatisfied by performances just as can an outer audience (Greenwald & Breckler, 1985; Schlenker, 1985). Unfortunately, such formulations seem to introduce a homunculus as the ghost in the machine. If the self is a schema or theory, then it cannot also be a little person inside watching the performances of the public person. This is not to say that people do not engage in rehearsals. Internalized reference groups may be imagined and rehearsals may be carried out *as if* they were present. However, performances are never for the sole purpose of satisfying or deceiving oneself.

Theories are not audiences and it does not make much sense to act in order to please a theory. It is instructive to consider the differences between a person and others as audiences. Both the person and others are in a position to observe the person's behavior, but only the person is privy to his or her private cognitions. On the other hand, a person is not directly able to observe the perceptions and inferences others make from the behavior that is observed.

The person is typically in the position of trying to influence others—to gain their liking, respect, acquiescence, or attitude change. Often the person and the other have differing values, goals, priorities, and constraints. While the person may be said to engage in self-persuasion (Burnstein & Vinokur, 1975), the conflicts of interests that are endemic in interpersonal relations are absent.

Secret agendas, a desire to manipulate and deceive others, the goal of getting others to mediate reinforcements that otherwise would not be attainable, as well as possession of different perspectives, information, and values contribute to important differences between the observations and evaluations of one's own behavior and the attributions made by others. Only by working out the details of how self-presentational behaviors when performed in the absence of others (absolutely private) affect self-theory, and the functions such self-presentations serve, will it be possible to empirically evaluate any hypotheses. That is, the assertion that self-presentations are performed for the self as audience is not sufficiently detailed to constitute a testable theory. Whether the details can be provided in a way that can avoid the problems presented here remains to be seen.

Sex Roles, Public Behavior, and Self

Sex differences in American society may be attributable at least in part to time spent in intimate versus impersonal relationships. During the 20th century in Western societies that were in the process of industrialization men have forayed out in public both to earn income and for leisure, while women were more apt to remain at home or with intimate others. Thus, men learned to suppress their emotions, perhaps to the point that they stopped feeling much even in intimate relationships. On the other hand, women, taught to be nurturant and oriented toward family and friends rather than a career out in public, more easily expressed emotions. This analysis, given the assumption that emotions play an important role in the development of self-theories, would suggest that men would be less authentic than women and would have less secure theories of the self.

The available evidence indicates that females are more likely to seek psychological treatment and have poorer self-concepts than do men (Franks & Burtle, 1974). While this evidence might appear contrary to the above analysis of the effects of public and private behavior on self-differences in emotional expression and self-evaluations, it rather suggests that cultural change involving the movement of women from family-oriented lifestyles to career orientations has created a problem of adjustment more difficult than those experienced by men. Because of socialization practices many women find it difficult not to express their emotions in public, and may incorporate into their self-theories the reactions occurring in both intimate and impersonal relationships. Women then find that they are caught in a Catch-22 situation. If they express emotions in public, they are perceived as acting inappropriately (or, derisively, like women), but if they are dispassionate and unemotional, they are perceived as cold and ruthless. This double-bind situation creates interpersonal difficulties and low self-esteem.

Self as Agent: The Relationship of Private Cognitions to Public Behavior

Self as Information Processor

For the most part I have been discussing the relationships between behavior, audiences, and the actor's construction of a theory of self. Much of the current interest in the self is focused on the organization and/or processing of information. The self directs attention to, selectively interprets, and remembers information, tends to take credit for and remember successes but denies and forgets failures, and through a kind of cognitive conservatism assimilates and remembers more consistency and unity to behavior than actually occurs (Greenwald, 1980).

The information-processing effects attributed to the self must be carefully conceptualized so as not to fall into circular or reductio ad absurdum logic traps. Is it that "the self" processes the information or can we conceive of the self as no more than an organization of information? Epstein (1973) conceived of the self as a theory, and as long as we do not worry about "who" it is that has the theory, we may avoid a logical trap and evade constructing a homunculus.

Gergen (1984) suggested that the self as agent is placed by some theorists in the position of searching for, coding, and sorting incoming information. At the same time a structural view of the self is maintained in the form of schemata or naive theories. The self as agent is frequently viewed as procuring information in a manner that is consistent with positive self-schemata. The idea that a person performs for his or her self as audience extends the functioning of the information-processing self so that it also *acts* to produce information that enhances self-esteem. The self becomes a trinity—three-in-one and one-in-three—including actor, information processor, and object of schemata. Apart from the theoretical difficulties associated with such a view, it must be asked if there is any way to evaluate it empirically.

The empirical data obtained relating the self to information-processing biases do not strongly establish a filtering mechanism in the sense of selecting information that gets into the system. It is plausible to suggest that people first perceive information and then retrospectively reorganize (or integrate) it into a coherent theory of the self. Subsequent recall is affected by the reorganization of information (Loftus, 1974), but it is still to be established that the phenomenological experience of the self is an important cause for subsequent social behavior.

Most theorists conceive of the self as both an object and an agent. Williams James and George Herbert Mead both distinguished between I and a Me of experience. There is no doubt that people do form conceptions of themselves, and we have examined how public and private experiences affect people's naive theories of the self. Some social psychologists assign the self the functions of forming self-identities appropriate to various circumstances, setting goals, and guiding behavior (e.g., Schlenker, 1985).

The self is considered by many social psychologists as a master controller of much or all of human behavior. Evidence that people develop feelings of self-efficacy or self-control has not been convincingly shown to be causally necessary for explaining other social behaviors. After reviewing the available evidence on the self as a regulator of behavior, Wylie (1979) concluded that attempts to link global self-conceptions or self-regard to subsequent behavior have led to preponderantly null results. However, she believes that more specific (less global) conceptions of the self may be crucial for explaining behavior. At the present time the available evidence does not provide a compelling case for a conception of the self as an important mediating factor in directing or controlling behavior.

Public and Private Self-Consciousness and Control Theory

The literature on public and private self-consciousness might be taken as an example of the type of research advocated by Wylie. According to Carver and Scheier (1985), self-consciousness "refers simply to the disposition to be aware of the self" (p. 149). Public self-consciousness refers to awareness of a social self, an object to which others respond. Private self-consciousness is an awareness of an internal, covert, and secret self not available to the scrutiny of others.

An elaborate "control theory" has been developed to indicate how focusing an individual's attention on private or public self-consciousness or eliciting the relevant disposition is associated with self-regulation of behavior (Carver & Scheier, 1985). It is assumed in this theory that a person who is high in private self-consciousness and focused on his or her self (and who is low in public self-consciousness) would show little "concern regarding self-presentation to other persons . . . [but] when this focus is tempered by an awareness of public self-aspects, there may occur instead an effort to present or portray that private self to others" (p. 169).

The bifurcation of the self into two selves having semi-independent agendas, and capable presumably of coordinating their goals or being in conflict with one another, shows a willingness among some contemporary social psychologists to develop enormously complex theories with many layers of inference between inferred processes and empirical data. Apart from the empirical problem of developing ways of testing the theoretical processes at every level of inference, one wonders in the context of our earlier discussions whether the traits of private and public self-consciousness would lead people to behave the same way in both intimate and impersonal relationships. It might be the case, for example, that persons high in public self-consciousness can let their hair down in front of family and friends, but not outside the small circle of intimates. Or, people who score high in private self-consciousness (and low in public self-consciousness) may be more emphatic in expressing their motives or values to impersonal others than to intimates because the latter already have formed stable impressions and such self-presentations would not be very effective if "out of character."

A simple way to avoid the complexities of self-consciousness or control theories is to suggest that individuals give differential value to observable and public characteristics, such as body image, facial beauty, and clothing, and to intrapsychic or private factors, such as values or motives. Indeed, Cheek and Briggs (1982) found strong correlations between paper-and-pencil measures of private and public self-consciousness and ratings of importance of characteristics associated with them. Thus, the higher the scores of subjects in private self-consciousness the greater the importance they attributed to internal factors as aspects of their identities. Also, the greater the importance attributed to material and social aspects of identity the higher the scores of subjects on the paper-and-paper measure of public self-consciousness.

Carver and Scheier (1985) have argued that the correlational data obtained by Cheek and Briggs (1982) do not establish cause and effect, and hence cannot be interpreted as evidence against control theory. However, the simplicity of the self-identity view is a strong argument in its favor. A conservative approach to theorizing in social psychology would be to make inferences regarding cognitive or dispositional factors rather grudgingly—only when there appears to be no other way to explain a given data domain. There may be no need to make a complex theory with a dual theory of private and public selves to explain the available data. A self-identity theory seems to be a simple alternative formulation of a large number of studies that does not require a theory of the self as controller of behavior. While self-observation may lead to self-inferences about traits, values, and identities, these theories of the self may have little or no correspondence with the actual causes of behavior.

Self, Consciousness, and Behavior

Some theories that place the self in the role of master controller of human social behavior assume that the self is fully conscious, a phenomenological self. A linkage is assumed between retrospective development of a theory of the self, which an actor presumably could articulate to another person, however limited or complex the theory and behavior. This is why self-esteem scales simply ask people what they think of themselves. It is assumed that people develop explanations of their own behavior, and because of a postulated need to behave consistently these self-theories become a basis for subsequent actions.

Most theories of the self must struggle with the concept of consciousness (or awareness). Is it simply a mirror reflecting events (or cognitions) but without content of its own (Sartre, 1957), or is it a reservoir having connections with other states of consciousness as psychoanalytic theory proposed (Freud, 1938)? Is consciousness active and originative of experiences, or is it a passive, observational, contemplative, and introspective faculty of the mind? Surely not all consciousness, whatever it is, consists of the self, but some theories of the self imply that the self is entirely conscious (e.g., Carver & Scheier, 1985).[2] Speculative questions like these bring out some of the ambiguities, metaphysical characteristics, and speculative aspects of "scientific" theories of self.

In the philosophy of action a distinction has been made between *a* reason and *the* reason (Davidson, 1963). Reasons people offer for their conduct, even when given sincerely, do not necessarily represent the actual justifications for their behavior. There is little basis for believing that people are sufficiently aware of the causes of their own behavior to provide accurate explanations to psychologists. If self-theories are for the most part constituted of explanations for our behavior, they are naive theories of psychology. Because such theories are not seriously tested under controlled conditions by their holders, they are more like lawyers' briefs than scientific theories. That is why they show strong biases in information processing. Prior information affects perceptions of subsequent information, not only in theories of the self, but in theories of almost anything else (Kuhn, 1962).

Self-theories depend for whatever predictive and explanatory power they claim to have on the content of what a person believes about his or her self. Since a person's view of his or her self depends upon cultural factors, it would follow logically that any social psychology that is based on a theory of the self would be mostly historical and not a transcultural and transhistorical science (Gergen, 1974).

Self-Esteem as Generalized Reinforcer

Tedeschi and Norman (1985) proposed that during development children imitate models who are effective in interpersonal interactions. To the extent that the imitated behaviors "live up" to those of the models, the individual is successful in influencing others, gains interpersonal rewards, and subsequently conceives of his or her self in positive reputational terms. This process allows the individual retrospectively to view his or her behavior as approximating an ideal, and it provides a basis for self-evaluation (self-esteem). Since available human models may establish a number of differing but effective identities, a large array of behaviors may be perceived as relevant for self-evaluations.

---

[2]The self has an effect on behavior only when the individual is self-focused.

Positive self-evaluations are experienced as reinforcing because they are associated with external reinforcements accruing from successful interpersonal behavior. Negative evaluations are experienced as punishing because they are associated with unsuccessful interpersonal behavior. In this way, through associations with many external reinforcements, self-evaluations become important as a form of generalized reinforcers. Thus, while the self is not postulated as a controller of behavior, self-evaluations, which take on positive and/or negative values in all cultures, are given a significant role in the explanation of social behavior.

The theory proposed by Tedeschi and Norman (1985) does not view the self as a master program that runs the computer. It gives the self a mostly retrospective and automated associationist role in explaining social behavior. It is a cautious approach to theorizing that tries to avoid proposing speculative, all-inclusive hypothetical and intraorganismic factors too complex to evaluate empirically with contemporary research methods.

Private and Public Manipulations in Laboratory Experiments

Researchers have often attempted to examine controversies between impression management and intrapsychic theories by manipulating the private or public nature of behavior (Tetlock & Manstead, 1985). The reasoning has been that subjects will behave differently in public than in private if impression management concerns are salient, but if effects are based primarily on cognitive factors no differences would occur.

An examination of the research procedures used to manipulate the public or private nature of behavior raises doubts about their validity. A favorite procedure is to allow subjects to remain anonymous in the sense that the experimenter does not know their names (Gaes, Kalle, & Tedeschi, 1978; Malkis, Kalle, & Tedeschi, 1982). Subjects may sign up for the experiment with a pseudonym and may be told not to sign any protocols, and the experimenter may tell the subjects that he or she does not want to know their names so as to maintain scientific objectivity. This procedure may well reduce the sense of accountability that subjects have for their behavior, but it is questionable whether the behavior could be considered "private." After all, a total stranger (i.e., the experimenter) has the subject under surveillance. Furthermore, there is a question regarding anonymity. The experimenter may not know the subject's name, but the latter is not invisible. The experimenter is typically someone whom subjects might encounter around the college campus or in the classroom. Thus, facial recognition, like fingerprints, can be used to identify the person.

Another procedure used to manipulate the private or public nature of behavior has been to have subjects fill out questionnaires without identifying themselves by name, place the questionnaires in envelopes, and mail them to some researcher at another location, typically at great distance from the testing site (Schlenker, Forsyth, Leary, & Miller, 1980). This procedure may reduce the concern subjects have about the researchers' reactions, but it may also reduce their sense of accountability for what they do. Unfortunately, the latter response is contrary to the goals of the researchers, who are interested in obtaining a sample of the kind of behavior subjects might perform in private (away from the intruding observations of strangers). In intimate (i.e., private) relationships, people have a stronger sense of accountability than when behaving anonymously in front of strangers. While researchers hope that removing the intrusion of a face-to-face interaction with an experimenter will induce greater revelations about "true" or "private" self or other cognitions, there is no evidence supporting the validity of such an assumption. Indeed, deindividuation theory proposes that anonymity reduces the awareness of individual identity and is associated with antisocial behaviors (Festinger et al., 1952; Zimbardo, 1970).[3]

Still another method of manipulating private and public conditions for subjects in experiments was developed by Helmreich & Collins (1968). Subjects were put in a room by themselves, were told to make an audiotape of a practice speech, and were also told they could erase the tape afterward. Thus, the speech would not be heard by anyone. Certainly this procedure reduces the impression management concerns of subjects, but it is not clear that the condition is one of privacy. Giving a speech is a public behavior, and practicing it means giving the speech *as if* there was an audience present. Rehearsing it may give the person confidence when an audience is actually present, but the rehearsal probably does not represent what the subject would do in intimate relationships and may not reveal "true" beliefs or attitudes.

Lie detectors have been developed to directly access the private attitudes of individuals. There is some question as to whether lie detectors do what they were designed to do, but they may induce subjects who believe in their validity to confess to beliefs they otherwise would not reveal in public (Lyyken, 1974). The bogus pipeline procedures developed by Jones & Sigall (1971) parallel those of a lie detector. Subjects are told an electronic apparatus can measure their attitudes from implicit muscle responses, and they are given a convincing demonstration of its apparent validity. The intent is to induce subjects to "confess" their private (i.e., "true") beliefs and attitudes. It is reasoned that subjects should believe that an experimenter would know their attitudes anyway through the measures taken by the electronic instruments, and should they not tell the "truth" the experimenter/psychologist might believe they lacked emotional stability or that they were liars. Essentially, there is nothing to be gained by deception because it will always be detected. Hence, even if one's private attitudes are socially despicable, the experimenter will be able to detect them, and it is better to have "wrong" attitudes and be perceived as honest or emotionally stable than to have "wrong" attitudes and be perceived as dishonest or emotionally unstable.

While questions have been raised about the validity of the bogus pipeline procedures (Cherry, Byrne, & Mitchell, 1976; Ostrom, 1973; Tetlock & Manstead,

---

[3]The procedure of embedding subjects in a mass testing situation and asking them not to identify themselves on a protocol probably creates feelings of anonymity, but it is still a public situation, one that may produce deindividuation.

1985), the evidence is encouraging. For example, in an experiment directed toward examining the validity of the bogus pipeline procedures, Quigley-Fernandez and Tedeschi (1978) found that subjects were much more likely to confess possession of illicit information (given to them by an experimental confederate) when they were hooked up to the bogus pipeline than when they were asked in face-to-face interviews or on paper-and-pencil questionnaires. Also, the validity of the bogus pipeline procedures is supported by a series of experiments designed to test hypotheses derived from impression management theory (see review by Tedeschi & Rosenfeld, 1981).

This quick review of procedures for manipulating private and public conditions in experiments indicates a need for developing ways for studying behavior in intimate social interactions. While the bogus pipeline is a promising development for studying the phenomenology of subjects, research techniques for understanding the interrelations of behavior in intimate and impersonal situations do not exist. Indeed, research on intimate *and* impersonal relationships, particularly in terms of self-concept and self-esteem, has not been systematically done.

Conclusions and Implications

What we believe the relationships are between public and private selves depends on what meaning we give to such terms. When "private" refers to the phenomenological experiences of the individual, two important problems are raised: (a) What is the relationship of public behavior to private conceptions of self? and (b) What is the relationship of private conceptions of self to subsequent behavior? Examination of these problems suggests that the first question is much simpler than the second. The ability of humans to engage in self-reflection and the use of language to form theories provides the basis for development of the self. The individual's beliefs and evaluations of himself or herself can be traced developmentally to social interactions with others. Although social psychologists have done a great deal to explore the relationships between behavior and subsequent beliefs about the self, little has been done to study the relative and differential impact of intimate and impersonal relationships on the development of self-concept and self-evaluation. It has been suggested in this chapter that two factors, perceived freedom and emotional arousal, are necessary accompaniments of behavior that individuals introject into their self-theories. Because intimate relationships are vested with greater emotion and require less control over emotions, they have a greater impact on development of the self.

The view of the self as a controller of behavior must grapple with the tendency to formulate theories placing a homunculus inside the actor. Those theories that avoid this logic trap are usually so sweeping or ambiguous that they are immune from empirical falsification. Questions regarding the linkage of phenomenological aspects of the self to subsequent behavior, and about the nature and functions of consciousness, have not been squarely faced by theorists of the self. No solutions are offered for these questions, but a conservative stance is taken, in which inferences are grudgingly made and the principle of parsimony is adopted as a strategy for staying close to the data. This stance does not deny an important role for the self in explaining social behavior, and indeed a theory of self-esteem based on the notion of its being a generalized reinforcer is suggested as a mechanism affecting behavior.

Acknowledgments. The author appreciates the comments and suggestions of Roy Baumeister, Richard Felson, and Valerie Melburg.

References

Aries, P. (1962). *Centuries of childhood: A social history of family life* (R. Baldick, Trans.) New York: Random House.

Baumeister, R.F., & Tice, D.M. (1986). Emotion and self-presentation. In R. Hogan & W.H. Jones (Eds.), *Perspectives in personality* (Vol. 2). Greenwich, CT: JAI Press.

Bem, D.J. (1972). Self-perception theory. In L. Berkowitz (Ed.), *Advances in experimental social psychology* (Vol. 6). New York: Academic Press.

Benn, S.I., & Gaus, G.F. (1983). The public and the private: Concepts and action. In S.I. Benn & G.F. Gaus (Eds.), *Public and private in social life*. New York: St. Martins Press.

Burnstein, E., & Vinokur, A. (1975). What a person thinks upon learning that he has chosen differently from others: Nice evidence for the persuasive arguments explanation of choice shifts. *Journal of Experimental Social Psychology, 11*, 412–426.

Carver, C.S., & Scheier, M.F. (1985). Aspects of self and the control of behavior. In B.R. Schlenker (Ed.), *The self and social life*. New York: McGraw Hill.

Cheek, J.M., & Briggs, S.R. (1982). Self-consciousness and aspects of identity. *Journal of Research in Personality, 16*, 401–408.

Cherry, F., Byrne, D., & Mitchell, H.E. (1976). Clogs in the bogus pipeline: Demand characteristics and social desirability. *Journal of Research in Personality, 10*, 69–75.

Confucius. (1938). *The wisdom of Confucius* (Lin Yutang, Ed. and Trans.). New York: Random House.

Cooley, C.H. (1902). *Human nature and the social order*. New York: Scribner.

Darwin, C. (1872). *The expression of emotions in man and animals*. London: J. Murray.

Davidson, D. (1963). Actions, reasons, and causes. *Journal of Philosophy, 60*, 685–700.

Douglas, W., & Gibbins, K. (1983). Inadequacy of voice recognition as a demonstration of self-deception. *Journal of Personality and Social Psychology, 44*, 589–592.

Ekman, P., & Friesen, W.V. (1975). *Unmasking the face*. Englewood Cliffs, NJ: Prentice-Hall.

Epstein, S. (1973). The self-concept revisited: Or a theory of a theory. *American Psychologist, 28*, 212–221.

Felson, R.B. (1981). Self and reflected appraisal among football players: A test of the Meadian hypothesis. *Social Psychology Quarterly, 44*, 116–126.

Festinger, L. (1954). A theory of the social comparison processes. *Human Relations, 7*, 117–140.

Festinger, L., Pepitone, A., & Newcomb, T. (1952). Some consequences of deindividuation in a group. *Journal of Abnormal and Social Psychology, 47*, 382–389.

Franks, V., & Burtle, V. (Eds.). (1974). *Women in therapy: New psychotherapies for a changing society*. New York: Brunner/Mazel.

Freud, S. (1938). *A general introduction to psychoanalysis*. New York: Garden City Publishing Co.

Gaes, G.G., Kalle, R.J., & Tedeschi, J.T. (1978). Impression management in the forced compliance situation: Two studies using the bogus pipeline. *Journal of Experimental Social Psychology, 14*, 493–510.

Gergen, K.J. (1974). Social psychology as history. *Journal of Personality and Social Psychology, 26*, 309–320.

Gergen, K.J. (1984). Theory of the self: Impasse and evolution. In L. Berkowitz (Ed.), *Advances in experimental social psychology* (Vol. 17). New York: Academic Press.

Gergen, K.J. (1985). The ethnopsychology of self-deception. In M.W. Martin (Ed.), *Self-deception and self-understanding*. Lawrence: University of Kansas Press.

Goffman, E. (1961). *Encounters*. Indianapolis, In: Bobbs-Merrill.

Greenwald, A.G. (1980). The totalitarian ego: Fabrication and revision of personal history. *American Psychologist, 35*, 603–613.

Greenwald, A.G., & Breckler, S.J. (1985). To whom is the self presented? In B.R. Schlenker (Ed.), *The self and social life*. New York: McGraw Hill.

Grice, H.P. (1969). Utterer's meaning and intentions. *Philosophical Review, LXVI*, 147–177.

Gur, R.C., & Sackheim, H.A. (1979). Self-deception: A concept in search of a phenomenon. *Journal of Personality and Social Psychology, 37*, 147–169.

Guthrie, E.R. (1952). *The psychology of learning* (rev. ed.). New York: Harper & Row.

Heidegger, M. (1962). *Being and time* (J. Macquarrie & E. Robinson, Trans.). New York: Harper & Row.

Helmreich, R.L., & Collins, B.E. (1968). Studies in forced compliance: Commitment and magnitude of inducement to comply as determinants of opinion change. *Journal of Personality and Social Psychology, 10*, 75–81.

Hochschild, A. (1983). *The managed heart: Commercialization of human feeling*. Berkeley: University of California Press.

Hogan, R. (1982). A socioanalytic theory of personality. In M. Page (Ed.), *Nebraska symposium on motivation*. Lincoln: University of Nebraska Press.

Hogan, R., & Cheek, J. (1982). Identity, authenticity, and maturity. In T.R. Sarbin & K.E. Scheibe (Eds.), *Studies in social identity*. New York: Praeger.

Hull, C.L. (1952). *A behavior system: An introduction to behavior theory concerning the individual organism*. New Haven, CT: Yale University Press.

Jones, E.E., & Davis, K.E. (1965). From acts to dispositions: The attribution process in person perception. In L. Berkowitz (Ed.), *Advances in experimental social psychology* (Vol. 2). New York: Academic Press.

Jones, E.E., & Sigall, H. (1971). The bogus pipeline: A new paradigm for measuring affect and attitude. *Psychological Bulletin, 76*, 349–364.

Kuhn, T. (1962). *The structure of scientific revolutions*. Chicago: University of Chicago Press.

Laird, J.D. (1974). Self-attribution of emotion: The effects of expressive behavior on the quality of emotional experience. *Journal of Personality and Social Psychology, 29*, 475–486.

Laird, J.D., Wagener, J.J., Halal, M., & Szegda, M. (1982). Remembering what you feel: The effects of emotion on memory. *Journal of Personality and Social Psychology, 42*, 646–657.

Lanzetta, J.T., Cartwright-Smith, J., & Kleck, R.E. (1976). Effects of nonverbal dissimulation on emotional experience and autonomic arousal. *Journal of Personality and Social Psychology, 33*, 354–370.

Lanzetta, J.T., & Orr, S.P. (1980). Influence of facial expression on the classical conditioning of fear. *Journal of Personality and Social Psychology, 37*, 1081–1087.

Loftus, E.F. (1974). *Memory*. Reading, MA: Addison-Wesley.

Lyons, J.O. (1978). *The invention of the self: The hinge of consciousness in the eighteenth century*. Carbondale: Southern Illinois University Press.

Lyyken, D.T. (1974). Psychology and the lie detector industry. *American Psychologist, 10*, 725–739.

Malkis, F.S., Kalle, R.J., & Tedeschi, J.T. (1982). Attitudinal politics in the forced compliance situation. *Journal of Social Psychology, 117*, 79–91.

Martin, M.W. (1985). General introduction. In M.W. Martin (Ed.), *Self-deception and self-understanding*. Lawrence: University of Kansas Press.

Mead, G.H. (1934). *Mind, self, and society*. Chicago: University of Chicago Press.

Moore, B., Jr.(1984). *Privacy: Studies in social and cultural history.* Armonk, NY: M.E. Sharpe.

Nisbett, R.E., & Wilson, T.D. (1977). Telling more than we can know: Verbal reports on mental processes. *Psychological Review, 84,* 231–259.

Ostrom, M.T.(1973). The bogus pipeline: A new *ignus fatuus? Psychological Bulletin, 79,* 252–259.

Quigley-Fernandez, B., & Tedeschi, J.T. (1978). The bogus pipeline as lie detector: Two validity studies. *Journal of Personality and Social Psychology, 36,* 247–256.

Rosenberg, M. (1979). *Conceiving the self.* New York: Basic Books.

Sartre, J.P. (1957). *Transcendence of the ego: An existentialist theory of consciousness.* New York: Farrar, Straus & Giroux.

Schlenker, R.B. (1980). *Impression management: The self-concept, social identity, and interpersonal relations.* Monterey, CA: Brooks/Cole.

Schlenker, B.R. (1982). Translating actions into attitudes: An identity-analytic approach to the explanation of social conduct. In L. Berkowitz (Ed.), *Advances in experimental social psychology* (Vol. 15). New York: Academic Press.

Schlenker, B.R. (1985). Identity and self-identification. In B.R. Schlenker (Ed.), *The self and social life.* New York: McGraw Hill.

Schlenker, B.R., Forsyth, D.R., Leary, M.R., & Miller, R.S. (1980). Self-presentational analysis of the effect of incentives on attitude change following counterattitudinal behavior. *Journal of Personality and Social Psychology, 39,* 553–557.

Scott, M.D., & Lyman, S. (1968). Accounts. *American Sociological Review, 33,* 46–62.

Sennett, R. (1978). *The fall of public man: On the social psychology of capitalism.* New York: Vintage.

Skinner, B.F. (1953). *Science and human behavior.* New York: Macmillan.

Swann, W.B., Jr. (1984). Self-verification: Bringing social reality into harmony with the self. In J. Suls & A.G. Greenwald (Eds.), *Psychological perspectives on the self* (Vol. 2). Hillsdale, NJ: Erlbaum.

Tedeschi, J.T., & Norman, N (1985). Social power, self-presentation, and the self. In B.R. Schlenker (Ed.), *The self and social life.* New York: McGraw Hill.

Tedeschi, J.T., & Rosenfeld, P. (1981). Impression management theory and the forced compliance situation. In J.T. Tedeschi (Ed.), *Impression management theory and social psychological research.* New York: Academic Press.

Tetlock, P.E., & Manstead, A.S.R. (1985). Impression management versus intrapsychic explanations in social psychology: A useful dichotomy? *Psychological Review, 92,* 59–77.

Trilling, L. (1973). *Sincerity and authenticity.* Cambridge, MA: Harvard University Press.

Triplett, N. (1897). The dynamogenic factor in pacemaking and competition. *American Journal of Psychology, 9,* 507–533.

Wilde, O. (1969). *The artist as critic: Critical writings of Oscar Wilde* (R. Ellmann, Ed.). New York: Random House.

Wylie, R.C. (1979). *The self-concept: Theory and research on selected topics* (rev. ed.). Lincoln: University of Nebraska Press.

Zimbardo, P.G. (1970). The human choice: Individuation, reason, and order versus deindividuation, impulse, and chaos. In W.J. Arnold & D. Levine (Eds.), *Nebraska Symposium on motivation* (Vol. 17). Lincoln: University of Nebraska Press.

The Nature of Self-Identification

Self-identification is the process, means, or result of showing oneself to be a particular type of person, thereby specifying one's identity (Schlenker, 1984, 1985a). Fixing and expressing identity involves systematically defining and categorizing oneself, bringing relevant evidence and experiences to bear. It is accomplished privately, through contemplation of oneself, and publicly, through self-disclosure, self-presentation, and other activities that serve to construct one's identity for audiences. Self-identification can be performed linguistically through statements or assertations, or iconically through the images created by task performances, dress, mannerisms, and so forth (Schlenker, 1980). Self-identification, as with any type of definition, results in the specification of unique qualities that distinguish oneself from most others (e.g., idiosyncratic characteristics that, at the extreme, might be sought by aspirants to the *Guinness Book of World Records*) as well as similarities to others. These similarities are the basis for one common submeaning of identification that relies on definition by analogy: the psychoanalytic notion of identifying with admired or feared others and using them as exemplars for conduct.

Elsewhere (see Schlenker, 1985a, for further discussion), I proposed that self-identification always occurs in a particular context that reflects the interaction of the *person* (e.g., the actor's self-concept, dispositional tendencies, values), the *situation* (e.g., opportunities for and constraints on the satisfaction of values; cues about applicable personal and social rules and roles), and one or more salient *audiences* for the activity. An initial assessment of these factors evokes for the actor or prompts the actor to formulate: (a) a goal or set of goals for the occasion, (b) a script or plan for goal accomplishment, and (c) a set of desired identity images (or schemata) that are embedded within the overall script or plan and mediate self-identifications. These propositions assert that self-identification is, on any particular occasion, an *activity*. It is not merely a reflection of the self-concept, nor is it simply a mindless reaction to situational pressures or a cunning action with Machiavellian intent. Self-identifications are contextually bound and influenced by the person, situation, and audience. Yet the actor extracts from them generalizations that, wittingly or unwittingly, comprise the self-concept, and once these generalizations are derived they in turn influence subsequent self-identifications.

The Concept of Identity

Self-identification constructs and expresses an identity. The concept of *identity* recognizes the mutual dependency of the private and public selves. Identity can be regarded as a theory of self that is formed and maintained through actual or imagined interpersonal agreement about what the self is like. Analogous to a scientific theory, its contents must withstand the process of consensual agreement by informed, significant observers (see Schlenker, 1985a, 1985b). Discussions of identity invariably invoke this process of triangulation between audiences. As examples:

Psychologist Erik Erikson: ". . . the conscious feeling of having a personal identity is
   based on two simultaneous observations: the immediate perception of one's self-
   sameness and continuity in time; and the simultaneous perception that others
   recognize one's self-sameness and continuity" (1959, p 23).
Philosopher Rom Harré: ". . . the sense of personal identity depends on a socially
   enforced theory of self by which a human being conceives a continuous coordina-
   tion of point of view and point of action" (1983, p. 41).
Sociologist Gregory Stone: "One's identity is established when others place him as
   a social object by assigning him the same words of identity that he appropriates for
   himself" (1962, p. 93).

The theme that emerges from these analyses is that identity is forged, expressed,
maintained, and modified in the crucible of social life, as its contents undergo the
process of actual or imagined observation, judgment, and reaction by audiences
(oneself and others). People's ideas about themselves are expressed and tested in
social life through their actions. In turn, the outcomes of these "tests" provide a
basis for crystallizing, refining, or modifying identity based in part on how believable or defensible these identity images appear to be.[1]
   With the concepts of self-identification and identity as background, the two
dimensions described previously are reexamined. These are the actor's motives and
the public or private nature of the behavior.

Motives Reconsidered: Desired Identity Images

In his "wager," Pascal provided a justification for why people should believe in God.
He argued that if people believe and God exists, they will ultimately gain limitless
rewards; if they believe and God does not exist, they have lost nothing. If people do

---

[1]Identity, like any theory, is both a *structure*, containing the organized contents of experience,
and an active *process* that guides and regulates one's thoughts, feelings, and actions
(Schlenker, 1985a). It influences how information is perceived, processed, and recalled (e.g.,
Greenwald & Pratkanis, 1984; Kihlstrom & Cantor, 1984; Markus, 1977), it acts as a script
to guide behavior (Schlenker, 1980, 1985a), and it contains standards against which one's
behavior can be compared and evaluated, thereby influencing one's affective state (Schlenker,
1985a). When the term "identity" refers to a person's cumulative theory of self, it appears
to be identical to how the term "self-concept" is usually used, especially by theorists who
have been influenced by James (1890) and Mead (1934). Epstein (1973) defined the self-
concept in precisely this way, as a self-theory. The connotations of identity, though, highlight
private and public triangulation, while the connotations of the self-concept suggest a more
private phenomenon. A distinction can be drawn between identity as a cumulative theory of
self and identity as it is situated or conceived in relation to particular other people in particular contexts (e.g., Hewitt, 1976). The former can be referred to interchangeably as identity
or the self-concept. The latter refers to a particular set of self-identifications that occur in
context; these are represented in memory as self-images (or self-schemata) if they refer to
generalized constructions about the self.

not believe and God exists, they ultimately will have lost everything; if they do not believe and God does not exist, they will have gained nothing. Although some theologians have discussed Pascal's wager in the category of justifications for the existence of God, it more properly is an example of a justification for beliefs. Beliefs do not exist without consequences, and these consequences are integrally related to why people come to hold one belief rather than another.

Incorporating consequences, Pragmatic philosophers such as William James (1907) and Charles Sanders Pierce (1878) linked the truth of an idea to its usefulness. For a belief to be true, it should be useful in permitting those who hold it to function effectively in the world. Although the Pragmatists did not discuss usefulness in precisely these terms, it seems appropriate to suggest that beliefs should produce a feeling of being able to understand, predict, and control events better than alternatives, and should provide a sense of satisfaction.

The two elements that emerge from a Pragmatic analysis of why people come to hold particular beliefs, and hence which ones are true to them, are (a) *believability*, or the extent to which the belief is a reasonably accurate construal of the salient evidence, and (b) *personal beneficiality*, or the extent to which it serves the holder's goals and values (Schlenker, 1980, 1982, 1985a). These two elements are components of *all* beliefs. Of course, different contexts may require weighing one of the components more heavily than the other (e.g., ambiguous evidence gives greater weight to the beneficiality component, whereas the expectation that one's beliefs may be challenged by an expert audience armed with persuasive evidence places greater weight on the believability component), but all beliefs contain both elements.

When applied to self-identification, the analysis suggests that within the range of potentially believable self-identifications, that is, the self of self-beliefs that can be justified and defended based on salient evidence, people endorse those that best serve their goals and values. I have termed these *desirable identity images* or *desirable self-identifications* (Schlenker, 1980, 1982, 1985a). (Schlenker [1980, 1981] presented a formula for assessing desirable identity images. Briefly, the formula takes into account the expected outcomes if a belief is correct minus the expected outcomes if a belief is incorrect, weighted by the perceived probability that the belief is correct versus incorrect, respectively.)

The concept of a desirable identity image does not suggest that people's fantasies dominate reality or that people unflaggingly express ideal images of self. Rather, people's self-identifications are bound by the requirement that they have a legitimate claim to the identity images, that is, that actors can justify and defend their claims about the self to audiences, including the self, by providing the appropriate evidence if called upon to do so. Desired images are somewhat glorified images of the self; images that are a bit too good to be true, yet that the actor is convinced are true (Greenwald & Breckler, 1985). In short, desirable identity images represent what people believe they *can be* and *should be* in particular contexts, and are influenced by personality factors, situational factors, and audience factors.

The context generates a set of desirable identity images and these images mediate people's self-identifications on the occasion. The proposition suggests an integrative perspective on three related debates about the motives underlying behavior:

1. Do people strive for accuracy or exhibit self-serving, motivated biases in their self-beliefs (Alicke, in press; Tetlock & Levi, 1982)?
2. Are people motivated to promote self-consistency or maximize self-esteem (S. C. Jones, 1973; Mettee & Aronson, 1974; Shrauger, 1974; Swann, 1985)?
3. Do people present the real self (as perceived) or the ideal self to others (e.g., compare Swann, 1985, with Baumeister, 1982)?

The opposite positions in these debates are usually regarded as theoretical alternatives. Proponents of each side have often argued that the motive they favor is the dominant one. They have tried to explain contrary results, which appear to support the potency of the opposite motive, by (a) introducing hypotheses that would also permit those results to be interpreted in terms of the favored motive, or (b) suggesting that the opposite motive exists but operates only within a more limited range of conditions as compared to the favored motive (see Schlenker, 1984).

The self-identification approach takes a different view. Each of the opposites describes phenomena that represent greater weight being placed on one of the two components, believability or personal beneficiality, of why people hold or assert particular beliefs (Schlenker, 1984, 1985a). Positions stressing accuracy give priority to the believability component, in that they emphasize relatively logical inferences from the evidence, often seemingly made at the expense of the implications for the self. Positions stressing esteem maximization give priority to the personal beneficiality component, in that they emphasize the protection and enhancement of esteem even at the expense of constructing or presenting valid views of the self. In contrast, the self-identification approach regards believability and beneficiality as coexisting components of all self-identifications. The problem is not to determine which "motive" exists or when one motive will dominate the opposite. Instead, the components can be viewed as factors in an equation, with their integration equaling the desirability of the self-identification. Different contexts (e.g., situations, audiences) and individual differences result in different weightings and values for the components (see Schlenker, 1980, 1981, for further discussion). For example, a glorifying self-identification that may seem believable when a person is alone at home may seem less believable when she is with expert, discerning others; the self-identification then would be more desirable and likely to be proffered in the first case than in the second. The desirability of an identity image is not a constant; it is a product of the moment, although it probably fluctuates only within a relatively restricted range for a given person. (A cataloging of the variables that appear to influence desirability is beyond the scope of this paper, and the beginnings of such a list are available elsewhere [e.g., Schlenker, 1980, 1982, 1985a].)

Private and Public Behavior Reconsidered: Audiences

Private and Public

Public behavior is significant. The silly little things people do at home alone are for personal consumption; they can chuckle in amusement without the diagnostic gaze of others. Public behavior can create a greater impact. In general, public as compared to private behavior is more committing, in that it is more difficult to revoke, implies that the actor will behave commensurately in the future, and implies that he or she has behaved similarly in the past (Goffman, 1959; Kiesler, 1971; Schlenker, 1975, 1980; Tedeschi, Schlenker, & Bonoma, 1971; Wicklund & Gollwitzer, 1982). It forces people to build a reputation, with or without their consent, by which they will be known and treated. In contrast, private behavior is easier to dismiss, trivialize, or forget if one is so inclined. Unless one is willing, private behavior means that one cannot be held accountable to others who might disapprove or condemn; or, for that matter, one cannot receive the commendations of others who might approve and praise. When people behave publicly, they offer evidence for others to contemplate, evaluate, and respond. The reactions of others must be integrated with one's own self-knowledge to form conclusions about the self. Consensual validation provides an important test of any theory, and identity is no exception.

Which creates a greater impact, public or private behavior? A persuasive argument can be made for the potency of public behavior (Baumeister, 1982; Baumeister & Jones, 1978; Goffman, 1959; Jones & Pittman, 1982; Kiesler, 1971; Schlenker, 1975; Tedeschi & Rosenfeld, 1981; Tedeschi et al., 1971; Wicklund & Gollwitzer, 1982). But in recognizing the committing aspects of public behavior, it may be too easy to forget that private behavior can also be diagnostic and create a significant effect. Indeed, self-enhancement and self-protection have been documented even under private conditions (e.g., Greenwald & Breckler, 1985; Riess, Rosenfeld, Melburg, & Tedeschi, 1981; Schlenker, Hallam, & McCown, 1983).

Hawthorne's Puritan tale of the *Scarlet Letter* tells of a woman branded by public condemnation and a man haunted by private guilt because of their mutual impropriety. The man was revered by the community at large. His identity and reputation were beyond reproach in virtually all of his public dealings, and the lone exception involved an audience who would never tell. Yet he suffered the torments of the damned because of his perceived failing. As a case study in the social psychology of private versus public behavior, the novel is enlightening. It is, of course, fiction and it describes a situation that mingles private and public concerns. For the man, the woman was a significant audience irrespective of her immediate presence and the community at large. Also, the perceived injustice of only one party publicly suffering for the vice of two was too much for his conscience to bear. And perhaps imaginings of community condemnation, if they were to know the truth, entered his thoughts. The cynic might even suggest that the man's private guilt emerged from the (unlikely) fear that the woman might disclose their affair. Irrespective, the inevitable drama is played out in this crossfire of private and public concerns. The novel illustrates the intertwined nature of private and public concerns, and highlights how different audiences play poignant roles in our lives. These salient audiences, present or imagined, may be a more significant determinant of self-identifications than the mere private or public nature of the activity.

Types of Audiences

Self-identification *always* involves one or more real or imagined audiences (Schlenker, 1980, 1982, 1984, 1985a). At least three types of audiences can be distinguished, and these vary in the degree to which they evoke private versus public concerns.

The first audience for self-identification is the self (Greenwald & Breckler, 1985; Hogan, 1982; Schlenker, 1980, 1984, 1985a; Snyder, Higgins, & Stucky, 1983). People's own internalized values, standards, and knowledge provide a basis for self-regulation and self-evaluation. Research on private self-attention (Carver & Scheier, 1981, 1985) and inner orientation (Hogan & Cheek, 1983) usually address the self-as-audience for the self-identification process.

A second audience consists of other people with whom one interacts. Others can influence actors' self-identifications when those others are present, when future interactions are anticipated, or when past interactions are contemplated. Theorists in the areas of self-presentation and self-disclosure have focused primarily on this category of audience. Research on public self-attention, which reflects concern about how one is being evaluated by others (Carver & Scheier, 1981, 1985), and outer orientation (Hogan & Cheek, 1983) usually addresses itself to the influence of immediate others, often others who are strangers.

A third audience is reference others who have achieved a special prominence in one's life (Schlenker, 1984, 1985a). Their opinions and standards are sufficiently respected that they are evoked as exemplars and evaluators across a wide variety of situations, and not solely when actors interact or expect to interact with them. Examples can include parents, best friends, spouse, children, admired mentors, and reference groups. Also in this category are others who one may never have met or who may not even exist, yet who are held up as models and perhaps judges for one's conduct. These can range from the child's concern about how Santa Claus might judge his actions to the adult's commitment to Jesus. These are often our heroes and heroines, who provide us with a sense of direction and dedication.

Reference others occupy an intermediate position between public and private concerns. Many reference others are real people or groups with whom we interact (or at least individuals who are believed to be real, e.g., Santa Claus). As such, we are concerned about their opinions and the type of information about us that comes to their attention. Yet we also admire them and many of their standards, even when these may differ from our own, and use them as exemplars for how to behave, basing our self-evaluations on how well or poorly we have measured up to them. For example, many soldiers during World War II reported that they conjured an image of John Wayne and tried to emulate his conduct during battle. Thus, reference others can provide both a public concern, serving as an evaluative audience who will judge our identities, and a private concern, serving as a model for conduct and self-evaluation.[2] Any particular reference other may evoke one or both of these concerns.

Greenwald and Breckler (1985) explicitly recognized the importance of reference others as an audience for self-presentations. They referred to reference group

[2]The distinction between other people and reference others as audiences can be regarded as reflecting (at least) the dimensions of the importance of the audience, its salience even when it is not physically present, and its capacity to serve as an admired exemplar as well as an evaluative source. In this sense, the distinction represents degrees of difference in multi-

audiences as the collective facet of the self (as compared to the private and public facets), noted that this facet contains both inner and outer components, and suggested that it serves as a source of central values. As Greenwald and Breckler indicated, social psychologists have conducted very little research on the impact of this audience on self-identifications.

When Is Each Audience Salient?

Personality, situational, and audience factors combine to determine which one(s) of these audiences are salient. Variables that focus people's attention on particular others or increase their concern about how they are perceived and evaluated by others are likely to increase the salience of others, including reference others. Personality variables that are likely to produce these effects include public self-consciousness (Carver & Scheier, 1981, 1985; Fenigstein, Scheier, & Buss, 1975; Greenwald & Breckler, 1985), outer orientation (Hogan & Cheek, 1983), fear of negative evaluation (Watson & Friend, 1969), social anxiety (Leary, 1983; Schlenker & Leary, 1982a, in press), needs for social approval (Crowne & Marlowe, 1964), high self-monitoring (M. Snyder, 1979), and authoritarianism (Greenwald & Breckler, 1985).

Situational variables in this category include the immediate presence of others, a camera that will record one's behavior for review by a particular group, the anticipation of an important interaction with others, a recent interaction in which one's identity was especially benefited or harmed, or a solo performance in which a group's attention is focused on oneself (Buss, 1980; Carver & Scheier, 1981, 1985; Greenwald & Breckler, 1985; Schlenker, 1980). Even when present, other people are likely to be more salient when they are more significant, such as those who are powerful, attractive, and expert (Jones & Wortman, 1973; Schlenker, 1980, 1984; Tedeschi & Norman, 1985).

Finally, even when they are not present, particular other people and reference others can be cued by their mention (e.g., their name), their relevance to a particular situation (e.g., a soldier before battle may think of John Wayne), their relevance to one's goals (e.g., a child drawing up a wish list at Christmas thinks of Santa), or their association with concepts that are currently activated in memory (e.g., a child sees a Christmas tree and thinks of Santa). Given that reference others are significant and likely to be associated in memory with a greater number of concepts, goals, and situations, they are more likely to be salient in their absence than is the average other person.

In contrast, the self-as-audience is made salient by variables that focus attention on the private self, focus attention on individualistic goals, or decrease concerns about how one appears to others. Personality variables that are likely to produce

---

dimensional space rather than an either-or categorization. (All three dimensions appear to be involved. Some important others who may be salient even in their absence still may not be evoked as reference others because they are not exemplars, as in the case of a policeman for a member of a juvenile gang.)

these effects include private self-consciousness, inner orientation (Hogan & Cheek, 1983), needs for achievement (Greenwald & Breckler, 1985), and a self-image of autonomy (Schlenker, 1980). Situational conditions that focus attention inward include the presence of a small mirror or listening to a tape recording of one's voice (Carver & Scheier, 1981, 1985; Greenwald & Breckler, 1985). Finally, the self-as-audience may be evoked by default when people are alone or in the presence of less significant audiences (those less powerful, attractive, expert).

Audience Influences on Self-Identification

The traditional view of an audience in much of the self-presentation literature is as a target for the machinations of actors intent on furthering their self-interests. Yet an audience does much more, even before an interaction gets underway and a true interplay of opinions and activities occurs. When an audience (including the self) is salient, it can influence self-identification in at least four ways: (a) it activates in memory relevant information about the self, the audience, and behavior, (b) it serves as a receptor for the packaging of that information, (c) it provides an evaluative framework for the self-identification, and (d) it influences expected outcomes.

Audiences as cues. Audiences cue relevant information in memory about oneself, the audience, and the audience's relationship to onself. Audiences thereby activate pertinent self-schemata, roles (e.g., a new parent's view of what parent should be to children), past experiences (e.g., the identity one has assumed in relation to a particular audience in the past), and possible goals that can be satisfied. Once this information is activated, actors draw upon it in their subsequent self-identifications to that audience. An audience is thus one of several factors—which also include the self-concept, personal goals, and situational cues—that cue contextually relevant information about the self.

A classic example of the cueing function of audiences is the college student who feels uncomfortable when she returns home on vacation and relates to her parents in terms of the old self-images and roles that she had once exercised instead of the new self-images and roles she has acquired since being on her own. Although examples abound, there has been relatively little research on the cueing function of audiences. A notable exception is the work of McGuire and his associates (McGuire, McGuire, Child, & Fujioka, 1978; McGuire, McGuire, & Winton, 1979; McGuire & Padawer-Singer, 1978) on the spontaneous self-concept. They found that people are most likely to list spontaneously characteristics of the self that distinguish them from salient comparison groups.

Research on private versus public self-attention is relevant to the cueing function in that it examines the antecedents and consequences of focusing on the private versus public self. Conditions that focus one's attention on an immediate audience of others (e.g., videotaping one's performance for display to classmates) make salient how the self appears to those others, prompting subjects to conform to expected roles (e.g., Carver & Scheier, 1985). In contrast, conditions that promote a focus of attention on the self-as-audience (e.g., a small mirror) make salient one's own beliefs and values, and prompt subjects to present the self in ways that reflect self-conceptions and other internal states (Carver & Scheier, 1985).

Audiences as receptors. After pertinent information about the self is salient, it must be communicated to the audience, who serve as a receptor for the information. To communicate effectively requires tailoring or fitting information to the audience's knowledge and value systems, using terms, symbols, and evidence that will be comprehensible to them. Further, to communicate persuasively requires that the information be presented in ways that are expected to be most likely to be accepted and least likely to be challenged by the audience given their knowledge and values. This process requires role-taking skill in being able to place oneself in the position of the audience and anticipate how they are likely to perceive various ways of packaging desired self-identifications.

The literature on self-presentation abounds with research on how subjects adjust their behaviors based on the target's perceived knowledge and values (e.g., Backman, 1985; Baumeister, 1982; Baumeister & Jones, 1978; Jones & Pittman, 1982; Jones & Wortman, 1973; Schlenker, 1975, 1980, 1984, 1985a; Schlenker & Leary, 1982b; Schlenker, Miller, & Leary, 1983; M. Snyder, 1979; Tedeschi & Norman, 1985; Tetlock, 1985; Tetlock & Manstead, 1985). Self-presentations represent packaged information that appears designed to accomplish the actor's goals in the context of the audience's knowledge and values. The actor's goals, of course, may involve communicating truthful or distorted information about the self.

There are individual differences in the ability to communicate information about the self effectively and persuasively. Cheek (1982) found that people who score high on both acting ability (a skill that should facilitate effective communication) and private self-consciousness (the tendency to focus on the private self and perhaps come to know it better) are best able to minimize discrepancies between their own perceptions of self and their identities as perceived by friends. Individual differences in role-taking skill should similarly increase the effectiveness of self-identifications (Cheek & Hogan, 1983; Hogan, Jones, & Cheek, 1985). Finally, individual differences in self-monitoring, the tendency to be sensitive to cues from others and motivated to use those cues for self-regulation and control (M. Snyder, 1979), and Machiavellianism (Christie & Geis, 1970) have been found to be related to the effective use of strategic self-presentation.

Audiences as evaluative frameworks. An audience provides an evaluative framework for assessing self-identifications (Greenwald & Breckler, 1985; Schlenker, 1980, 1985a). That is, the audience is expected to observe, judge, and react to the activity, using particular standards for judgment and then responding appropriately with approval or disapproval and perhaps positive or negative sanctions. In this sense, the audience draws one's attention to a particular set of beliefs, behavioral prototypes, standards, and potential consequences relevant to the self-identification. The knowledge, standards, and rules that comprise this evaluative framework can be one's own (self-as-audience), a reference other's, another person's or group's, or a combination or compromise of these.

There is considerable commonality between the concept of self-attention and the notion of an audience as an evaluative framework, although there are also differences (Carver & Scheier, 1985; Greenwald & Breckler, 1985). In the case of self-attention, attention is first focused on the private or public self, because of a dispositional tendency or a situational cue; then an evaluative process begins based on the pertinent reference values (Carver & Scheier, 1985). In contrast, the idea of an audience as an evaluative framework suggests that a salient audience *draws* attention to the appropriate private or public reference values (Greenwald & Breckler, 1985). Despite this difference in emphasis and sequencing (attention to the private or public self preceding or following an evaluative orientation), the empirical implications of the two approaches largely overlap; both ultimately expect that attention will be focused on the private or public self and that an evaluative orientation occurs.

Audiences and outcome implications. Finally, audiences influence people's expectations of outcomes following self-identifications (Schlenker, 1980, 1984, 1985a; Schlenker & Leary, 1982a, in press). Self-identification outcome expectations represent the perceived likelihood that one's self-identifications will meet or exceed the appropriate personal or social standards. If people believe their self-identifications do so, they experience positive affect, feel good about themselves, and anticipate positive evaluations or positive sanctions from the audience. These positive experiences are a direct function of the importance of the standards, the extent to which the performance exceeds the standards, and the extent to which the actor attributes responsibility for the performance to the self as opposed to situational conditions or luck (Schlenker, 1985a; Schlenker & Leary, 1982a). If people believe their self-identifications will not meet the appropriate standards, they experience negative affect, feel bad about themselves, and anticipate negative evaluations or negative sanctions from the audience. These negative experiences are a direct function of the importance of the standards, the size of the discrepancy between the standards and the performance, and the extent to which the actor attributes responsibility for the failure to himself or herself rather than situational conditions or luck (Schlenker, 1985a; Schlenker & Leary, 1982a).

The Influence of the Private Self on Self-Presentations

A traditional view has regarded public self-identifications as *expressions* of the self-concept, and accounted for instances where the self-identification diverges from the self-concept by citing situational pressures. An alternative view has regarded public self-identifications as under the control of situational contingencies, and demoted the self-concept by viewing it as an epiphenomenon. Instead, self-identifications should be regarded as *activities* (thoughts or behaviors) *that occur in particular social contexts and are multiply determined.* They are influenced by (a) the actor's personality, including the self-concept, (b) the actor's goals and affective state, (c) the situation, and (d) salient audiences (Schlenker, 1980, 1984, 1985a). These four factors interact to determine the self-identification that occurs at a particular moment in time. Once a specific self-identification has occurred, it can in turn influence the self-concept (as is considered shortly), as well as the actual or perceived state of the audience, the situation, and the actor's goals and affective state.

The question of when the self-concept will be expressed in public self-identifications can be addressed in this context. More appropriately, the question becomes: When will aspects of the self-concept be salient and weighed heavily relative to the other factors as a determinant of self-identifications?

Personality and the Self-Concept

Self-images (or self-schemata) vary in their *importance*, that is, the extent to which they are related to valued outcomes, and their *centrality*, that is, the extent to which they subsume other related information about the self (e.g., Rosenberg, 1979; Schlenker, 1985a). Images of the self that are more important and central have usually been formed and stabilized over years of personality development through their continued use and subsequent validation by significant others, and they form the core of the self-concept (Hogan, 1982). Self-images that are more important and central are more likely to be activated in memory by contextual cues, and hence to be salient in any particular context. They are therefore more likely to be represented in people's self-identifications across a variety of situations. The sense of continuity bestowed by one's identity seems partly due to the influence of these important and central self-images.

Research on social cognition has provided findings that are consistent with the hypothesized effects of importance and centrality. Schemata that have been *frequently used* in the past are more available and likely to be activated in the present (e.g., Higgins & King, 1981). Further, schemata that have been *recently used* are more likely to be activated in the present; recent usage primes a schema in memory and makes it more accessible in a current context (e.g., Wyer & Srull, 1981). Of course, frequently used schemata are also more likely to have been used recently (Fiske & Taylor, 1984). Given that important and central self-images are more likely to have been frequently used, and probably used recently, their accessibility in memory should be increased. Irrespective of their overall importance and centrality, however, self-images that have been recently used (e.g., because of a just-elapsed interaction) will be more likely to be activated in the present by internal or external cues.

Related to frequency is the amount of direct behavioral experience the actor has had enacting the behaviors associated with the self-image. Some self-images are played out primarily in one's imagination; by choice or lack of opportunity the actor has not gained much experience behaviorally constructing and defending these images in public. Other self-images have been formed and shaped through behavioral experience. Fazio and Zanna (1981) have found that attitudes based on direct behavioral experience are relatively more accessible in memory, likely to be activated by situational cues, and likely to guide later behaviors than are attitudes based on indirect experience. The same might be expected of self-images, which are attitudes about self.

Contexts cue or activate particular self-schemata (e.g., Fiske & Taylor, 1984). Situations, audiences, and personal goals can all cue information in memory and thereby activate elements of the self-concept. Because of the specificity of these effects, they are discussed shortly in relation to the appropriate cueing agent.

Personality dispositions also play a role in the self-identification process. I have already discussed dispositional tendencies that focus attention on the self, making contextually relevant self-beliefs salient. Once salient, these self-images are more likely to be expressed in public self-identifications.

Personal Goals and Affective State

Given an individual's goals on an occasion, some self-images will be associated with goal achievement while others will be unassociated. For example, a junior executive who has the goal of rapid personal advancement in his or her company may regard such attributes as hard work, initiative, sound judgment, cleverness, and sociability as associated with the goal. The goal will then cue these self-images, thereby activating them in memory, and they will be more likely to be contained in public self-identifications.

There has been virtually no research on the impact of an actor's goals on the activation of particular self-images. However, research indicates that, when forming judgments of other people, a perceiver's goals influence the schemata that are activated (e.g., Cantor & Mischel, 1979; Jeffrey & Mischel, 1979); and that cueing a particular role context (e.g., professional life versus family life) activates schemata that are associated with the goals of the pertinent roles (e.g., schemata relevant to the business world versus parenting) (Trzebinski, McGlynn, Gray, & Tubbs, 1985). It would therefore be reasonable to expect that an actor's goals similarly activate asociated self-images.

Actor's moods and state of positive or negative affect will similarly influence the self-images that are salient. Affective states increase the accessibility in memory of commensurately toned information (Isen, 1984; Snyder & White, 1982). People who experience positive affect are more likely to focus on positive information about the self, while those who are experiencing negative affect are more likely to focus on negative information. In support of this idea, Snyder and White (1982) found that people in an elated mood tended to remember pleasant life experiences, while those in a depressed mood tended to remember sad and unpleasant experiences. Similarly, Mischel, Ebbesen, and Zeiss (1973) found that subjects who experienced a recent success attended more to their personality assets and less to their liabilities than did subjects who experienced a recent failure.

Situational and Audience Factors

Situations and audiences provide the context for self-identifications. (The impact of audiences has already been discussed, so the present section primarily concentrates on situational factors.) Contexts influence, in at least two ways, the extent to which elements of the self-concept will be expressed in public self-identifications

(Schlenker, 1984, 1985a). First, they do so through the opportunities and constraints they present. Situations and audiences both offer possibilities for satisfying
or thwarting values and goals, and present actors with behavior–outcome contingencies. When these contingencies involve public self-identifications, as in the case of
a job interview or important date, people are more likely to present themselves in
ways that maximize expected rewards and minimize expected costs (Baumeister,
1982; Jones & Pittman, 1982; Jones & Wortman, 1973; Schlenker, 1980; Tedeschi,
1981; Tedeschi & Norman, 1985). The more important the values and goals are, and
the clearer the contingency is between relevant outcomes and particular types of
self-presentations, the more likely it is that self-presentations will be influenced by
the situation and audience rather than the self-concept.

Secondly, situations (as well as audiences) influence self-identifications through
their capacity to cue particular goals, scripts or plans, and identity images, thereby
making them salient and activating associated information in memory. The cued
information can be of a more personal nature, such as elements of the self-concept,
or it can be of a more social nature, such as socially appropriate goals, scripts, and
roles that a person in the situation is expected to enact (irrespective, to some degree,
of the person's feelings or self-concept).

Situations can be said to have "personalities" (Bem & Funder, 1978), in that
specific traits are perceived as highly relevant to them (e.g., a battle evokes images
of bravery or cowardice; a party evokes images of gregariousness or shyness). Alexander and his associates (Alexander & Rudd, 1981; Alexander & Wiley, 1981) have
shown that subjects can identify normatively desirable social identities for given situations. Further, actors in these situations are evaluated more positively when their
behaviors more closely correspond with those of the most desirable social identity
for the situation. The situation itself thereby cues associated information about the
self, social roles, and social expectations in memory, and makes salient the contingencies between particular public self-identifications and outcomes.

Whether the self-concept will influence self-presentations depends on (a) the
balance of personal versus social information that is activated in memory, and (b)
the importance of the behavior–outcome contingencies on the occasion. Actors are
more likely to present themselves as the situation dictates when their options are
seemingly restricted, as in cases of highly structured situations that cue relevant
social roles and provide actors with less flexible social scripts, and situations that
involve important behavior–outcome contingencies. Actors are more likely to
present themselves consistently with their self-conceptions when their options are
greater, as in cases of less structured situations that permit a greater latitude of identities, and situations with less important behavior–outcome contingencies.

Conclusions

Conceptualizing self-identifications as activities shifts attention from the private
self per se to the personal and social influences on people's thoughts and behaviors. Situations, audiences, and personal characteristics (personality, self-concept,
goals, and affective state) combine to determine the self-identification that occurs

on a given occasion. Once the self-identification occurs, it can in turn influence the self-concept.

The Influence of Self-Presentations on the Self-Concept

Early social philosophers and psychologists (Baldwin, 1897; James, 1890) emphasized that the self is the product and reflection of social life. Symbolic interactionists (Cooley, 1902; Mead 1934), role theorists (Sarbin & Allen, 1968), dramaturgists (Goffman, 1959), and neo-Freudians (Sullivan, 1953) developed this theme to propose that people's private self-conceptions are constructed in part from the roles they enact, the public selves they project, and the self-relevant feedback they receive from others. Understanding the nature of the self-conception was held to be largely dependent on understanding the types of social experiences from which it is inferred.

Related Grounds for the Relationship

With this suggestive background of prior thought, it is somewhat surprising that very little research has examined the impact of people's public self-presentations on their private self-appraisals. However, several lines of related research, examining the relationship between behaviors and subsequent attitude change, suggest that self-appraisals will be strengthened or modified by self-presentations. Studies indicate a significant relationship between people's publicly enacted roles and their general attitudes toward role-relevant issues (Lieberman, 1956; Phillips, 1973; Sarbin & Allen, 1968). These largely correlational findings appear to be due to at least two influences: People select roles that are congruent with their values, attitudes, and personal attributes (Cheek & Hogan, 1983; Rosenberg, 1979; Secord & Backman, 1965; Swann, 1983), and also change their attitudes to make them more compatible with the roles they publicly enact (Janis, 1968; Lieberman, 1956).

Experimental studies have provided more definitive evidence indicating that role-playing a particular attitudinal position produces role-congruent attitude change (Elms, 1967; Janis, 1968). Attitudes are, under conditions that are considered shortly, strengthened or polarized following proattitudinal actions (e.g., Kiesler, 1971; Schlenker, 1982; Schlenker & Goldman, 1982) and made more consistent with counterattitudinal actions (Collins & Hoyt, 1972; Cooper & Fazio, 1984; Schlenker, 1982; Wicklund & Brehm, 1976). Indeed, self-generated information appears to be more effective in producing attitude change (e.g., Janis, 1968; Wicklund & Brehm, 1976), better recall of relevant details (Greenwald & Pratkanis, 1984), and more enduring attitudes that are more resistant to subsequent attitude change (Wood, 1982) than does passive exposure to comparable information. Explanations of these effects have been offered by self-perception theory (Bem, 1972), biased scanning approaches (Janis, 1968; Jones, Rhodewalt, Berglas, & Skelton, 1981), dissonance theory (Festinger, 1957; Wicklund & Brehm, 1976), and self-identification theory (Schlenker, 1982).

Self-Presentations and Self-Evaluations

This background of prior theory and relevant research makes it reasonable to expect that people's public self-presentations will also influence their private self-appraisals. The few studies (Gergen, 1965; Jones et al., 1981; Upshaw & Yates, 1968) that have explicitly examined the relationship have focused on changes in global self-evaluations as a consequence of self-presentational activities. These pioneering studies have been valuable in demonstrating that (a) self-presentations can affect subsequent self-appraisals, at least in terms of producing changes in global self-evaluations, (b) these changes are fairly robust and occur in a variety of situations, and (c) these changes are maximized when people's self-presentations occur under conditions of high decision freedom (Jones et al., 1981) or receive approval (Gergen, 1965).

In the first such study, Gergen (1965) found that subjects whose positive self-presentations were socially reinforced by an interviewer later evidenced more positive self-regard than did those who were not reinforced. In addition, it was found that, when subjects' self-presentations were reinforced, those who had exaggerated their self-descriptions under instructions to ingratiate later evidenced as high a level of self-evaluation as did subjects who had presented themselves under instructions to be accurate.

One interpretation of these findings was offered by E. E. Jones (1964), who suggested that, "Persons tend to exaggerate the perceived representativeness or felt sincerity of any performance which elicits approval" (p. 67), even if "they have distorted their self-picture in the attempt to gain this approval" (p. 58). This explanation implies that the actual *contents* of self-conceptions are modified to bring them in line with the *contents* of the self-presentations. Consistent with this explanation, Jones, Gergen, and Davis (1962) had earlier found that subjects rated their prior self-presentations to an interviewer as more accurate (i.e., self-descriptive) when they believed they had made a favorable rather than an unfavorable impression.

In contrast, Upshaw and Yates (1968) suggested that self-esteem should be temporarily raised following the successful completion of any task, such as trying to make a particular impression on another person and then receiving feedback that one has done so. They suggested that the changes in self-regard observed by Gergen represent feelings of heightened self-efficacy or the momentary flush of success rather than a change in self-appraisals that reflects the specific content of the self-presentation. To test their interpretation, they asked subjects to complete a personality test in a way that would cause a computer to give them very positive or very negative personality feedback, and subsequently received either a very positive or very negative profile. In support of their predictions, subjects' self-evaluations (as assessed on a measure of social desirability) were highest when they had accomplished their goal, that is, they tried for a positive evaluation and received it or tried for a negative evaluation and received it.

The study by Upshaw and Yates demonstrates the impact of successful goal completion on self-regard (see also Carver, 1979). It also illustrates the difficulty in drawing definitive conclusions about the precise effects of self-presentations on self-beliefs when (a) self-presentations are diffuse, encompassing numerous attribute dimensions, and (b) measures are taken only of global self-evaluations. Of course, the findings of Upshaw and Yates do not invalidate the interpretation of Gergen and Jones. Self-presentations may affect both corresponding self-beliefs and feelings of self-efficacy, and different contexts may make one or both relatively salient. The task used by Upshaw and Yates, a "game" context of fooling a computer where the feedback seems impersonal and undiagnostic, seems to be the type of situation that would emphasize "winning" and not the relevance of self-presentations to self-beliefs. The task used by Gergen, creating a positive impression on an interviewer who provides personal feedback after an interaction, is less of game and would make self-presentations appear to be relevant to self-beliefs.

More recently, Jones et al. (1981) conducted an interesting set of studies that examined the effects of self-deprecation as well as self-enhancement. In their first two studies, they found that subjects matched the self-enhancing or self-deprecating presentations given by models. When self-evaluations were later assessed, a carry-over effect was obtained, with subjects shifting their self-evaluations in the direction of the positivity–negativity of their self-presentations.

A third study examined conditions under which these carry-over effects would be maximized or minimized. In the context of a simulated job interview, subjects were given high or low choice about presenting themselves in a self-enhancing or self-deprecating fashion. Subjects also either gave their own in-role responses to the interviewer's forced-choice questions (self-referencing condition) or were told to give a set of preplanned role responses (non-self-referencing condition). It was found that, when subjects presented themselves self-enhancingly, they raised their self-evaluations in the self-referencing condition but not in the non-self-referencing condition; choice in selecting the role had no effect on self-evaluations. In contrast, when subjects presented themselves self-deprecatingly, they lowered their self-evaluations in the high-choice condition but not in the low-choice condition; the self-referencing condition had no effect on self-evaluations.

In explaining these results, Jones et al. argued that different processes accounted for the effects of self-enhancement versus self-deprecation; biased scanning was engaged after self-enhancement while dissonance was produced by self-deprecation. Their biased scanning variant of self-perception theory indicates that "situational cues elicit overt behaviors, and these behaviors, more compatible with some potential features of the self than others, render those compatible features salient" (1981, p. 419). The "crucial ingredient" in determining whether biased scanning will occur after a self-presentation is "whether the behavior is seen as 'owned' by the actor and reflective of his or her contemporary view of self," and not "whether an individual has or has not the freedom to engage in the suggested behavior" (p. 419).

Jones et al. also argued that the self is asymmetrically structured, with favorable self-descriptions more likely to be regarded as compatible with the self than unfavorable self-descriptions. If unfavorable self-presentations are more clearly discrepant from existing self-views, they will be more likely to arouse dissonance. The amount of dissonance that is generated will be directly related to the amount of perceived choice in selecting the role that was performed. Subjects therefore lower their self-evaluations to reduce dissonance only when they choose to engage in self-derogation.

This provocative interpretation was admittedly speculative and required assumptions about the structure of the self, the domain of each theory, and the link between the theories and the independent variables. With regard to the theory–variable linkage: Why would the choice variable, which has been repeatedly argued to influence self-perception (Bem, 1972), not be applicable to the biased scanning variant? Why would self-referencing, which involves *choice* in the selection of the contents of the role, be irrelevant to dissonance? Jones et al. do not provide answers, but instead appear to assign each variable to a different theory. Further, it is not clear why subjects in the self-deprecation condition would reduce dissonance by lowering their self-evaluations rather than employing an alternative mode of dissonance resolution, such as misperceiving their behavior as less counterattitudinal than it actually was (Scheier & Carver, 1980) or perceiving a greater obligation to perform the behavior (Verhaeghe, 1976). Indeed, dissonance theorists (e.g., Aronson, 1969) have argued that the elements of the self-concept are resistant to change and would usually be a least-preferred mode of reducing dissonance.

One possible reason for the pattern of results is that attributions of the *self-representativeness* of the behavior may have been influenced by the interaction of the three independent variables. Choice has been shown to interact with the social desirability of behavior to determine the extent to which attitudes are inferred from the behavior. Observers' attributions of an actor's attitudes are affected by the actor's choice in selecting a debate role when the role is socially undesirable (analogous to a negative self-presentation) but not when the role is socially desirable (analogous to a positive self-presentation) (Jones & Harris, 1967). Choice is therefore a more important attributional cue when behaviors are negative rather than positive. Self-referencing, in contrast, may be a more important cue when the behavior is positive rather than negative. Self-derogation is such a socially unexpected action that the actor is distinguished from other people primarily on the basis of choosing to perform the role, not on the basis of its precise details. Positive self-presentations, however, are more common and expected. Actors are distinguished from other people not on the basis of choosing to perform the behavior, which almost everyone would do, but on the basis of the precise details of the self-presentation and the freedom one had in selecting those details.

If this analysis is correct, then subjects in the Jones et al. (1981) study may simply have shifted their self-feelings in the direction of their behavior whenever the behavior seemed to be representative of the self. The representativeness of the behavior is a dimension that is relevant to both self-perception theory and dissonance theory. Therefore, either theory could be used to explain the results; or, following Jones et al., one might suggest that each theory is limited to a particular province.

It is clear that additional research is needed to clarify the issues and to examine the precise impact of self-presentations on both global self-evaluations and the content of self-appraisals. These issues and ambiguities aside, however, the work of E. E. Jones and his associates is important in demonstrating the impact of situational cues in eliciting self-presentations, and the subsequent impact of those behaviors on self-evaluations. In addition, they cogently argue that more than one process may be involved. With this background in mind, I now turn to a self-identification approach to the area.

Self-Identification as an Active Versus Passive Process

The self-identification process can vary in the extent to which it involves active assessment of the self, situation, and audience during the selection and construction of desired identity images (Schlenker, 1980, 1984, 1985a). Most everyday situations are relatively routinized and people's activities proceed without extensive thought about and assessment of the self and relevant contextual features (e.g., James, 1890; Langer, 1978; Schlenker, 1980, 1984, 1985a). Examples include dealing with familiar settings in the company of familiar and supportive others, performing frequently encountered tasks, and enacting frequently performed roles. Self-identifications then occur rather automatically, without prior thought and planning, based on scripts that have been used repeatedly and successfully in similar past contexts (and that contain the pertinent identity images for these contexts). They comprise modulated, habitual patterns of self-identifying behavior that may, at one time, have been practiced with care, but now form part of the actor's arsenal of activities. Unless problems are perceived as the script unfolds, self-identification proceeds according to the script. In this more passive, nonreflective mode, self-identifications draw largely from private self-images and frequently enacted roles, and they rarely represent a clear break from values or self-beliefs. To the extent that these self-identifications influence private self-appraisals, they are likely to do so through a more passive process without accompanying reflection, such as by the activity making a particular self-image salient, rather than by a more active process of contemplation and rationalization.

There are other occasions, however, when people expend considerable thought and planning on their performances, such as before an important date or speech, and are especially alert during the performance itself, vigilantly assessing themselves and the context and determining how they are doing. There are also occasions that might otherwise be routine in which problems develop during the performance and generate active assessment. At least two factors seem to produce active assessment of self-presentations (Schlenker, 1985a, in press). First is the *importance* of the values, goals, and identity images that exist on the occasion. As these increase in importance, so does the extent to which the occasion marshals the actor's mental resources. Second is the magnitude of any anticipated or encountered *impediments* to goals, scripts or plans, and the construction of desired identities. Impediments can spring from uncertainties, doubts, or threats that are relevant to a performance. A situation may be novel or unfamiliar, causing actors puzzlement about how to behave; an audience may be intimidating, causing actors to wonder about how they will come across; actors may doubt their ability to achieve their goals, causing them to expect failure; actors may be uncertain about their standing on particular attributes, causing them to reflect on their actual characteristics. As these examples illustrate, impediments can arise from personality, situational, and audience factors.

When they do occur, people engage in increased assessment of the factors relevant to the impediment.

The increased processing of information produced by these conditions implicates a more active and motivated (goal-directed) type of cognitive activity than is implied by the less thoughtful and more routine passive mode (Schlenker, 1980, 1984, 1985a, in press). *Active assessment produces more intensified processing of information pertinent to the problem, including information about one's identity. Further, it produces attempts to reconcile this information with one's desired identity images as best as possible.* The increased thought and motivation to construct desired identity images thereby focuses attention on the self, produces contemplation of the relevant self-images, and is guided by the pursuit of "truth about the self" in terms of the compromise between believability and beneficiality.

The distinction between active and passive modes has precedence in the literature on persuasion (Petty & Cacioppo, 1981) and attitude change following counterattitudinal behavior (Fazio, Zanna, & Cooper, 1977). Petty and Cacioppo proposed that persuasion occurs in one of two ways: via a central route that involves active processing, thoughtful consideration, and evaluation of arguments and evidence; or via a more passive, peripheral route in which salient situational features, such as the characteristics of the source of the message, influence reactions in a nonthoughtful manner. They proposed that the ego importance of the information contained in the communication is a major determinant of whether processing occurs by the central route (for ego-involving messages) or the peripheral route (for uninvolving messages). Ego importance falls in the present category of the importance of the relevant values, goals, and identity images. In a related vein, Fazio et al. proposed that, when counterattitudinal actions fall within an individual's latitude of acceptance on a topic, and hence are not greatly discrepant from existing beliefs, attitude change takes place via a passive self-perception process in which attitudes are simply inferred from behaviors. When counterattitudinal actions fall within an individual's latitudes of rejection on an issue, and hence are clearly discrepant from prior beliefs, attitude change takes place via the motivated process of dissonance reduction, which involves rationalization. Large discrepancies between actions and attitudes can be regarded as a subtype of the present category of impediments, since they both raise uncertainties about what the actor is "really like" and threaten desired identity images (Schlenker, 1982).

The Passive Mode: Processes

When people are in the passive, or nonthoughtful, mode, public self-identifications can influence private self-appraisals. The effects, however, appear to represent straightforward processes of self-perception and cognitive salience, not active ratiocination such as contemplating the "truth" about oneself, ruminating about existing self-images, or rationalizing events. At least two interrelated processes appear to be involved. Public self-identifications can (a) initiate a self-perception process in which self-images are inferred from the behavior (Bem, 1972; Jones et al., 1981; Kelley, 1967), and (b) activate behavior-relevant self-images in memory, making them more accessible (Fazio, Effrein, & Falender, 1981; Fazio, Herr, & Olney, 1984).

Self-perception. Cues that generate the inference that a behavior is representative of the self (i.e., descriptive of enduring personal characteristics) will produce a shift in the corresponding self-belief in the direction of the behavior or, if a self-belief already corresponds with the behavior, strengthen that self-belief, making it more accessible in memory and resistant to change. This proposition is consistent with the tenets of self-perception theory (Bem, 1972), Kelley's (1967) covariance model of attribution, and the biased scanning variant of self-perception theory (Jones et al., 1981). (The conditions that produce an inference of representativeness are considered shortly.)

Research on self-perception, which indicates that people infer their attitudes from their behaviors when situational pressures are minimal (see Bem, 1972), is consistent with the above proposition, although few of these studies have dealt directly with beliefs about the self. The few studies that are germane to self-appraisals lend support to the proposition. First, studies that have examined the impact of self-presentations on self-evaluations focused on the role of social approval (Gergen, 1965; Jones et al., 1962) and, more recently, the self-referencing quality of self-enhancement (Jones et al., 1981). It may be concluded from these studies that people's self-evaluations are altered when self-presentations are regarded as representative of an enduring personal characteristic (i.e., approval provides consensual agreement about the self-characterization; self-referencing suggests that the self-presentation reflects internal attributes). Second, Turner and Gordon (1981) found that the "true self" is usually associated with behaviors that are perceived as unpremeditated and spontaneous, while the "spurious self" is associated with behaviors that are seen as calculated or the result of external requirements.

Activating self-schemata. Fazio et al. (1984) suggested that attitudinal inferences from behavior "produce an attitude that is highly accessible in memory, that is, one that can serve as a strong, unambiguous internal cue" (p. 278). In examining attitude-behavior consistency, Fazio et al. found that behaviors that were freely chosen, as opposed to required, facilitated subjects' subsequent judgments, as measured by the latency of response to attitudinal inquiries on the dimension represented by the behavior. Behaviors that are freely selected are likely to be perceived as internally caused, and hence be representative of personal characteristics (Bem, 1972; Kelley, 1967). In contrast, behaviors that were required did not improve subsequent response speed. These findings suggest that when behaviors are perceived as representative of the self, a self-perception process occurs in which corresponding attitudes are formed, activated, and/or strengthened. These attitudes, in turn, become readily accessible in memory and are likely to influence subsequent activities.

In a related vein, Fazio et al. (1981) asked subjects a set of questions that were designed to elicit, and did elicit, either extraverted or introverted responses. Subsequently, subjects completed questionnaires that assessed introversion versus extraversion and also had the opportunity to interact with another subject (actually a confederate) in a waiting room situation where behavioral measures of introversion-extraversion could be gathered (e.g., who initiated the conversation, how much the subject talked, judges' ratings of the subjects' introversion-extraversion). It was found that subjects who had undergone extraverted as opposed to introverted questioning during the interview subsequently rated themselves as more extraverted and actually behaved in a more extraverted fashion. Their freely chosen self-descriptions during the interview seemed to activate the relevant concept in memory and permitted it to guide their subsequent actions.

When self-schemata are activated by a self-perception process, the information they contain (e.g., past behaviors, experiences) is more accessible in memory, facilitating relevant judgments and guiding the actor's activities. Dlugolecki and Schlenker (1985) examined the impact of self-presentations on self-appraisals, recall, and behavior. Subjects were told that the experiment was a training exercise for graduate students who were learning interview techniques and who believed that the subjects were applicants for a research assistant position. Half the subjects were interviewed under instructions to create a positive impression of their sociability, an attribute supposedly important for the position. (Subjects were given high choice about selecting the self-enhancing role and could provide their own in-role answers to the interviewer's questions, thereby maximizing the likelihood of self-inferences of sociability.) The remaining subjects were told about the emphasis on sociability but were not interviewed. Subsequently, the following measures were taken: (a) anonymous self-reports of sociability, self-esteem, and other attributes (e.g., leadership, intelligence); (b) behavioral measures of sociability in a waiting room situation with another subject (actually a confederate), which included whether the subject initiated a conversation, how much he or she talked, and judge's ratings of the subjects' sociability; and (c) an anonymous behavioral recall measure that asked subjects to list five behavioral experiences that they had had in the past (outside the experimental setting) that were relevant to sociability and to indicate how sociable each example suggested they were.

As compared to subjects who did not present themselves to the interviewer, those who presented themselves as sociable later described themselves as being more sociable and actually behaved more sociably with the confederate in the waiting room, being more likely to initiate a conversation, talking more often, and being rated by judges as more sociable. They thus not only described themselves as more sociable, but this self-image guided their behavior in a different setting. In addition, subjects who had presented themselves, as compared to those who had not, later recalled past behaviors that typified greater sociability, as rated both by the subjects and by judges who read and evaluated the incidents that were listed. Their self-presentations apparently activated a self-image of high sociability that made prior highly sociable past experiences accessible in memory. Finally, no differences were obtained between the self-presentation and no-self-presentation conditions on measures of self-esteem, of unrelated attributes such as leadership ability or intelligence, or of affect, such as happy-sad and cheerful-depressed. The effects of the self-presentation therefore were specific to the self-image that was contained in the self-presentation, did not generalize across all attributes, and could not have been mediated merely by momentary increases in self-esteem or positive affect.

Forming and strenghtening self-beliefs through self-perception. The cumulative body of research on self-perception processes indicates that attitudes can be formed (Bem, 1972) and strengthened, that is, made more accessible in memory (Fazio et al., 1984) and more resistant to change (Kiesler, 1971), by one's behaviors. The traditional view advanced by some advocates of self-perception theory is that attitudes and other internal states are largely an epiphenomenon, arising after one's behaviors, and are relatively unstable, continually being erased and recreated by one's actions. In contrast, Fazio et al. (1984) noted that it "is ironic that an individual's undergoing what is described as a radical behaviorist process has the outcome of strengthening the attitude, making it more of an accessible, internal cue and, hence lessening the need to rely on a similar process in the future" (p. 284). Research on the activation of attitudes in memory as a consequence of self-perception contributes to a picture of the self as a somewhat more stable, less situationally determined, entity.

The Passive Mode: When Do Self-Presentations Influence Self-Appraisals?

When will people's behaviors influence their self-appraisals through the processes of self-perception and the activation of self-schemata? The answer requires examination of the conditions that produce the inference that a self-presentation is representative of the self; and also the conditions that override the process by activating preexisting self-images, which reduce or eliminate the need to infer internal states from behaviors.

Representativeness. When self-presentations appear to be representative of the self, that is, descriptive of enduring personal characteristics, corresponding self-images are formed, strengthened, or activated. Research has indicated that people are more likely to attribute their behaviors to internal states (e.g., traits, attitudes) when they appear to be personally responsible for the behavior. Greater personal responsibility is created when: (a) an action occurs under conditions of high rather than low choice, especially when the behavior is less expected or desirable (Bem, 1972; Collins & Hoyt, 1972; Kelley, 1967); (b) the specific content of the action is not constrained by situational requirements (Jones et al., 1981); (c) the action appears to be spontaneous rather than calculated (Turner & Gordon, 1981); (d) monetary payments for the action are either small or excessively large and suggestive of immoral activity rather than an appropriate compensation (Kelley, 1967; Schlenker, 1982; Schlenker, Forsyth, Leary, & Miller, 1980); and (e) the behavior has been consistently emitted across a variety of situations (Kelley, 1967; C. R. Snyder, 1985; Snyder et al., 1983). These contextual conditions lead to an inference of an internal rather than external origin for the act and heighten feelings of personal responsibility.

In addition, a self-presentation is more likely to be perceived as representative of the self when it receives consensual agreement from others indicating that they validate it as compared to when they stand mute about it (Schlenker, 1980). An audience who provides favorable, approving feedback after positive self-presentations (Gergen, 1965) or a sad nod of agreement following negative self-presentations indicates that they support and accept as accurate the identity that was offered. These tacit or explicit opinions serve to enhance the perceived representativeness of the self-presentation. Indeed, Jones et al. (1962) found that positive self-presentations that received approval were regarded as more self-descriptive than those that did not. Of course, not all audiences serve as potent cues for representativeness. The opinions of gullible, unknowledgeable others receive less weight than those of knowledgeable, discerning others. Consequently, perceived representativeness will be enhanced when the validating audience is more significant to the actor, being more competent, attractive, or powerful (Schlenker, 1980) and consisting of a larger rather than smaller number of others (Backman, Secord, & Pierce, 1963).

Strength of prior self-beliefs. Bem (1972) introduced a qualifier to self-perception theory by postulating that the process would occur when "internal cues are weak, ambiguous, or uninterpretable" (p. 2). Strong, well-defined internal states presumably override the self-perception process by providing salient private information that forms the basis for judgments. Indeed, self-perception has been found to occur primarily under conditions of internal uncertainty (Chaiken & Baldwin, 1981; Green, 1974) and/or low importance of the judgment (Taylor, 1975). For example, Chaiken and Baldwin (1981) found that subjects inferred their religious attitudes from their freely chosen behaviors only when they had weak initial attitudes, as determined by low affective-cognitive consistency. Subjects with strong initial attitudes (high affective-cognitive consistency), in contrast, relied on these for their subsequent activities and did not demonstrate a self-perception effect. In a slightly different vein, Taylor (1975) found that subjects inferred their attitudes toward another person from bogus physiological feedback only when they anticipated no future consequences of their attitudes. When future consequences were anticipated, subjects engaged in a more thoughtful reevaluation of their attitudes in which the bogus feedback played a minimal role. Taylor suggested that a self-perception process is likely to occur only when attitudes and their consequences are unimportant or inconsequential.

What factors constitute a strong, well-defined self-schema or initial attitude about the self? Several dimensions have been isolated. Attitudes about the self can be regarded as stronger when: (a) they are more important to the individual because they fulfill personal needs and goals, and are related to valued outcomes (Greenwald & Breckler, 1985; Schlenker, 1982, 1984, 1985a; Taylor, 1975; Wicklund & Gollwitzer, 1982); (b) they are more central to the individual's self-conception, encompassing numerous subsidiary self-images (Rosenberg, 1979; Schlenker, 1984, 1985a); (c) they have been formed through personal experience on the dimension, as opposed to having been contemplated in the abstract (Fazio & Zanna, 1981); (d) they exhibit high rather than low consistency between the affective and cognitive components (Chaiken & Baldwin, 1981); and (e) the individual expresses high rather than low certainty in his or her standing on the dimension (Markus, 1977; Swann, 1985). Each of these factors increases the accessibility of prior self-schemata and thereby overrides the self-perception process.

When strong prior attitudes are relevant to a particular situation (i.e., likely to be cued by contextual features), they appear to take precedence over behaviors as a guide for subsequent self-identifications. Attitudes of more moderate strength, however, may still override the self-perception process if they are activated by internal or external cues. Situational cues, such as instructing a person to think about his or her relevant attitudes (Snyder & Swann, 1976), or personality dispositions that focus people on the private self (Carver & Scheier, 1981, 1985; Greenwald & Breckler, 1985; Hogan & Cheek, 1983) increase the likelihood that contextually relevant attitudes will be activated, even when these might otherwise be less than especially strong.

Discrepancies between attitudes and behaviors. If behaviors are clearly discrepant from prior attitudes, will self-perception occur? Fazio et al. (1977) proposed that a self-perception process is applicable only when behaviors are not greatly discrepant from prior attitudes. Operationally, they predicted that behaviors that fall within people's latitude of acceptance on a dimension (i.e., the range of values that people would endorse as being descriptive of and in tune with their favored position) will evoke a self-perception process. However, behaviors that fall within people's latitudes of rejection on a dimension (i.e., the range of values that people regard as undescriptive and opposed to their favored position) produce dissonance, an active process that involves motivated rationalization. Behaviors that are clearly discrepant from prior attitudes make those attitudes more salient than they would otherwise be and highlight the discrepancy, producing a situation in which more active processing is needed to account for the problem. Jones et al. (1981) endorsed this interpretation and, as discussed earlier, applied it to the effects of self-presentations. The results of experiments by Fazio et al. (1977), Jones et al. (1981), and Woodyard (1972) are consistent with these hypotheses.

The Active Mode: Processes

In contrast to the passive mode, the active mode involves a more thoughtful consideration of the implications of one's self-presentations and the contexts in which they occur. It constitutes a more intensive processing of information that goes beyond surface features and involves argumentation (documenting and counterarguing) designed to reaffirm desired identity images (Schlenker, in press). This assessment engages both the cognitive and motivational facets of the actor's identity.

The goal of the assessment is to construct desired identity images. In other words, it is to arrive at the "truth about the self," with truth defined in terms of the combination of believability ("Based on salient evidence, is this the type of person I really am?") and beneficiality ("Is this the type of person I really want to be?"). Evidence and aspirations become fused in the integration, and actors' conclusions identify the "best" type of person they can be given the self-presentation, the context, and the salient evidence (Schlenker, 1980, 1985a, in press).

When active processing occurs, it has the potential to influence self-conceptions. However, the possible impact is less straightforward than is the case in the passive mode. In the passive mode, the question is, when will people's self-presentations produce a strengthening or corresponding shift in private self-appraisals versus have little impact on the private self? In the active mode, however, the more intensive processing can produce internalization, no change, or even a boomerang effect, where self-appraisals shift in a direction opposite to the self-presentation (e.g., as when a person counterargues against an undesirable self-presentation and contemplates information that would discount it and reaffirm desired identity images). The possibility of a boomerang effect produced by self-presentations has not been previously considered in the literature, although the general phenomenon has been documented in the area of attitude change (Petty & Cacioppo, 1981).

Further, situational cues and audience feedback may play a more complex role in influencing self-appraisals. In the passive mode, cues that lead to the attribution that a self-presentation is representative rather than unrepresentative of the self produce greater correspondent change in self-appraisals. The self-inference process is rather straightforward and cues are taken at face value; for example, if cues suggest an internal origin for the action, an attribution is made to dispositional characteristics. Although this "logical basis" for drawing conclusions may be used in the active mode, greater thought permits people to go beyond face value and rationalize their acts. Schlenker (1980, 1982, 1985a) proposed that *when the behavior pertains to an important identity image, people are likely to resist the inference that a desirable self-presentation is unrepresentative of self or an undesirable one is representative of self.* In resisting the inference, people construct accounts for the event that preserve or reaffirm their desired identities and negate the impact of cues that would lead to an alternative conclusion (Schlenker, 1980, 1982, in press).

In order to explore the implications of active processing, consider two types of events that are important to the self and that can create problems during the self-identification process. These are occasions when: (a) self-presentations threaten the self, and (b) self-presentations potentially benefit the self but their implications are ambiguous.

Active Processing and Threats to the Self

Identities are potentially threatened when undesirable information can be associated with the self (Schlenker, 1980, 1982). Self-presentations are undesirable to the extent that they violate personal or social standards for conduct, including the standards for claiming desired identity images (e.g., a transgression violates the image of being a moral, rule-abiding individual). Such actions can generate negative consequences for the self (e.g., they can produce anxiety, embarrassment, or shame, result in disapproval, and make the actor appear to be incompetent, unattractive, immoral, or otherwise different than he or she desires to appear) and/or for other people (e.g., harming or deceiving others). Self-presentations are more closely associated with the self when they appear to be representative rather than unrepresentative of the actor's characteristics. For example, high association is created when self-presentations occur under conditions of high personal responsibility or when audiences appear to regard the behavior as descriptive of the actor's characteristics. When undesirable information can be associated with the self, a failure to neutralize the potential problem has negative repercussions for identity.

Intensified processing and accounting. When potential problems arise, an active assessment of self, situation, and audience is triggered that produces (a) an intensified search for, processing and recall of, and sensitivity to pertinent information, (b) an increased salience of relevant personal or social standards against which actors compare their performance, and (c) an explanation of the potential difficulty that seeks to reconcile the undesired information with the relevant personal or social standards (Schlenker, 1985a, in press). When active processing begins, people become increasingly sensitive to nuances and implications of information that they may not have previously noticed or considered. In addition, prior self-schemata and the subsumed self-beliefs, experiences, and standards that are relevant to the occasion become salient. The increased accessibility of this self-information provides a rich data base for defining and attempting to deal with the problem.

At the outset of assessment, people search for information in a fashion that is biased toward supporting their desired identity images. M. Snyder (1984) has documented people's selective tendency to seek and obtain confirmation for their hypotheses through a biased search-and-examination process. Desired beliefs about the self occupy a central position in people's cognitive worlds, so it is not surprising that they will usually search for self-relevant information in a manner that generates support (see Swann, 1983, 1985). When potential threats occur, the propensity appears to be heightened, motivating people to seek additional documentation that will buttress their desired identity images. A variety of research suggests a selective search, both in one's memory and in the environment, when potential threats are encountered. For example, Frey (1981) showed that, when people's identities are threatened by their purported poor performance on an intelligence test, they tend to seek out information that derogates the validity of the test, thereby eliminating the problem. Pyszczynski, Greenberg, and LaPrelle (1985) found that, after failure, people most prefer to examine social comparison information when they believe others did poorly on the test rather than well.

People process information more thoroughly and recall it better when it pertains to the self than when it is irrelevant to the self (Greenwald, 1980; Greenwald & Pratkanis, 1984). This pervasive egocentric sensitivity to information is enhanced in the face of problems: Potential threats generate more intensified processing of relevant information than would otherwise occur. Research supports the proposition and indicates that information processing can be facilitated when people confront potential threats. Wyer and Frey (1983) found that subjects display better recall of self-threatening information than nonthreatening information. They argued that this more in-depth processing is used in people's attempts to counterargue and refute the implications of the information, thereby preserving desired identity images. Similarly, Swann and Hill (unpublished, described in Swann, 1983) found that subjects who received self-discrepant feedback from others made self-descriptive judgments faster than those who received self-confirming feedback or no feedback. These results suggest that potential threats to the self increase the accessibility of the relevant identity images in memory, making them more likely to guide the actor's subsequent judgments and actions. Indeed, Swann and Read (1981) and Swann and Hill (1982) found that subjects who received self-disconfirming feedback from audiences, as compared to those who received self-confirming feedback, were subsequently most likely to try to reaffirm these images by acting in a self-validating manner. Their actions appeared to be designed to change the opinion of the evaluator and thereby eliminate the problem.

Active assessment also increases the salience of personal or social standards for performance (Carver, 1979; Carver & Scheier, 1981; Schlenker, 1984, 1985a, in press; Schlenker & Leary, 1982a, in press). Self-presentations are compared against these standards and, if they fall short, negative affect is generated. Actors feel tense and anxious, and may experience a lowering of global self-feelings until the threat is eliminated or reduced. These negative self-feelings are greater to the extent that the potential threat is of greater magnitude and actors perceive that they will be unable to reduce its impact on their identity.

Active assessment also generates an explanation of the potential threat that attempts to reconcile the undesired information with the personal and social standards that appear to have been violated (Schlenker, 1980, 1982, in press). These self-serving explanations are termed *accounts*. Two general classes of accounts are *excuses*, which attempt to minimize the actor's personal responsibility for the event (e.g., blaming the behavior on situational pressures; attributing a negative evaluation from others to their incompetence or ill will), and *justifications*, which attempt to minimize the undesirability of the event by underestimating its consequences or reinterpreting the event itself (e.g., claiming that little harm was done, or that the behavior was not as it may have appeared, as in the case of a joke).

The literature on defensive biases in attribution (e.g., Weary Bradley, 1978) can be viewed as the study of excuses (Schlenker, 1980, 1982; C. R. Snyder, 1985). The literature on attitude change following behavior that harms others can be regarded as the study of justifications (see Schlenker, 1980, 1982). In the literature on counterattitudinal behavior, subjects have been found to employ both excuses and justifications as means of rationalizing their actions (see Schlenker, 1982, for a review). For example, subjects excuse their actions by stating that they were under obligation to comply with the experimenter's request (Verhaeghe, 1976) or by accepting feedback from observers that suggests their behavior was constrained even though the subjects did not initially perceive it as such (Riess & Schlenker, 1977). Justifications used by subjects include shifting their attitudes on the topic to demonstrate greater agreement with their behavior, thereby making the behavior appear less deceitful or harmful, and misperceiving the behavior itself, regarding it as less discrepant from their prior attitudes (e.g., Scheier & Carver, 1980; Schlenker et al., 1980).

The impact on self-appraisals. Whether or not potential threats will influence sub-sequent self-appraisals depends on the magnitude of the problem and the perceived likelihood that it can be successfully resolved (Schlenker, in press). Potential threats that are easily eliminated produce no change in self-appraisals. When counterattitu-dinal behavior occurs in a context of minimal personal responsibility or no negative consequences, attitudes are not influenced by the behavior (e.g., Collins & Hoyt, 1972; Schlenker, 1982). These "potential threats" are impotent because they occur without undesired implications for identity; either no harm was done or the actor is not accountable for the behavior. Indeed, little or no negative affect appears to accompany these conditions (Cooper & Fazio, 1984) and self-evaluations appear to be unchanged by them (Jones et al., 1981). The threat is readily dispelled by virtue of salient situational features that can be quickly identified during assessment.

In contrast, stronger potential threats produce more intensive cognitive and behavioral activities that can magnify one's strengths or weaknesses. When people's prior self-images on the relevant dimensions are important, strong, and well defined, a large supply of image-supporting information is potentially available in memory. Active processing makes this information salient, and counterarguing occurs to explain and defuse the potential threat. Excuses and justifications are generated to account for the undesired behavior, such as citing a perceived obliga-tion to perform the behavior or play the role. These accounts serve to protect prior self-images such that they *do not have to change to accommodate the behavior.*

This analysis of active processing differs from an alternative interpretation offered by Jones et al. (1981). They proposed that public self-derogation that falls in an individual's latitude of rejection on the dimension arouses dissonance, and *self-images will shift in the direction of the behavior* in order to reduce the dissonance. The self-identification approach, in contrast, suggests that a corresponding change in self-images usually will not occur under these conditions because accounts will be generated to reduce the threat. Indeed, dissonance theorists (Aronson, 1969) have usually argued that the self-concept comprises cognitive elements that are especially resistant to change. Hence, when dissonance occurs, alternative modes of dis-sonance resolution, analogous to the present categories of excuses and justifica-tions, will be employed. Therefore, to the extent that prior self-images are important, strong, and well defined, they are unlikely to shift to accommodate highly discrepant behavior.[3]

---

[3]The results of Jones et al. (1981) do not aid in distinguishing between these interpretations. Although they found that subjects lowered their global self-evaluations after a globally nega-tive self-presentation, it is not clear whether these findings reflected (a) a downward shift in the content of self-beliefs produced by the self-presentation, or (b) a short-term, generalized lowering of global self-feelings produced by the negative affect associated with self-derogations that appear to be representative of self. Such negative affect should momentarily occur until the actor has successfully resolved the problem through accounts and the reaffir-mation of self. In addition, it is unclear whether subjects had strong, well-defined attitudes on the dimensions that were involved and regarded these dimensions as high in importance.

An interesting implication of active processing is that an undesirable self-presentation may actually *strengthen* people's self-images on the dimension. When prior self-images are important, strong, and well defined, a large supply of refuting information is potentially available in memory. The behavior activates this information, magnifies the examination of it, and generates counterarguing in the attempt to reaffirm the desired images. The result is a strengthening (i.e., greater subsequent accessibility in memory and greater resistance to change) or even polarization of desired identity images. Identity is thereby asserted at the expense of the threat. Consistent with this reasoning, Tesser (1978) documented that greater thought about a particular attitude tends to polarize it. In the case of undesirable self-presentations, the polarization of attitudes represents a boomerang effect, in which self-appraisals are shifted in a direction opposite the behavior.

Spivak and Schlenker (1985) found evidence of a boomerang effect following undesirable self-presentations. In their study, some of the subjects were induced to present themselves negatively on the important dimension of social sensitivity. The self-presentation occurred in the context of cues that indicated it was either representative (i.e., play the negative role, but try to be truthful, thinking of yourself on a day when you are down about your sensitivity) or unrepresentative (i.e., play the role, even if you have to lie, but don't be so outrageous that it is not credible). The representativeness manipulation produced equally negative self-presentations, but the two groups differed appropriately in the degree to which they said they lied. Subjects were subsequently asked to rate their social sensitivity on an anonymous questionnaire.

The negative self-presentation should be more self-threatening, and hence generate greater assessment and counterarguing, when it might be seen as diagnostic rather than undiagnostic of self. The results supported this reasoning. As compared to a control group who did not present themselves, subjects in the unrepresentative cue condition showed no change, but subjects in the representative cue condition significantly *increased* their self-ratings of social sensitivity. The former subjects could simply dismiss the behavior as a legitimate lie requested by the experimenter. The latter subjects, in comparison, polarized their self-appraisals and thereby reaffirmed desired images. These findings are opposite what might be expected based on a simple self-inference process in which self-appraisals are shifted in the direction of behaviors that appear to be representative of self.

There has been no research to explore the boundaries of a boomerang effect. The present analysis suggests that it will be most likely to occur after undesirable self-presentations when prior self-images are important, strong, and well defined. These conditions provide an impetus for counterarguing and increase the likelihood that desired identity images can be reaffirmed successfully. Successful counterarguing is also likely to be facilitated when the environmental context for the activity is supportive, as in cases where friends or family assist the actor in reaffirming desired identity images (Schlenker, in press).

Under what conditions will self-appraisals shift in the direction of undesirable self-presentations? To the extent that prior self-images on the dimension are weak and held with uncertainty, a strong threat indicating that the self-presentation is representative of self will be more difficult to defuse. The examination of relevant information is then likely to reveal an inadequate data base that makes counter-arguing difficult. Actors may begin to doubt their desired standing on the dimension and their ability to maintain it. These doubts will be enhanced when the context for the activity is unsupportive (Schlenker, in press), as when the behavior is public, other people are perceived to be discerning and critical, the actor has not established a "good" prior reputation on the dimension, and the situation is seen as more diagnostic in nature (e.g., a "test" rather than a "game"). Low expectations of being able to counteract the threat produce anxiety, and actors become trapped in a process of intensified self-assessment that is likely to magnify their weaknesses (Schlenker, in press; Schlenker & Leary, 1982a). The result is likely to be a change in self-appraisals on the dimension in the direction of the undesirable self-presentation. When particular identity images are highly important to the actor, they are difficult to abandon on the basis of a single undesirable self-presentation even if they are poorly documented. However, continued strong threats are likely to have a cumulative impact and produce changes in self-appraisals. Research is needed on these hypotheses.

Are positive deviations threatening? Are self-presentations that flagrantly overesti-mate (positively) one's attributes also a threat, or are threats confined to those that flagrantly underestimate (negatively) one's attributes? There are grounds for con-cluding that excessively positive self-presentations (e.g., those that fall within an individual's latitude of rejection on the dimension) will generate a threat, even though the magnitude of that threat may not be as great as that of negative self-presentations because of its positive nature. Excessively positive self-presentations can create personal and interpersonal problems (see Schlenker, 1980, 1984, 1985a; Schlenker & Leary, 1982a, in press). They commit actors to personal and social standards they doubt they can meet, and they make it difficult to document claims to these images in the face of tests and impediments. Self-assessment will produce negative affect and self-criticism when actors consider the extent to which they will fall short of the high interpersonal expectations. Therefore, to the extent that exces-sively positive self-presentations commit actors to standards that they doubt they will be able to maintain, they pose a threat and arouse anxiety. Actors will attempt to account for them in ways that maintain and protect their prior identity images, such as by rejecting the extent to which the aggrandizing self-presentation is self-representative. Indeed, people reject overly enhancing praise from others that might commit them to continued superior performance (S. C. Jones, 1973; Kanouse, Gum-pert, & Canavan-Gumpert, 1981).

Active Processing and Potential Benefits to Self

Impediments to desired identity images are also created when events block recogni-tion of one's perceived attainments (Schlenker, 1980, 1982, in press; Schlenker & Schlenker, 1975). When people have pretensions of claiming highly desired identity images (i.e., those that are important, personally beneficial, and seemingly believable), their aspirations are thwarted if they confront problems. The problems can include the skeptical remarks of doubting others (e.g., his promotion was due to politics or luck rather than merited) or contextual cues that appear to deny personal responsibility (e.g., her contribution to charity was pressured by the solicitor rather than motivated by altruistic concerns) or undermine the importance of the attainment (e.g., her contribution was minimal and will not really be of much help). In the absence of impediments, actors can proceed with their plans with the confidence that their claims to desired identity images are secure. When impediments occur, actors' plans are disrupted, their recognition is questioned, and active processing occurs to reaffirm the desired identity images and remove the impediment.

It is proposed that identity-thwarting impediments (e.g., dealing with the insinuations of others that one's promotion was unmerited) produce effects that are analogous to those generated by more overt types of identity-threatening impediments (e.g., dealing with the loss of one's job and its implications of incompetence). The impediment engages that active mode and produces (a) intensified processing of relevant information, (b) a comparison of the identity that has been created because of the impediment with the relevant personal and social standards, (c) an explanation of the impediment that is designed to reconcile it with the standards, and (d) other activities designed to reaffirm the desired identity images. In comparison to the extensive literature on the consequences of overt threats to self, there has been less research on the consequences of identity-thwarting impediments. The literature that does exist, though, supports the complementarity of these types of impediments.

People prefer to receive credit for identity-bolstering events and usually construct self-serving explanations of them. *Acclamations* are self-serving explanations of an event that indicate why important standards have been met or exceeded (Schlenker, 1980, 1982, 1985a, in press). Two forms of acclamations are *entitlements*, which attempt to maximize personal responsibility for the event; and *enhancements*, which affirm the identity-bolstering qualities of the event. Entitlements are illustrated by the tendency to attribute successes to personal rather than situational causes (e.g., Weary Bradley, 1978), while enhancemetns are illustrated by the tendency to overvalue one's own accomplishments relative to the comparable accomplishments of others (Rosenberg, 1979) or to regard one's own motives for a behavior as "better" than the motives of others (Schlenker, Hallam, & McCown, 1983).

Being denied credit for an accomplishment is upsetting and generates counterarguing. Sicoly and Ross (1977) found that subjects who believed they had performed well on a test (a) took high personal responsibility for the accomplishment and (b) derogated others who assigned them less responsibility than they had taken, thereby countering the challenge. The complementary reactions occurred after failure: subjects who believed they had performed poorly on the test (a) took low personality responsibility for their performance and (b) derogated others who assigned them higher responsibility.

Undesired audience feedback also seems to increase the accessibility of relevant self-images in memory, to produce attempts to reaffirm desired identity images, and to mobilize behaviors in ways designed to eliminate the impediment. Identity-discrepant as opposed to identity-validating feedback from audiences has been found to cause subjects to make identity-descriptive judgments faster, to be more resistant to the feedback, and to polarize their self-descriptions and dramatize their actions in ways that assert desired identity images (Gollwitzer & Wicklund, 1985; Swann & Hill, 1982; Swann & Read, 1981).

One of the unusual implications of the self-identification analysis is that it suggests a possible reversal of the traditional relationship between personal responsibility and attitude change. From an attributional standpoint, people "are" what they are responsible for doing. It has been largely taken for granted that greater responsibility for an act produces greater attitude change to justify the act (Bem, 1972; Collins & Hoyt, 1972; Cooper & Fazio, 1984; Wicklund & Brehm, 1976). However, these analyses ignore people's ability to influence their environments by anticipating the reactions of audiences and acting in ways that can alter attributions that might otherwise be likely. People resist the inference that a desirable self-presentation is unrepresentative of self, just as they do the inference that an undesirable self-presentation is representative of self. When self-presentations are highly desirable, situational cues that block recognition are hypothesized to generate active processing and lead to an assertion of these desired identity images. Thus, cues suggesting lower rather than higher responsibility for important, desired actions likely to strengthen or polarize desired identity images (Schlenker, 1980, 1982, in press; Schlenker & Goldman, 1982; Schlenker & Riess, 1979; Schlenker & Schlenker, 1975).

This hypothesis has been supported in the area of attitude change. Schlenker and Schlenker (1975) induced subjects to praise another person, who actually was rather plain and ordinary, under conditions of low or high importance of the act (i.e., they either would not or would meet and interact with the other). Further, the behavior occurred under conditions of low or high choice. According to self-perception theory, subjects should have inferred more positive attitudes toward the other when choice was high. However, as had been predicted by the self-identification approach, subjects evidenced the most positive attitudes toward the other when the action was important and occurred under conditions of low choice. In a conceptually similar study of proattitudinal behavior by Schlenker and Goldman (1982), subjects delivered a proattitudinal communication on a topic about which they felt strongly, and the behavior was elicited under conditions of low or high choice. When the importance of the behavior was emphasized by stressing persuasiveness, it was found that subjects polarized their attitudes, becoming even more strongly in favor of the topic, in the low-choice but not the high-choice condition.

In the most direct evidence to date, Spivak and Schlenker (1985) found a "reverse representativeness" effect of self-presentations. Some of the subjects in their study presented themselves positively on the dimension of social sensitivity, and the self-presentation was elicited under conditions suggesting that the behavior was either representative or unrepresentative of self. When anonymous self-ratings of their social sensitivity were later assessed, it was found that subjects polarized their self-appraisals in the unrepresentative cue condition, rating themselves higher than subjects in a control group who did not present themselves. In contrast, subjects in the representative cue condition, who did not confront an impediment to their desired self-identification, evidenced no shift in self-appraisals.

These results indicate that self-appraisals can be polarized when impediments thwart desirable self-presentations. The boundary conditions for the effect have not been explored, however, and future research is needed. It is proposed that the effect is most likely to occur when (a) the behavior pertains to important, strong identity images that the individual has pretensions of claiming, and (b) impediments arise that weaken these claims. These conditions generate active processing and equip the actor with a supportive data base for dispelling the problem and reaffirming desired images of self. A second unexplored issue concerns whether self-appraisals are strengthened, even though they are not polarized, when a highly desirable self-presentation is not impeded. Spivak and Schlenker (1985) did not find a shift in self-appraisals in the representative cue condition. Nonetheless, the corresponding self-images may have been *strengthened*, in the sense of becoming more accessible in memory, more likely to influence future behavior, or more resistant to subsequent attack.

Summary

Self-identification is the process, means, or result of fixing and expressing one's identity, both privately through self-reflection and publicly through self-disclosure and self-presentation. Self-identification is an *activity* that *always* occurs in a particular context, which reflects the transaction between the *person* (e.g., his or her self-images, dispositional tendencies, goals, mood), an *audience* (self, real or imagined others), and the *situation* (e.g., situational opportunities and constraints). In combination, these factors determine the self-identifications that occur on a particular occasion. They cue relevant sets of identity images, provide opportunities for and constraints on the construction of desired identity images, provide an evaluative framework for performances, and influence actors' outcome expectations.

Traditional analyses have viewed public self-identification (e.g., self-presentations and self-disclosures) from the perspective of either the private self or situational pressures. Person views regard self-identifying activities as expressions of self-conceptions and look to the situation only to explain occasions where public activities deviate from private beliefs. Situational views regard self-identifying activities as under the control of situational contingencies and see the self-concept largely as an epiphenomenon that emerges after the behavior in order to describe or justify it. In contrast, the self-identification approach views self-identification as a transaction between the person and the environment. The question is not if self-conceptions influence self-identifications or when the behavioral expression of self-conceptions is purest. It is, when will aspects of the self-concept be salient and weighted heavily relative to other factors (considerations generated by the situation and real or imagined audience) as a determinant of self-identifications? This analysis shifts attention from the private self per se to the combined personal and social influences on behavior. In addition, attention is shifted from simply the private or public nature of the activity to the examination of the context for the activity; indeed, it is argued that the salient audience (real or imagined) for the activity may be as important a determinant of the activity as its private or public nature.

Once a particular self-identification has occurred, it can in turn influence the self-concept (as well as the audience and situation). The self-identification process varies in the extent to which it involves a passive versus active assessment of the self, situation, and audience. The passive mode is most likely to occur when self-identifications are less important and no impediments arise to one's self-identifying activities. Under these conditions, self-identifications are more routine and draw largely from private self-images and frequently enacted roles. Public self-presentations can then initiate a self-perception process in which corresponding self-images are strengthened and made more accessible in memory. The strengthening of self-images occurs primarily when cues suggest that the behavior is representative of self.

In contrast, the active mode occurs when self-identifications are more important or impediments arise to one's self-identifying activities. Active assessment produces (a) more intensified processing of pertinent information and (b) attempts to reconcile this information with one's desired identity images. People examine information to arrive at the "truth about the self," with truth defined in terms of the combination of believability ("Is this the type of person I am?") and beneficiality ("Is this the type of person I really want to be?"). When active processing occurs, people are likely to resist the inference that a desirable self-presentation is unrepresentative of self or an undesirable one is representative of self. A boomerang effect can result, in which self-appraisals are shifted in a direction opposite the self-presentation, as people attempt to reaffirm desired identity images (e.g., when highly undesirable self-presentations appear to be representative of self). Further, in contrast to traditional analyses that indicate that attitudes are changed primarily when behaviors appear to be representative of self, it is suggested that self-appraisals can be influenced by actions that appear to be unrepresentative (e.g., people polarize their self-appraisals to reaffirm desirable identity images if a desirable self-presentation appears to be unrepresentative). These "counterintuitive" effects have been demonstrated in research, but future work is needed to test hypotheses that describe their boundary conditions.

Acknowledgments. Thanks are extended to Mark Alicke and Roy Baumeister for their helpful comments on an earlier draft of this chapter.

References

Alexander, C. N., Jr., & Rudd, J. (1981). Situated identities and response variables. In J. T. Tedeschi (Ed.), *Impression management theory and social psychological research*. New York: Academic Press.

Alexander, C. N., Jr., & Wiley, M. G. (1981). Situated activity and identity formation. In M. Rosenberg & R. H. Turner (Eds.), *Social psychology: Sociological perspectives*. New York: Basic Books.

Alicke, M. D. (in press). Public explanation and private ratiocination: Communication between the public and private selves. In R. H. Hogan & W. H. Jones (Eds.), *Perspectives in personality: Theory, measurement, and interpersonal dynamics* (Vol. 2). Greenwich, CT: JAI Press.

Aronson, E. (1969). The theory of cognitive dissonance: A current perspective. In L. Berkowitz (Ed.), *Advances in experimental social psychology* (Vol. 4). New York: Academic Press.

Backman, C. W. (1985). Identity, self-presentation, and the resolution of moral dilemmas: Towards a social psychological theory of moral behavior. In B. R. Schlenker (Ed.), *The self and social life*. New York: McGraw-Hill.

Backman, C. W., Secord, P. S., & Peirce, J. R. (1963). Resistance to change in the self-concept as a function of consensus among significant others. *Sociometry, 26*, 102–111.

Baldwin, J. M. (1897). *Social and ethical interpretations*. New York: Macmillan.

Baumeister, R. F. (1982). A self-presentational view of social phenomena. *Psychological Bulletin, 91*, 3–26.

Baumeister, R. F., & Jones, E. E. (1978). When self-presentation is constrained by the target's prior knowledge: Consistency and compensation. *Journal of Personality and Social Psychology, 36*, 608–618.

Bem, D. J. (1972). Self-perception theory. In L. Berkowitz (Ed.), *Advances in experimental social psychology* (Vol. 6). New York: Academic Press.

Bem, D. J., & Funder, D. C. (1978). Predicting more of the people more of the time: Assessing the personality of situations. *Psychological Review, 85*, 485–501.

Buss, A. H. (1980). *Self-consciousness and social anxiety*. San Francisco: Freeman.

Buss, A. H., & Briggs, S. R. (1984). Drama and the self in social interactions. *Journal of Personality and Social Psychology, 47*, 1310–1324.

Cantor, N., & Mischel, W. (1979). Prototypes in person perception. In L. Berkowitz (Ed.), *Advances in experimental social psychology* (Vol. 12). New York: Academic Press.

Carver, C. S. (1979). A cybernetic model of self-attention processes. *Journal of Personality and Social Psychology, 37*, 1251–1281.

Carver, C. S., & Scheier, M. F. (1981). *Attention and self-regulation: A control-theory approach to human behavior*. New York: Springer-Verlag.

Carver, C. S., & Scheier, M. F. (1985). Aspects of self and the control of behavior. In B. R. Schlenker (Ed.), *The self and social life*. New York: McGraw-Hill.

Chaiken, S., & Baldwin, M. W. (1981). Affective–cognitive consistency and the effect of salient behavioral information on the self-perception of attitudes. *Journal of Personality and Social Psychology, 41*, 1–12.

Cheek, J. M. (1982). Aggregation, moderator variables, and the validity of personality tests: A peer-rating study. *Journal of Personality and Social Psychology, 43*, 1254–1269.

Cheek, J. M., & Hogan, R. (1983). Self-concepts, self-presentations, and moral judgments. In J. Suls & A. G. Greenwald (Eds.), *Psychological perspectives on the self* (Vol. 2). Hillsdale, NJ: Erlbaum.

Christie, R., & Geis, F. L. (Eds.) (1970). *Studies in Machiavellianism*. New York: Academic Press.

Collins, B. E., & Hoyt, M. F. (1972). Personal responsibility-for-consequences: An integration and extension of the "forced compliance" literature. *Journal of Experimental Social Psychology, 8*, 558–593.

Cooley, C. H. (1902). *Human nature and the social order*. New York: Scribners.

Cooper, J., & Fazio, R. H. (1984). A new look at dissonance theory. In L. Berkowitz (Ed.), *Advances in experimental social psychology* (Vol. 17). New York: Academic Press.

Crowne, D. P., & Marlowe, D. (1964). *The approval motive*. New York: Wiley.

Dlugolecki, D., & Schlenker, B. R. (1985). *The impact of self-presentations on subsequent self-appraisals: General or specific effects?* Unpublished manuscript, University of Florida, Gainesville.

Elms, A. C. (1967). Role playing, incentive, and dissonance. *Psychological Bulletin, 68*, 132–142.

Epstein, S. (1973). The self-concept revisited: Or a theory of a theory. *American Psychologist, 28*, 404–416.

Erikson, E. H. (1959). Identity and the life cycle. In G. S. Klein (Ed.), *Psychological issues*. New York: International Universities Press.

Fazio, R. H., Effrein, E. A., & Falender, V. J. (1981). Self-perceptions following social interaction. *Journal of Personality and Social Psychology, 41*, 232–242.

Fazio, R. H., Herr, P. M., & Olney, T. J. (1984). Attitude accessibility following a self-perception process. *Journal of Personality and Social Psychology, 47*, 277–286.

Fazio, R. H., & Zanna, M. P. (1981). Direct experience and attitude-behavior consistency. In L. Berkowitz (Ed.), *Advances in experimental social psychology* (Vol. 14). New York: Academic Press.

Fazio, R. H., Zanna M. P., & Cooper, J. (1977). Dissonance and self-perception: An integrative view of each theory's proper domain of application. *Journal of Experimental Social Psychology, 13*, 464–479.

Fenigstein, A., Scheier, M. F., & Buss, A. H. (1975). Public and private self-consciousness: Assessment and theory. *Journal of Consulting and Clinical Psychology, 43*, 522–527.

Festinger, L. (1957). *A theory of cognitive dissonance*. Evanston, IL: Row, Peterson.

Fiske, S. T., & Taylor, S. E. (1984). *Social cognition*. Reading, MA: Addison-Wesley.

Frey, D. (1981). The effect of negative feedback about oneself and cost of information on preference for information about the source of this feedback. *Journal of Experimental Social Psychology, 17*, 42–50.

Gergen, K. J. (1965). Interaction goals and personalistic feedback as factors affecting the presentation of self. *Journal of Personality and Social Psychology, 1*, 413–424.

Goffman, E. (1959). *The presentation of self in everyday life*. New York: Doubleday.

Gollwitzer, P. M., & Wicklund, R. A. (1985). Self-symbolizing and the neglect of others' perspectives. *Journal of Personality and Social Psychology, 48*, 702–715.

Green, D. (1974). Dissonance and self-perception analyses of "forced compliance": When two theories make competing predictions. *Journal of Personality and Social Psychology, 29*, 819–828.

Greenwald, A. G. (1980). The totalitarian ego: Fabrication and revision of personal history. *American Psychologist, 35*, 603–618.

Greenwald, A. G., & Breckler, S. J. (1985). To whom is the self presented? In B. R. Schlenker (Ed.), *The self and social life*. New York: McGraw-Hill.

Greenwald, A. G., & Pratkanis, A. R. (1984). The self. In R. S. Wyer & T. K. Srull (Eds.), *Handbook of social cognition* (Vol. 3). Hillsdale, NJ: Erlbaum.

Harré, R. (1983). Identity projects. In G. M. Breakwell (Ed.), *Threatened identities*. New York: Wiley.

Hewitt, J. P. (1976). *Self and society: A symbolic interactionist social psychology*. Boston: Allyn and Bacon.

Higgins, E. T., & King, G. A. (1981). Accessibility of social constructs: Information-processing consequences of individual and contextual variability. In N. Cantor & J. F. Kihlstrom (Eds.), *Personality, cognition, and social interaction*. Hillsdale, NJ: Erlbaum.

Hogan, R. (1982). A socioanalytic theory of personality. In M. Page (Ed.), *Nebraska symposium on motivation*. Lincoln: University of Nebraska Press.

Hogan, R., & Cheek, J. M. (1983). Identity, authenticity, and maturity. In T. R. Sarbin & K. E. Scheibe (Eds.), *Studies in social identity*. New York: Praeger.

Hogan, R., Jones, W. W., & Cheek, J. M. (1985). Socioanalytic theory: An alternative to armadillo psychology. In B. R. Schlenker (Ed.), *The self and social life*. New York: McGraw-Hill.

Hogan, R., & Sloan, T. (1985). Self-presentation and personality: A reply to Buss and Briggs. Unpublished manuscript, University of Tulsa.

Isen, A. M. (1984). Toward understanding the role of affect in cognition. In R. S. Wyer & T. K. Srull (Eds.), *Handbook of social cognition.* Hillsdale, NJ: Erlbaum.

James, W. (1890). *The principles of psychology.* New York: Holt.

James, W. (1907). *Pragmatism.* New York: Longmans-Green.

Janis, I. L. (1968). Attitude change via role-playing. In R. P. Abelson, E. Aronson, W. J. McGuire, T. M. Newcomb, M. R. Rosenberg, & P. H. Tannenbaum (Eds.), *Theories of cognitive consistency: A sourcebook.* Chicago: Rand McNally.

Jeffery, K. M., & Mischel, W. (1979). Effects of purpose on organization and recall of information in person perception. *Journal of Personality, 47,* 397–419.

Jones, E. E. (1964). *Ingratiation.* New York: Appleton-Century-Crofts.

Jones, E. E., Gergen, K. J., & Davis, K. E. (1962). Some determinants of reactions to being approved or disapproved as a person. *Psychological Monographs, 76,* (2, Whole No. 521).

Jones, E. E., & Harris, V. A. (1967). The attribution of attitudes. *Journal of Experimental Social Psychology, 3,* 2–24.

Jones, E. E., & Pittman, T. S. (1982). Toward a general theory of strategic self-presentation. In J. Suls (Ed.), *Psychological perspectives on the self* (Vol. 1). Hillsdale, NJ: Erlbaum.

Jones, E. E., Rhodewalt, F., Berglas, S., & Skelton, J. A. (1981). Effects of strategic self-presentation on subsequent self-esteem. *Journal of Personality and Social Psychology, 41,* 407–421.

Jones, E. E., & Wortman, C. (1973). *Ingratiation: An attributional approach.* Morristown, NJ: General Learning Press.

Jones, S. C. (1973). Self- and interpersonal evaluations: Esteem theories versus consistency theories. *Psychological Bulletin, 79,* 185–199.

Kanouse, D. E., Gumpert, P., & Canavan-Gumpert, D. (1981). The semantics of praise. In J. H. Harvey, W. Ickes, & R. F. Kidd (Eds.), *New directions in attribution research* (Vol. 3). Hillsdale, NJ: Erlbaum.

Kelley, H. H. (1967). Attribution theory in social psychology. In D. Levine (Ed.), *Nebraska symposium on motivation.* Lincoln: University of Nebraska Press.

Kiesler, C. A. (1971). *The psychology of commitment.* New York: Academic Press.

Kihlstrom, J. F., & Cantor, N. (1984). Mental representations of the self. In L. Berkowitz (Ed.), *Advances in experimental social psychology* (Vol. 17). New York: Academic Press.

Langer, E. J. (1978). Rethinking the role of thought in social interaction. In J. H. Harvey, W. Ickes, & R. F. Kidd (Eds.), *New directions in attribution research* (Vol. 2). Hillsdale, NJ: Erlbaum.

Leary, M. R. (1983). *Understanding social anxiety: Social, personality, and clinical perspectives.* Beverly Hills, CA: Sage.

Lieberman, S. (1956). The effects of changes in roles on the attitudes of role occupants. *Human Relations, 9,* 385–402.

Markus, H. (1977). Self-schemata and processing information about the self. *Journal of Personality and Social Psychology, 35,* 63–78.

McGuire, W. J., McGuire, C. V., Child, P., & Fujioka, T. (1978). Salience of ethnicity in the spontaneous self-concept as a function of one's ethnic distinctiveness in the social environment. *Journal of Personality and Social Psychology, 36,* 511–520.

McGuire, W. J., McGuire, C. V., & Winton, W. (1979). Effects of household sex composition of the salience of one's gender in the spontaneous self-concept. *Journal of Experimental Social Psychology, 15,* 77–90.

McGuire, W. J., & Padawer-Singer, A. (1978). Trait salience in the spontaneous self-concept. *Journal of Personality and Social Psychology, 33,* 743–754.

Mead, G. H. (1934). *Mind, self, and society.* Chicago: University of Chicago Press.

Mettee, D. R., & Aronson, E. (1974). Affective reactions to appraisal from others. In T. L. Huston (Ed.), *Foundations of interpersonal attraction.* New York: Academic Press.

Mischel, W., Ebbesen, E. B., & Zeiss, A. R. (1973). Selective attention to the self: Situational and dispositional determinants. *Journal of Personality and Social Psychology, 27*, 129–142.

Petty, R. E., & Cacioppo, J. T. (1981). *Attitudes and persuasion: Classic and contemporary approaches.* Dubuque, IA: William C. Brown.

Phillips, N. E. (1973). Militarism and grassroots involvement in the military-industrial complex. *Journal of Conflict Resolution, 17*, 625–655.

Pierce, C. S. (1878). How to make our ideas clear. *Popular Science Monthly, 12*, 286–302.

Pyszczynski, T., Greenberg, J., & LaPrelle, J. (1985). Social comparison after success and failure: Biased search for information consistent with a self-serving conclusion. *Journal of Experimental Social Psychology, 21*, 195–211.

Riess, M., Rosenfeld, P., Melburg, V., & Tedeschi, J. T. (1981). Self-serving attributions: Biased private perceptions and distorted public descriptions. *Journal of Personality and Social Psychology, 41*, 224–231.

Riess, M., & Schlenker, B. R. (1977). Attitude change and responsibility avoidance as modes of dilemma resolution in forced compliance settings. *Journal of Personality and Social Psychology, 35*, 21–30.

Rosenberg, M. (1979). *Conceiving the self.* New York: Basic Books.

Sarbin, T. R., & Allen, V. L. (1968). Role theory. In G. Lindzey & E. Aronson (Eds.), *The handbook of social psychology* (2nd ed., Vol. 1). Reading, MA: Addison-Wesley.

Scheier, M. R., & Carver, C. S. (1980). Private and public self-attention, resistance to change, and dissonance reduction. *Journal of Personality and Social Psychology, 39*, 390–405.

Schlenker, B. R. (1975). Self-presentation: Managing the impression of consistency when reality interferes with self-enhancement. *Journal of Personality and Social Psychology, 32*, 1030–1037.

Schlenker, B. R. (1980). *Impression management: The self-concept, social identity, and interpersonal relations.* Monterey, CA: Brooks/Cole (Distributed by Krieger Publishers, Melbourne, FL).

Schlenker, B. R. (1981, August). *Self-presentation: A conceptualization and model.* Paper presented at the 89th Annual Meetings of the American Psychological Association, Los Angeles.

Schlenker, B. R. (1982). Translating actions into attitudes: An identity-analytic approach to the explanation of social conduct. In L. Berkowitz (Ed.), *Advances in experimental social psychology* (Vol. 15). New York: Academic Press.

Schlenker, B. R. (1984). Identities, identifications, and relationships. In V. Derlega (Ed.), *Communication, intimacy and close relationships.* New York: Academic Press.

Schlenker, B. R. (1985a). Identity and self-identification. In B. R. Schlenker (Ed.), *The self and social life.* New York: McGraw-Hill.

Schlenker, B. R. (1985b). Introduction: Foundations of the self in social life. In B. R. Schlenker (Ed.), *The self and social life.* New York: McGraw-Hill.

Schlenker, B. R. (in press). Threats to identity: Self-identification and social stress. In C. R. Snyder & C. E. Ford (Eds.), *Coping with negative life events: Clinical and social psychological perspectives.* New York: Academic Press.

Schlenker, B. R., Forsyth, D. R., Leary, M. R., & Miller, R. S. (1980). Self-presentational analysis of the effects of incentives on attitude change following counterattitudinal behavior. *Journal of Personality and Social Psychology, 39*, 553–577.

Schlenker, B. R., & Goldman, H. J. (1982). Attitude change as a self-presentation tactic following attitude-consistent behavior: Effects of choice and role. *Social Psychology Quarterly, 45*, 92–99.

Schlenker, B. R., Hallam, J. R., & McCown, N. E. (1983). Motives and social evaluation: Actor-observer differences in the delineation of motives for a beneficial act. *Journal of Experimental Social Psychology, 19*, 254–273.

Schlenker, B. R., & Leary, M. R. (1982a). Social anxiety and self-presentation: A conceptualization and model. *Psychological Bulletin, 92*, 641–669.

Schlenker, B. R., & Leary, M. R. (1982b). Audiences' reactions to self-enhancing, self-denigrating, and accurate self-presentations. *Journal of Experimental Social Psychology, 18*, 89–104.

Schlenker, B. R., & Leary, M. R. (in press). Social anxiety and communication about the self. *Journal of Language and Social Psychology.*

Schlenker, B. R., Miller, R. S., & Leary, M. R. (1983). Self-presentation as a function of the validity and quality of past performance. *Representative Research in Social Psychology, 13*, 2–14.

Schlenker, B. R., & Riess, M. (1979). Self-presentation of attitudes following commitment to proattitudinal behavior. *Human Communication Research, 5*, 325–334.

Schlenker, B. R., & Schlenker, P. A. (1975). Reactions following counterattitudinal behavior which produces positive consequences. *Journal of Personality and Social Psychology, 31*, 962–971.

Secord, P. F., & Backman, C. W. (1965). Interpersonal approach to personality. In B. H. Maher (Ed.), *Progress in experimental personality research* (Vol. 2). New York: Academic Press.

Shrauger, J. S. (1975). Responses to evaluation as a function of initial self-perceptions. *Psychological Bulletin, 82*, 581–596.

Sicoly, F., & Ross, M. (1977). Facilitation of ego-biased attributions by means of self-serving observer feedback. *Journal of Personality and Social Psychology, 35*, 734–741.

Snyder, C. R. (1985). The excuse: An amazing grace? In B. R. Schlenker (Ed.), *The self and social life*. New York: McGraw-Hill.

Snyder, C. R., Higgins, R. L., & Stucky, R. J. (1983). *Excuses: Masquerades in search of grace*. New York: Wiley-Interscience.

Snyder, M. (1979). Self-monitoring processes. In L. Berkowitz (Ed.), *Advances in experimental social psychology* (Vol. 12). New York: Academic Press.

Snyder, M. (1984). When belief creates reality. In L. Berkowitz (Ed.), *Advances in experimental social psychology* (Vol. 18). New York: Academic Press.

Snyder, M., & Swann, W. B., Jr. (1976). When actions reflect attitudes: The politics of impression management. *Journal of Personality and Social Psychology, 34*, 1034–1042.

Snyder, M., & White, P. (1982). Moods and memories: Elation, depression, and the remembering of the events of one's life. *Journal of Personality, 50*, 149–167.

Spivak, R., & Schlenker, B. R. (1985). *The impact of self-presentations on self-appraisals: Self-inference of self-affirmation?* Unpublished manuscript, University of Florida, Gainesville.

Stone, G. P. (1962). Appearance and the self. In A. M. Rose (Ed.), *Human behavior and social processes*. Boston: Houghton Mifflin.

Sullivan, H. S. (1953). *Conceptions of modern psychiatry*. New York: Norton.

Swann, W. B., Jr. (1983). Self-verification: Bringing social reality into harmony with the self. In J. Suls & A. G. Greenwald (Eds.), *Psychological perspectives on the self* (Vol. 2). Hillsdale, NJ: Erlbaum.

Swann, W. B., Jr. (1985). The self as architect of social reality. In B. R. Schlenker (Ed.), *The self and social life*. New York: McGraw-Hill.

Swann, W. B., Jr., & Hill, C. A. (1982). When our identities are mistaken: Reaffirming self-conceptions through social interaction. *Journal of Personality and Social Psychology, 43*, 59–66.

Swann, W. B., Jr., & Read, S. J. (1981). Self-verification processes: How we sustain our self-conceptions. *Journal of Experimental Social Psychology, 17*, 351–372.

Taylor, S. E. (1975). On inferring one's own attitudes from one's behavior: Some delimiting conditions. *Journal of Personality and Social Psychology, 31*, 126–131.

Tedeschi, J. T. (Ed.). (1981). *Impression management theory and social psychological research*. New York: Academic Press.

Tedeschi, J. T., & Norman, N. (1985). Social power, self-presentation, and the self. In B. R. Schlenker (Ed.), *The self and social life*. New York: McGraw-Hill.

Tedeschi, J. T., & Rosenfeld, P. (1981). Impression management theory and the forced compliance situation. In J. T. Tedeschi (Ed.), *Impression management theory and social psychological research*. New York: Academic Press.

Tedeschi, J. T. Schlenker, B. R., & Bonoma, T. V. (1971). Cognitive dissonance: Private ratiocination or public spectacle? *American Psychologist, 26*, 685–695.

Tesser, A. (1978). Self-generated attitude change. In L. Berkowitz (Ed.), *Advances in experimental social psychology* (Vol. 11). New York: Academic Press.

Tetlock, P. E. (1985). Toward an intuitive politician model of attribution processes. In B. R. Schlenker (Ed.), *The self and social life*. New York: McGraw-Hill.

Tetlock, P. E., & Levi, A. (1982). Attribution bias: On the inconclusiveness of the cognition-motivation debate. *Journal of Experimental Social Psychology, 18*, 68–88.

Tetlock, P. E., & Manstead, A. S. R. (1985). Impression management versus intrapsychic explanations in social psychology: A useful dichotomy? *Psychological Review, 92*, 59–77.

Trzebinski, J., McGlynn, R. P., Gray, G., & Tubbs, D. (1985). The role of categories of an actor's goals in organizing inferences about a person. *Journal of Personality and Social Psychology, 48*, 1387–1397.

Turner, R. H., & Gordon, S. (1981). The boundaries of the self: The relationship of authenticity in the self-conception. In M. D. Lynch, A. A. Norem-Hebeisen, & K. J. Gergen (Eds.), *Self-concept: Advances in theory and research*. Cambridge, MA: Ballinger.

Upshaw, H. S., & Yates, L. A. (1968). Self-persuasion, social approval, and task success as determinants of self-esteem following impression management. *Journal of Experimental Social Psychology, 4*, 143–152.

Verhaeghe, H. (1976). Mistreating other persons through simple discrepant role playing: Dissonance arousal or response contagion. *Journal of Personality and Social Psychology, 34*, 125–137.

Watson, D., & Friend, R. (1969). Measurement of social-evaluative anxiety. *Journal of Consulting and Clinical Psychology, 33*, 448–457.

Weary Bradley, G. (1978). Self-serving biases in the attribution process: A reexamination of the fact or fiction question. *Journal of Personality and Social Psychology, 36*, 56–71.

Wicklund, R. A., & Brehm, J. W. (1976). *Perspectives on cognitive dissonance*. Hillsdale, NJ: Erlbaum.

Wicklund, R. A., & Gollwitzer, P. M. (1982). *Symbolic self-completion*. Hillsdale, NJ: Erlbaum.

Wood, W. (1982). Retrieval of attitude-relevant information from memory: Effects on susceptibility to persuasion and on intrinsic motivation. *Journal of Personality and Social Psychology, 42*, 798–810.

Woodyard, H. D. (1972). Self-perception, dissonance, and premanipulation attitudes. *Psychonomic Science, 29*, 193–196.

Wyer, R. S., Jr., & Frey, D. (1983). The effects of feedback about self and others on the recall and judgments of feedback-relevant information. *Journal of Experimental Social Psychology, 19*, 540–559.

Wyer, R. S., Jr., & Srull, T. K. (1981). Category accessibility: Some theoretical and empirical issues concerning the processing of social stimulus information. In E. T. Higgins, C. P. Herman, & M. P. Zanna (Eds.), *Social cognition: The Ontario Symposium* (Vol. 1). Hillsdale, NJ: Erlbaum.

Chapter 3
Four Selves, Two Motives, and a Substitute Process Self-Regulation Model

Roy F. Baumeister and Dianne M. Tice

In this chapter, we present an outline of self-presentation theory: the basic units, the main motives, and the causal processes. We propose, first, that there are two types of self-presentational motive, one aimed at impressing or manipulating the audience, the other aimed at claiming a certain public identity and reputation. Second, we distinguish the four main conceptual units that constitute the various selves of self-presentation. These are the public self, the self-concept, the actual or behavioral self, and the ideal self. Finally, we discuss self-presentation in the context of how people control their own behavior, including analysis of how self-presentational processes can replace other causal processes.

Two Motives

Early research on self-presentation focused on how an individual would adapt his or her behavior to the preferences and expectations of an audience. The success of this research approach (exemplified in the work of E. E. Jones, James Tedeschi, and their colleagues and students) convinced people of the importance of the individual's motive to please and impress other people.

A major expansion of interest in self-presentation took place in connection with the growth of research on the self. Interest in the self promoted an interest in self-presentation as something other than strategic manipulation of audiences (and other than as alternative explanations for past studies of various social behaviors). Self-presentation began to be thought of by some scholars as one of the major processes of the self. Schlenker (1980) described self-presentation as a matter of claiming identity, and Hogan (1982) described it as one of the two or three most important personality processes. The point of these views is that self-presentation is an essential and decisive part of becoming who you want to be. In important ways, the self exists as communicated to others.

Thus, self-presentation refers to two quite different types of motivations. Most self-presentation researchers now accept some form of the distinction between playing to the audience and expressing or constructing one's public identity. This distinction was articulated by Baumeister (1982a) as "pleasing the audience" versus "self-construction." Recently, Tedeschi and Norman (1985) categorized self-presentation ploys as being either tactical or strategic in the military sense of the terms—meaning that the behaviors were designed to further either short-term or long-term goals, respectively. Greenwald and Breckler (1985) distinguished between self-presentation geared to others and self-presentation aimed at the self. A similar distinction has been argued persuasively by Carver and Scheier (1981) in terms of self-awareness. Schlenker's and Hogan's ideas embody the long-range, identity-creating goals of self-presentation. Another example of the self-construction component of self-presentation is Wicklund and Gollwitzer's (1982) work on symbolic self-completion. Wicklund and Gollwitzer proposed that the creation and fulfillment of the self necessarily involve "social reality"; in other words, being acknowledged and recognized by others (which is one of the goals of self-presentation) is an essential part of constructing the self (see Gollwitzer's chapter in this volume). All these views are different formulations of the distinction between the two types of self-presentational motives, one based on the expressive goals of the self and the other based on the demands or expectations of the immediate audience.

Unfortunately, much of the research community still thinks of self-presentation as only the audience-oriented kind. A good example is a recent article by Buss and Briggs (1984), which paradoxically sought to treat "expression" of the self as the opposite of self-presentation.

Our point is that current work on self-presentation generally acknowledges and embodies the distinction between two motive types, one centered on the audience and the other guided by the long-range expressive goals of the self. It is worth adding that both motives have undergone conceptual advances for which there is a lot of empirical work yet to be done. For example, Baumeister's (1982a) term "pleasing the audience" seems too narrow in light of the work by Jones and Pittman (1982), who proposed that self-presentation can be geared to the audience without trying to make a good impression. Intimidation and supplication, in their terms, present the self in undesirable and unpleasing ways in order to manipulate the audience. The term "pleasing the audience" should therefore probably be changed to something like "playing to the audience" to encompass the additional motivations proposed by Jones and Pittman (1982). Empirical work on intimidation and supplication strategies is scant at present, and the conceptual understanding of the motive "playing to the audience" would benefit from further experimental investigation.

Four Selves

We have spoken of self-presentation as one process of constructing the self, but it is worth asking: What is the self in self-presentation? The answer is not simple. Each person has four versions or components of the self, each of which can independently affect self-presentation. We discuss each of these four selves in three steps: first we define the term, then we suggest what causes it to differ from the other selves, and finally we show how it affects self-presentation behavior. It is worth mentioning here that the four selves that we propose are identified merely as heuristics. We do not mean to imply that they are unchanging, unified structures.

The Public Self

The first self is what is typically called the public self. This is the totality of how one is known to others—one's reputation and public roles. It is partly the product of self-presentation, but it also affects and contains subsequent self-presentations, such as by creating commitments (e.g., Tedeschi, Schlenker, and Bonoma, 1971) and creating public assumptions and expectations (e.g., Baumeister & Jones, 1978).

The Private Self

The public self is no surprise as a component of self-presentation theory. It is the private self, though, that is conceptually problematic. The private self has three relevant meanings: self-concept, the actual self, and the ideal self.

Self-concept. The self-concept is our second version of the self. It differs from the public self as the result of several causes and processes. One is secrecy or other nondisclosure of self; the person simply refuses or fails to communicate some belief about himself or herself. Another source of discrepancy between the public self and the self-concept is the actor-observer bias (Jones and Nisbett, 1971), which entails that others will see you differently than you see yourself. Greenwald's (1980) self-serving bias of beneffectance—the tendency to see oneself as responsible for good, as opposed to bad, outcomes—is a similar cognitive bias that may cause self-concepts to differ from public selves. A third source of discrepancy between the public self and self-concept is that self-presentation may often be deliberately distorted or falsified.

More work is needed on how the self-concept is related to self-presentation. The obvious hypothesis is that people mostly tend to present themselves as they know themselves. This obvious hypothesis is often wrong. People often fail to present themselves in honest consistency with their self-conceptions (Schlenker, 1975). We know too, that the causal arrow can point in the opposite direction. Self-concepts can be altered by self-presentation. For example, Jones, Rhodewalt, Berglas, and Skelton (1981) demonstrated that subjects who were induced to act in either a self-enhancing or self-deprecating manner in an interview setting showed corresponding self-concepts on a subsequent self-rating inventory. Fazio, Effrein, and Falender (1981) found similar results in a study in which subjects participated in an interaction that was biased to produce either introverted or extraverted behavior on the part of the subject. This behavior led to differences in self-concept that, in turn, seem to have led to differences in later behavior. In a related vein, we demonstrated that self-presentation can produce real attitude change in a dissonance paradigm (Baumeister & Tice, 1984).

It is true that people do disclose their honest beliefs about themselves at times. But we suggest that, before there can be a new model of the relation between self-concept and self-presentation, further study is needed on two issues. First, the role of self-concept in processing information must be related to self-presentation. Second, the relation between self-presentational behavior and self-esteem needs further clarification. There are two ways of looking at this relationship between self-esteem and self-presentational behavior. First of all, how does level of self-esteem affect self-presentational style? Some of our recent work has indicated that people with high self-esteem tend to be more sensitive to self-presentational concerns than people with low self-esteem (Baumeister & Tice, 1985; Baumeister, 1982b; Tice & Baumeister, 1985). Another way of looking at this relationship is to ask how self-presentation affects self-esteem. The Jones et al. (1981) study described above demonstrated that acting (self-presenting) in a self-enhancing manner can lead to higher self-esteem while acting in a self-deprecating manner can result in low self-esteem.

The actual self. The third self that we are proposing is the actual or behavioral self. The actual self is the reality of the person in the sense of behaviors, traits, and individual differences or characteristics. The actual self may differ from the self-concept for several reasons. One is self-deception (Gur & Sackeim, 1979). People may also use the defensive attributional strategy of self-handicapping (Jones & Berglas, 1978) to protect their self-concepts from seeing unflattering aspects of their actual selves. Because self-handicapping consist of putting barriers in the way of one's own success, one is actually increasing the chances of failure for the actual self while protecting the self-concept. For example, if a student is unsure about how she will perform on her first exam in graduate school, she may go out drinking the night before the exam in order to provide an excuse to protect her self-concept of competence in case of failure. If she fails, she can reason, "It isn't that I don't have the ability to perform well; my poor grade is due to my hangover and lack of study—a temporary situation." A hangover, or inadequate studying, actually does decrease the chances of a successful performance on the exam, however. The student has increased her chances of failing on the level of the actual self while protecting and possibly enhancing (if she should succeed despite the handicap) her self-concept. Self-handicapping is thus one strategy that may result in discrepancies between the self-concept and the actual self.

The self-concept is a product of inferences, inductions, and interpretations, many of which are subject to systematically motivated distortions and biases. Failures of introspection will also result in discrepancies between the self-concept and the actual self. Indeed, to the extent that Nisbett and Wilson (1977) are correct about the poverty of introspection, one should not have much faith in the congruence between the self-concept and the actual self.

Another source of discrepancy between the actual self and the self-concept is the false consensus effect. If you think that everyone is the same as you in some way, then you will not think of that attribute as a distinctive trait. For example, if you are an especially optimistic person, the false consensus effect may lead you to believe that most other people are optimistic, too. You will therefore not consider optimism distinctive, and it won't be part of your self-concept even though it is part of your actual self.

The actual self differs from the public self for the same reasons that the self-concept differs from the public self—secrecy or nondisclosure, actor-observer bias, and deliberate or strategic falsifications in self-presentation. In addition, all the various attributional biases contribute to this discrepancy because an attributional bias means that others will not see you as you really are. Indeed, to the extent that people make the fundamental attributional error (Ross, 1977), that is, infer traits that are not there, the public self will differ from the actual self.

In a sense there is no need to talk about the relation between the actual self and self-presentation because the actual self constitutes the behavior that also comprises self-presentation. But there is another, less obvious part of that relationship. The actual self includes the stable individual core of personality, that is, real traits, real skills, and real affective predispositions. There are important individual differences in the skills, styles, and patterns of self-presentation (Hogan, 1982; Jones & Pittman, 1982; Snyder, 1974). At the very least, these place individual limits on the malleability of the social chameleon.

The ideal self. The fourth self is the one that serves as the goal state for the other three, namely the ideal self. Your ideal self is the person that you would like to be, having the attributes you would like to have. The ideal self differs first of all from the actual self because people all fall short of their goals. Such imperfection is part of the human condition and forms the basis and inevitability of ontological guilt (Heidegger, 1927). The ideal self differs from the self-concept according to one's perceived faults and failings, which in turn depend on one's degree of honesty with oneself. The ideal self differs from the public self depending on one's honesty with others as well as relative skill at making a desired impression.

The point of the ideal self is that you try to make each of your other selves identical with the ideal self. The most difficult task is to make your actual self equal your ideal self. That is accomplished by diligent self-improvement, that is, altering your behavior. Making the self-concept match the ideal self can be done in either of two ways: You change your actual self by altering your behavior and then perceive that you have done so, or you convince yourself that you are better than you actually are using rationalization, selective perception and memory, and so forth. Finally, the public self is made equal to the ideal self either by perfecting the actual self and then letting others find this out, or, more realistically, by means of strategic, self-enhancing self-presentations. This last is how the ideal self affects self-presentational behavior—it furnishes the image of self that one seeks to present to others.

Thus the relation between the ideal self and the other three selves is as a goal state that guides change. The relations among the other three selves also needs to be explicated, although that is not purely a task of self-presentation theory. Such relations among public self, self-concept, and actual self include reflected appraisal (Shrauger & Schoeneman, 1979), self-perception (Bem, 1972), role demands and public expectations, and many others. No doubt change in one of those three selves reverberates through both the others, although perhaps not in straightforward or obvious ways.

Some Reflections on the Four Selves

As we mentioned, these four selves are proposed as heuristics. We do not mean to imply that each of the selves (or components of the self) that we have identified is a solitary, unchanging, unified concept or a monolithic entity. Rather, we have identified these aspects of the self merely for the sake of convenience—it is more expedient to talk about the different processes of self-presentation if we can refer to these different aspects of the self. There are real differences, for example, between what people think of themselves and what someone else thinks of them; between what people think of themselves and what they would like to be like; or between reputation and actual behavior. We have used these four selves as concepts to think about these differences.

In particular, we do not want to imply that any of the four selves is unified or internally consistent. The self (whether public, private, or ideal) may contain conflicts and contradictions. Studying such inner contradictions may be a valuable way to learn about the relationships among the four selves. As a first step we offer the following brief model.

Inconsistency can easily arise in the ideal self. An individual may admire two qualities or identities and may aspire to both. Latent contradictions may not emerge until the individual attempts to translate these ideals into action—in other words, attempts to make the actual self congruent with both goals. For example, a person may find it desirable to be ambitious, hard driving, and success oriented, but at other times the person may admire and desire a relaxed, easygoing, and casual attitude. The person's ideal self may thus come to embody both the hard driving and easygoing qualities. But while it may be easy to admire both qualities, it is hard to act out both of them simultaneously. They make conflicting prescriptions about how to behave in various situations, such as whether to persist at a task when bored or fatigued. Thus, latent conflicts may emerge at the behavioral level (see Baumeister, Shapiro, & Tice, 1985). One may compartmentalize one's behavior, acting out the different ideals at the different times, but such a coping strategy introduces inconsistency into the public self. Thus, in our example, some people may see the individual acting in a casual, easygoing fashion, whereas others see the individual acting ambitious and driven. This pattern may gradually lead others to see the individual as hypocritical when they discover these inconsistencies. Others' reactions may force the individual to face the issue of inconsistency both within his or her self-concept and in relation to others.

Thus, inconsistency may spread from the ideal self into the behavioral self and the public self, and from there into the self-concept. Perhaps only then does the individual try to resolve the problem at its source, by choosing between the conflicting ideals.

Self-Regulation and Substitute Process

In this section, we argue that self-presentation provides one causal route to various behaviors. The same behaviors can often be effected by other routes, however. Thus, self-presentation can substitute for other causal processes. We suggest that this substitution of processes can best be understood by placing self-presentation in the context of the self-regulation of behavior.

Self-Presentation as Substitute for Causal Processes

As noted in the Preface to this book, self-presentation gained popularity (or notoriety, depending on your point of view!) as an alternative explanation for various phenomena in social psychology. In other words, researchers often explained their effects on the basis of intrapsychic processes, but others then suggested that the effects were caused by self-presentational motives. Typically, someone would show that the effect was dependent on self-presentation by showing that it was reduced or eliminated in a private, confidential, or anonymous setting. To dispute the self-presentational interpretation, researchers would then try to show that the same effect could be obtained in the absence of self-presentational factors (we present several examples shortly).

Consider the logic beneath such a controversy. Demonstrating a difference between public and private situations does not prove that self-presentation is a *necessary* cause of that behavior. It does not disprove the potential contribution of purely intrapsychic processes. Likewise, showing that a given behavior can be produced in the absence of self-presentation does not prove self-presentation to be irrelevant, although it does show that self-presentation is not a necessary cause. Although the rule of parsimony leads scientists to prefer to think each behavioral pattern must derive from a single, constant process, we argue that this view is often untenable. Social reality may not be as simple as the rule of parsimony inclines one to think. The same behavioral pattern may in fact derive in different circumstances from different causal processes. Self-presentation and intrapsychic motives may often be just such alternative causal pathways. We think that no simpler explanation is adequate to handle several well-studied domains. Let us consider some examples.

Dissonance. Cognitive dissonance was originally proposed as an intrapsychic process (Festinger, 1957). In that view, the mind is endowed with motivations to achieve and preserve consistency. When people behaved in certain ways, therefore, they would revise their attitudes if necessary in order to make their attitudes consistent with their actions (e.g., Festinger & Carlsmith, 1959). This intrapsychic view was disputed by self-presentation theorists, who argued that people were motivated to maintain the public reputation of consistency (Tedeschi et al., 1971). In this view, self-presentational concerns led to the public expression of attitudes consistent with recent behavior, either as an insincere pretext (e.g., Gaes, Kalle, & Tedeschi, 1978), or as genuine attitude change (e.g., Baumeister, 1982a).

Evidence accumulated that dissonance was affected by self-presentational manipulations (e.g., Gaes et al., 1978; Schlenker, Forsyth, Leary, & Miller, 1980). Still, did this evidence signify that self-presentation was a necessary part of the dissonance process? Some theorists began to argue that self-presentation could not explain all the dissonance effects (Schlenker, 1982; Cooper & Fazio, 1984), and some evidence provided suggestive support for that view (Paulhus, 1982).

In a direct test, Baumeister & Tice (1984) varied both publicness (relevant to self-presentation) and choice (relevant to intrapsychic processes), in order to ascertain which was a necessary cause of dissonance. Apparently neither one is necessary. Attitude change was found in a public, no-choice condition, and it was found in a private, high-choice condition. This result indicates that similar degrees of attitude change can derive from quite different causal processes. One process appears to depend on self-presentational motivations. The other involves private feelings of personal responsibility and can work even in the clear absence of self-presentational motivations.

Reactance. Brehm (1966) proposed his theory of psychological reactance as an intrapsychic process. In that original view, the mind is endowed with motivations to preserve its freedom and range of options, so it resists and resents threats to that freedom. This view was disputed by self-presentation theorists, who argued that the main motivation was to preserve the *appearance* of freedom. They provided evidence that reactance occurred mainly in connection with public threats to one's freedom and with public responses to such threats (Baer, Hinkle, Smith, & Fenton, 1981). Thus, as with cognitive dissonance, the behavioral pattern was reduced or mitigated by removal of self-presentational concerns. But such evidence does not prove that self-presentation is a necessary cause of reactance.

In a careful review, Wright and Brehm (1982) concluded that self-presentation cannot account for all reactance phenomena. Although the self-presentational motive to preserve the public impression of freedom can be a powerful cause of reactance, it is dispensable. Reactance can occur in private situations. Once again, therefore, we argue that multiple causal pathways can produce similar effects.

Social facilitation. Involvement in academic controversies is a mixed blessing. Such controversies attract attention that can benefit one's career, but one also tends to make enemies and that can be harmful. Perhaps the ideal solution has been found by C. Bond, who recently waged a controversy with himself. In 1982, he published experimental evidence that self-presentation is a powerful cause of social facilitation effects (i.e., intensification of behavior due to the presence of other people). In 1983, he and Titus published a meta-analytic review concluding that self-presentation contributes little or nothing to social facilitation.

We are concerned here with the reasoning in the latter article (Bond & Titus, 1983). The main argument is that the size of the social facilitation effect is no larger in studies that include self-presentational factors than in studies where self-presentation is absent. Bond and Titus reasoned that if self-presentation does not increase the size of social facilitation effects, then its contribution is negligible, and therefore its causal role must be trivial or nonexistent. This is sound reasoning *if* one accepts the parsimonious principle that each behavior derives from a single causal process. But of course we are disputing that principle. If one accepts our hypothesis that multiple causal pathways can lead to the same behaviors, then it is possible to reconcile the findings of Bond and Titus (1983) with those of Bond (1982) and others who have demonstrated the importance of self-presentation for producing social facilitation effects. The same effects, with the same effect sizes, can arise either from a process that is driven by self-presentational motivations such as concern over evaluation by others, or from a process driven by arousal caused by the mere presence of others.

Self-Regulation

The picture that emerges from the above examples portrays self-presentation as one causal process that can substitute for others. Often the same behavior can be produced by self-presentational motivations and processes as by other processes. Obviously, self-presentation does not always produce the same results as other (intrapsychic) processes, but it can and often it does.

We suggest that the capacity of self-presentation to be a causal substitute can be understood by considering self-presentation in the context of self-regulation of behavior. To do this, we shall adapt the hierarchical model of action identification proposed by Vallacher and Wegner (1985). These authors suggested that any given action can be identified at various levels, from the mundane and mechanical to the grandiose, abstract, and long-term. For example, the same activity can be thought of as "moving my fingers" or "typing numbers" (low-level identification), as "creating a computer file" or "analyzing some data" (medium level), or as "conducting research" and "advancing my career" (high level). Consistent with Carver and Scheier (1981), they proposed that the low levels are understood as means of accomplishing the high-level goals, and high levels direct the lower levels. Self-regulation, then, is understood as the process whereby low-level or immediate behaviors are guided by the long-term, high-level goals and projects.

Earlier, we suggested that there are two types of self-presentational motive. One, self-construction, must be considered here as a high-level project, for it involves the long-term and abstract goal of publicly claiming a certain identity and reputation. The other, pleasing the audience, is an intermediate to high-level goal that is subservient to other goals of making friends and influencing others so as to obtain various rewards for oneself. Thus, self-presentation can be regarded as two systems of relatively high-level projects that can take over and direct immediate activities.

The capacity of self-presentation to take over and direct particular behaviors can best be seen in cases in which self-presentation alters the behavioral outcome rather than produces the same result. To illustrate this, we digress briefly and give one example. Baumeister, Cooper, and Skib (1979) had subjects solving anagrams in a situation in which they were told explicitly that they were not expected to be very successful. The basis for this expectancy of poor performance was presented as either a desirable or an undesirable trait, and self-presentation was manipulated by varying the publicness of the situation. The immediate goal of solving anagrams was to solve as many as possible, and most subjects appeared to do that reasonably well. Significantly fewer anagrams were solved, however, in the public condition linking the failure expectancy to a desirable trait. For these subjects, the self-presentational desire to communicate to others that they possessed the desirable trait overrode the intrinsic goal of solving anagrams. Working on the puzzles was transformed from "trying to find correct answers" into "making a public statement about my personal qualities," resulting in the observed change in behavior.

Thus, when self-presentational motives are engaged, they direct behavior, whereas behavior will be guided by other processes and motives when self-presentation is not engaged. What causes self-presentational motives to come into play? First, the public nature of the situation. Second, the fact that the situation contains possible implications about the self. Third, the symbolic relevance of the situation (including threats) to one's aspired identities.

Certain circumstances can be desirable according to several different long-term goals. Consistency between one's attitudes and one's actions, for example, can be a means of preserving the respect and esteem of others, or it can be a means of justifying one's actions to oneself, or it can be a means of keeping one's life conveniently simple to understand. The attempt to accomplish such consistency by means of cognitive dissonance reduction can therefore arise from any one of several high-level motives. Hence the patterns of multiple independent causality that we described earlier in this paper.

In conclusion, then, self-presentation is one (actually two) of several systems for guiding and regulating one's immediate behavior. It is a powerful one, for it tends to take precedence over some other motivational systems. Still, there are times when it is simply irrelevant, and at these times the other motives and processes will guide behavior. When the situation engages self-presentation, however, its processes will substitute for others and determine the course of action.

References

Baer, R., Hinkle, S., Smith, F., & Fenton, M. (1980). Reactance as a function of actual versus projected autonomy. *Journal of Personality and Social Psychology, 38,* 416–422.

Baumeister, R. F. (1982a). A self-presentational view of social phenomena. *Psychological Bulletin, 91,* 3–26.

Baumeister, R. F. (1982b). Self-esteem, self-presentation, and future interaction: A dilemma of reputation. *Journal of Personality, 50,* 29–45.

Baumeister, R. F., Cooper, J., & Skib, B. A. (1979). Inferior performance as a selective response to expectancy: Taking a dive to make a point. *Journal of Personality and Social Psychology, 37,* 424–432.

Baumeister, R. F., & Jones, E. E. (1978). When self-presentation is constrained by the target's knowledge: Consistency and compensation. *Journal of Personality and Social Psychology, 36,* 608–618.

Baumeister, R. F., Shapiro, J. P., & Tice, D. M. (1985). Two kinds of identity crisis. *Journal of Personality, 53,* 407–424.

Baumeister, R. F., & Tice, D. M. (1984). Role of self-presentation and choice in cognitive dissonance under forced compliance: Necessary or sufficient causes? *Journal of Personality and Social Psychology, 46,* 5–13.

Baumeister, R. F., & Tice, D. M. (1985). Self-esteem and responses to success and failure: Subsequent performance and intrinsic motivation. *Journal of Personality, 53,* 450–467.

Bem, D. (1972). Self-perception theory. In L. Berkowitz (Ed.), *Advances in experimental social psychology* (Vol. 6). New York: Academic Press.

Bond, C. F. (1982). Social facilitation: A self-presentational view. *Journal of Personality and Social Psychology, 42,* 1042–1050.

Bond, C. F., & Titus, L. J. (1983). Social facilitation: A meta-analysis of 241 studies. *Psychological Bulletin, 94,* 265–292.

Brehm, J. (1966). *A theory of psychological reactance.* New York: Academic Press.

Buss, A. H., & Briggs, S. R. (1984). Drama and the self in social interaction. *Journal of Personality and Social Psychology, 47,* 1310–1324.

Carver, C. S., & Scheier, M. F. (1981). *Attention and self-regulation: A control theory approach to human behavior.* New York: Springer-Verlag.

Cooper, J., & Fazio, R. H. (1984). A new look at dissonance theory. In L. Berkowitz (Ed.), *Advances in experimental social psychology* (Vol. 17, pp. 229–266). New York: Academic Press.

Fazio, R. H., Effrein, E. A., & Falender, V. J. (1981). Self-perceptions following social interaction. *Journal of Personality and Social Psychology, 41,* 232–242.

Festinger, L. (1957). *A theory of cognitive dissonance.* Stanford, CA: Stanford University Press.

Festinger, L., & Carlsmith, J. M. (1959). Cognitive consequences of forced compliance. *Journal of Abnormal and Social Psychology, 58,* 203–210.

Gaes, G. G., Kalle, R. J., & Tedeschi, J. T. (1978). Impression management in the forced compliance situation. Two studies using the bogus pipeline. *Journal of Experimental Social Psychology, 14,* 493–510.

Greenwald, A. G. (1980). The totalitarian ego: Fabrication and revision of personal history. *American Psychologist, 35,* 603–613.

Greenwald, A. G., & Breckler, S. J. (1985). To whom is the self presented? In B. R. Schlenker (Ed.), *The self and social life* (pp. 126–145). New York: McGraw-Hill.

Gur, R. C., & Sackheim, H. A. (1979). Self-deception: A concept in search of a phenomenon. *Journal of Personality and Social Psychology, 37,* 147–169.

Heidegger, M. (1927). *Sein und zeit.* [Being and time]. Tuebingen, W. Germany: Max Neimeyer Verlag.

Hogan, R. (1982). A socioanalytic theory of personality. In M. Page & R. Dienstbier (Eds.), *Nebraska symposium on motivation* (pp. 55–90). Lincoln: University of Nebraska Press.

Jones, E. E., & Berglas, S. (1978). Control of attributions about the self through self-handicapping strategies: The appeal of alcohol and the role of underachievement. *Personality and Social Psychology Bulletin, 4,* 200–206.

Jones, E. E., & Nisbett, R. E. (1971). *The actor and the observer: Divergent perceptions of the causes of behavior.* Morristown, NJ: General Learning Press.

Jones, E. E., & Pittman, T. S. (1982). Toward a general theory of strategic self-presentation. In J. Suls (Ed.), *Psychological perspectives on the self* (Vol. 1, pp. 231–262). Hillsdale, NJ: Erlbaum.

Jones, E. E., Rhodewalt, F., Berglas, S., & Skelton, J. A. (1981). The effects of strategic self-presentation on subsequent self-esteem. *Journal of Personality and Social Psychology, 41,* 407–421.

Nisbett, R. E., & Wilson, T. D. (1977). Telling more than we can know: Verbal reports on mental processes. *Psychological Review, 84,* 231–259.

Paulhus, D. (1982). Individual differences, self-presentation, and cognitive dissonance: Their concurrent operation in forced compliance. *Journal of Personality and Social Psychology, 43,* 838–852.

Ross, L. D. (1977). The intuitive psychologist and his shortcomings: Distortions in the attribution process. In L. Berkowitz (Ed.), *Advances in experimental social psychology* (Vol. 10). New York: Academic Press.

Schlenker, B. R. (1975). Self-presentation: Managing the impression of consistency when reality interferes with self-enhancement. *Journal of Personality and Social Psychology, 32,* 1030–1037.

Schlenker, B. R. (1980). *Impression management: The self-concept, social identity, and interpersonal relations.* Monterey, CA: Brooks/Cole.

Schlenker, B. R. (1982). Translating actions into attitudes: An identity-analytic approach to the explanation of social conduct. In L. Berkowitz (Ed.), *Advances in experimental social psychology* (Vol. 15). New York: Academic Press.

Schlenker, B. R., Forsyth, D. R., Leary, M. R., & Miller, R. S. (1980). Self-presentational analysis of the effects of incentives on attitude change following counterattitudinal behavior. *Journal of Personality and Social Psychology, 39,* 553–577.

Shrauger, J. S., & Schoeneman, T. J. (1979). Symbolic interactionist view of the self-concept: Through the looking glass darkly. *Psychological Bulletin, 86,* 549.

Snyder, M. (1974). The self-monitoring of expressive behavior. *Journal of Personality and Social Psychology, 30,* 526–537.

Tedeschi, J. T., and Norman, N. (1985). Social power, self-presentation, and the self. In B. R. Schlenker (Ed.), *The self and social life.* New York: McGraw-Hill.

Tedeschi, J. T., Schlenker, B. R., & Bonoma, T. V. (1971). Cognitive dissonance: Private ratiocination or public spectacle? *American Psychologist, 26,* 685–695.

Tice, D. M., & Baumeister, R. F. (1985). Self-esteem, self-handicapping, and self-presentation: The benefits of not practicing. Unpublished manuscript, Case Western Reserve University.

Vallacher, R. R., & Wegner, D. M. (1985). *A theory of action identification.* Hillsdale, NJ: Erlbaum.

Wicklund, R. A., & Gollwitzer, P. M. (1982). *Symbolic self-completion.* Hillsdale, NJ: Erlbaum.

Wright, R. A., & Brehm, S. S. (1982). Reactance as impression management: A critical review. *Journal of Personality and Social Psychology, 42,* 608–618.

Chapter 4

Self-Presentation and Self-Evaluation: Processes of Self-Control and Social Control

Robert M. Arkin and Ann H. Baumgardner

No topical area of social psychology has struggled with the issue of public versus private selves more than has the theoretical and empirical work in the area of self-presentation. The several other chapters in this book that deal expressly with self-presentation, or allude to the management of one's public persona, attest to this. Indeed, it seems inevitable that interest in a class of behaviors characterized as self-presentational would lead to interest in how, and how well, what is inside the individual gets outside in the form of a social self. Further, whether private and public selves are parallel in content and process, and how they may interrelate, have become central questions in the impression management literature. These questions provided the impetus for this chapter.

The term "self-presentation" refers to the process of establishing an identity through the appearance one presents to others. People are constantly engaged in presenting an appearance, either intentionally or unintentionally, honestly or deceitfully, to actual or imagined others; consequently, virtually all behavior could be viewed as presentational.

Not surprisingly, this all-encompassing view of self-presentation, which seems to exclude little if anything, has led to considerable controversy. Those researching self-presentational phenomena and observers from afar (i.e., those working in more traditional and established literatures in social psychology) have both found it wanting. In amoebalike fashion, the grand theory of self-presentation takes on literature after literature, accounting for and incorporating the basic findings and being nourished by them. This tends to occur whenever it seems some phenomenon might have a self-presentational basis.

This all-encompassing approach has stimulated debate and concern about the proper boundaries of self-presentation theory, and how to delimit the definition. The all-encompassing approach may have enjoyed the side effect of broadening the audience for and recognition of self-presentation as a viable explanatory vehicle. Nevertheless, such a broad definition may well lead to disillusionment in the long run.

In the recent past there has already been criticism of the lack of clarity of the self-presentation "viewpoint" (Tetlock & Manstead, 1985). There have also been attempts to distinguish genuine and authentic behavior from presentational pretense (Buss & Briggs, 1984), and public displays of the private self (e.g., Swann & Ely, 1984) from straightforward attempts to achieve a desirable image (e.g., Baumeister, 1982). Our purpose in the present chapter is to examine both the antecedents of self-presentation and the consequences of self-presentational behavior for linkages between private selves and public selves. By examining these relationships explicitly we hope to achieve two ends.

First, we hope to arrive at a definition of self-presentation that is neither so all-encompassing and grand theoretic nor so particular (e.g., pretense) as to be useless or restricting. Second, we provide an organizational schema we hope is useful for understanding some of the similarities and differences between several types of self-presentation and some related phenomena. In so doing, we are able to review briefly and discuss some of the most exciting and novel findings in contemporary social psychology. Finally, the residual effect of self-presentation on self-concept is reviewed briefly. A distinction between the social foundations and personal foundations of self-concept is drawn and the role of bias in internalization via both routes is discussed.

Social Control and Personal Control

In the literature on self-presentation, it is quite common to find manipulations of the relative public scrutiny of some behavior. It has been assumed that impression management occurs only when people believe that others can observe their behavior, or will learn of it at some time in the future. Presumably, intrapsychic processes (e.g., dissonance, reactance, attitude change) are operative in strictly private circumstances whereas interpersonal processes (i.e., self-presentation) are operative in public settings. Accordingly, behaviors that occur in public but not in private are interpretable as self-presentational, whereas behaviors that occur in private and public circumstances to an equal extent (or that occur strictly in private) are interpretable as intrapsychic.

Tetlock and Manstead (1985) found this view wanting. Their grounds for complaint were twofold. First, some self-presentation formulations (e.g., Schlenker, 1980) allow for self-presentation to the self, or to internalized and imagined audiences, a psychological process that "could occur under conditions of total experimental anonymity" (Tetlock & Manstead, 1985, p. 64). Second, they noted that manipulations of the publicness or privateness of behavior surely have an impact on intrapsychic processes (e.g., arousal, dissonance, self-awareness) and that public contexts are therefore not free of private, intrapsychic elements. In short, manipulations of the relative publicness versus privateness of behavior are impure and incapable of definitively separating self-presentation from other phenomena.

We are inclined to go a step further. Specifically, we propose that motives that are strictly social in origin and motives that originate intrapsychically are orthogonal to the relative publicness or privateness of the context in which behavior occurs. By uncoupling the motivational basis of behavior from the setting in which it occurs, it seems that certain insights can be gained. In particular, similarities and dissimilarities between several types of self-presentational behaviors, and between self-presentation and some other related phenomena, can be made somewhat clearer. Therefore, an organizational schema unconfounding setting and motivational basis for behavior is presented later in the chapter. For the moment, we turn to our main theme.

A single motivational principle seems to link the wide array of self-presentational, and related non-self-presentational, actions: the *seeking and maintaining of personal control, or effectance* (e.g., White, 1959). Whether the individual is attempting to achieve long-term material gain or momentary pleasure, it seems that one's goal in life must be to function effectively, behaving in ways that will maximize pleasure and minimize pain. To accomplish this, a person must have some measure of personal control over his/her own actions and the environment (Bandura, 1977; Langer, 1983). Two types of personal control have recently been proposed (Rothbaum, Weisz, & Snyder, 1982): primary control and interpretive control.

Primary Control

In primary control, Rothbaum et al. (1982) focused on attempts to bring the environment into line with one's wishes. In the case of self-presentation, direct attempts to influence others' impressions of oneself clearly constitute instances of primary control. Approval is sought, disapproval avoided, certain inferences about oneself promoted and others deflected, solely to pave the way toward smooth social relations and the social rewards others are able to provide. Such positive outcomes may, of course, be realized in other ways (e.g., Machiavellian manipulation, exchange of goods or services), but self-presentation is a relatively cost-effective and socially sanctioned means of social influence.

The motivational basis of image control has historically been characterized as the quest for social approval. In a related way, disapproval avoidance has been viewed as the motivational basis for certain forms of protective or defensive self-presentational ploys (Arkin, 1981). For instance, excuses, apologies, modesty, and conformity have been characterized as protective ploys, motivated by the avoidance of disapproval. Conversely, claiming responsibility for positive outcomes, presenting oneself as expert, and many other such behaviors have been characterized as assertive ploys, driven by the quest for social approval (Baumeister, 1982).

The need for social approval may be viewed as founded in conditioning (e.g., Jellison & Gentry, 1978), in that approval is characteristically associated with material and social rewards and disapproval is associated with punishment. Power and influence over others (Tedeschi & Norman, 1985) and achieving material or monetary gain (Jellison, 1981) are commonly posed as the motivational basis of self-presentation. Sociobiologists argue that maintaining social approval has survival value for both the individual and the species (e.g., Wilson, 1978).

Aside from its motivational basis, as the literature on self-presentation has grown and matured subtle distinctions in the specific nature of self-presentation have been explored. For instance, it has recently been proposed that people employ several different stylistic sorts of presentational ploys (e.g., intimidation, ingratiation, self-promotion) each designed to foster a certain specific inference, such as likable, competent, or helpless (Jones & Pittman, 1982). Yet, such inferences are desirable only because they are part of an overall strategy of "getting one's way" in social relations.

Tedeschi and Norman (1985) argued that different presentational ploys come into play depending upon whether short-term or long-term gains are salient. The metaphor is borrowed from the military, where *tactical actions* are taken for limited short-term goals, while *strategic actions* are directed toward a longer range plan. For instance, ingratiation (e.g., flattery) is a tactic designed to arouse a particular emotion in the target (liking) that will translate into action beneficial to the presenter in the short run; fostering an impression of trustworthiness is a strategic maneuver designed to reap benefits only in the distant future.

Regardless of its specific nature, the intent of such *self-promotive* self-presentation[1] is to influence the impression of self formed by others in order to serve some social motive (i.e., social power, social approval).

Interpretive Control

Rothbaum et al. (1982) also coined the term "secondary control." It refers to instances in which individuals opt to bring themselves in line with the environment, rather than vice versa. They posed *predictive control* as one form of secondary control. For example, predictive control can be achieved, and can protect against disappointment, when an individual opts to attribute failing performance or uncontrollable outcomes to limited ability. This attribution produces an expectation of continuing failure, but it serves to avert the discomfort of high expectations that are dramatically violated by surprising, perhaps jarring, unanticipated failure. Similarly, *illusory control*, another type of secondary control, can be achieved through attributions to luck. Attributions to chance permit an individual to reserve energy and emotional investment for other situations, ones in which they can capitalize on ability. The fortunes of "lady luck" are satisfactory for the time being.

Whereas primary control involves overt behavioral strategies, these forms of secondary control involve interpretive control (Rothbaum et al., 1982). With interpretive control, a person strives to understand and derive meaning from seemingly uncontrollable circumstances. Interpretive control, then, is the use of cognitive gymnastics in order to accept, accommodate, and adjust to an undesirable reality. Nevertheless, all forms of secondary control and primary control constitute efforts to sustain rather than relinquish a perception of personal control.

---

[1]Our use of the term "self-promotion" should not be confused with the way that Jones and Pittman (1982) used it. Theirs is a more specific and restrictive meaning.

In addition to the forms of interpretive control specified by Rothbaum et al. (1982), we propose another. Specifically, we suggest that individuals engage in interpretive control that is not devoted to accommodation, but instead serves to sustain an individual's belief (however illusory that belief might be) in his/her *power to exert influence over future events*. Rather than attempts to accommodate to uncontrollable events, then, this form of interpretive control is designed to sustain an "illusion of control" (Langer, 1983) and the possibility of primary control in future circumstances. In short, an individual must *believe* in his/her own efficacy; if he/she does not, the likelihood of initiating potentially rewarding actions and continuing such actions to their completion may be diminished (e.g., Bandura, 1977; Deci, 1975). In the extreme, this may even lead to the sort of inaction associated with learned helplessness (e.g., Peterson & Seligman, 1984; Seligman, 1975).

Thus, Rothbaum et al. (1982) emphasized interpretive control that involves relinquishing one's ability to exert effective primary control in the future (e.g., lack of ability attributions, attributions to luck, attributions to powerful others); we emphasize a form of interpretive control that involves asserting one's *potential* for effective control in the future (e.g., lack of effort attributions; see Baumgardner, Heppner, & Arkin, 1986.

Our distinction is similar to one drawn in another context by Langer (1983). Langer noted that some attributional interpretations are easy to make, are comforting, and are therefore seductive. In the case of divorce, for example, the attribution "It was my ex-spouse's fault" is comforting in the short run, yet it ignores the process involved in the disintegration of the marriage. It is also focused on an uncontrollable feature of the individual's circumstances.

Langer found that more process-oriented divorcees, who viewed the relationship as at fault, were more successful at coping with their divorce. This occurred despite the fact that these individuals were assuming more personal responsibility for the negative event than were divorcees oriented more toward spouse-focused attributions. The relationship-focused divorcees were also more active afterward, happier, and more positive in their feelings toward their ex-spouse than the spouse-attribution-oriented divorcees.

In our estimation, these benefits are traceable to an attribution that permits a feeling of hopefulness, of future controllability, of effectance and the utility of effort in future relationships. It is analogous to the benefits of lack-of-effort attributions for failure at achievement tasks; lack-of-ability attributions and task-difficulty attributions are stable and uncontrollable by nature, and therefore cannot inspire hope.

Clearly, the way an individual construes self-relevant events can contribute to (or detract from) a sense of personal control. For instance, in the self-serving bias (see Arkin, Cooper, & Kolditz, 1980) people attribute their successes to personal factors; by doing so, it has been argued, people ensure feelings of control over their present and future outcomes (see Weary & Arkin, 1981). A sense of personal causation (for positive outcomes) is an important factor contributing to a sense of personal efficacy (Deci & Ryan, 1980). In contrast, a feeling of personal causation for negative outcomes has been characterized as the most debilitating pattern of self-relevant ideation (Beck, 1967). This is particularly true if the causal responsibility is assigned to a stable element of the self (such as one's ability or competence; see Abramson, Seligman, & Teasdale, 1978).

In sum, then, having a self-view that is favorable, as well as having a stable and certain concept of one's capabilities, makes future, further instrumental action (i.e., primary control) *seem* possible.

Summary

To summarize, there is considerable evidence that people strongly value and are reluctant to relinquish the perception of control. Primary control, where individuals strive to bring the environment in line with their own wishes, is preferred. Rothbaum et al. (1982) added that, when primary control is deemed unattainable, people do not merely abandon all efforts at exerting control. These authors introduced the idea of secondary control, in which individuals strive to bring themselves in line with environmental forces.

We have added another brand of interpretive control beyond Rothbaum et al.'s (1982) ingenious two-process theory; the version of intepretive control we pose is neither entirely primary nor entirely secondary. It is argued that people strive, when primary control is unattainable or problematic, to sustain their perception of their potential for effective primary control in the future (see Langer, 1983, also). Further, it was argued that a self-conception that is favorable, as well as stable, certain, and reliable, makes future instrumental action based on one's capabilities seem useful.

In the next section of the chapter the application of these notions to the topic of self-presentation is explored.

An Organizational Schema

In Figure 4-1 we have organized our earlier distinctions between context and motivational bases for behavior in a two-dimensional matrix. Instances of motives that are purely social and motives that originate intrapsychically are characterized as orthogonal to the private or public nature of the context in which the behavior occurs. Primary control, in the form of self-promotive instances of self-presentation, is located in the upper right corner of the matrix. This cell constitutes behaviors driven by social motives, and that are expressly directed toward others. The balance of the cells of the matrix may be viewed as different brands of the sort of interpretive control we proposed above. Before launching into detailed descriptions of the content and basis of each cell, we present a brief abstract of the sort of reinterpretation of these literatures we undertake.

For instance, in the case of self-deception, which falls in the individualistic motivation-private settings cell, an individual may arrange circumstances to foster some preferred inferences about himself/herself, or change his/her estimation of the importance of some attribute or trait. The purpose is, in both instances, to avoid the

Setting

	Private	Public
Social (Interpersonal) Origin	Rehearsals	Self-Promotion
Individualistic (Intrapsychic) Origin	Self-Deception	Self-Expression/ Self-Construction

Motivational Basis of the Phenomena

Figure 4-1. Two-dimensional matrix of the motivational bases for behavior.

implication of admitting deficiencies in some arena. By extension, the purpose of such behavior is based on the desire to avoid feelings of helplessness and the goal is to avoid having to give up hope of being effective in the future.

In the individualistic motives-public settings cell, we have placed processes of self-confirmation. According to Swann and Ely (1984, p. 1288), "people's self-concepts serve as an important means of predicting and controlling their social worlds," and people will go to great ends to ensure that their self-concepts are not shaken, and that they are not rendered doubtful. Doubt may be preferable to certain failure. Nevertheless, it is even more advantageous to avoid doubt whenever possible. Charles Sanders Pierce (1868) argued that doubt can be almost as paralyzing a state as the confident self-attribution of incompetence. Once again, then, such an individualistic motive can be construed as energized by the individual's desire to sustain a sense of possibility, a sense of hope and efficacy.

Finally, in the case of social motives and private settings, we propose that individuals often attempt a task (in private) to see if it can be done, or adopt a stance or assume a role (in private) to see if it works. These sorts of behaviors, which are private but stem from social motives, serve the purpose of testing the limits of one's potential public image and therefore enhancing one's viability when genuine social opportunities and challenges are posed. This is a type of empathic attempt to see oneself as others may see one, anticipating the likely reception to one's public persona. In this sense, private rehearsal constitutes interpretive control rather than primary control.

In the next few pages we amplify this organizational schema and offer illustrations for each of the types of interpretive control we have proposed.

Private Settings–Social Motives

A professional actor must rehearse his/her part, block actions, and imagine executing the role prior to ensemble performance. Similarly, the ordinary social performer also enacts performances in private to discern the points of vulnerability, the subjective likelihood of success, and other aspects of the genuine social enterprise. This can occur in one's mind's eye, so to speak, as when one rehearses privately and inaudibly the opening to a telephone conversation just prior to dialing. It may also include verbal and audible dialogues, such as Woody Allen is fond of putting in his films, in which the individual playacts both parts.

Such private rehearsals are often highly simplified versions of public behavior. Yet, the essential elements, especially the elements that the individual may be most concerned about executing successfully, are probably present.

These presentations directed toward an imaginary audience in private settings, as a form of interpretive control, would be difficult to research. We suspect that subjects rarely feel very private in experimental cubicles and would not be inclined to engage in open rehearsal of forthcoming behavior. Further, it would be difficult to access the trail of private thoughts that would constitute such a rehearsal process.

Nevertheless, it seems that such private rehearsals exist and that creative and clever investigators may be able to uncover illustrations (see Cacioppo & Petty, 1981). Tetlock and Manstead (1985) suggested that there may be important individual differences in the extent to which people engage in such a process (e.g., individual differences in social anxiety or in private or public self-consciousness). This may be one means by which researchers interested in such a process can uncover it.

For purely practical reasons, though, it may be more important for researchers and theorists merely to acknowledge the possibility of such rehearsals. In so doing, they will be forced to consider the limitations of inductions of publicness of behavior as a means to identify impression management. To the extent that such a class of behaviors exists, comparisons of private and public behavior may not be as revealing as they seem at first blush (see Tetlock & Manstead, 1985).

Private Settings–Individualistic Motives

Traditionally, social psychologists have adopted a perspective on human social behavior that emphasizes rationality, information seeking, and a preference for certainty, accuracy, and a complete understanding of one's fit with both the physical and social environment. This orientation is reflected in the longstanding impact of Festinger's (1954) theory of social comparison processes, Trope and Burnstein's (e.g., Trope, 1975) work on diagnosticity, Kelley's (e.g., 1971) theoretical and empirical work on models of attribution processes, Petty and Cacioppo's (1981) Elaboration Likelihood Model of persuasion, and numerous other guiding theortical orientations in the subdiscipline.

Naturally, throughout the years there have been many attempts to show the less rational side of human social behavior. For instance, some have argued that attributions about oneself are shaped by self-esteem motives (Weary & Arkin, 1981), that people will selectively avoid information that might produce dissonance (see Wicklund & Brehm, 1976), even that people occasionally prefer an ambiguous to a certain interpretation of their own qualities and preferences (Snyder & Wicklund, 1981) and avoid information that would provide certainty about their capabilities and potentials (Arkin & Baumgardner, 1985). Nevertheless, even when bias is acknowledged and studied intensively, it is often construed as unfortunate misapplications of principles of inference, deduction, and logic that otherwise serve the individual well (see Nisbett & Ross, 1980).

Presently, the credibility of views of social information processing that incorporate motivational biases, especially ones that characterize some behavior as outright self-deception, is increasing. Indeed, the term self-deception is gaining currency in both the psychological literature (e.g., Martin, 1985) and in contemporary popular literature (e.g., Goleman, 1985).

To illustrate, there is evidence that individuals will select actions that are diagnostic of favorable outcomes, even though they know full well that the actions themselves do not and cannot cause the outcomes (Quattrone & Tversky, 1984). In one experiment, subjects immersed their arms in a chest of circulating ice-cold water before and after they had engaged in physical exercise. Subjects who had learned in between trials that a long life expectancy was associated with an increase in tolerance increased their length of immersion. Those subjects who learned that life expectancy was associated with decreases in tolerance decreased their duration of immersion (Quattrone & Tversky, 1984). There was also evidence that subjects denied their intent to foster the comforting diagnosis of longevity, enabling them to infer with abandon that the test of ice water tolerance was a valid index of their life expectancy.

Seemingly, instead of seeking to learn something accurate about their likely longevity, subjects were inclined to "cheat" in such a way that the more favorable outcome (a long life) was diagnosed. Quattrone and Tversky (1984) argued that, given an opportunity, people will abandon useful, accurate, and diagnostic information in favor of information that is comforting, flattering, or enhancing.

This demonstration is consistent with Gur and Sackeim's (1979) recent definition of self-deception. They characterize self-deception by the following criteria: 1) the individual simultaneously holds two contradictory beliefs; 2) the individual is not aware of holding one of the beliefs; and 3) the lack of awareness is motivated. In the study carried out by Quattrone and Tversky (1984), it seems that people selected actions to facilitate inferring an auspicious antecedent cause; to accept the inference as valid, though, they also had to "render themselves unaware of having selected the action just to infer the cause" (p. 239).

The strategic behavior known as self-handicapping shares many features with the Quattrone and Tversky (1984) demonstration of self-deception. Self-handicapping (Jones & Berglas, 1978) refers to an individual's attempt to reduce threat to esteem by actively seeking or creating factors that interfere with performance, and thus provide a persuasive explanation for potential failure (Arkin & Baumgardner, 1985). People will handicap themselves when such a maneuver can serve self-presentational ends (Baumgardner, Lake, & Arkin, 1985; Kolditz & Arkin, 1982). It has not yet been demonstrated that self-handicapping occurs in purely private contexts, however (see Arkin & Baumgardner, 1985).

If it does occur in private, it could qualify as an illustration of self-deceptive interpretive control. Specifically, the inference (of doubt, rather than incompetence) is likely to be most comforting to the extent that the individual can deny that he/she is the origin of the handicap. To the extent that people deny their part in putting a handicap in place, self-handicapping in private contexts would seem to live up to the Gur and Sackeim (1979) definition of self-deception.

Interestingly, Tesser's (e.g., 1980) *Self-Evaluation Maintenance Model* also seems amenable to characterization as an instance of self-deception. Tesser proposed that individuals will change the dimensions along which they define themselves in order to enhance or sustain their self-esteem. Specifically, some dimension (e.g., tennis-playing skill) will become less central to self-definition to the extent that another performs better than oneself on that dimension, and particularly if that other is perceived as similar to oneself in general respects.

In a study by Tesser and Paulhus (1983), subjects were led to believe that they were either similar or dissimilar to one another. Each subject then received private information that he/she had either done quite well or quite poorly on a "cognitive perceptual integration" task. Subsequently, each subject met privately with an interviewer who communicated a belief that the subject had either done quite well or quite poorly *independent of* the subject's actual performance feedback. Subjects' private evaluations of the test were then assessed.

As predicted, subjects who believed they outperformed another subject indicated that the test was more relevant than did subjects who believed they had been outperformed; this effect was more pronounced for subjects led to believe their partner was similar to them. Perhaps more intriguing, subjects also rated the test as more relevant when the interviewer believed they outperformed the other subject even when the subject knew he/she had not outperformed that other subject at all.

Subjects in this study seem to have engaged in self-deception. In an apparent effort to bolster self-esteem, they denied the falsity of positive feedback. To the extent that the subjects suppressed, forgot, or never registered the change in self-concept, this finding would seem to be consistent with the current conceptualization of self-deception.

Public Settings–Individualistic Motives

The idea that individuals use social relations in the service of intrapsychic motives is certainly not new. Social comparison theory (Festinger, 1954), attribution theory (Goethals & Darley, 1977), and theories about the self-regulation of affect (Cialdini & Kenrick, 1976) all posit the social setting as a place to satisfy various intrapsychic motives.

Likewise, several theories that include image management components acknowledge the role of social relations in meeting goals that are essentially intrapsychic or individualistic in nature. In particular, research addressing processes of self-verification (Swann, 1984), self-construction (Baumeister, 1982), and self-esteem maintenance (Tessser, 1980) all address this relationship.

Swann (e.g., 1984) asserted that, as children begin to fashion a coherent self-conception, they become invested in seeing to it that their self-concept is not shaken and does not change in any radical way. Further, when people have fairly confident self-views, they strive to verify these views when possible; Swann calls these processes self-verification.

To illustrate, Swann and Hill (1982) found that, when individuals received feedback from others that was highly discrepant from their own self-conception, they actively sought to reject, refute, and undermine its credibility. Specifically, when another participant (a confederate) characterized the subject as either rather dominant or rather submissive, subjects whose self-conceptions were discrepant, and who were given the opportunity to undermine this assessment, did so. Self-conceived "dominants" who had been construed as submissive became all the more assertive; self-conceived "submissives" who had been mislabeled became all the more docile. In short, the subjects' presentations of self were designed to reaffirm their own privately held conceptions of self. The presentation to others was merely the vehicle for accomplishing this.

In a similar way, Swann and Read (1981) found that people who regarded themselves as likable acted to undermine negative appraisals from significant others; more surprising, those who viewed themselves as dislikable presented themselves in a way that would undermine positive appraisals they had received. In short, Swann and Read (1981) found that people were no less likely to try to verify negative conceptions of self than to attempt verifying positive self-conceptions.

In sum, people seem to insulate themselves "against self-discrepant feedback by actively soliciting feedback that supports their self-views" (Swann & Ely, 1984, p. 1287). They accomplish this, at least in part, through self-presentation.

Tesser's (e.g., 1980) *Self-Evaluation Maintenance Model*, which we characterized previously as an instance of self-deception, predicts that people are motivated to protect or enhance their *self-evaluation* rather than their *self-concept* (as Swann's theory predicts). Indeed, a major tenet of the model is that "people will change their self-definition in order to protect or to enhance their self-evaluation" (Tesser & Paulhus, 1983, p. 673). In several of the studies in this research program, there appear to be public components to this behavior. Specifically, what an audience believes about an individual's performance seems to affect the individual's reports of the relevance of that performance dimension, regardless of the subject's own private beliefs (Tesser & Paulhus, 1983).

According to this model, then, self-esteem reigns supreme and self-concept is slave to that master. In this specific way, the two approaches (Swann's and Tesser's) are profoundly different from one another. Further, it appears the Self-Evaluation Maintenance Model could be categorized in either the lower right or lower left quadrants (or both) of our schema. In contrast, it seems that the self-verification model fits neatly only as a social process designed to satisfy individualistic motives (i.e., only in the lower right quadrant). Nevertheless, while different in some respects, the two theories and programs of research share significant properties. We return to these shortly.

Another approach that poses individualistic motives, expressed through a public forum, is Baumeister's (1982) notion of self-construction. He proposed public expressions of self to be a means of approximating as nearly as possible one's ideal self. To accomplish this, people are motivated to convince others that they approximate their ideal selves. According to one formulation (Jones, Rhodewalt, Berglas, & Skelton, 1981), this is one avenue by which people can attempt to persuade themselves of that. However, Baumeister (1982) focused on a somewhat different process, one akin to the process of self-verification. He argued that part of constructing (i.e., becoming) a certain self-conceptualization involves public recognition of oneself as personifying that quality. This viewpoint bears a strong resemblance to Gollwitzer and Wicklund's notion of social reality construction (see Chapter 7 by Gollwitzer in this volume).

One essential feature separates self-promotive self-presentation and self-construction. When guided by self-construction, rather than self-promotion, the individual's own ideal self is the criterion by which a favorable presentation of self is estimated (rather than, for instance, the approval of significant others).

Baumeister (1982) noted that self-promotive self-presentation and self-construction often overlap and coincide, but are just as often contradictory in their implications. For instance, people frequently yield to social influence in certain instances (as in the typical conformity study), but refuse to yield to social influence in other circumstances (as in the typical study of reactance). He interpreted such differences as reflecting the conflicting motives of "pleasing the immediate audience and constructing one's public self" (p. 21). In a similar way, Buss and Briggs (1984) have recently argued for an enhanced theoretical role for the concept of expressiveness. They argue that "it would be folly for psychologists to neglect offstage behavior" (p. 1322), which, in their view, constitutes authenticity and the expression of character.

Summary

To recapitulate, we have argued that self-presentation is an active form of social influence. Yet, at the same time, certain types of presentation of self (e.g., self-verification, self-esteem maintenance, self-construction) can be viewed as sharing more conceptually with such nonpresentational behaviors as self-deception and private rehearsal than with the self-promotive sort of self-presentation.

To illustrate, the Self-Evaluation Maintenance Model predicts that people are motivated to sustain or enhance their self-evaluation through processes of self-deception or processes of self-presentation. Loosely speaking, people can accomplish this by adjusting their self-concept, privately or publicly. Conversely, the push toward self-verification, self-construction, and self-deception (e.g., self-handicapping) is based upon the idea that individuals want to sustain a coherent view of self, one that is neither beseiged by doubts nor uncomfortably far from the ideal self. While these notions appear to be in conflict, they share certain properties. Both views propose intrapsychic motives. In each case, the motive underlies an array of behavioral phenomena reflecting processes of self-regulation. The crucial question remaining is whether there is some conceptually meaningful feature linking the various processes of self-regulation.

As suggested above, the interlinking utility of maintaining self-esteem, sustaining a coherent self-concept, approximating one's ideal self, fending off a clear and certain but unflattering self-evaluation, and the like is to self-regulate one's sense of personal efficacy, control, and therefore hope. The absence of self-esteem, the presence of a vague or uncertain self-concept, and the failure to avoid unflattering assessments of one's own capabilities are already known to be associated with feelings of helplessness and hopelessness (e.g., Abramson et al., 1978; Arkin, Kolditz, & Kolditz, 1983).

Self-Promotion and Self-Concept

The relationship between self-concept and behavior was explicit in the three cells of the organization schema characterized as interpretive control. In contrast, in the fourth case (self-promotive self-presentation), little was known until recently about the impact of presentational behavior upon an audience, the presenter's perception of the others' response, and—most important—the influence of the presenter's behavior upon his/her self-concept. Indeed, some theorists have proposed two quite separate selves, a public one and a private one (Scheier & Carver, 1983), implying that processes of self-presentation may actually be independent of private self-regard.

In the recent past, however, these issues have been addressed, partly reflecting a general resurgence of interest in the self and social cognition. The present section is devoted to reviewing briefly this aspect of the relationship between private self and public self.

It is useful to distinguish at the outset between two sorts of routes to internalization of self-presentational behavior. These routes reflect recurring themes in the self-concept literature. Broadly speaking, these are analogous to the "looking-glass self" (Cooley, 1902; Mead, 1934) or "social self" (James, 1890) on the one hand, and the self rising from private ratiocination on the other. According to the first view, the self is a "product and reflection of social life" (Shrauger & Shoenemann, 1979, p. 549). According to the second, there is no such primacy of others as sources of information about the self. Instead, in these more contemporary views individuals are construed as increasingly reliant on internal cognitive processes exclusive of social relations (e.g., Bem, 1967, 1972; Duval & Wicklund, 1972; Festinger, 1957; Jones & Nisbett, 1972; Ross, 1977; Wicklund & Brehm, 1976).

It is not the purpose of the present section to argue that there are two distinct selves. Instead, the distinction between social and personal refers only to two routes, characterized as social versus personal here, by which people may come to adopt (i.e., "internalize") certain private views based upon their public presentations of self. This distinction between the *social foundations* and the *personal foundations* of self-concept and self-evaluation is illustrated in the top and bottom halves of the model appearing in Figure 4–2.

Turning first to the personal foundations, the model specifies that individuals interpret their own self-presentations much as an outside observer would. These interpretations are, theoretically, independent of others' reactions to the self-presentation; in short, internalization along this route is not mediated by the judgments of others.

The social foundations of internalization involve similar linkages with one additional feature. Instead of directly observing one's own self-presentations, this route involves the presenter interpreting others' reactions to his/her behavior. Thus the

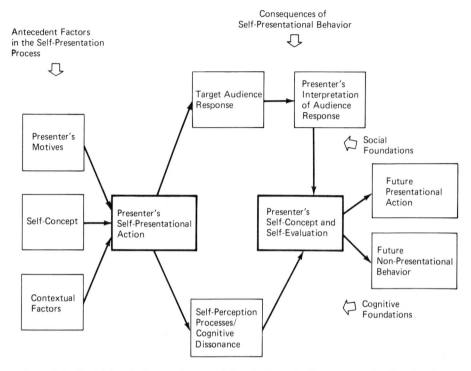

Figure 4-2. Social foundations and personal foundations of self-concept and self-evaluation.

link between self-presentation and self-concept may be viewed as posing one mediator (i.e., presenter interpretation) through the personal route, and two mediators (i.e., others' reactions and the presenter's interpretation of those reactions) through the social route.

Personal Route to Internalization of Self-Presentation

Several studies have shown that individuals exhibit carry-over effects (e.g., Fazio, Effrein, & Falender, 1981; Gergen, 1965; Jones et al., 1981; Upshaw & Yates, 1968). The term "carry-over effect" refers to cases in which an individual adopts privately what he/she displays publicly. Explanations for this effect have been derived from self-perception theory (Bem, 1967), a variant of self-perception theory (Jones, et al., 1981), and certain reinterpretations of cognitive dissonance theory (Wicklund & Brehm, 1976).

According to self-perception theory, the self-concept is malleable. The presenter merely observes his/her own behavior, as an outside observer might, and infers self-conception from that behavior. Jones et al. (1981) argued in favor of a variant of self-perception theory, termed "biased scanning" (Janis & Gilmore, 1965). According to this biased scanning viewpoint, situational cues make certain features of the self more available in memory and, consequently, these features are given more weight in subsequent self-reflection.

However, changes in self-concept resulting from self-perception processes should depend on whether the individual views the self-presentation as a reflection of his/her own self-concept. For example, if an individual believes that he/she is simply playacting, and that the performance cannot be indicative of his/her true self, then a corresponding shift in self-concept should not occur.

According to cognitive dissonance formulations, carry-over effects involve attempts on the part of the actor to reduce discrepancies between a salient self-presentation and a conception of self. Thus, if a presenter exhibits behaviors that do not seem typical of his/her underlying predispositions, and if he/she feels responsible for those behaviors, then changes in self-concept to match the presentational behaviors should occur.

Jones et al. (1981) argued that changes in self-concept due to the arousal of cognitive dissonance should be influenced by factors such as perceived choice and responsibility for the self-presentational behavior. According to Wicklund and Brehm (1976), if an individual does not feel personally responsible for the discrepant behavior, or does not feel that there was sufficient choice to engage or not engage in the behavior, then dissonance should not result and self-concept should remain unchanged.

Two investigations have been undertaken to examine the impact of self-perception versus cognitive dissonance processes on carry-over effects (Jones et al., 1981; Rhodewalt & Agustsdottir, 1985). Jones et al. (1981) led subjects to believe that they were assisting the experimenter by playing the role of a job applicant in an interview. The interviewer allegedly did not know that the interview was contrived. Subjects were instructed to make either a self-enhancing or self-deprecating impression. In order to test the dissonance explanation, half the subjects were told they could withdraw from the experiment (high choice) and half were told the experiment necessitated their dissimulation (low choice). The biased scanning hypothesis was evaluated by instructing half the subjects to think of themselves on a particularly good day or particularly bad day and then to improvise their self-enhancing or self-deprecating performance as it might occur on the basis of those memories. Their responses were then provided to yoked subjects, matched on initial self-esteem. The yoked subjects were instructed to treat these responses as if they were their own. For each pair of subjects, then, the self-presentation was equally discrepant from how they normally viewed themselves; the self-presentation was supposed to reflect prior, personal knowledge of their own behavior only for the subjects who had reflected on their own personal experience.

Jones et al. (1981) replicated earlier findings (e.g., Gergen, 1965; Upshaw & Yates, 1968) by uncovering a clear carry-over effect: subjects showed corresponding shifts in self-esteem ratings as a function of self-presentation. Interestingly, both biased scanning and dissonance reduction seemed to account for the effect, but in different circumstances. When subjects were instructed to self-enhance, it appeared that biased scanning accounted for the positive self-esteem shifts; self-enhancing subjects showed an increase in self-esteem only if they self-referenced (referred to

their own behavior) during the interview. Yoked subjects in the self-enhancing conditions showed no carry-over effect. When subjects were instructed to self-
deprecate, however, it appeared that dissonance reduction accounted for the negative self-esteem shifts; self-deprecating subjects showed a decrease in self-esteem
only if they believed they had a clear choice in deciding to engage in the presentational behavior.

Rhodewalt and Agustsdottir (1985) provided an interesting extension of this study.
They divided subjects into depressed and nondepressed groups. For nondepressed
subjects, their findings were identical to those reported by Jones et al. (1981).
However, the findings for depressed subjects were the mirror image. Carry-over
effects for self-enhancing presentations seemed mediated by dissonance reduction
whereas those for self-deprecating presentations seemed mediated by self-
perception. According to the authors, this difference is attributable to depressed
subjects' negative self-concepts. Self-enhancing presentations were discrepant from
their negative self-views for depressed subjects, resulting in cognitive dissonance.
Self-deprecating presentations were congruent with self-views for the depressed
subjects, producing biased scanning processes.

Whether the basis is dissonance reduction, self-perception, or some facsimile, it
seems evident that presenters sometimes adopt internally and privately what they
project externally and publicly. Without regard to others' reactions, presenters carry
over and internalize their own behaviors and experience corresponding shifts in self-
esteem.

Social Route to Internalization of Self-Presentation

In the social route, an actor must first notice, perceive, and then interpret others'
reactions to his/her self-presentational behaviors. In the following paragraphs,
audience reaction to self-presentations, and actors' subsequent interpretations of
those reactions, are discussed briefly. Together, these sets of findings paint a fairly
sensible picture of this social route to internalization.

Audience reactions to self-presentations. With regard to the first step in the social
route, it seems clear that audiences do not ordinarily provide direct feedback to
presenters regarding the effectiveness of their presentational behaviors. This is particularly true when the presentation is less effective than intended (Blumberg, 1972;
Tesser & Rosen, 1972, 1975). In other words, if an audience disapproves of a given
behavior this disapproval is unlikely to be communicated directly. It is apparently
normative for people to mask their disapproval.

The power of such a norm has been demonstrated recently. Instead of direct forms
of disapproval, these studies point to more indirect forms of feedback, leaked in the
form of nonverbal behavior. Disapproving audiences may mask their disapproval of
a presenter as best they can, but still reveal it to some extent through channels they
cannot control.

Gotlib and Robinson (1982) had subjects interact with depressed and nondepressed target persons. They found that subjects were quite positive in terms of

direct verbal feedback toward all targets. However, in terms of more subtle and indirect nonverbal measures, subjects showed more negative reactions toward depressed targets. They smiled less often, demonstrated less interest, and showed less pleasantness in their facial expressions with depressed targets.

This suggests that people may encounter difficulty deciphering the impact of their self-presentations on others. Individuals who receive negative nonverbal messages about their self-presentations may register the disapproval but be unaware of the immediate cause of it. The presenter may feel rejected but not know at all why. The others' verbal behavior, which is designed to be positive and approving, belies one's own self-presentation as the cause of the subtle feeling of rejection. Further, nonverbal behavior is often registered but without any awareness of the process (e.g., Birdwhistell, 1970; Schneider, Hastorf, & Ellsworth, 1979), which would be likely to contribute to the presenter's sense of confusion.

Presenters' reactions to audience feedback. It appears that individuals generally tend to accept feedback from others (e.g., Darley & Fazio, 1980; Snyder & Swann, 1978a, 1978b). Research addressing *expectancy confirmation* (Darley & Fazio, 1980) and *behavioral confirmation* (Snyder & Swann, 1978a, 1978b) has shown that subjects adopt, or internalize, qualities that others ascribe to them. For instance, the individual who receives feedback that he/she is an extravert will incorporate that assessment and actually exhibit more extraverted behaviors subsequently (Fazio et al., 1981).

In the Fazio et al. (1981) study, subjects first interacted with an experimenter who indicated that the subject was either an introvert or an extravert. Following this, subjects completed a self-description inventory and then interacted with a confederate in a different setting. Subjects in this study changed their self-descriptions to conform to the experimenter's feedback. Moreover, the confederate's ratings indicated that subjects also showed corresponding shifts in behavior (see Snyder, Campbell, & Preston, 1982; Snyder & Swann, 1978a, 1978b; Snyder, Tanke, & Berscheid, 1977).

At the same time it also appears that individuals seek to disconfirm feedback regarding their self-presentations if it is clearly discrepant from their own private self-conceptions (e.g., Swann, 1984). In addition, individuals may also interpret feedback in a way that serves their own esteem needs. It is fairly common to find that individuals enjoy hearing positive things about themselves, seek such information and, on occasion, misread feedback from others in the service of self-esteem (Bradley, 1978; Greenwald, 1980; Greenwald & Breckler, 1985). Perhaps, then, people simply attend more closely to positive feedback and less closely to negative feedback from others.

Sicoly and Ross (1977) provided a suggestive illustration of such a distortion. In their study, subjects either succeeded or failed a social sensitivity task. They subsequently received feedback from a confederate who assigned them either more or less responsibility for the success or failure than they assigned themselves. Subjects who received diminished responsibility ratings for failure or inflated responsibility ratings for success rated the confederate's judgment as highly accurate. Subjects were seemingly motivated to enhance or protect esteem and accomplished this by rejecting negative feedback and embracing positive feedback.

Tesser and Paulhus (1983) provided a comparable example of such a bias. Subjects in this study readily accepted audience feedback if it was positive. They did so even though it was utterly clear that the feedback was false.

Both Sicoly and Ross (1977) and Tesser and Paulhus (1983) found that individuals were more receptive to positive than negative audience feedback. Their findings suggest that presenters do not merely react passively and logically to the feedback they receive from others. Rather, they suggest that people actively seek information and prefer to accept inferences that are desirable or comforting to hear (see Arkin, Gleason, & Johnston, 1976).

Summary

The impact of self-presentational behavior on subsequent self-concept follows two paths. Along the personal route, individuals observe and interpret their own self-presentations and, as a result, sometimes internalize these through self-perception and cognitive dissonance processes. Along the social route, an audience reacts to a given self-presentational behavior; the presenter then perceives, interprets, and often internalizes that assessment.

Room for bias exists in both the social route and personal route to internalization. Both these sources of self-serving bias might lead to a false sense of confidence in one's self-presentational efficacy. To the extent this is true, people may be inclined to internalize more of their presentations of self than warranted (particularly when those presentations of self confirm one's self-image and/or are positive in nature). In this sense, then, it seems arguable that even the aftermath of forms of control that are primary reflect instances of interpretive control. Indeed, signals that one's efforts to exert primary control fell short would be more disconcerting than failures to achieve effective interpretive control. This may explain the powerful normative pressure for social observers to engage in "face-work" (Goffman, 1959) rather than be completely forthcoming in their interpersonal evaluations. People seem to sense correctly that unadulterated honesty may have dramatic repercussions.

Summary and Conclusions

Self-presentation is a compelling area of research and theory for a variety of reasons. Not least of all, the theoretical and empirical work in self-presentation has centered attention on the issue of public selves versus private selves. In the present chapter we examined both some of the antecedents of self-presentation and some of the consequences of self-presentation looking for specific linkages between the private self and the public self.

Social control and personal control were distinguished. In self-promotive self-presentation, social control is exerted. Individuals attempt to establish an identity through the appearance presented to others for reasons of social motivation (i.e., to pave the way toward smooth social relations and the social rewards others are able to provide). The self-promotive brand of self-presentation was likened to Rothbaum et al.'s (1982) notion of primary control (i.e., attempts to bring the environment in line with one's wishes). Other, more recent accounts of self-presentational behavior—as well as some other related behaviors (e.g., self-deception)—were characterized as driven by self-regulation of a sense of personal control. These phenomena were categorized as a form of interpretive control (Rothbaum et al., 1982) and as motivated by the desire to sustain one's belief in the power to exert influence over future events. A self-conception that is favorable, as well as stable, certain, and reliable, can serve such a belief system. Achieving such a self-conception through self-presentation was interpreted in this chapter as an instance of behavioral self-regulation.

Toward the end of the chapter the residual effect of self-presentation on self-concept was reviewed briefly; here again, it was argued that presentations of self that confirm one's self-image and/or are positive in nature are most likely to be internalized as an accurate reflection of self. In this way, even the aftermath of instances of primary control reflect interpretive control as well. In short, processes of self-regulation of a sense of personal control were interpreted as occurring in both the arenas of self-perception and self-presentation.

While the evidence for the role of control motivation (interpretive control) in self-presentation is circumstantial at present, the linkages between private self and public self analyzed here suggest the utility of considering this motivational factor in future theory and research.

References

Abramson, L. Y., Seligman, M. E. P., & Teasdale, J. D. (1978). Learned helplessness in humans: Critique and reformulation. *Journal of Abnormal Psychology, 87*, 49–74.

Arkin, R. M. (1981). Self-presentation styles. In J. T. Tedeschi (Ed.), *Impression management theory and social psychological research* (pp. 311–333). New York: Academic.

Arkin, R. M., & Baumgardner, A. H. (1985). Self-handicapping. In J. H. Harvey & G. W. Weary (Ed.), *Attribution: Basic issues and applications* (pp. 169–202). New York: Academic.

Arkin, R. M., Cooper, H. M., & Kolditz, T. (1980). A statistical review of the literature concerning the self-serving attribution bias in interpersonal situations. *Journal of Personality, 48*, 435–448.

Arkin, R. M., Gleason, J. M., & Johnston, S. (1976). Effect of perceived choice, expected outcome, and observed outcome of an action on the causal attributions of actors. *Journal of Experimental Social Psychology, 12*, 151–158.

Arkin, R. M., Kolditz, T., & Kolditz, K. (1983). Attributions of the test-anxious student: Self-assessments in the classroom. *Personality and Social Psychology Bulletin, 9*, 271–280.

Bandura, A. (1977). Self-efficacy: Toward a unifying theory of behavioral change. *Psychological Review, 84*, 191–215.

Baumeister, R. F. (1982). A self-presentational view of social phenomena. *Psychological Bulletin, 91*, 3–26.

Baumgardner, A. H., Heppner, P. P., & Arkin, R. M. (1986). The role of causal attribution in personal problem solving. *Journal of Personality and Social Psychology, 50*, 636–643.

Baumgardner, A. H., Lake, E., & Arkin, R. M. (1985). Claiming mood as a self-handicap: The influence of spoiled and unspoiled public identity. *Personality and Social Psychology Bulletin, 11*, 349–357.

Beck, A. T. (1967). *Depression: Clinical, experimental, and theoretical aspects.* New York: Hoeber.

Bem, D. J. (1967). Self-perception: An alternative interpretation of cognitive dissonance phenomena. *Psychological Review, 74*, 183–200.

Bem, D. J. (1972). Self-perception theory. In L. Berkowitz (Ed.), *Advances in experimental social psychology* (Vol. 6). New York: Academic.

Birdwhistell, R. L. (1970). *Kinesics and context.* Philadelphia: University of Pennsylvania Press.

Blumberg, H. H. (1972). Communication of interpersonal evaluations. *Journal of Personality and Social Psychology, 23*, 157–162.

Bradley, G. W. (1978). Self-serving biases in the attribution process: A reexamination of the fact or fiction question. *Journal of Personality and Social Psychology, 36*, 56–71.

Buss, A. H., & Briggs, S. R. (1984). Drama and the self in social interaction. *Journal of Personality and Social Psychology, 47*, 1310–1324.

Cacioppo, J. T., & Petty, R. E. (1981). Social psychological procedures for cognitive response assessment: The thought listing technique. In T. V. Merluzzi, C. R. Glass, & M. Genest (Eds.), *Cognitive Assessment* (pp. 181–192). New York: Guilford.

Cialdini, R. B., & Kenrick, D. T. (1976). Altruism as hedonism: A social development perspective on the relationship of negative mood state and helping. *Journal of Personality and Social Psychology, 34*, 907–914.

Cooley, C. H. (1902). *Human nature and the social order.* New York: Scribner and Sons.

Darley, J. M., & Fazio, R. H. (1980). Expectancy confirmation processes arising in the interaction sequence. *American Psychologist, 35*, 867–881.

Deci, E. L. (1975). *Intrinsic motivation.* New York: Plenum.

Deci, E. L., & Ryan, R. M. (1980). The empirical exploration of intrinsic motivation processes. In L. Berkowitz (Ed.), *Advances in Experimental Social Psychology* (pp. 40–81). New York: Academic.

Duval, S., & Wicklund, R. A. (1972). *A theory of objective self-awareness.* New York: Academic.

Fazio, R. H., Effrein, E. A., & Falender, V. J. (1981). Self-perception following social interaction. *Journal of Personality and Social Psychology, 41*, 232–242.

Festinger, L. (1954). A theory of social comparison processes. *Human Relations, 40*, 427–448.

Festinger, L. (1957). *A theory of cognitive dissonance.* Stanford, CA: Stanford University Press.

Gergen, K. J. (1965). Interaction goals and personalistic feedback as factors affecting the presentation of self. *Journal of Personality and Social Psychology, 1*, 413–424.

Goethals, G. R., & Darley, J. M. (1977). Social comparison theory: An attributional approach. In J. M. Suls & R. L. Miller (Eds.), *Social comparison processes* (pp. 259–278). New York: Hemisphere.

Goffman, E. (1959). *The presentation of self in everyday life* (Rev. ed.). New York: Doubleday.

Goleman, D. (1985). *Vital lies, simple truths: The psychology of self-deception.* New York: Simon & Schuster.

Gotlib, I. H., & Robinson, L. A. (1982). Responses to depressed individuals: Discrepancies between self-report and observer-rated behavior. *Journal of Abnormal Behavior, 91*, 231–240.

Greenwald, A. G. (1980). The totalitarian ego: Fabrication and revision of personal history. *American Psychologist, 35*, 603–618.

Greenwald, A., & Breckler, S. J. (1985). To whom is the self presented? In B. Schlenker (Ed.), *The self and social life* (pp. 126–145). New York: McGraw-Hill.

Gur, R. C., & Sackeim, H. A. (1979). Self-deception: A concept in search of a phenomenon. *Journal of Personality and Social Psychology, 37*, 147–169.

James, W. (1890). The principles of psychology. New York: Dover.

Janis, I. L., & Gilmore, J. B. (1965). The influence of incentive conditions on the success of role playing in modifying attitudes. *Journal of Personality and Social Psychology, 1*, 17-27.

Jellison, J. M. (1981). Reconsidering the attitude concept: A behavioristic self-presentation formulation. In J. T. Tedeschi (Ed.), *Impression management theory and social psychology research* (pp. 107-126). New York: Academic.

Jellison, J. M., & Gentry, K. W. (1978). A self-presentation interpretation of the seeking of social approval. *Personality and Social Psychology Bulletin, 4*, 227-230.

Jones, E. E., & Berglas, S. (1978). Control of attributions about the self through self-handicapping strategies: The appeal of alcohol and the role of underachievement. *Personality and Social Psychology Bulletin, 4*, 200-206.

Jones, E. E., & Nisbett, R. E. (1972). The actor and the observer: Divergent perceptions of the causes of behavior. In E. E. Jones, D. E. Kanouse, H. H. Kelley, R. E. Nisbett, S. Valins, & B. Weiner (Eds.), *Attribution: Perceiving the causes of behavior.* Morristown, NJ: General Learning Press.

Jones, E. E., & Pittman, T. S. (1982). Toward a general theory of strategic self-presentation. In J. Suls (Ed.), *Psychological perspectives on the self* (Vol. 1, pp. 231-262). Hillsdale, NJ: Erlbaum.

Jones, E. E., Rhodewalt, F., Berglas, S., & Skelton, J. A. (1981). Effects of strategic self-presentation on subsequent self-esteem. *Journal of Personality and Social Psychology, 41*, 407-421.

Kelley, H. H. (1971). Attribution in social interaction. In E. E. Jones, D. E. Kanouse, H. H. Kelley, R. E. Nisbett, S. Valins, & B. Weiner (Eds.), *Attribution: Perceiving the causes of behavior.* New York: General Learning Press.

Kolditz, T. A., & Arkin, R. M. (1982). An impression management interpretation of the self-handicapping strategy. *Journal of Personality and Social Psychology, 43*, 492-502.

Langer, E. J. (1983). *The psychology of control.* Beverly Hills, CA: Sage.

Martin, M. W. (Ed.). (1985). *Self-deception and self understanding: New essays in philosophy and psychology.* Lawrence: University of Kansas Press.

Mead, G. H. (1934). *Mind, self, and society.* Chicago: University of Chicago Press.

Nisbett, R. E., & Ross, L. (1980). *Human inference: Strategies and shortcomings of social judgment.* Englewood Cliffs, NJ: Prentice-Hall.

Peterson, C., & Seligman, M. E. P. (1984). Causal explanations as a risk factor for depression: Theory and evidence. *Psychological Review, 91*, 347-374.

Petty, R. E., & Cacioppo, J. T. (1981). *Attitudes and persuasion: Classic and contemporary approaches.* Dubuque, IA: William C. Brown.

Pierce, C. S. (1868). Questions concerning certain faculties claimed for man. *Journal of Speculative Philosophy, 2*, 103-114.

Quattrone, G. A., & Tversky, A. (1984). Causal versus diagnostic contingencies: On self-deception and on the voter's illusion. *Journal of Personality and Social Psychology, 46*, 237-248.

Rhodewalt, F., & Agustsdottir, S. (1985). *On the structure of the phenomenal self: The effects of self-presentation on subsequent self-esteem.* Unpublished manuscript, University of Utah.

Ross, L. (1977). The intuitive psychologist and his shortcomings: Distortions in the attribution process. In L. Berkowitz (Ed.), *Advances in Experimental Social Psychology* (Vol. 10, pp. 174-214). New York: Academic.

Rothbaum, F., Weisz, J. R., & Snyder, S. S. (1982). Changing the world and changing the self: A two-process model of perceived control. *Journal of Personality and Social Psychology, 42*, 5-37.

Scheier, M. F., & Carver, C. S. (1983). Two sides of the self: One for you and one for me. In J. Suls & A. G. Greenwald (Eds.), *Psychological perspectives on the self* (Vol. 2). Hillsdale, NJ: Erlbaum.

Schlenker, B. R. (1980). *Impression management: The self-concept, social identity, and interpersonal relations.* Monterey, CA: Brooks-Cole.

Schneider, D. J., Hastorf, A. H., & Ellsworth, P. C. (1979). *Person perception.* Reading, MA: Addison-Wesley.

Shrauger, J. S., & Schoeneman, T. J. (1979). Symbolic interactionist view of the self-concept: Through the looking glass darkly. *Psychological Bulletin, 86,* 549–573.

Seligman, M. E. P. (1975). *Helplessness: On depression, development, and death.* San Francisco: Freeman.

Sicoly, F., & Ross, M. (1977). Facilitation of ego-biased attributions by means of self-serving observer feedback. *Journal of Personality and Social Psychology, 35,* 734–741.

Snyder, M., Campbell, B. H., & Preston, E. (1982). Testing hypotheses about human nature: Assessing the accuracy of social stereotypes. *Social Cognition, 1,* 256–272.

Snyder, M., & Swann, W. B., Jr. (1978a). Behavioral confirmation in social interaction: From social perception to social reality. *Journal of Experimental Social Psychology, 14,* 148–162.

Snyder, M., & Swann, W. B., Jr. (1978b). Hypothesis-testing processes in social interaction. *Journal of Personality and Social Psychology, 36,* 1202–1212.

Snyder, M., Tanke, E. D., & Berscheid, E. (1977). Social perception and interpersonal behavior: On the self-fulfilling nature of social stereotypes. *Journal of Personality and Social Psychology, 35,* 656–666.

Snyder, M. C., & Wicklund, R. (1981). Attribute ambiguity. In J. H. Harvey, W. J. Ickes, & R. F. Kidd (Eds.), *New directions in attribution research* (Vol. 3, pp. 199–224). Hillsdale, NJ: Erlbaum.

Swann, W. B., Jr. (1984). Question for accuracy in person perception: A matter of pragmatics. *Psychological Review, 91,* 457–477.

Swann, W. B, Jr., & Ely, R. J. (1984). A battle of wills: Self-verification versus behavioral confirmation. *Journal of Personality and Social Psychology, 46,* 1287–1302.

Swann, W. B., Jr., & Hill, C. A. (1982). When our identities are mistaken: Reaffirming self-conceptions through social interaction. *Journal of Personality and Social Psychology, 43,* 59–66.

Swann, W. B., Jr., & Read, S. J. (1981). Self-verification processes: How we sustain our self-conceptions. *Journal of Experimental Social Psychology, 17,* 351–372.

Tedeschi, J. T., & Norman, N. (1985). Social power, self-presentation, and the self. In B. Schlenker (Ed.), *The self and social life* (pp. 293–322). New York: McGraw-Hill.

Tesser, A. (1980). *A self-evaluation maintenance model of social behavior.* Unpublished manuscript, University of Georgia.

Tesser, A., & Paulhus, D. (1983). The definition of self: Private and public self-evaluation management strategies. *Journal of Personality and Social Psychology, 44,* 672–682.

Tesser, A., & Rosen, S. (1972). Similarity of objective fate as a determinant of the reluctance to transmit unpleasant information: The MUM effect. *Journal of Personality and Social Psychology, 23,* 46–53.

Tesser, A., & Rosen, S. (1975). The reluctance to transmit bad news. In L. Berkowitz (Ed.), *Advances in experimental social psychology,* (Vol. 8, pp. 193–232). New York: Academic.

Tetlock, P. E., & Manstead, A. S. R. (1985). Impression management versus intrapsychic explanations in social psychology: A useful dichotomy? *Psychological Review, 92,* 59–77.

Trope, Y. (1975). Seeking information about one's own ability as a determinant of choice among tasks. *Journal of Personality and Social Psychology, 32,* 1004–1013.

Upshaw, H. S., & Yates, L. A. (1968). Self-persuasion, social approval, and task success as determinants of self-esteem following impression management. *Journal of Experimental Social Psychology, 4,* 143–152.

Weary, G., & Arkin, R. M. (1981). Attributional self-presentation. In J. H. Harvey, W. Ickes, & R. F. Kidd (Eds.), *New directions in attribution research* (Vol. 2, pp. 223–246). Hillsdale, NJ: Erlbaum.

White, R. W. (1959). Motivation reconsidered: The concept of competence. *Psychological Review, 66*, 297–333.
Wicklund, R. A., & Brehm, J. W. (1976). *Perspectives on cognitive dissonance*. Hillsdale, NJ: Erlbaum.
Wilson, E. O. (1978). On human nature. Cambridge, MA: Harvard University Press.

Chapter 5
On the Convergence of Public and Private Aspects of Self

Abraham Tesser and Janet Moore

This chapter deals with some issues concerning the correspondence of the self one presents to others and what one believes to be "true" of the self. That is, we are concerned with the discrepancy between what Baumeister and Tice (Chapter 3, this volume) call the public self and the self-concept. Our interest in these issues stems from a theory of social behavior known as the self-evaluation maintenance (SEM) model. First, we briefly describe the model and its implications for views of the self. Then we review a test of the model that raises the question of whether the predicted (and obtained) changes in the self represent changes in the public self (with the goal of creating a particular impression) or changes in the self-concept (with the goal of private self-evaluation maintenance). A couple of studies designed to address this question suggest that one's public self and one's self-concept tend to be similar. In the second half of the chapter we examine some reasons why the self-concept and the public self tend to converge. The convergence may be due to the potential of being found out when presenting a false, favorable public self, information overloads, the self-concept constraining the public self, the public self constraining the self-concept, and third factors constraining both the public self and the self-concept in similar ways.

The Self-Evaluation Maintenance (SEM) Model

The SEM model assumes that people want to maintain a positive self-evaluation. It specifies two processes that affect that self-evaluation: The reflection process and the comparison process. Both of these processes involve the closeness and performance of another person. Sometimes the good performance by a close individual raises one's self-evaluation by *reflection*. The person who brags about his cousin the great piano player, or about his neighbor who almost won a Nobel prize, is engaging in reflection. On the other hand, the good performance of a close other can sometimes lower self-evaluation by *comparison*. When an individual makes a 70 on an exam on which a friend made an 85, he or she does not take joy in that friend's accomplishment but rather feels bad by comparison.

The reflection process and the comparison process depend on the same two variables but have opposite effects. The good performance of another can inflate self-evaluation through reflection or lower self-evaluation by comparison. The model argues, however, that these two processes are not always equally important. The variable that determines the relative importance of the reflection and comparison processes is the relevance of the other person's performance to one's own self-definition. If the other person's performance is on a dimension that is important to one's self-concept, the comparison process will be important and the individual will suffer by comparison with a close other's better performance. On the other hand, if the other person's performance is on a dimension that is not important to one's self-concept, one is more likely to bask in reflected glory of that person's good performance.

The model goes on to suggest that persons change each of the three parameters in order to maintain a positive self-evaluation. That is, one might alter the relationship with another person. One might interfere with another person's good performance or facilitate that performance, or one might change his or her self-concept to make a performance dimension more or less relevant. More detailed discussions of the model and more comprehensive reviews of the evidence are available elsewhere (e.g., Tesser, 1986; Tesser & Campbell, 1983) so we do not attempt a summary here. Rather, we focus on one prediction and then examine some research that concerns whether the behavior associated with that prediction can best be described as serving an intrapsychic need for self-evaluation maintenance or a self-presentational need to look competent. The model assumes that people strive for both private and public self-evaluation and that the dynamics are pretty much alike.

What does the model predict about the construction of the self? This has to do with the relevance parameter. That is, to what extent is a performance dimension more or less relevant to one's self-definition (Tesser & Campbell, 1983)? With respect to self-definition the model predicts that the better another's (relative) performance on a particular dimension, the less self-definitional that dimension will be to the individual. And, the relationship between the other's performance and one's own self-definition will be more pronounced with increasing closeness of the other person. For example, if another child plays the piano better than 12-year-old Mary, according to the model Mary should decide that piano playing is not important to her, particularly if the other child and she are close (e.g., friends or relatives).

Tesser and Campbell (1980) tested these hypotheses by giving female subjects an opportunity to perform on a "social sensitivity" task and on an "esthetic judgment" task with a female confederate. Some subjects were led to believe that the confederate was very similar to them. Other subjects were led to believe that the confederate was very dissimilar. Each subject learned that she and the confederate performed at the same level (below average) on one task. On the other task, the subject's *absolute* level of performance was a little better (average), but the confederate's absolute level of performance was much better (clearly above average). In sum, subjects learned that their performance was poor but identical to that of the confederate on one task and average but inferior to that of the confederate on the other task.

There were three dependent measures of self-definition: choice of task for additional work, an interview regarding self-definition, and change in rating of the relevance of both task dimensions to subjects' self-definition. The results supported the hypotheses on the choice measure and the change in relevance measure but not on the interview measure. Subjects reduced the relevance of the dimension on which the confederate outperformed them. Further, this effect was more pronounced in the similar condition (close) than the dissimilar condition (distant). This was true despite the fact that the task on which the confederate outperformed the subject was also the task on which the subject herself performed better in an absolute sense. Thus, subjects' self-definitions moved away from the task on which they themselves did better (absolute performance) and toward the task on which their *relative* performance was better.

Public Versus Private Self-Evaluation Maintenance

This study by Tesser and Campbell (1980) raises an interpretational question that is important for present purposes. Did the subjects' behavior reflect attempts to maintain private self-evaluation or did it simply reflect attempts to evoke a positive evaluation from the experimenter (impression management)? The fact that the interview measure (taken by an interviewer who was not present during the experimental manipulations) did not show the predicted effects but the choice measure (taken by the experimenter) did show the effects is consistent with an impression management interpretation.

Our working assumption has been that public and private self-evaluation maintenance processes are generally similar. That is, an actor's behavior is intended to provide similar information to the self and to an audience. Before developing the theoretical underpinnings of that argument, however, we attempt to empirically assess the importance of public image management motives relative to private self-evaluation maintenance motives.

The observation that an individual behaves in a way that is consistent with the SEM model before an audience (as in Tesser & Campbell, 1980) does not allow an inference of whether the behavior is in the service of public image management or private self-evaluation maintenance. One way of disentangling these motives is to independently vary what an individual believes about the quality of his or her own performance and what he or she thinks an audience believes about that performance (but see Tetlock & Manstead, 1985). To the extent that public evaluation of self is important, what the audience is presumed to believe about the individual should be consequential in his behavior; to the extent that private self-evaluation is important, what the individual believes (regardless of audience beliefs) should be consequential.

The necessary conditions were set up by Tesser and Paulhus (1983). Subjects were given feedback that they had done better or worse than either a similar or dissimilar other on a dimension called Cognitive Perceptual Integration (CPI). Subjects were told that they would be interviewed by the experimenter's supervisor. When the experimenter entered the subjects' scores in the computer for the supervisor, he became confused about the order in which to enter them. The subjects were told that the information the supervisor reads about their performance may be wrong but they were asked not to reveal the mistake. In this way it was possible to vary independently what the subjects believed about their own performance and what the supervisor, an audience, believed about their performance.

What the participants told the supervisor was affected by both what the participants believed about their performances and what they thought the supervisor believed about their performances. That is, regardless of what the supervisor believed, the subjects told the supervisor that CPI was personally more important when the subjects knew they outperformed an other (particularly a similar other) than when they knew the other had outperformed them. Similarly, regardless of what the subjects knew about their own relative performances, they told the supervisor that CPI was more personally important when they thought the supervisor believed they (the subjects) had outperformed the other. These data suggest that the kinds of changes in behavior associated with the SEM model can serve both public and private motives.

The effects of public versus private motives on the enactment of behavior were disentangled another way also. In most instances one does not know the extent to which behavior is under the control of public or private motives. Suppose that the investigators supply the motive. For example, the subject is given a public motive; i.e., the subject's task is to behave so as to make an audience think he or she is competent. We can then observe the behavior under ordinary circumstances (when the motive is not supplied) and when the motive is supplied.

Suppose that when the public motive is supplied the behavior enacted is different from the behavior enacted under ordinary circumstances. Here one can infer that the behavior is *not* (at least not totally) ordinarily under the control of that same public motive. A less informative observation is that the behavior is the same regardless of whether the motive is supplied or not. If this occurs it would be tempting to infer that the behavior must ordinarily be under the control of a public motive. However, such an inference is merely *plausible*. We cannot rule out the possibility that private motives are ordinarily important but that they produce the same behaviors as do public motives (see Baumeister & Tice, 1984; Ross, MacFarland, Conway, & Zanna, 1984).

A study in which subjects were given scenarios in which the protagonist was described as either psychologically close or distant to a comparison other was recently completed by Tesser and Barbee (in preparation). The comparison other was described as either performing better than or at about the same level as the protagonist. The subject's goal was to advise the protagonist about the level of relevance to self-definition of the performance dimension and the extent to which to claim a better or poorer performance in order to create an image of competence in an audience who was aware of the closeness and performance of the other.

As indicated earlier, the SEM model predicts an interaction between the closeness and performance of the comparison other on self-definition. The advice the subject gave the protagonist in the Tesser and Barbee study is consistent with this prediction and with the outcomes of previous studies in which no motive was supplied.

Because subjects were provided with the goal of creating a public image of competence in this study and the results are like the original studies, it is plausible (but not necessary) to assume that the behavior in the original studies may have been directed by a public image management motive.

Recall that the SEM model is systemic. We would like to touch on one other aspect of it with regard to this particular study—performance. Again, the subject's goal was to advise the protagonist how to behave in order to appear competent. This time the scenarios differed in terms of the closeness of the other and the relevance of the performance dimension to the protagonist's self-definition. Also, the subject was to advise the protagonist about the extent to which he should claim a better or poorer performance than the comparison other.

The model suggests that when relevance to self-definition is high the potential for suffering by comparison is high. Therefore, one should derogate the other's performance, particularly when the other is close. When relevance to self-definition is low, the chance to bask in another's reflected glory is high so the actor should enhance the other's performance, particularly when the other is close. In this case the advice given to the protagonist was *opposite* to what was predicted by the model and what was found in previous studies in which no motive was supplied (e.g., Tesser and Smith, 1980; Tesser and Campbell, 1982). In the case of affecting another's performance one *must* conclude that the subject's goal in the previous research could not have been entirely to create a public impression of competence.

In sum, the evidence indicates that both public and private motives are served by the behaviors associated with the model. What is more, given the way in which the research was conducted, it is possible to conclude that there is a good bit of overlap in the functional relationships driving behavior related to public and private goals. Given a set of antecedent conditions a desire for public *or* for private image maintenance produces similar social behaviors.

In a similar vein, a tenet of Schlenker's (1982) identity-analytic theory is that persons offer explanations for their conduct when it violates either personal or private standards and that often these standards converge. Additionally, Schlenker proposed that persons may present one impression in one situation and another image in another situation, but that these are merely aspects of the large theoretical structure of the self. Baumeister (1982) has suggested that the social behaviors that appear to be for the benefit of an audience also may be driven by self-fulfillment (private) motives; specifically, a person attempts to become his or her ideal self by convincing others that he or she "really" is like the ideal self. In short, the insight that public and private selves will tend to converge is hardly novel.

On the Convergence of the Public Self and the Self-Concept

In doing the research associated with the SEM model we have come to the conclusion that public behavior and the self-concept are driven by similar forces and will ordinarily be similar. Although we do not agree totally with Tetlock and Manstead (1985) that research attempting to delineate intrapsychic mechanisms from public image management tactics is doomed to failure, we wholeheartedly agree with their conclusion that research ought to address questions concerning the circumstances when one or the other motive will be preeminent. Our focus on the pages to follow is slightly different from but consistent with the spirit of their admonition. Rather than concern ourselves with shifting motives, we simply speculate on the circumstances under which the public self and the self-concept will converge and when they will diverge.

We assume that a major goal of public behavior is to create a positive impression. Clearly other goals are possible. Gollwitzer (Chapter 7, this volume) mentions such goals: the facilitation of social interaction (e.g., Goffman, 1959); the establishment of interpersonal power (e.g., Jones & Pittman, 1982); and the establishment of a cross-situational identity as an effective influencer (e.g., Schlenker, 1985) in addition to the goal of creating a positive impression. However, desire for social approval has been studied most (e.g., Crowne & Marlowe, 1964; Jellison & Gentry, 1978; Paulhus, 1984; Schlenker, 1980; Tedeschi, 1981) and has been the goal most commonly assumed. Since, for present purposes, it is convenient to focus on only one motive we have chosen to focus on the motive of winning approval.

The Dilemma in Creating a Positive Impression

There is a potential conflict in enacting behaviors intended to win social approval. If an audience sees a self-presentation as being inconsistent with the actor's actual self, there is the possibility that the actor will be seen as a manipulator, braggart, or liar. (For purposes of the present discussion we treat self-concept, actual self, and private self as synonymous even though there are often good reasons for distinguishing them; see Baumeister & Tice, Chapter 3, this volume.) None of these views is flattering. This is the crux of a dilemma. An enactment of the self intended to produce approval can actually produce disapproval if the audience thinks the enactment is false. Therefore, the actor attempting to curry favor must be very careful not to appear deceptive (Jones, 1964). What does this dilemma imply regarding the convergence of the public self and the self-concept?

One can construe a presentation of self that is different from one's self-concept as deception. Also, there is an extant literature on deception. We are beginning to learn about the nonverbal concomitants of deception (e.g., Ekman & Friesen, 1974; Zuckerman, DeFrank, Hall, Larrance, & Rosenthal, 1979), the physiological correlates of deception (e.g., Waid & Orne, 1980), and the personality correlates of successful deceivers (e.g., DePaulo & Rosenthal, 1979). However, there is very little research on the circumstances under which persons are more or less likely to lie. A first step in that direction was taken by Ulvedal, Millar, & Tesser (1984). In a preliminary study they found that the self-reported probability of lying decreased with the probability of being detected and the cost of being detected; lying increased with the anticipated gain associated with a successful deception.

There is some self-presentation research that addresses the first factor, the probability of being detected. If one's audience is to witness one's future performance then the probability of a false self-presentation being detected is higher than if one's audience will not witness one's future performance. Thus, there should be greater convergence between the self-concept and the public self under conditions of future contact. Schlenker (1975) manipulated self-concept, i.e., expectations for future task success, and whether an audience would learn of subsequent performance. He found greater similarity between self-concept and public self in the future knowledge condition than in the future ignorance condition.

Just as the probability for detection increases with future surveillance, it can also increase with an audience's knowledge of past behavior. For example, if an audience has seen one fail at a task, presenting oneself as good at the task may not be believable. Baumeister and Jones (1978) gave subjects good or bad personality feedback, thereby manipulating their self-concepts. They also manipulated whether or not the subject believed that an audience had seen the previous feedback. As expected, they found that when the subject believed that the audience was familiar with their past there was no attempt to present a positively inflated public self on dimensions related to the feedback. In fact, there was a unidimensional, modest public self-presentation across *both* positive and negative feedback conditions. Even more intriguing is a pattern of "compensation" that was observed. Although subjects who were given negative feedback did not present an inflated public self to a knowledgeable audience on dimensions related to the feedback, they did show an inflated public self on dimensions unrelated to the feedback, dimensions on which the audience was ignorant.

Taken together, these studies suggest that persons are less likely to be deceptively self-serving with people who know something of their past and with people who will know something of their future. That is, an individual's public self and private self are more likely to converge with people who know the individual, i.e., most people with whom he or she is acquainted. The Baumeister and Jones data further suggest that one must be careful in specifying the dimensions of self-presentation; under the same conditions, different dimensions of the self behave differently.

In the Baumeister and Jones study self-presentation differed on arbitrarily selected dimensions of the self, i.e., those on which the experimenter chose to manipulate audience knowledge and those that did not happen to enter into that manipulation. Are there also aspects of the self that are generally (cross-situationally) more or less likely to be the locus of deceptive self-presentation? Are there aspects of the self that are more easily verified than other aspects of the self? Thoughts and feelings are less verifiable than behaviors and biographical "facts" such as number of siblings. Therefore, one might expect less discepancy between public self and self-concept with respect to the latter aspects of the self than with respect to the former aspects. Indeed, there is evidence from the applied psychometric literature that "objective" biographical items are less likely to be faked and show less change when respondents are instructed to create a particular image (Owens, 1976). What is interesting about these items is that persons fake them less even when they believe that there is no way of checking up on the accuracy of their statements (Saunder, Shaffer, & Owens, 1984).

It is interesting to note in this context that persons do not see behaviors and thoughts and feelings as equally valid indicators of the self. While many psychologists would argue that behavior is the sine qua non of the self, the work of Susan

Andersen (1984; Andersen & Ross, 1984) suggests that people believe they have revealed more about themselves when they reveal their thoughts and feelings than their behaviors; and, they believe they have learned more about another when they learn about that other's thoughts and feelings than about his or her behavior. If these findings are taken with the findings from the Saunder et al. (1984) study, it appears that persons are likely to be deceptive about those aspects of the self that are subjectively the most important and diagnostic.

Another way to deal with the question of whom we deceive about what is to focus on the potential gain or loss associated with a particular self-presentational episode. Millar and Tesser (1985) argued that persons deceive others about different things. Every individual is in a number of relationships and each relationship has associated with it a different set of expectations concerning his or her behavior. Every individual also has a set of expectations for his or her own behavior that is different from that associated with any single relationship. Let us assume that if others discover that an individual has violated their expectancies it would result in a costly disruption of the relationship. The general hypothesis is that one deceives particular people about the behaviors that violate their particular expectations. The individual's own expectations should have little impact on deception.

In order to test their hypothesis about deception, Millar and Tesser had subjects rate the extent to which a parent, a former employer, and they themselves held an expectation that prohibited each of 32 behaviors. They were also asked to indicate the likelihood that they would lie to their parent or to their employer about each behavior if they had engaged in the behavior. For each subject two regression equations were computed: likelihood of lying to a parent was regressed on parent's expectations, employers' expectations, and self-expectations (across the 32 behaviors); and likelihood of lying to an employer was regressed on the same three predictors. The results were quite supportive. The expectations accounted for about 40% of the variance in likelihood of lying. Further, as predicted, parent's expectations were a more important determinant of lying to a parent than employer's or self-expectations; employer's expectations were a more important determinant of lying to an employer than parent's or self-expectations. Parental expectation was a stronger predictor of lying to a parent than lying to an employer; employer's expectations were a more important determinant of lying to an employer than lying to a parent, and self-expectation was not significantly different from zero in either equation.

The Millar and Tesser results support the conclusion of the Baumeister and Jones (1978) study. Discrepancies between self-concept and public self, i.e., deception, are not unidimensional. Different areas of the self produce different levels of discrepancy. The Baumeister and Jones study suggests that these differences are partially due to audiences' knowledge (probability of detection); the Millar and Tesser study suggests that differences are partially due to differences in audience expectation (potential cost–gain). Because different audiences have differential access to information and differential expectations, both studies suggest that areas of deception will differ with audiences.

We have reviewed evidence that suggests that the convergence between public self and self-concept will vary with the probability of the public performance being believed and the potential gain associated with a discrepant public self. Perhaps more interesting is the notion that these two variables can interact to affect the discrepancy between self-concept and public self. This interaction is predicated on the inherent conflict associated with presenting a discrepant public self. If the audience believes the self that is presented to them, the presenter or actor stands to reap certain rewards from the audience. For example, meeting the expectations of the audience could gain the audience's approval. If the audience does not believe the public self, however, the actor stands to lose favor with the audience, i.e., the actor may be seen as a fake, liar, or braggart.

Increasing the importance of a positive impression should increase the conflict. Thus, when one believes that the discrepancy is difficult to detect, the greater the importance of creating a positive impression the greater should be the discrepancy between public and private selves. On the other hand, when the probability of detection (and being labeled a liar) is high, the greater the importance of creating a positive impression the less the discrepancy between public and private selves. For example, Tom is more likely to present himself in a job interview as having outstanding computer skills, when in fact they are only mediocre, if he desperately wants the job and knows that the interviewer is not likely to check on the validity of his claims. If Tom knows, however, that the interviewer probably will call a previous employer to check on past performance, then the more Tom wants the job the less likely he is to inflate his computer skills during the interview.

In sum, if the goal of public self-presentation is to procure a positive evaluation, then presenting a public self that is discrepant from the self-concept is problematic because if deception is detected the positive self-presentation will result in a negative evaluation. The likelihood that one will indeed portray a discrepant public self varies inversely with the probability of detection and directly with the incentive for such a portrayal. Thus, people are unlikely to dissimulate with audiences who are familiar with their past or potentially knowledgeable about their future, such as in most lasting relationships. However, holding surveillance constant, they are likely to dissimulate with respect to expectations that are important to the relationship.

Cognitive Loads and Convergence of Public Self and Self-Concept

There is an old but convincing literature that suggests that beyond some optimal level cognitive loads are aversive (see Zuckerman, 1979a for a recent review of these theories). We believe that from a cognitive perspective it is generally difficult to keep track of and integrate the implications of even a single, private view of self. Creating additional, public selves will often result in an aversive cognitive overload. Therefore, public and private selves will often tend to be the same.

If this line of reasoning is correct several hypotheses follow. For example, one might expect fewer or smaller differences between the public self and one's self-concept as the ability to deal with complexity decreases. That is, where the actor is already deluged with much information or where the actor is fatigued or distracted, the additional complexity associated with presenting a discrepant public self ought to be particularly noxious and avoided. Aids to memory or information processing should reduce loads and make it easier for an actor to deal with the complexity associated with a discrepant public self. Thus, actors who have committed a particular discrepant public self to memory, or those who have prompts or cues, should be more likely to exhibit a discrepancy than actors who must ad lib or attempt to remember a single performance. Another factor that might increase cognitive load is the diversity of potential audiences. As one's audience increases in heterogeneity, the number of different public selves necessary to engender positive regard will also increase with attendant increases in complexity. Therefore, since cognitive overloads are aversive one would expect less discrepant self-presentations when it is necessary to deal with a variety of audiences. Although the effects of cognitive overloads on the impressions persons form of others have been studied recently (e.g., Bargh & Thein, in press; White & Carlston, 1983), we could find no studies of these effects on self-presentation.

The literature also indicates that affect (positive or negative) sums with the amount of "information" in producing an overall cognitive load (e.g., Schroder, Driver, & Streufert, 1967). This being the case, we would expect less discrepancy between self-concept and public self under circumstances that produce strong emotion. That is, people who are depressed, or fearful, or elated ought to be more likely to enact their self-concept rather than a discrepant public self. Again, this is an area ripe for empirical study.

The Self-Concept Constrains the Public Self

The self-concept and the public self will often be similar because the self-concept biases the way one sees the world. There is a substantial literature on projection (Sherwood, 1981) and on what has come to be known as the false consensus effect (Ross, Greene, & House, 1977). These literatures suggest that persons tend to assume that others are similar to them. There is also a voluminous literature documenting the relationship between similarity and attraction (Byrne, 1971). If an individual wants someone to like him or her and assumes the other person is similar to his or her self-concept (the false consensus effect), then it would be to the individual's advantage to make his or her public self similar to his or her private self. On the other hand, if the individual does not assume that the other is similar to his or her self-concept (i.e., there is little projection), but he or she wants to be liked by the other, then the self that is presented is likely to be one that wins the audience's favor but is discrepant from the private self. In other words, the degree of discrepancy between the public self and the private self depends on the magnitude of projection. If this is the case, then factors that influence the magnitude of projection also should affect the public self-private self discrepancy.

The two factors that have been found to interact to influence the magnitude of projection are awareness of certain aspects of self and closeness of an audience. When one is aware of one's shortcomings, one projects more to a close other than when one is not aware. When an individual is not aware of shortcomings, more projection tends to occur to an outgroup or distant other. If we take only one of these circumstances and look at the implications for the public-private discrepancy, then the more one is aware of a personal inadequacy the more one will project to a close other, and thus, the smaller will be the discrepancy between the private self and the self that is presented to a close other.

Contrary to the above argument, while there tends to be a much larger projection effect for opinionlike issues than on performance quality (Marks & Miller, 1983), we would not necessarily expect greater private-public self similarity on opinion items than on performance dimensions. People tend to believe that they are better than others on important (or relevant) performance dimensions (Tesser & Campbell, 1982). So if they present what they believe about their own performances, that should generate a positive impression that would not be discrepant from the private self.

The self-concept also constrains the public self simply because it is available for public enactment. According to Markus (e.g., Markus & Sentis, 1982), there are aspects of the self-concept called self-schemata. These aspects are responded to faster, held with greater confidence, and are more resistant to persuasion than are other descriptors of self that could be, but are not, self-schematic. For example, Markus found that persons who were schematic with respect to the trait *independence* were more extreme in their endorsement of traits related to independence, responded faster with the judgment "me"-"not me" to such traits in a reaction time task, and were less persuaded by a message arguing against their independence than persons who were aschematic regarding this trait. Further, Bargh (1982) has shown that information relevant to the self-concept affects cognitive processing even when the individual is not consciously aware of that information. Information that is available (Tversky & Kahneman, 1974) or chronically accessible (Higgins, King, & Mavin, 1982) tends to have an impact in the construction of ongoing behavior. Thus, even if an individual is not particularly motivated to enact his or her self-concept, the self-concept, being available, will influence the public self.

Schematic aspects of the self-concept not only constrain the public self because they are available for enactment, but they also provide an interpretive function that could impact the public self. Any particular situation or action can be interpreted in many different ways. For example, if John gives Mary an answer on a test item he could be seen as dishonest, or as friendly, or as trying to show off, or as flaunting authority, or as exhibiting an internal locus of control, and so on. Bem and Allen (1974) have suggested that different persons have different "equivalence classes" of behavior. Thus, someone who is self-schematic with respect to independence, for example, is likely to interpret the world in terms of independence-dependence and to construe different episodes as equivalent if an interpretation in terms of "independence" makes them similar. Such a person is likely to interpret John's behavior in terms of flaunting authority rather than friendliness or honesty.

The self-presentational response one makes to a situation is entirely dependent on the meaning of the situation. If one's self-concept influences the meaning of the situation then one's self-concept will also influence one's public self. The example of John may help to clarify the relationship between self-schemata and public behavior.

If the interpreter of John's behavior happens to be the classroom teacher, then construing John's behavior as defiance of authority is likely to result in attempts by the teacher to reinstate himself or herself as an authority figure, i.e., to present an image of an authority figure. Again, the teacher's self-schemata influenced the way John's behavior was interpreted, which affected the self the teacher presented to John.

The Public Self Constrains the Self-Concept

There is a set of arguments for the convergence of public and private selves that comes from the idea that the public self constrains the self-concept. If one presents a public self that is discrepant from the self-concept, there are important, well-documented psychological processes that are set into motion and have as their culmination an alteration of the private self (self-concept) so that it is consistent with the public self. These processes are dissonance reduction and self-perception. According to the theory of cognitive dissonance, when an individual's behavior is inconsistent with a belief, an uncomfortable affective state is aroused. If the public self is inconsistent with the self-concept or one's beliefs about oneself, then a state of dissonance should be aroused that the individual is motivated to alleviate. One way of relieving the dissonant state is to make one's self-belief or self-concept consistent with one's public self. Self-perception theory, on the other hand, hypothesizes that when individuals' feelings or attitudes are ambiguous they observe their own behavior and then infer their internal state. Consequently, persons may use their public presentations as indications of their "real selves," thereby impacting the self-concept.

The role of these processes in determining self-concept change following from public self-presentation was tested in a recent study by Jones, Rhodewalt, Berglas, and Skelton (1981). These researchers first manipulated persons' self-presentations and then measured changes in self-esteem. In a series of experiments subjects were induced to behave in either a self-deprecating or self-enhancing manner during an interview. Subsequent ratings of self-esteem reflected the prior manipulation of self-presentation; persons who behaved in a self-deprecating manner reported lower self-esteem than they had reported at an earlier administration of the same scale while persons who displayed self-enhancing behavior reported higher self-esteem.

The authors then attempted to tease out the effects of self-perception processes and dissonance reduction on the changes in self-esteem resulting from the self-presentational behavior. They reasoned that, if dissonance were responsible for the change, then whether participants had a choice to participate in the interview should be an important determinant of self-esteem change. On the other hand, if self-perception processes were operative then choice should be unimportant. The variable that would be important for self-perception theory, however, would be whether the individual saw the self-presentational behavior as reflective of the "true" self; i.e., whether the behavior was "owned" by the individual. What Jones et al. unexpectedly found was that self-perception seemed to be responsible for the self-concept changes when subjects were induced to behave in a self-enhancing manner while dissonance reduction appeared to be operative when subjects had publicly presented themselves in a self-deprecating manner. While aspects of the authors' reasoning seem somewhat unclear, the study does offer convincing evidence that self-presentation results in changes in the self-concept. Additionally, there is some support for the role of dissonance reduction and self-perception processes as mediators of the self-concept changes that result from public behavior.

There is another facet of dissonance research that suggests that the public self can affect the private self. A long-standing controversy in the cognitive dissonance literature has concerned whether the obtained attitude change in forced-compliance studies results from a desire to appear consistent to the audience or a motivation to be consistent within oneself (Baumeister, 1982; Paulhus, 1982; Tedeschi, Schlenker, & Bonoma, 1971). In a recent study by Baumeister and Tice (1984) both self-presentational needs and the need to be internally consistent were found to be sufficient to produce dissonance reduction. However, even when attitude change resulted from self-presentational concerns, the change was maintained in situations where there was no audience. The authors suggested that perhaps the attitude change that was originally self-presentationally motivated may have resulted in "real" attitude change. This study offers further support for the notion that the private self (self-concept) can be altered by self-presentation.

The convergence of public and private selves as a result of dissonance and self-perception processes is set into motion by the individual's *own* public behavior. Is it also the case that one's public self will bring one's private self into line even when the individual had no part in creating the public self? From a theoretical perspective the answer is yes. There is evidence from a diverse literature that indicates that the public enactment of a behavior, even a behavior that is not freely chosen, elicits certain responses from others that, in turn, contribute to the person's self-concept. Certainly, the symbolic interactionist position is that one's definition of oneself is the reflection of the way others respond to one (Mead, 1934; Scheff, 1974). Additionally, work in the area of role theory (Sarbin & Allen, 1968) suggests that the societal role one is forced to assume, one's public behavior, can affect one's self-concept. For example, the bank executive who returns to college for an advanced degree is no longer treated as a person in authority but must assume the role of "student" and behave accordingly. Eventually the banker may come to view himself as "student" rather than as a person in a position of authority.

Research on the behavioral confirmation phenomenon also support this notion that the responses one elicits from others can impact the self-concept. For example, in the Snyder, Tanke, and Berscheid study (1977) subjects were led to believe that targets were either attractive or unattractive. Subjects' beliefs were manipulated and were unrelated to the target's actual appearance. Results showed that subjects interacted differently with targets they believed to be attractive and those they believed to be unattractive, which elicited differential behavior from the targets. More importantly, targets believed to be attractive began to behave like attractive persons and targets believed to be unattractive also behaved according to subjects' expectation. We also have evidence of such processes form our own laboratory. In the study by Tesser and Paulhus (1983) subjects were confronted with an audience who had received arbitrary feedback about their relative performance on a task. Regardless of whether the audience's beliefs were accurate or inaccurate from the subject's perspective, the audience's beliefs affected the subject's behavior under circumstances where the subject believed he was alone and unobserved. Since the subject was unaware of being observed, his behavior was interpreted as reflecting his own private view of self.

External Constraints on the Public Self and the Self-Concept

To the extent that external variables have similar impact on both the self-concept and the private self there will be a convergence between these two selves. We have argued that a pervasive goal for the public self is to engender positive regard. Persons want others to like them, respect them, and think they are competent. There is more than ample documentation that these are the kinds of things individuals also wish to believe about themselves. The literatures on self-serving biases in attribution (Zuckerman, 1979b), beneffectance (Greenwald, 1980, and self-evaluation maintenance (Tesser, 1986) are all examples of this. Since the goals of both public self and self-concept are often the same, it seems reasonable to expect convergence to be the rule rather than the exception.

Assuming that equivalence of goals can cause convergence, we would expect greater convergence between the self-concept and the public self when the values of the audience are seen to be similar to the values of the self. Thus, there ought to be greater convergence when an audience is from the same as opposed to a different reference group as the self. There ought to be greater convergence on behaviors for which there are generally agreed upon values than upon behaviors that are matters of taste.

While the similarity of goals for the public and private self may result in a convergence of the two, neither of these may correspond to the "true" or "real" self. That is, the sameness of goals may cause parallel distortions in the public self and the self-concept so that both end up discrepant from the "true" personality in the same way. For example, parallel inflated appraisals of competence may exist in the self-concept and the public self. Take for instance the example of Tom, who wants to get a job as a computer programmer. Tom's self-presentational goal is to appear competent in the area of computer programming. The appearance Tom hopes to create for others is quite similar to the belief he would like to hold about himself. Tom's computer skills, however, are only mediocre, but the goal to appear to be competent leads to similar distortions of skills to the public and to himself.

Reality constraints (Walster, Berscheid, & Barclay, 1967; Tesser, 1976) also limit what an individual can incorporate into the self-concept and what can be publicly displayed. If a student failed a course, for example, it is difficult for him to believe that he is good in that subject and it would also be difficult for him to tell his schoolmates that he is good in the subject. If a 5'2" woman weighs 170 pounds, it will be difficult for her to believe that she is svelte and it will be difficult to convince others that she is svelte.

There are also social structural variables that constrain public and private selves in the same way. For example, roles lead to constrained behaviors for both role partners. The self as related to these roles is thereby constrained in both its public and private aspects.

Summary

In sum, we have argued that one's public self and one's self-concept will ordinarily tend to converge. Several factors that might produce this convergence have been discussed. One factor is the dilemma associated with creating a deceptive positive impression: One may appear to be faking and thereby destroy the very goal for which the presentation was enacted. Therefore, greater convergence is expected when the probability of detection of deception is high and when the stakes for deception are low. Convergence may also be expected because maintaining a public self that is different from one's self-concept can result in a noxious information overload. Different forms of constraint may also result in convergence. The self-concept tends to produce information-processing effects that constrain the public self. The public self, in turn, through a variety of processes including dissonance, self-perception, and labeling, tends to constrain the self-concept. Finally, both the public self and the self-concept are often influenced (constrained) by the same external factors.

References

Andersen, S. M. (1984). Self-knowledge and social inference: II. The diagnosticity of cognitive-affective and behavioral data. *Journal of Personality and Social Psychology, 46,* 294–307.

Andersen, S. M., & Ross, L. (1984). Self-knowledge and social inference: I. Perceptions of cognitive-affective and behavioral data. *Journal of Personality and Social Psychology, 46,* 280–293.

Apsler, R. (1975). Effects of embarrassment on behavior toward others. *Journal of Personality and Social Psychology, 32,* 145–153.

Bargh, J. A. (1982). Attention and automaticity in the processing of self-relevant information. *Journal of Personality and Social Psychology, 43,* 425–436.

Bargh, J. A., & Thein, R. D. (1985). Individual construct accessibility, person memory, and the recall-judgment link: The case of information overload. *Journal of Personality and Social Psychology, 49,* 1129–1146.

Baumeister, R. F. (1982). A self-presentational view of social phenomena. *Psychological Bulletin, 91,* 3–26.

Baumeister, R. F., & Jones, E. E. (1978). When self-presentation is constrained by the target's prior knowledge: Consistency and compensation. *Journal of Personality and Social Psychology, 36,* 608–618.

Baumeister, R. F., & Tice, D. M. (1984). Role of self-presentation and choice in cognitive dissonance under forced compliance: Necessary or sufficient causes? *Journal of Personality and Social Psychology, 46,* 5–13.

Bem, D. J., & Allen, A. (1974). On predicting some of the people some of the time: The search for cross-situational consistencies in behavior. *Psychological Review, 81,* 506–520.

Byrne, D. (1971). *The attraction paradigm.* New York: Academic Press.

Cialdini, R. B., & Richardson, K. D. (1980). Two indirect tactics of image management: Basking and blasting. *Journal of Personality and Social Psychology, 39,* 406–415.

Crowne, D. P. & Marlowe, D. (1964). *The approval motive: Studies in evaluative dependence.* New York: Wiley.

DePaulo, R. M., & Rosenthal, R. (1979). Telling lies. *Journal of Personality and Social Psychology, 37,* 1713–1722.

Ekman, P., & Friesen, W. V. (1974). Detecting deception from the body or face. *Journal of Personality and Social Psychology, 29,* 288–298.

Goffman, E. (1959). *The presentation of self in everyday life.* Garden City, NY: Doubleday.

Greenwald, A. G. (1980). The totalitarian ego: Fabrication and revision of personal history. *American Psychologist, 35,* 603–618.

Higgins, E. T., King, G. A., & Mavin, G. H. (1982). Individual construct accessibility and subjective impressions and recall. *Journal of Personality and Social Psychology, 43,* 35–47.

Jellison, J. M., & Gentry, K. A. (1978). Self-presentation interpretation of the seeking of social approval. *Personality and Social Psychology Bulletin, 4,* 227–230.

Jones, E. E. (1964). *Ingratiation.* New York: Irvington Publishers, Inc.

Jones, E. E., & Pittman, T. S. (1982). Toward a general theory of self-presentation. In J. Suls (Ed.), *Psychological perspectives on the self* (Vol. 1). Hillsdale, NJ: Erlbaum.

Jones, E. E., Rhodewalt, F., Berglas, S., & Skelton, J. (1981). Effects of strategic self-presentation on subsequent self-esteem. *Journal of Personality and Social Psychology, 41,* 407–421.

Marks, G., & Miller, N. (1983). *Thinking one's abilities are unique and one's opinions are common.* Paper presented at the meeting of the American Psychological Association, Anaheim, CA.

Markus, H., & Sentis, K. (1982). The self in social information processing. In J. Suls (Ed.), *Psychological perspectives on the self* (Vol. I). Hillsdale, NJ: Erlbaum.

Mead, G. H. (1934). *Mind, self, and society.* Chicago: University of Chicago Press.

Millar, K., & Tesser, A. (1985). *The consequences of violated expectations: Sometimes lying, sometimes guilt, sometimes both.* Unpublished paper, University of Georgia.

Owens, W. A. (1976). Background data. In M. D. Dunnette (Ed.), *Handbook of industrial and organization psychology.* Chicago: Rand-McNally.

Paulhus, D. L. (1982). Indiviual differences, self-presentation, and cognitive dissonance: Their concurrent operation in forced compliance. *Journal of Personality and Social Psychology, 44,* 1253–1265.

Paulhus, D. L. (1984). Two-component model of socially desirable responding. *Journal of Personality and Social Psychology, 46,* 598–609.

Ross, L., Greene, D., & House, P. (1977). The "false consensus effect": An egocentric bias in social perception and attribution processes. *Journal of Experimental Social Psychology, 13,* 279–301.

Ross, M., McFarland, C., Conway, M., & Zanna, M. (1984). Reciprocal relation between attitudes and behavior recall: Committing people to newly formed attitudes. *Journal of Personality and Social Psychology, 45,* 257–267.

Sarbin, T. R., & Allen, V. L. (1968). Role theory. In C. Linzey and E. Aronson (Eds.), *Handbook of social psychology* (Vol. 1). Reading, MA: Addison-Wesley.

Saunders, V., Shaffer, G. S., & Owens, W. A. (1984). *Additional evidence for the accuracy of biographical information: Long-term retest and observer ratings.* Unpublished paper, University of Georgia, Athens.

Scheff, T. J. (1974). The labelling theory of mental illness. *American Sociological Review, 39,* 444–452.

Schlenker, B. R. (1975). Self-presentation: Managing the impression of consistency when reality interferes with self-enhancement. *Journal of Personality and Social Psychology, 32,* 1030–1037.

Schlenker, B. R. (1980). *Impression management.* Monterey, CA: Brooks/Cole.

Schlenker, B. R. (1982). Translating actions into attitudes: An identity-analytic approach to the explanation of social conduct. In L. Berkowitz (Ed.), *Advances in experimental social psychology* (Vol. 15). New York: Academic Press.

Schlenker, B. R. (1985). Identity and self-identification. In B. R. Schlenker (Ed.), *The self and social life.* New York: McGraw-Hill.

Schroder, H. M., Driver, M. J., & Streufert, S. (1967). *Human information processing.* New York: Holt, Rinehart & Winston.

Sherwood, G. G. (1981). Self-serving biases in person perception: A reexamination of projection as a mechanism of defense. *Psychological Bulletin, 90,* 445–459.

Snyder, M., Tanke, E. D., & Berscheid, E. (1977). Social perception and interpersonal behavior: On the self-fulfilling nature of social stereotypes. *Journal of Personality and Social Psychology, 35,* 656–666.

Tedeschi, J. T. (1981). *Impression management theory and social psychological research.* New York: Academic Press.

Tedeschi, J. T., Schlenker, B. R., & Bonoma, T. V. (1971). Cognitive dissonance: Private ratiocination or public spectacle? *American Psychologist, 26,* 685–695.

Tesser, A. (1976). Thought and reality constraints as determinants of attitude polarization. *Journal of Research in Personality, 10,* 183–194.

Tesser, A. (1986). Some effects of self-evaluation maintenance on cognition and action. In R. M. Sorrention & E. T. Higgins (Eds.) *The handbook of motivation and cognition: Foundations of social behaviors.* New York: Guilford Press.

Tesser, A., & Barbee, A. (in preparation). *Appearing competent: On the public nature of self-evaluation maintenance processes.*

Tesser, A., & Campbell, J. (1985). A self-evaluation maintenance model of student motivation. In C. Ames & R. Ames (Eds.), *Research on motivation in education: The classroom milieu.* New York: Academic Press.

Tesser, A., & Campbell, J. (1982). Self-evaluation maintenance and the perception of friends and strangers. *Journal of Personality, 50,* 261–279.

Tesser, A., & Campbell, J. (1983). Self-definition and self-evaluation maintenance. In J. Suls & A. G. Greenwald (Eds.), *Psychological perspectives on the self* (Vol. 2, pp. 1–31). Hillsdale, NJ: Erlbaum.

Tesser, A., Campbell, J., & Smith, M. (1984). Friendship choice and performance: Self-evaluation maintenance in children. *Journal of Personality and Social Psychology, 46,* 561–574.

Tesser, A., & Paulhus, D. (1983). The definition of self: Private and public self-evaluation management strategies. *Journal of Personality and Social Psychology, 44,* 672–682.

Tesser, A., & Smith, J. (1980). Some effects of task relevance and friendship on helping: You don't always help the one you like. *Journal of Experimental Social Psychology, 16,* 582–590.

Tetlock, P. E., & Manstead, A. S. (1985). Impression management versus intrapsychic explanations in social psychology: A useful dichotomy? *Psychological Review, 92,* 59–77.

Tversky, A., & Kahneman, D. (1974). Judgment under uncertainty: Heuristics and biases. *Science, 185,* 1124–1131.

Ulvedal, K., Millar, M., & Tesser, A. (1984). *The effects of perceived situational factors on self-reports of deceptive behavior.* Paper presented at the 30th meeting of the Southeastern Psychological Association, New Orleans, LA.

Waid, W. M., & Orne, M. T. (1980). Individual differences in electrodermal lability and the detection of information and deception. *Journal of Applied Psychology, 65,* 1–8.

Walster, E., Berscheid, E., & Barclay, A. M. (1967). A determinant of preference among modes of dissonance reduction. *Journal of Personality and Social Psychology, 7,* 211–215.

White, J. D., & Carlston, D. E. (1983). Consequences of schemata for attention, impressions, and recall in complex social interactions. *Journal of Personality and Social Psychology, 45,* 538–549.

Zuckerman, M. (1979a). *Sensation seeking: Beyond the optimal level of arousal.* Hillsdale, NJ: Erlbaum.

Zuckerman, M. (1979b). Attribution of success and failure revisited, or: The motivational bias is alive and well in attribution theory. *Journal of Personality, 47,* 245–287.

Zuckerman, M., DeFrank, R. S., Hall, J. A., Larrance, D., & Rosenthal, R. (1979). Facial and vocal cues of deception and honesty. *Journal of Experimental Social Psychology, 15,* 378–396.

Chapter 6
Self-Presentation and the Phenomenal Self: On the Stability and Malleability of Self-Conceptions

Frederick T. Rhodewalt

In the Woody Allen film *Zelig*, the central character is the quintessential self-presenter, "a human chameleon," who took on the characteristics, mannerisms, and even the appearance of those with whom he interacted. Although Leonard Zelig's self-presentational strategy was a device designed to protect his true "self" from rejection, the viewer gradually learns that Zelig's public ploys left him with no self to protect. To a lesser extent most people are a little like Zelig in that on many occasions their strategic self-presentations do alter their self-conceptions. In our work, my colleagues and I consistently observe what we have termed the *carry-over effect* (Jones, Rhodewalt, Berglas, & Skelton, 1981; Rhodewalt & Agustsdottir, 1986; see also Gergen, 1967). That is, when subjects engage in strategic self-presentations in order to create a specific impression of themselves in another, there is typically a shift in subjects' self-conceptions in the direction of the self-presentational episode.

Most research in the area of self-presentation has focused on the strategies employed in the service of presenting an intended or desired image of the self (Jones & Pittman, 1982; Tedeschi & Norman, 1983). In contrast, the present chapter is concerned with the issues of *when* and *how* people's public self-presentations *carry over* to modify their private selves. In this chapter a theory is developed to account for the way in which self-presentations may lead to both momentary and more long-lasting shifts in one's self-concept. Considered at the same time is the equally important issue of how self-conceptions can appear on the one hand so malleable and on the other so well structured and stable. This paradox is used as the vehicle by which the theory is presented. I continue by drawing some of the implications of the model for the self in social interaction settings. Highlighted in this discussion is the interplay between self-presentation and interpersonal processes that contribute to stability and change in self-conceptions. Finally, the chapter concludes with a discussion of theory and research on selected individual differences hypothesized to mediate the carry-over effect.

A Process Model of Self-Presentation and the Phenomenal Self

Stable Self Versus Malleable Self

The issue of interest in this chapter is the influence of public presentations of the self on one's private self-conceptions. Intertwined in this topic are questions about the precise nature of the self as a psychological construct. For example, implicit in the carry-over effect is the idea that the self is highly mutable. The view of the self as constantly changing appears to be at odds with current cognitive research on the self. In this section there is first a consideration of the evidence for a stable and well-structured self and then a review of research on self-presentation that suggests that the self is highly mutable. With this backdrop, a theory of self-presentation and the phenomenal self is proposed that integrates these two perspectives on the self. The section closes with a report of research derived from the model.

The stable self. A casual reading of the current research literature in social cognition provides a fairly consistent picture of the self as being represented in memory in an organized, integrated, schematic form much like one's representations of other individuals or situations (Kihlstrom & Cantor, 1983; Markus, 1977; Markus & Sentis, 1982; Rogers, 1981). For instance, in a series of important studies, Markus (1977) presented evidence that individuals with self-schemata in a particular domain (i.e., dependence-independence) processed information about themselves much more efficiently and were more resistant to schema-incongruent information than were aschematic people without such well-developed knowledge structures with respect to independence. Although the notion of self-knowledge structures appears to be well supported, there is considerable debate about the details of how this knowledge is structured and represented in memory (see Kihlstrom & Cantor, 1983, for a review). Is the self unitary or a "confederation" (Greenwald & Pratkanis, in press) of independent but integrated selves? Does self-knowledge take the form of a set of self-schemata (Markus & Sentis, 1982), a hierarchical category (Rogers, 1981), or an associative network (Bower & Gilligan, 1979)? These are a few of the questions that currently occupy theorists of the cognitive self. However, an assertion that runs through all of this work is that the self is well structured, stable and, fairly consistent across time (Cheek & Hogan, 1983).

Factors in addition to the integrity of the memorial representation of one's self-knowledge contribute to the stability of the self. Rather than automatically facilitating the processing of self-relevant information, the self actively distorts or resists contradictory information to appear consistent. For example, Greenwald (1980) has described a set of cognitive biases underlying what he termed the "totalitarian ego." Biases such as viewing oneself as instrumental for good but not bad outcomes (beneffectance) or assimilating new information to fit existing self-schemata (cognitive conservatism) contribute collectively to the stability of self-conceptions. In addition, the very nature of our social encounters also facilitates the image of a stable self. That is, one's self-conceptions play an active role in reciprocally determining the social context in which self-knowledge is generated. In a series of studies, Swann and his colleagues (Swann, 1983; Swann & Ely, 1984; Swann & Hill, 1982;

Swann & Read, 1981a, 1981b) have shown that people create through their self-presentational strategies and choices of people and interaction settings a "social reality" that verifies their beliefs about themselves.

In brief, this very selective and abbreviated review highlights the fact that self-conceptions are thought to be highly structured, stable, and resistant to disconfirming information if indeed it ever arises.

Self-presentation and the malleable self. In contrast to the position that the self is well organized and stable is an earlier tradition that places greater emphasis on the social dynamics of one's self-conceptions. This perspective arrives at the conclusion that the self is socially malleable and in a continual state of flux. The antecedents for this position are found in Erving Goffman's (1959) dramaturgical analogy and the pragmatic view of William James (1890). According to Goffman the "face" that one presents varies from audience to audience. Each "face" reflects a different "social self" shifting from scene to scene. Similarly, James observed that "a man has as many social selves as there are individuals who recognize him and carry an image of him in their head" (p. 294).

Not only is it true that social situations modify the presentation of oneself, as these authors observed, but there is an abundance of evidence that inidicates that as one's self-presentational behavior changes so does one's own conception of self.[1] Direct evidence for the impact of self-presentation on self-concept can be found in a study by Gergen (1967) in which he had subjects participate in an interview. Half of the subjects were instructed to make a good impression on the interviewer and half were told to help the interviewer get to know them. The interviewer responded to all subjects in the self-enhancement condition and half of the subjects in the accurate-self condition by reinforcing positive self-characterizations. Later, on an ostensibly unrelated measure of self-esteem, subjects viewed themselves more positively if they had received positive feedback regardless of whether their initial impression management motive was self-enhancement or self-accuracy.[2] Thus self-presentations that lead to positive reinforcement produce positive shifts in self-esteem.

Scattered among the wealth of research on the self-fulfilling prophesy is further evidence for the power of the social interaction sequence in shaping one's self-conceptions through self-presentational behavior. Fazio, Effrein, & Falender (1981)

---

[1] More broadly, it appears as if our identities are constantly constructed and modified through social interaction. In addition to self-presentational behavior (Gergen, 1967; Jones et al., 1981), social comparison processes (Morse & Gergen, 1970; Rhodewalt & Comer, 1981) and induced affect (Natale & Hantas, 1982) have also been shown to alter subjects' subsequent self-conceptions.

[2] Self-concept conventionally refers to all aspects of knowledge concerning who one is, and self-esteem refers more specifically to the evaluation of who one is. Despite this distinction, self-concept and self-esteem are used interchangeably in this chapter because our work typically studies changes in the individual's self-concept along an evaluative dimension.

set out to examine the effects of responding to a constrained or channeled interaction on a target's self-perceptions. Subjects participated in an interview in which they responded to a set of questions designed to elicit either introverted or extraverted self-descriptions. When later responding to a trait inventory in an allegedly unrelated context, subjects who had undergone the extravert interview thought of themselves as more extraverted while subjects who had responded to the introvert interview thought of themselves as more introverted (see also Snyder & Swann, 1978). Fazio et al. offered a self-perception explanation for their demonstration of the carry-over effect that is strikingly similar to the account presented in this chapter. They suggest that responding to introverted or extraverted questions made the subjects consider their own introverted or extraverted behavior in a biased manner. When subjects were subsequently asked to think about themselves on the dimension of introversion-extraversion, instances of introverted or extraverted behavior were differentially more salient to them and, thus, influenced their self-perceptions.

These studies indicate that principles of reinforcement and differential accessibility appear to mediate the carry-over effect in certain self-presentational contexts. My colleagues' and my research has taken a different slant on the effects of self-presentation on self-conceptions (Jones et al., 1981; Rhodewalt & Agustsdottir, 1986). We have been concerned with how the self-presenter reconciles a strategically enacted public performance with the kind of person he or she really is. Consider Marty, who is applying for a position as a used car salesman and belives that the job requires a person who is outgoing, confident, and friendly while conveying sincerity and trustworthiness. Marty's task is to make a self-enhancing presentation at the employment interview so that he creates this desired image in the mind of his future employer. How will Marty come to terms with this strategic self-enhancing performance vis-à-vis his private self-appraisal?

In the example, Marty is faced with the self-attributional task of inferring the implications, if any, of his behavior for the self. It was hypothesied that the perceived legitimacy of the self-presentation was the diagnostic dimension in this regard (Jones & Pittman, 1982). Marty in effect asks himself what the typical person would have done in that situation. If the answer is that anyone in that situation would be equally self-enhancing, then Marty would judge his self-enhancing performance as being legitimate but not terribly informative about himself. However, if Marty feels no one else would have behaved similarly—that the self-presentation was more than what was called for by the situation—then the behavior should have consequences for how he views himself. Marty might feel guilt or shame and thus, experience a decline in self-esteem. Or, he may alter his self-conceptions by elevating them to be more consistent with the presented self.

These two alternatives were explored by Jones and Berglas (Jones et al., 1981, Experiment I). Subjects were interviewed for a position as an encounter group observer, and were led to believe that whether or not they received the job would be determined by how favorable an impression they made on the interviewer. Either prior to or after the interview subjects were shown a video supposedly excerpted from earlier interviews. The perceived legitimacy of the subject's self-enhancing interview behavior was manipulated by showing three interviewees being either uniformly self-enhancing (high perceived legitimacy) or uniformly self-deprecating (low perceived legitimacy). Each subject then was motivated to present himself in positive terms and led to believe that others behaved the same or differently in the interview. It was predicted that subjects who received the consensus information prior to the interview would modify their self-presentations accordingly and not display any carry-over on subsequent self-esteem. However, subjects who learned of the consensus information after their interviews would be confronted with a different situation. The high perceived legitimacy subjects—those who saw others being self-enhancing—would perceive high consensus (Kelley, 1967) and not feel pressure to change their self-conceptions in response to their self-presentations. In contrast, low perceived legitimacy subjects—those who self-enhanced and then learned that all others self-deprecated—would modify their self-conceptions to be consistent with their self-presentations.

Postexperimental measures of self-concept were collected in a neutral setting ostensibly unrelated to the interview. The consensus information had a marked effect on subjects' interview behavior if it was presented prior to the interview. Subjects who saw others being self-enhancing were self-enhancing themselves and subjects who saw others being self-deprecating behaved likewise. In contrast to predictions, receiving the consensus information after the interview had no effect on subjects' self-esteem. Subjects who learned after the fact that their self-enhancing behavior was non-normative did not respond to the inconsistency between self-presentation and self-conceptions by raising their self-esteem.

Equally surprising were the results for subjects who received the consensus information prior to engaging in the interview. The consensus information clearly affected the subjects' interview behavior, which, in turn, carried over to their self-esteem when assessed in a neutral context. It appeared that it was the performance of the self-presentational behavior and not the consensus information itself that produced the self-concept change.

In light of these unexpected findings a replication investigation was undertaken to determine if the results could be produced with a somewhat different procedure (Jones et al., 1981, Experiment II). The cover story in this study was that we were interested in the nonverbal behavior of graduate student interviewers and that the subject was to serve as a "confederate" and aid the experimenter by role-playing a job applicant. Subjects were instructed to play the role so as to give the interviewer a favorable impression of them. Again the legitimacy of the self-enhancing presentation was manipulated by providing information about the behavior of earlier interviewees.

The findings were strikingly similar to those in Experiment I. Subjects who saw others being self-enhancing were self-enhancing themselves while subjects who saw others being self-deprecating were themselves self-deprecating during the interview. More important, all subjects, regardless of the perceived legitimacy of their interview behavior, displayed carry-over correspondent with their self-presentations.

In brief, these studies dramatically illustrate the robustness of the carry-over effect. In contrast to the well-structured and stable self characterized in the social cognition research, the picture of the self depicted by the self-presentation studies is one that is shifting and highly mutable.

The Phenomenal Self

The problem then is, how can the self be well structured and stable and yet be as malleable as the foregoing survey of self-presentation studies indicates? In this chapter, it is proposed that the apparent contradiction may be resolved by recognizing the difference between underlying stable representations of the self and the experience of the self. This distinction is not completely original. Other writers have commented on the self that is in one's awareness. For instance, Scheier and Carver (1981, 1983) have written extensively about self-consciousness, which encompasses both the individual's awareness of inner thoughts, feelings, and beliefs and the awareness of oneself as a social object. The prominence of oneself in consciousness continually shifts as one's attention shifts from a focus outward on the situation to a focus on the individual as an entity in the situation. Closer to the present discussion, however, is McGuire's work on the spontaneous self-concept (McGuire & McGuire, 1981, McGuire, McGuire, Child, & Fujioka, 1978; McGuire & Padawer-Singer, 1976). In the typical study McGuire asks the individual to generate an open-ended self-description. It is of particular interest here that situational factors such as context or group composition have a remarkable influence on people's immediate experience of themselves. If the subject is atypical with regard to some reference group (for example, younger than the rest of the group members), then that factor (e.g., age) will be prominent in that individual's spontaneous self-concept. In brief, all of these writers have emphasized the experiential aspect of the self rather than how the self is represented in memory.

For present concerns, however, Jones and Gerard's (1967) description of the *phenomenal self* provides a working definition of the self that can accommodate the stable and mutable aspects of one's self-conceptions. In their usage, the phenomenal self refers to "a person's awareness, arising out of his interactions with the environment, of his own beliefs, values, attitudes, the links between them, and the implications for his behavior" (p. 716). Every person has available to them an integrated representation of who they are that *may* be used for the interpretation of their present behavior and serves as a guide for future acts. When in awareness, the phenomenal self represents a summary statement of the self-relevant information that is currently accessible. Stability is facilitated by two sources. First, the catalogue of self-relevant information from which the currently experienced self is drawn is fairly constant across time and modality. Second, people's interactions with others who see them in terms of stable traits or attributes tend to be limited and repetitive so that people receive somewhat consistent social feedback about who they are. However, because one's available self-knowledge is too vast to fit in awareness at any one moment, situational and motivational cues render certain aspects of the self more accessible than others and lead to moment-to-moment shifts in the phenomenal self. Finally, as noted by Jones and Pittman (1982), there is a gradual evolution of the phenomenal self over time to incorporate new behaviors. The moment-to-moment shifts in the phenomenal self most often go unnoticed by the self-perceiver. People's sense of continuity and self-consistency limit such momentary vacillations from being entertained in awareness. Although their senses of identity feel stable over time, people nevertheless periodically recognize that they are, for example, not as liberal but much less selfish than they once were.

Self-Presentation and the Phenomenal Self

With this working definition of the phenomenal self in mind, one may now turn to the central question: What are the effects of public self-presentations on private self-appraisals and how are these effects mediated?

It is proposed that underlying the experienced or phenomenal self are many plausible selves. That is, people have a range of attributes, past behaviors, and experiences that underlie their present self-conceptions. In the model, all potentially available self-knowledge stored in memory will be referred to as the latitude of acceptance of the phenomenal self (see Hovland, Harvey, & Sherif, 1957). It should be emphasized that the model does not specify the form of the memorial representation of the self but rather recognizes the presence of such representations. Regardless of the structure of self-knowledge, it is assumed that it can enter into awareness as a constantly shifting sequence of salient foci. This view is consistent with current descriptions of the self as an organized set of interconnected but differentially accessible schemata (Markus & Sentis, 1982). For the sake of illustration, Fig. 6-1 arranges this information along a dimension of favorability. All information within the latitude of acceptance is *available* in memory and the X indicates the phenomenal self or currently *accessed* information for the hypothetical person.

Although the self-knowledge that one has available to oneself is vast, it has its limits. For each individual there is a range of possible self-defining experiences that are not currently incorporated into his or her own idiosyncratic self-concept. I may think of myself as a fairly good tennis player. This self-conception is based on a wide

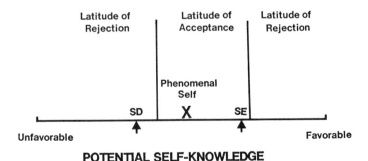

Figure 6-1. Latitudes of acceptance and rejection of the phenomenal self. Rhodewalt, F., & Agustsdottir, S., 1986. Copyright © 1986 by the American Psychological Association. Reprinted by permission.

range of positive and negative experiences with tennis. Nonetheless, I have never suffered the humiliation of being defeated by my 3-year-old son, nor have I experienced the ecstasy of winning Wimbledon (nor the local city tournament, for that matter). Both favorable and unfavorable information that is not well represented with regard to the self falls into the latitudes of rejection of the phenomenal self (refer to Fig. 6-1).

Self-presentational behavior then, can occupy one of two possible relationships to the phenomenal self. First, it may fall within the latitude of acceptance. That is, current public displays may reflect available self-referent knowledge and, thus, should render that knowledge more accessible in self-reflection. One's self-presentation, on the other hand, may portray a self that is in the individual's latitude of rejection. In this case the person's self-presentation is in conflict with his or her private conceptions of self. It is proposed that either self-presentational circumstance can potentially lead to a shift in one's view of oneself. However, the process by which the shift occurs will be different depending on whether the presentation was in the individual's latitude of acceptance or rejection.

According to the model, self-presentations within the latitude of acceptance should influence the phenomenal self through a variant of self-perception that seems to be captured best by the term "biased scanning" (Janis & Gilmore, 1965). Biased scanning in more current terms reflects the idea of differential accessibility of potentially available self-knowledge. That is, self-presentations within the latitude of acceptance serve to make certain congruent aspects of self-relevant information more accessible. In turn, this more easily accessed information is given greater weight in later private self-reflection.

In contrast, it is suggested that discrepant self-presentations in the latitude of rejection arouse cognitive dissonance (Festinger, 1957; Wicklund & Brehm, 1976). That is, shifts in the phenomenal self are responses to the inconsistency between current self-presentations and prior self-knowledge. Factors such as perceived choice and responsibility should influence the carry-over effect for presentations in the latitude of rejection.

One of the important influences on the development of this line of thinking is a study by Fazio, Zanna, and Cooper (1977). The issue that concerned these researchers was the dissonance versus self-perception controversy in the attitude change literature. In a clever demonstration, Fazio et al. provided evidence that self-perception processes best explained attitude change when the attitudinal discrepancy was in the individual's latitude of acceptance (Hovland et al., 1957). When the attitude-discrepant behavior fell in the subject's latitude of rejection, however, cognitive dissonance processes mediated attitude change. While the Fazio et al. (1977) study served as a prototype for the present model, an important difference should be highlighted. In contrast to the traditional self-perception view that involves an inferential process, differential accessibility of self-referent information is more automatic. That is, according to self-perception theory, behavior in the latitude of acceptance is informative only if it occurs under low situational constraint. The present biased scanning view requires only that the self-referent information be accessed into working memory.

Experimental Support for the Model

Two investigations have been conducted in which the elements of the model have been shown to mediate the carry-over effect. (To be honest, the first study led inductively to the generation of the model.) In this investigation, Jones and I (Jones et al., 1981, Experiment III) attempted to pit the differential accessibility explanation for the carry-over effect against the cognitive dissonance interpretation. The subjects in this study thought they were assisting the experimenter by playing the role of an applicant for an undergraduate research assistantship. The "graduate student interviewer" alledgedly did not know that the interview was contrived. Subjects were instructed to make either a positive or negative impression (role assignment) on the interviewer. Making a negative impression appeared reasonable because subjects thought that the experimenter was interested in the interviewer's nonverbal behaviors in that type of interaction. Cognitive dissonance was manipulated by instructing half of the subjects that the choice to play the role was up to them and they could decline at that point if they so desired. The remaining half of the subjects were told that the purposes of the experiment necessitated their dissimulation. The biased scanning hypothesis was evaluated by having half of the subjects improvise their responses to the interview. That is, depending upon role assignment, subjects were asked to think of themselves on a good or bad day and then respond to the interviewer's queries. This manipulation was intended to make positive or negative self-relevant information differentially accessible. Each self-referencing subject had a yoked counterpart who was matched on initial self-esteem and who was provided the responses of the self-reference subject to role-play during the interview. Thus for each pair of subjects the self-presentation was equally discrepant from how they normally viewed themselves, but for only one subject was the self-presentation likely to make accessible greater prior self-knowledge. Part of the interview protocol was an oral administration of the Self-Evaluation Triads test (Gergen, 1962), which was also used as the premeasure of self-esteem. After the interview, the experimenter returned and asked as a favor for a colleague at another university if the subject would mind completing a packet of questionnaires. Included in the packet was the postmeasure of self-esteem, which the subject answered anonymously in private and then sealed in an addressed envelope to be mailed by a secretary.

The results of this investigation are displayed in Table 6-1. As indicated in the top portion of the table, subjects were successful at presenting a self-enhancing or self-deprecating performance. With regard to the carry-over of these self-presentations on subsequent self-conceptions, both dissonance and biased scanning processes accounted for self-esteem change. If subjects were self-deprecating, those who felt that they had chosen to play the role (high choice) displayed a decline in self-esteem whereas those who were assigned the role (low choice) showed no carry-over. Interestingly, whether the self-deprecating performance was improvised or simply role-played made no difference.

The picture for self-enhancement was completely reversed. If the subject was conveying a positive image to the interviewer, then the degree to which the performance was self-referent accounted for the positive carry-over on self-esteem. Self-

Table 6-1. Interviewers Rating of Self-Presentation and Mean Changes in Self-Esteem Pretest to Interview and Pretest to Postinterview.

Rating Context	High Choice		Low Choice	
	Self-Reference	Yoked	Self-Reference	Yoked
During interview				
Self-enhancing				
Inteviewer's rating	4.3	3.8	3.6	4.1
Interview behavior	22.8	22.0	39.3	37.0
Self-deprecating				
Interviewer's rating	−1.8	−2.9	−1.0	−2.7
Interview behavior	−26.2	−28.9	−36.9	−39.1
Anonymous post				
Self-enhancing	18.1	−0.2	25.7	11.1
Self-deprecating	−13.1	−16.1	8.7	−4.7

From Jones, E.E., et al. (1981). Copyright © 1981 by the American Psychological Association. Adapted by permission.

referencing subjects displayed a significant increase in self-esteem regardless of whether they were in the high- or low-choice conditions. Yoked subjects showed no such shifts in self-concept. Correlational analyses supported the differential accessibility interpretation of the self-referencing effect. It was reasoned that if self-referencing is making self-relevant information more accessible, then the amount of self-referencing (i.e., the extremity of the self-presentation) should correlate positively with the amount of subsequent change in self-esteem. Consistent with this thinking, self-enhancing subjects who improvised their response had significant positive correlations between the extremity of their interview behavior and subsequent self-esteem change. Self-deprecating subjects displayed no such relationship between the extremity of their self-presentation and subsequent shift in the phenomenal self.

In summary then, self-enhancing subjects in this study who improvised their self-presentations shifted their self-conceptions in a positive direction because the self-referent behavior made positive features within their latitudes of acceptance more accessible. Yoked self-enhancing subjects did not display positive carry-over because their performance did not access as much positive self-relevant information.

One will note that the hypothetical latitude of acceptance depicted in Fig. 6-1 is somewhat asymmetrically constructed. The assumption of an asymmetrical latitude of acceptance is necessary in order to interpret the results of this investigation in terms of the model. It seems reasonable that, for most of the subjects in this study, creating a negative impression for another person is an act with which they had little experience and it should have been inconsistent with how they usually viewed themselves. Accordingly, only when subjects were made to feel responsible for their self-presentational behaviors in the latitude of rejection did they display a decline in self-esteem. Low-choice subjects whose behaviors were also in their latitudes of rejection did not experience the discrepancy between self-conceptions and interview presentation and, thus, did not change their self-esteem in the service of dissonance reduction. These subjects could point to the situation as justification for their behavior.

If the latitudes of acceptance–rejection analogy is accurate then it should be possible to induce people to be so self-enhancing that their behavior is within their positive latitude of rejection or minimally self-deprecating and within their latitude of acceptance. Dissonance variables would then be expected to account for positive carry-over and biased scanning would mediate negative carry-over. Just such a proposition was tested by Sjöfn Agustsdottir and me (Rhodewalt & Agustsdottir, 1986). Rather than attempt to scale each individual's latitude of acceptance and rejection for self-relevant information, we took an individual difference perspective on these issues. Recent theory and research suggested that depressed individuals could be expected to have relatively broad latitudes of acceptance for negative self-relevant information and narrow latitudes for positive content. Based on Beck's (Beck, Rush, Shaw, & Emery, 1979) self-schema model of depression, Kuiper and his colleagues have presented evidence that clinically depressed patients possess self-schemata comprised largely of negative self-knowledge (Kuiper, MacDonald, & Derry, 1983).

Agustsdottir and I replicated the Jones et al. procedure with subjects preselected for level of depression. While expecting to reproduce the earlier finding (Jones et al., 1981, Experiment III) for nondepressed subjects, we predicted the data for depressed subjects would conform to the hypothetical phenomenal self depicted in Fig. 6-2. Inducing a depressed subject to be self-enhancing would be in the subject's latitude of rejection and thus dissonance arousing. In contrast, self-deprecating behavior should be within the subject's latitude of acceptance and, accordingly only those behaviors that trigger differential accessibility of negative content (self-referencing) would produce the negative carry-over to self-esteem.

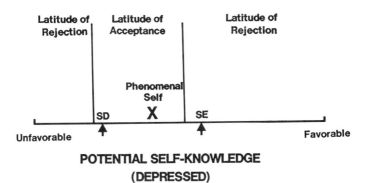

SE=Self-Enhancement, SD=Self-Deprecation

Figure 6-2. Hypothesized latitudes of acceptance and rejection for depressed individuals.

In addition to replicating the previous study (Jones et al., 1981, Experiment III), the results for depressed subjects strongly supported the predictions. Self-enhancing depressed subjects showed an increase in self-esteem only if they had chosen to engage in the self-presentation. Those depressed subjects who engaged in a self-deprecating presentation during the interview later displayed a decline in self-esteem only if they had self-referenced by improvising the presentation.

In accord with the model, correlations between the extremity of the self-presentation during the interview and the amount of carry-over on the phenomenal self were again computed. As one will recall, it is assumed that if the self-referencing effect is being mediated by the increased accessibility of self-relevant knowledge then the more information that is accessed the greater the shift in self-esteem. Nondepressed subjects who were self-referencing within their latitude of acceptance (self-enhancement) experienced greater positive shifts in self-esteem the more they self-enhanced during the interview. Self-deprecating nondepressed subjects showed no such relationship. Depressed subjects, who we argued were operating within their latitude of acceptance when self-deprecating, also showed the expected relationship between behavior and self-esteem only if they improvised (self-referenced) during the interview. Surprisingly, self-enhancing depressed subjects showed the positive behavior–self-esteem correlation but only in the high-choice condition. With one exception, then, the correlational analysis supported the differential accessibility interpretation of the effects of self-referencing within the latitude of acceptance. This one exception is returned to during the examination of individual differences and the phenomenal self. For the moment, the available data, although limited, indicate that the latitudes of acceptance–rejection analogy provides a useful framework in which to examine the interplay between one's conception of oneself and one's social world.

The Phenomenal Self in Social Interaction

In this section the implications of the process model of the phenomenal self for the stability versus malleability of self-conceptions in the stream of social discourse are reviewed.

Social Interaction and the Latitude of Acceptance

Permit me to return for a moment to the definition of the phenomenal self that has guided our investigations. In its present conception the phenomenal self has several important components. First, it is a potentially available awareness of past acts, values, attitudes, beliefs, and their implications for current behavior. As Jones and Pittman (1982) noted, the phenomenal self is primarily social in nature and vulnerable to reflected social pressure for stability and consistency. Despite these pressures, the phenomenal self displays moment-to-moment shifts in content.

Finally, it appears to undergo more enduring long-term modification of self-knowledge. The framework described in this chapter can accommodate all of these seemingly disparate aspects of the phenomenal self. That is, the model includes a self that is both static and dynamic and both automatic (mindless) and mindful (Langer & Newman, 1979).

The latitude of acceptance is the underlying core of the phenomenal self. Current contextual cues, behaviors, and affect serve to increase the relative accessibility or salience of one facet of the self over others. To the extent that other people and situations provide consistent cues, the individual will display apparent consistency and stability of self-relevant behavior. Nonetheless, within any individual's experience is enough contextual variation and varied social feedback to shift the person's focus among social selves (e.g., academic to parent to athlete) and within self categories (e.g., the thrill of victory and the agony of defeat).

Are these momentary shifts in self-conception so readily observed in the laboratory little more than epiphenomena with no potential long-term significance? I would argue no, but only in circumscribed instances. One will recall that when subjects in the Fazio et al. (1981) study responded to interview questions that focused either on introverted or extraverted behaviors, they demonstrated the carry-over effect in that they later displayed corresponding shifts in their self-conceptions. More important was the finding that subjects then conveyed these altered self-images to a naive perceiver. In a similar vein, Snyder and Swann (1978) found that when they led perceivers to expect their interaction partners to be either hostile or nonhostile these expectations were subtly transmitted during the interaction so that the partner confirmed the initial expectation. Not only was the partner's behavior modified during the interaction, the partners then conveyed the hostile or non-hostile impression to a naive perceiver during a subsequent encounter. In some instances, then, it is possible that one's momentary self-concept will be perpetuated through social interaction feedback.

In addition to its influence on social feedback, momentary shifts in the phenomenal self can lead to the acquisition of information or the performance of additional behavior that bolsters and sustains the temporary view of the self. For instance, Mischel, Ebbeson, and Zeiss (1973) provided subjects with success or failure feedback. After administering the feedback, selective attention to the self was examined by giving the subjects the opportunity to look at information about personal assets and liabilities. Compared to failure-feedback and no-feedback subjects, subjects who received success feedback spent nearly twice as much time reviewing information about their assets.

More recently, Wright and Mischel (1982) had subjects work on a task for which they received success or failure feedback. While working on the tasks and learning of their performance, subjects were induced to experience either a positive, neutral, or negative mood. The dependent measures included a variety of variables designed to assess differences in the way that self-referent information had been processed. Included were measures of future performance expectancies, goal setting, and recall of past performances. As expected, performance feedback predictably influenced these variables. More important, induced mood contributed independently to these effects; positive-mood subjects offered the highest estimates of past successes and the most positive global self-evaluations. Negative-mood subjects gave the lowest estimates of success and the most unfavorable self-evaluations. More central to the present discussion was the finding that induced mood led to very different expectations for future success, with positive-mood subjects reporting higher expectations than negative-mood subjects. Although the pertinent data were not collected, it is likely that subject's expectancies would influence their performance in future situations and thus, provide additional feedback consistent with their current self-view.

A third study provides an additional piece of evidence that bears on the potential importance of momentary fluctuations in the self. Campbell and Fairey (1985) asked high- and low-self-esteem subjects to image and explain hypothetical success or failure experiences and then solve a series of anagrams. Success explanations increased subjects' own performance expectancies and actual performance, and failure explanations decreased expectancies and performance. However, these findings were qualified by the subjects' initial levels of self-esteem. Success explanations uniformly elevated both high- and low-self-esteem subjects' expectancies and performance. Failure explanations, in contrast, only influenced low-self-esteem subjects. It is interesting to note that subsidiary analyses of the attributional content of the hypothetical explanations indicated that high-self-esteem subjects were self-serving, taking credit for success while blaming failure on external causes. Low-self-esteem subjects offered approximately the same proportion of self-attributions for failure as they did for success. In the terminology of the current model, low-self-esteem subjects had broader latitudes of acceptance for negative self-referent information and this feature accounted for the self-esteem differences in response to failure situations.

In combination, the studies described above highlight another issue to which I alluded earlier. It appears that the phenomenal self is asymmetrically constructed, with the average person having a broader latitude of acceptance for positive than for negative self-relevant knowledge. Because positive information is more available in memory it is more easily made accessible by current contextual cues and behavior than is negative self-knowledge. In his description of the "totalitarian ego," Greenwald (1980) listed a group of biases employed by the self in the service of maintaining a favorable self-image. In large part, these biases entail the generation of causal explanations that permit one to take credit for esteem-enhancing outcomes and deflect responsibility for esteem-threatening feedback. It is suggested here that the asymmetrically constructed phenomenal self facilitates this process. That is, when people encounter positive feedback they automatically have accessible to them many other instances of themselves in positive situations (what Mischel refers to as the "warm glow"). Because negative self-relevant information is not as automatically accessible, it is likely to be experienced as schemata incongruent and thus instigate an attributional search for the cause (Hastie, 1984). In other words, self-serving attributions may be in part a consequence of the availability heuristic (Tversky & Kahneman, 1974).

Returning for a moment to the main theme of this section, it is contended that the importance of moment-to-moment shifts in self-conceptions for behavior and social interaction should not be underestimated. It seems apparent that in many circumstances these initially temporary fluctuations in the self can take on a more enduring status.

Social Interaction and the Latitude of Rejection

Although it is possible that momentary shifts in the self may endure through social interaction, it is proposed that the more permanent modifications of the self occur through incongruent information being internalized through dissonance reduction. As Hastie (1984) has demonstrated, inconsistent information—presumably including self-relevant information in the latitude of rejection—instigates attributional processing. Attributional processing, in turn, results in a stronger memory trace for the inconsistent material, especially if the attribution locates the cause of the inconsistent behavior within the actor (Crocker, Binns, & Weber, 1983). In terms of self-discrepant presentations, high-choice subjects who are confronted with inconsistent self-relevant information should be most likely to encode that material in memory because dissonance reduction has already led the subject to conclude that the inconsistent behavior is self-revealing.

Of course, it is recognized that, although the model specifies that dissonance-mediated modifications of the self should persist over time, there is no direct evidence to this effect. However, in earlier work employing the induced compliance paradigm, Higgins, Rhodewalt, and Zanna (1979) found dissonance-motivated attitude change to persist for a 2-week period. More recently, Axsom and Cooper (1985) examined the role of dissonance reduction in producing weight loss through effort justification. Of interest here is the fact that significant effects of the experimental conditions on weight loss were observed at a 1-year follow-up. Axsom and Cooper explained this surprising finding by suggesting that dissonance reduction led to an increase in the perceived importance or desirability of weight loss for the dieter. Although highly speculative at this point, it seems likely that changes in self-conceptions resulting from dissonance reduction will remain over time.

Nonetheless, as anyone who has endeavored to conduct dissonance research will attest, it requires a delicate arrangement of features of the behavioral context to engender dissonance. This reality probably militates against dissonance-motivated self-concept changes in most instances of self-discrepant behavior. The situation must elicit a self-discrepant act from the person without providing obvious cues to its situational determination. It is when people believe that they freely performed the behavior or instigated the contradictory feedback that they will alter their self-conceptions in response to dissonance motivation. If people do not believe that the behavior or feedback is accurately self-diagnostic, then they will be motivated to distort, discredit, or dilute the discrepant information by engaging in self-verifying behavior (Swann & Ely, 1984; Swann & Hill, 1982).

Individual Differences in the Effects of Self-Presentation on the Phenomenal Self

The major assertion of this chapter is that people's public self-presentations frequently influence how they later privately view themselves. Should we expect the effects of any given self-presentation to be the same for all individuals? In anticipation of the research surveyed in this section, the answer is clearly no. According to the model, self-presentational behavior influences the phenomenal self through two very different processes. Behavior within the latitude of acceptance impinges on the phenomenal self via the cognitive mechanism of differential accessibility. Behavior in the latitude of rejection alters self-conceptions through the motivational avenue of dissonance reduction. The impact of self-presentational behavior on the phenomenal self should then be mediated by cognitive and motivational differences in the way people process information about themselves.

Differences in Self-Schemata Content

With respect to any given attribute one's current self-presentation may be consistent, inconsistent, or irrelevant to one's existing conception of oneself (Lord, Gilbert, & Stanley, 1982; Markus, 1977). The process model of the phenomenal self is concerned with those presentations that are either self-congruent or incongruent. How one deals with self-presentations that are irrelevant to the self poses an interesting question. One possibility is that traditional self-perception processes (Bem, 1972) would determine whether or not the self-presentational episode had any meaning for the self. Internal cues in this situation presumably are unclear about where one stands with regard to the attribute implied by the self-presentation. People should then simply observe their behavior and the circumstances of its occurrence and infer their traits and characteristics in much the same way they infer their attitudes from behavior. However, because most social behavior is open to multiple interpretations, it is likely that one will construe most self-presentations as relevant to some existing dimension of the self. In most cases, then, the self-presentation will be either consistent or inconsistent with an aspect of the self.

The Rhodewalt and Agustsdottir (1986) investigation employed depressed subjects because it was assumed that level of depression reflected differences in the content of self-relevant knowledge. Subsidiary analyses from this study mentioned earlier might provide some insight into the interplay between behavior and self-knowledge that is not well formed or easily accessible in memory. As noted previously, depressed individuals differ from nondepressed individuals in that their self-schemata contain more negative and less positive information (Kuiper et al., 1983). It is noteworthy that subjects in the Rhodewalt and Agustsdottir study were only mildly depressed, because these individuals fall somewhere between nondepressed and clinically depressed individuals, with self-schemata that contain both positive and negative information.

The reader will recall that Rhodewalt and Agustsdottir's depressed subjects who self-enhanced displayed the carry-over effect only if they believed they chose to play the role, a finding that was interpreted as indicative of behavior that was inconsistent with self-relevant knowledge. However, within the high-choice self-enhancing conditions it was found that the extremity of the self-presentational behavior was correlated with the magnitude of the carry-over effect for those depressed subjects who were self-referencing. While Kuiper and Derry (1982) reported that the self-schemata of mildly depressed subjects contain both positive and negative information, they also noted that positive information is not processed as efficiently as negative information. In a similar vein, Ingram, Smith, and Brehm (1983) demonstrated that success feedback did not activate positive self-relevant information for mildly depressed subjects as it did for nondepressed subjects.

How might one account for these findings? Many forms of social and performance feedback are ambiguous with regard to the self. That is, many of our outcomes need not be automatically categorized as self-relevant. It may be only when one's attributional analysis indicates that the behavior is self-diagnostic that the ambiguous but potentially meaningful feedback becomes more self-relevant and thus increases the accessibility of now-consistent information. Presumably self-schemata are built up through repeated experience with feedback from one's social world. Many studies attest to the fact that people often manifest consistent individual differences in the way in which they attribute their behavior (see Rhodewalt & Comer, 1981 for discussion). Some individuals are consistently self-serving in their attributions while others appear habitually to make self-attributions for most of their outcomes (Rhodewalt, 1984). Thus differences among individuals in their tendency to view unfavorable public behavior as self-revealing should differentiate, in part, those who will experience dissonance after a self-descrepant act from those who will not.

These speculations might be particularly meaningful with regard to depression. That is, a "depressive attributional style" (Peterson & Seligman, 1984) might be instrumental to the formation of the depressed self-schema by increasing the frequency of instances when negative events will be viewed as self-relevant and consequently, stored in self-referent form.

Self-Esteem

The empirical evidence presented in support of the present model indicates that one's self-presentations often lead to positive or negative shifts in self-evaluation. It should be the case, then, that one's level of self-esteem or habitual level of self-evaluation (Coopersmith, 1967; Shrauger, 1975) is an important mediator of the effects of self-presentation on the phenomenal self. In this regard, self-esteem is thought to be similar to depression in that low-self-esteem individuals' self-schemata contain more negative self-referent information than the self-schemata of high-self-esteem individuals. Evidence consistent with this proposition may be found in the Campbell and Fairey (1985) investigation. One will recall that asking subjects to imagine and explain a hypothetical failure resulted in lower performance expectancies and lower actual performance only for low self-esteem subjects. It is suggested here that such a manipulation made other instances of failure more accessible for low-self-esteem subjects, and it was the presence of this information that contributed to the decreased expectancies. For high-self-esteem subjects failure experiences are in the latitude of rejection, and imagining a hypothetical failure presumably would not lead to differential accessibility for congruent experiences. In fact, Campbell and Fairey (1985) reported that high-self-esteem subjects gave significantly fewer characterological attributions for imagined failure than did low-self-esteem subjects, indicating that these subjects do not think of failure in terms of the self. It is likely that these factors account for Campbell and Fairey's failure to observe "carry-over" from imagining a failure experience to performance expectancies for high-self-esteem individuals.

This interpretation has potentially important implications for the body of research that has been concerned with the effects of performance feedback on the subsequent performance of high- and low-self-esteem subjects. A survey of selected findings indicates that, relative to their high-self-esteem counterparts, failure feedback leads low-self-esteem subjects to display poorer subsequent performance (Baumeister & Tice, 1985; Schalon, 1968; Shrauger & Sorman, 1977), decreased task persistence (Shrauger & Sorman, 1977), and lowered expectancies for future performance (McFarlin & Blascovich, 1981). Those studies that demonstrate a reversal of these effects either prevent the subject from focusing on the feedback as self-relevant (Brockner & Hulton, 1978) or force the subject to remain engaged in the task long enough to experience a success for which the low-self-esteem subject feels responsible (Shrauger & Sorman, 1977). In the former example, biased scanning of the self is circumvented and in the latter case the subject is forced to self-attribute feedback that is possibly inconsistent with the current phenomenal self.

These conjectures raise two related issues. First, an attempt has been made to interpret the differential effects of performance feedback on the self-perceptions of high- and low-self-esteem people. Additional research is required to determine what, if any, are the effects of performance feedback on the moment-to-moment shifts in one's "phenomenal self-esteem." Second, although the present model was developed to account for the effects of self-presentations on self-conceptions, the discussion of self-esteem and performance feedback illustrates that the model may provide a useful framework in which to study the relations between the self and a variety of social behaviors.

Self-Complexity

Recent work by Linville (1982) highlights the importance of the organization of self-knowledge and is pertinent to the discussion of the effects of self-presentation on the phenomenal self. She has provided evidence that people vary with respect to the "complexity" with which they represent information about themselves and others. The greater the number of feature sets or number of branches in a hierarchical representation of the self the greater the complexity of the self-representation. Self-complexity appears to be related to variability in biased scanning of the self. For example, when Linville (1982) led subjects to believe that they had either succeeded or failed at a test of intelligence, low-self-complexity subjects displayed far greater feedback-congruent changes in mood and self-appraisals than did high-complexity subjects. Returning to self-presentational behavior, one would predict that positive and negative carry-over should be much greater for people who have simplistically organized conceptions of self than for people with more articulated and complex self-conceptions.

Repression–Sensitization

Jones and Gerard (1967) emphasized that the phenomenal self waxes and wanes in awareness. This suggests that consistent differences in attention to, or awareness of, the self should mediate the effects of self-presentation on self-conceptions. Moreover, a motivational analysis would suggest that self-attention should vary according to the specific nature of the self-relevant information. In the cognitive view attentional styles should vary only as a function of the salience or intensity of the self-relevant cues in the context or situation while the motivational view would predict that attentional style should interact with the context.

Support for the importance of motivational differences can be found in the Mischel et al. (1973) study of the effects of success and failure feedback on subsequent selective attention to the self. These authors reasoned that the impact of the feedback would be mediated by the subject's characteristic level of repression-sensitization (Byrne, 1964). Repressors typically avoid threatening stimuli while sensitizers approach such situations. In general, Mischel et al. found that success experiences led to greater attention to assets and less attention to liabilities. However, this finding was qualified by whether the subject was a repressor or sensitizer. Repressors spent more time on assets and less on liabilities than did sensitizers. Moreover, repressors were somewhat unaffected by success and failure feedback in their allocation of attention to the self. In contrast, sensitizers were dramatically affected by prior performance feedback. After success experiences, sensitizers spent more time attending to assets than they did after failure experiences and after failure spent significantly more time reviewing liabilities. Extending these findings to self-presentational behavior, one would expect sensitizers to display greater carry-over than repressors for presentations within their latitude of acceptance. At the same time, the Mischel et al. (1973) data suggest that sensitizers might have broader latitudes of acceptance for negative information. They should also experience greater dissonance when their behavior falls into the latitude of rejection. This later prediction stems from the fact that repressors are more likely to employ denial and thus refuse to feel responsible for the self-discrepant act (see Zanna & Aziza, 1976). While this discussion is speculative with regard to self-presentation, repression–sensitization does serve to illustrate the potential importance of motivational factors in the shifting foci of the phenomenal self.

Self-Consciousness

Repression and sensitization are ego-defensive styles of coping with threat. Placing motivational concerns aside, people also vary in the extent to which the self is in awareness or prominent in their thinking. Self-consciousness (Fenigstein, Scheier,

& Buss, 1975; Scheier & Carver, 1983) is an individual difference construct that involves differences in self-attention. In their original statement of objective self-awareness theory, Duval and Wicklund (1972) proposed that one's focus of attention could be directed outward on the environment or inward to the self as an object in the environment. Several studies indicate that manipulations designed to increase objective self-awareness, such as placing a mirror in front of the subject, also increase the tendency to use self-relevant information in speech (Carver & Scheier, 1978; Davis & Brock, 1975). This indicates that self-referent knowledge is more accessible when one is objectively rather than subjectively self-aware.

More recently, Fenigstein et al. (1975) have argued that there are consistent dispositional tendencies for individuals to be more or less chronically self-aware. They use the term self-consciousness to differentiate this disposition from the transient states of objective and subjective self-awareness. Moreover, Fenigstein et al. distinguish between two orthogonal types of self-consciousness. Private self-consciousness refers to an awareness of one's private thoughts and feelings while public self-consciousness concerns one's awareness of the self as a social object. The findings of several studies are of particular interest to our concern with the effects of self-presentational behavior on self-conceptions. Hull and Levy (1979) found that, compared to low-private-self-conscious subjects, people high in private self-consciousness have easier access to self-referent knowledge. High-private-self-conscious individuals also report that the traits and other information that constitute their self-images are more important than do their low-private-self-conscious counterparts (Cheek & Briggs, 1982). Taken together, these findings suggest that a person who is characteristically high in private self-consciousness will be most influenced by his or her self-presentational behavior. For these people self-referent knowledge is always very close to awareness. Thus behavior as well as other contextual cues should easily trigger differential accessibility. On those occasions when they are induced to present themselves in a self-discrepant way, they should experience dissonance and incorporate the discrepant act into their self-images.

What of those individuals who are chronically aware of their public selves? Research indicates that high-public-self-conscious people also have well-articulated and easily accessible self-knowledge structures. The difference is that these self-schemata contain information about public and physical identity rather than traits and feelings. In addition, individuals high in public self-consciousness are more accurately aware of the impact their behavior is having upon others (Tobey & Tunnell, 1981). These findings indicate that the processes by which self-presentational behavior molds the phenomenal self should be similar for high-public- and high-private-self-conscious people. However, the processes should be initiated by different cues in the situation. For the high-public-self-conscious person cues about the public implications of his or her behavior and the reactions of others should lead to differential accessibility of various aspects of the public self and moment-to-moment changes in self-conceptions. Of course, if the public implications of the self-presentational episode are too self-discrepant then the person should experience dissonance. People who are characteristically low in both public and private consciousness should possess a collection of somewhat murky self-conceptions that are largely impervious to contextual variation in self-relevant cues.

Self-Monitoring

Self-monitoring (Snyder, 1974, 1979) is a trait dimension that represents the combination of self-presentational and self-attentional differences. The high-self-monitoring individual is simultaneously sensitive to situational cues to appropriate behavior and skillful at monitoring his or her own expressive behavior in accordance with these cues. Low self-monitors' behavior seems to be guided more by their own beliefs, values, and attitudes. Several features of self-monitoring appear particularly relevant to our discussion of the effects of self-presentational behavior on one's self-image. First, people high in self-monitoring are more aware of the situational determination of their behavior (Jones & Baumeister, 1976). Second, high self-monitors report greater situation-to-situation behavioral variability (Snyder & Monson, 1975) and display lower attitude–behavior consistency than do low self-monitors (Zanna, Olsen, & Fasio, 1980). At the same time high self-monitors are less likely to experience dissonance-motivated attitude change following counterattitudinal behavior (Snyder & Tanke, 1976). Finally, low self-monitors appear to have richer and better articulated self-schemata than do high self-monitors (Snyder & Cantor, 1980).

How does all of this bear on self-presentational behavior? Although high self-monitors should be more skilled at enacting strategic self-presentations, it is probable that in most instances these public displays will have little impact on their self-conceptions. Because high self-monitors are very attuned to the situational demands guiding their behavior, these individuals should experience few instances where they feel responsible for self-discrepant acts. At the same time, the phenomenal selves of high self-monitors should be relatively unaffected by behaviors within their latitude of acceptance. Snyder and Cantor's findings suggest that self-referent knowledge may not be as automatically accessible for high self-monitors as it is for lows. Moreover, when attempting to convey an impression of oneself to another, high and low self-monitors are likely to rely on different sources of knowledge to guide their self-presentations. High self-monitors are apt to think of a prototypical other with regard to the trait in question while low self-monitors are likely to think of the trait in themselves (Snyder & Cantor, 1980). Thus the self-presentation of the low self-monitor will be more self-referent and lead to greater focused accessibility of presentation-congruent self-knowledge than will the corresponding self-presentation of a high self-monitor. Because of their proclivity to display attitude–behavior consistency low self-monitors should also be more disturbed by self-discrepant acts and, thus, display dissonance-motivated self-concept change.

Summary

The individual difference constructs surveyed in this section are not presented as an exhaustive list. Rather they were selected as exemplars of the kinds of person characteristics or information-processing differences that are thought to mediate the effects of people's self-presentations on their subsequent self-images. The investigation of these differences within the process model of the self outlined in this chapter should be mutually beneficial to both personologists and those interested in the more social aspects of the self.

Conclusion

In this chapter I have considered the issues of *when* and *how* people's self-presentations alter their private self-conceptions. The mere fact that people's public displays often lead to shifts in their self-conceptions fosters a characterization of the self as socially mutable. Yet, there is a wealth of experience, theory, and research that supports the view that one's identity is stable and consistent over time. I have argued that there is no one-to-one correspondence between the experience of self and the underlying stable representations of the self-concept. Rather, I proposed that the phenomenal self—the self in one's awareness—is comprised of ever-shifting salient facets of one's identity. Self-presentational behavior and the circumstances of its occurrence combine to form an important source of contextual information that can render self-knowledge differentially accessible. At the same time the phenomenal self is based on existing knowledge of traits, feelings, behaviors, and experiences. There are instances, then, when one's self-presentations convey a self that is discrepant with the phenomenal self.

A process model of the phenomenal self in social interaction was proposed to account for self-presentationally induced shifts in self-conception. The phenomenal self is depicted as possessing latitudes of acceptance and rejection of self-referent knowledge. Empirical evidence was described that demonstrated that self-presentational behavior for which there is a correspondent representation in self-referent memory instigates momentary shifts in the phenomenal self through the cognitive mechanism of differential accessibility. Self-presentations that portray a self that is discrepant with well-represented images of the self (i.e., in the latitude of rejection) lead to changes in the phenomenal self through dissonance reduction.

Next, I attempted to place the phenomenal self in the stream of social interaction by highlighting the reciprocal relationships between one's sense of self and the emerging social context. Finally, I suggested several personality traits that deserve attention as mediators or moderators of the carry-over effect of self-presentation on the phenomenal self.

Acknowledgments. I wish to extend my deepest appreciation to Ned Jones for introducing me to, and stimulating my thinking about, the issues addressed in this chapter. I also wish to thank Martin Chemers and Craig Hill for their thoughtful comments on an earlier version of this chapter.

References

Axsom, D, & Cooper, J. (1985). Cognitive dissonance and psychotherapy: The role of effort justification in inducing weight loss. *Journal of Experimental Social Psychology, 21,* 149–160.
Baumeister, R.F., & Tice, D.M. (1985). Self-esteem and responses to success and failure: Subsequent performance and intrinsic motivation. *Journal of Personality, 53,* 450–467.

Beck, A.T., Rush, A.J., Shaw, B.F., & Emery, G. (1979). *Cognitive therapy of depression*. New York: Guilford Press.

Bem, D.J. (1972). Self-perception theory. In L. Berkowitz (Ed.), *Advances in experimental social psychology* (Vol 6, pp 1–62). New York: Academic Press.

Bower, G.H., & Gilligan, S.G. (1979) Remembering information related to one's self. *Journal of Research in Personality, 13*, 420–432.

Brockner, J., & Hulton, A.J.B. (1978). How to reverse the vicious cycle of low self-esteem: The importance of attentional focus. *Journal of Experimental Social Psychology, 14*, 564–578.

Byrne, D. (1964). Repression–sensitization as a dimension of personality. In B.A. Maher (Ed.), *Progress in experimental personality research*. New York: Academic Press.

Campbell, J.D., & Fairey, P.J. (1985). Effects of self-esteem, hypothetical explanations, and verbalization of expectancies on future performance. *Journal of Personality and Social Psychology, 48*, 1097–1111.

Carver, C.S., & Scheier, M.F. (1978). Self-focusing effect of dispositional self-consciousness, mirror presence, and audience presence. *Journal of Personality and Social Psychology, 36*, 324–332.

Cheek, J.M., & Briggs, S.R. (1982). Self-consciousness and aspects of identity. *Journal of Research in Personality, 16*, 401–408.

Cheek, J.M., & Hogan, R. (1983). Self-concepts, self-presentations, and moral judgments. In J. Suls & A.G. Greenwald (Eds.), *Psychological perspectives on the self* (Vol. 2, pp. 249–273). Hillsdale, NJ: Erlbaum.

Coopersmith, S. (1967). *The antecedents of self-esteem*. San Francisco: Freeman.

Crocker, J., Binns, D., & Weber, R. (1983). Person memory and causal attributions. *Journal of Personality and Social Psychology, 44*, 55–66.

Davis, D., & Brock, T.C. (1975). Use of first person pronouns as a function of increased objective self-awareness and prior feedback. *Journal of Experimental Social Psychology, 11*, 381–388.

Duval, S., & Wicklund, R.A. (1972). *A theory of objective self-awareness*. New York: Academic Press.

Fazio, R.H., Effrein, E.A., & Falender, V.J. (1981). Self-perceptions following social interactions. *Journal of Personality and Social Psychology, 41*, 232–242.

Fazio, R.H., Zanna, M.P., & Cooper, J. (1977). Dissonance and self-perception: An integrated view of each theory's proper domain of application. *Journal of Experimental Social Psychology, 13*, 464–479.

Fenigstein, A., Scheier, M.F., & Buss, A.H. (1975). Public and private self-consciousness: Assessment and theory. *Journal of Consulting and Clinical Psychology, 43*, 522–527.

Festinger, L. (1957). *A Theory of Cognitive Dissonance*. Evanston, IL: Row, Peterson.

Gergen, K.J. (1962). *Interaction goals and personalistic feedback as factors affecting the presentation of the self*. Unpublished doctoral dissertation, Duke University.

Gergen, K.J. (1967). Interaction goals and personalistic feedback as factors affecting the presentation of self. *Journal of Personality and Social Psychology, 1*, 413–424.

Goffman, E. (1959). *The presentation of self in everyday life*. New York: Anchor Books.

Greenwald, A.G. (1980). The totalitarian ego: Fabrication and revision of personal history. *American Psychologist, 28*, 404–416.

Greenwald, A.G., & Pratkanis, A.R. (1984). The self. In R.S. Wyer & T.K. Srull (Eds.), *Handbook of Social Cognition*. Vol. 3. Hillsdale, NJ: Erlbaum.

Hastie, R. (1984). Causes and effects of causal attribution. *Journal of Personality and Social Psychology, 46*, 44–56.

Higgins, E.T., Rhodewalt, F., & Zanna, M.P. (1979). Dissonance motivation: Its nature, persistence, and reinstatement. *Journal of Experimental Social Psychology, 15*, 16–34.

Hovland, C.I., Harvey, O.J., & Sherif, M. (1957). Assimilation and contrast effects in reaction to communication and attitude change. *Journal of Abnormal and Social Psychology, 55*, 244–252.

Hull, J., & Levy, A. (1979). The organizational functions of the self: An alternative to the Duval and Wicklund model of self-awareness. *Journal of Personality and Social Psychology, 37*, 756–768.

Ingram, R., Smith, T.W., & Brehm, S.S. (1983). Depression and information processing: Self-schemata and the encoding of self-relevant information. *Journal of Personality and Social Psychology, 45*, 412–420.

James, W. (1890). *The principles of psychology.* New York: Holt.

Janis, I.L., & Gilmore, J.B. (1965). The influence of incentive conditions on the success of role playing in modifying attitudes. *Journal of Personality and Social Psychology, 1*, 17–27.

Jones, E.E., & Baumeister, R.F. (1976). The self-monitor looks at the ingratiator. *Journal of Personality, 44*, 654–674.

Jones, E.E., & Gerard, H.B. (1967). *Foundations of social psychology* (p. 716). New York: Wiley.

Jones, E.E., & Pittman, T.S. (1982). Toward a general theory of strategic self-presentation. In J. Suls (Ed.), *Psychological perspectives on the self* (Vol. 1, pp. 231–262). Hillsdale, NJ: Erlbaum.

Jones, E.E., Rhodewalt, F., Berglas, S., & Skelton, J.A. (1981). Effects of strategic self-presentation on subsequent self-esteem. *Journal of Personality and Social Psychology, 41*, 407–421.

Kelley, H.H. (1967). Attribution theory in social psychology. In D. Levine (Ed.), *Nebraska symposium on motivation* (Vol. 15). Lincoln: University of Nebraska Press.

Kihlstrom, J.F., & Cantor, N. (1983). Mental representations of the self. In L. Berkowitz (Ed.), *Advances in experimental social psychology* (Vol. 17, pp. 1–47). New York: Academic Press.

Kuiper, N.A., MacDonald, M.R., & Derry, P.A. (1983). Parameters of a depressive self-schema. In J. Suls & A.G. Greenwald (Eds.), *Psychological perspectives on the self* (Vol. 2, pp. 191–217). Hillsdale, NJ: Erlbaum.

Kuiper, N.A., & Derry, P.A. (1982). Depressed and nondepressed content self-reference in mild depressives. *Journal of Personality, 50*, 67–79.

Langer, E., & Newman, H.M. (1979). The role of mindlessness in a typical social psychology experiment. *Personality and Social Psychology Bulletin, 5*, 295–298.

Linville, P.W. (1982). Affective consequences of complexity regarding the self and others. In M.S. Clark & S.T. Fiske (Eds.), *Affect and cognition* (pp. 79–109). Hillsdale, NJ: Erlbaum.

Lord, C.G., Gilbert, D.T., & Stanley, M.A. (1982, August). *Individual self-schemas and processing information about the self.* Paper presented at a meeting of the American Psychological Association, Washington, DC.

Markus, H. (1977). Self-schemata and processing information about the self. *Journal of Personality and Social Psychology, 35*, 63–78.

Markus, H., & Sentis, K. (1982). The self in social information processing. In J. Suls (Ed.), *Psychological perspectives on the self* (Vol. 1, pp. 41–70). Hillsdale, NJ: Erlbaum.

McFarlin, D.B., & Blascovich, J. (1981). Effects of self-esteem and performance feedback on future affective preferences and cognitive expectations. *Journal of Personality and Social Psychology, 40*, 521–531.

McGuire, W.J., & McGuire, C.V. (1981). The spontaneous self-concept as affected by personal distinctiveness. In M.D. Lynch, A.A. Norem-Hebeisen, & K. Gergen (Eds.), *Self-concept: Advances in theory and research.* Cambridge, MA: Ballinger.

McGuire, W.J., McGuire, C.V., Child, P., & Fujioka, T. (1978). Salience of ethnicity in the spontaneous self-concept as a function of one's ethnic distinctiveness in the social environment. *Journal of Personality and Social Psychology, 36*, 77–90.

McGuire, W.J., & Padawer-Singer, A. (1976). Trait salience in the spontaneous self-concept. *Journal of Personality and Social Psychology, 33*, 743–754.

Mischel, W., Ebbesen, E.E., & Zeiss, A.R. (1973). Selective attention to the self: Situational and dispositional determinants. *Journal of Personality and Social Psychology, 27,* 129–142.

Morse, S.J., & Gergen, K.J. (1970). Social comparison, self-consistency, and the presentation of self. *Journal of Personality and Social Psychology, 16,* 148–159.

Natale, M., & Hantas, M. (1982). Effects of temporary mood states on selective memory about the self. *Journal of Personality and Social Psychology, 42,* 927–934.

Peterson, C., & Seligman, M.E.P. (1984). Causal explanations as a risk factor for depression: Theory and evidence. *Psychological Review, 91,* 347–374.

Rhodewalt, F. (1984). Self-involvement, self-attribution, and the Type A coronary-prone behavior pattern. *Journal of Personality and Social Psychology, 47,* 662–670.

Rhodewalt, F., & Agustsdottir, S. (1986). The effects of self-presentation on the phenomenal self. *Journal of Personality and Social Psychology, 50,* 47–55.

Rhodewalt, F., & Comer, R. (1981). The role of self-attribution differences in the utilization of social comparison information. *Journal of Research in Personality, 15,* 210–220.

Rogers, T.B. (1981). A model of the self as an aspect of the human information processing system. In N. Cantor & J. Kihlstrom (Eds.), *Personality, cognition, and social interaction* (pp. 193–214). Hillsdale, NJ: Erlbaum.

Schalon, C.L. (1968). Effect of self-esteem upon failure following performance stress. *Journal of Consulting and Clinical Psychology, 32,* 497.

Scheier, M.F., & Carver, C.S. (1981). Private and public aspects of the self. In L. Wheeler (Ed.), *Review of personality and social psychology* (Vol. 2, pp. 189–216). Beverly Hills, CA: Sage.

Scheier, M.F., & Carver, C.S. (1983). Two sides of the self: One for you and one for me. In J. Suls & A.G. Greenwald (Eds.), *Psychological perspectives on the self* (Vol. 2, pp. 123–157). Hillsdale, NJ: Erlbaum.

Shrauger, J.S. (1975). Responses to evaluation as a function of initial self-perceptions. *Psychological Bulletin, 82,* 581–596.

Shrauger, J.S., & Sorman, P.B. (1977). Self-evaluation, initial success and failure, and improvement as determinants of persistence. *Journal of Consulting and Clinical Psychology, 45,* 784–795.

Snyder, M. (1974). The self-monitoring of expressive behavior. *Journal of Personality and Social Psychology, 30,* 526–537.

Snyder, M. (1979). Self-monitoring processes. In L. Berkowitz (Ed.), *Advances in experimental social psychology* (Vol. 12). New York: Academic Press.

Snyder, M., & Cantor, N. (1980). Thinking about ourselves and others: Self-monitoring and social knowledge. *Journal of Personality and Social Psychology, 39,* 222–234.

Snyder, M., & Monson, T.C. (1975). Persons, situations, and the control of social behavior. *Journal of Personality and Social Psychology, 32,* 637–644.

Snyder, M., & Swann, W.B. (1978). Behavioral confirmation in social interaction: From social perception to social reality. *Journal of Experimental Social Psychology, 14,* 148–162.

Snyder, M., & Tanke, E.D. (1976). Behavior and attitude: Some people are more consistent than others. *Journal of Personality, 44,* 501–517.

Swann, W.B. (1983). Self-verification: Bringing social reality into harmony with the self. In J. Suls & A.G. Greenwald (Eds.), *Psychological perspectives on the self* (Vol. 2, pp. 33–66). Hillsdale, NJ: Erlbaum.

Swann, W.B., & Ely, R. (1984). A battle of wills: Self-verification versus behavioral confirmation. *Journal of Personality and Social Psychology, 46,* 1287–1302.

Swann, W.B., & Hill, C.A. (1982). When our identities are mistaken: Reaffirming self-conceptions through social interactions. *Journal of Personality and Social Psychology, 43,* 59–66.

Swann, W.B., & Read, S.J. (1981a). Acquiring self-knowledge: The search for feedback that fits. *Journal of Personality and Social Psychology, 41,* 1119–1128.

Swann, W.B., & Read, S.J. (1981b). Self-verification processes: How we sustain our self-conceptions. *Journal of Experimental Social Psychology, 17,* 351–372.

Tedschi, J.T., & Norman, N. (1983). Social power, self-presentation, and the self. In B. Schlenker (Ed.), *The self and social life.* (pp. 293–322). New York, McGraw-Hill.

Thomas, W.I. (1928). *The Unadjusted Girl.* Boston: Little-Brown.

Tobey, E.L., & Tunnell, G. (1981). Predicting our impressions on others: Effects of public self-consciousness and acting, a self-monitoring subscale. *Personality and Social Psychology Bulletin, 7,* 661–669.

Tversky, A., & Kahneman, D. (1974). Judgement under uncertainty: Heuristics and biases. *Science, 185,* 1124–1131.

Wicklund, R.A., & Brehm, J.W. (1976). *Perspectives on cognitive dissonance.* Hillsdale, NJ: Erlbaum.

Wright, J., & Mischel, W. (1982). Influence of affect on cognitive social learning person variables. *Journal of Personality and Social Psychology, 43,* 901–914.

Zanna, M.P., & Aziza, C. (1976). On the interaction of repression–sensitization and attention in resolving cognitive dissonance. *Journal of Personality, 44,* 577–593.

Zanna, M.P., Olson, J.M., & Fazio, R.H. (1980). Attitude–behavior consistency: An individual difference perspective. *Journal of Personality and Social Psychology, 38,* 432–430.

Chapter 7
Striving for Specific Identities:
The Social Reality of Self-Symbolizing

Peter M. Gollwitzer

Striving for specific identities (e.g., lawyer, mother, pious person) is not a strategic effort at self-presentation, but is rather a nonstrategic approach to self-construction. To understand which form such self-constructive efforts need to take in order to be effective, it is necessary to examine how individuals conceive of the intended identity goal state. My analysis of this issue—which draws on Lewin's ideas on goal striving—suggests that people define the goal of possessing a certain identity as located on the plane of social reality. That is, one feels it is necessary that others be aware of one's claim to possession of a particular identity.

However, individuals engaged in identity-related goal striving see in others nothing more than a passive witness of their efforts. This rather rudimentary form of relating to others is rooted in the special motivational force that instigates identity striving: a person's commitment to identity attainment. To highlight the unique nature of identity striving, I shall compare it with strategic forms of self-presentation. In sharp contrast to strategic self-presentation, identity striving does not necessitate a strong concern with the thoughts and feelings of the audience addressed.

The Subjective Conceptions of Identity Goals

The meaning of particular identities is ultimately derived from society, for an integral part of our socialization process involves learning what is expected of persons holding a particular identity. Moreover, the social community tends to teach its members unambiguous definitions of the various identities, since dual or triple definitions create misunderstandings among its members, hamper productive interactions, and only serve to split the community (Inkeles, 1968).

Individuals who are committed to an identity conceive of that identity in terms of a goal state, whose attainment requires not only possession of the potential to enact identity-relevant behaviors, but also the ability to maintain that potential over time. However, the key question with regard to identity attainment is whether these individuals also feel that *others* need to know about such potential before it is possible to lay claim to identity possession. In order to investigate the extent to which a sense of possessing an intended identity is dependent upon others' awareness of the individual's potential to enact identity-relevant behaviors, it is necessary to reflect back on the psychology of goal-striving as presented by the Lewinian school.

The Social Reality Concept of Lewin's Berlin Group

Mahler's (1933) operationalization of Lewin's (1926) ideas on goal striving led to the development of a methodology that is most useful in addressing the issue of individual representations of goals. Mahler claimed that individual goal conceptions can be unveiled by analyzing activities that are substitutable for original goal striving. The experimental paradigm she introduced (see also Lissner, 1933; Ovsiankina, 1928) was quite simple in nature: Subjects were instructed to perform a certain task, such as to build a playhouse from wooden blocks, to solve a mathematical problem with pencil and paper, or to construct meaningful sentences from word lists. Shortly after beginning the task, subjects were interrupted and asked to solve a substitute task. They were then allowed to return to the interrupted, original task. Of interest was whether subjects would take advantage of this opportunity to *complete* the original task.

Mahler postulated that whenever subjects experience a correspondence between the quality of the goal served by solving the *substitute* task and the quality of the goal served by working on the *original* task, they are no longer inclined to return to the original task since substitute completion has occurred. Accordingly, in the event that solving a substitute task reduces the frequency of resumption of the original task, it can be inferred that the goal of the original task entails qualities that are served by the substitute task performed.

Furthermore, Mahler suggested that tasks differ with respect to whether their solutions need to be shown to *others* for a feeling of task completion to emerge. For example, whether the building of a house out of wooden blocks is considered to be completed is not dependent on whether anyone else ever notices the finished house. However, when solving a certain task is interpreted by the individual as a test of intelligence, of creativity, or of any other self-related attribute, it is necessary that others take notice of the solution in order for a sense of completion to occur. Mahler therefore maintained that all *self*-related goals are located on what she referred to as the *plane of social reality*. No sense of having reached these goals occurs as long as relevant task solutions do not become a social fact through being noticed by others.

In experiments on this issue, Mahler applied the substitution paradigm such that the substitute tasks employed either served or did not serve goals located on the plane of social reality. For example, when the original task involved such activities as solving mathematical problems or constructing creative sentences from lists of words on a piece of paper, the substitute tasks required that individuals solve these problems either through silent deliberation or by speaking aloud. For both types of tasks, speaking aloud proved to be the more effective substitute task with respect to suppressing the resumption of the original task. Mahler interpreted these findings as indicative of the fact that subjects conceived of the original goals as located on the plane of social reality. That is, subjects not only sought to find solutions to mathematical or creative problems, but also wanted *others* (in this case the experimenter) to know that they were smart or creative. Thus, only solving the substitute tasks aloud provided a sense of having attained the self-related goals of being smart or creative to which subjects had aspired while working on the original tasks.

It appears, therefore, that having people engage in substitute activities that are either noticed by others or remain unnoticed is a simple and straightforward approach to determining whether the original activity served a goal that is located on the plane of social reality.

Exploring the Concept of Social Reality in the Realm of Identity-Related Goal Striving

Striving for particular identity goals requires the execution of identity-related activities. It is possible, for example, to strive for a specific identity through the exercise of identity-related social influence (e.g., an academic psychologist may engage in teaching psychology), by displaying material symbols (e.g., a pious person may wear a golden cross), through the fulfillment of the daily duties associated with a particular identity (e.g., a baker bakes bread), by simply making a verbal claim to possession of a particular identity (e.g., "I am a baker"; Gollwitzer, Wicklund, & Hilton, 1982), or through the acquisition of the skills and tools associated with an identity (e.g., an educational background in music theory and a fine-quality instrument for a musician).

Symbolic self-completion theory (Wicklund & Gollwitzer, 1982, 1983; Gollwitzer & Wicklund, 1985b) provides a theoretical framework for the analysis of identity-related striving. It is assumed that identity goals are composed of an entire set of indicators of attainment, referred to as the *symbols* of that identity, for they tend to carry a meaning that goes far beyond the purely physical, sensory experience of that indicator. Wearing a white coat, for example, triggers a more-or-less universal reaction in others that goes beyond the white coat's physical qualities, for it symbolizes to others that they are dealing with a physician.

To acquire one of the many societally defined identity goals, it is necessary to accumulate its symbols. Clearly, social identities are so broadly defined (e.g., pious person) that one is generally not in a position to acquire *all* of the indicators of an identity. Consequently, it is always possible to continue striving for an identity-related goal through the acquisition of further relevant symbols. Self-completion theory refers to such identity-constructing efforts as *self-symbolizing* activities.

Thus, to investigate whether people conceive of identity goals as located on the plane of social reality, subjects are first given the opportunity to engage in a self-symbolizing activity. In order to vary whether these efforts become a social fact, subjects are then placed in a situation where self-symbolizing is either noticed by others or simply remains unnoticed. Given that identity goals are located on the plane of social reality, striving for an identity in front of an audience should provide a stronger sense of possessing the intended identity than striving in the absence of an audience. To determine whether this is the case, self-symbolizing individuals are finally provided with a further opportunity to strive for the intended identity in order to observe the extent to which self-symbolizing efforts persist.

The impact of social reality on self-symbolizing efforts. In the first experiment conducted on this issue (Gollwitzer, 1986a, Study 1), female undergraduates who had expressed the intent to raise a family were asked to write down personal skills relevant to succeeding as a mother (e.g., "I love to cook") in order to prepare themselves for an exchange of personal information with a partner subject. Subjects were either informed that their self-descriptions would be carefully studied by the partner subject, or they were shown that their self-descriptions had been discarded and therefore would not become known to others. By placing subjects' self-descriptions under these two conditions, it was possible to vary whether subjects' self-symbolizing activities were noticed by others, and consequently, whether these efforts became a social fact.

Thereafter, subjects were given the opportunity to engage in further self-symbolizing by completing a personality profile questionnaire. The experimenter handed them a semantic differential type of personality questionnaire on which a sample profile was drawn, and explained that the sample profile represented the ideal personality for a mother (i.e., successful mothers have a personality profile similar to this sample profile). The experimenter had, however, merely fabricated the personality profile so as to describe a person with five positive and five negative traits. Subjects were then instructed to rate their own personality traits on this questionnaire.

When initial self-symbolizing (i.e., the written self-descriptions of mother-related personal skills) was not made known to the partner subject, subjects felt compelled to engage in further self-symbolizing by drawing their own personality profile similar to the ideal mother profile provided, thereby claiming possession of the personality attributes characteristic of ideal mothers. However, subjects whose initial self-descriptions were noticed by the partner subject ascribed attributes to themselves on the personality profile questionnaire that were at variance with the ideal mother profile. Evidently, self-symbolizing that remains unnoticed, and thus does not become a social fact, is less effective in furnishing subjects with a sense of possessing the intended identity than self-symbolizing that is noticed by others. Since it is necessary that others be aware of identity striving in order to acquire a stronger sense of goal attainment, it can be inferred that individuals conceive of identity goals as located on the plane of social reality.

Considering that in the present study initial self-symbolizing occurred only with respect to identity-related self-descriptions, and not in terms of actual identity-related performances, it is conceivable that taking notice of self-symbolizing might have failed to enhance people's sense of possessing the intended identity if subjects had instead been given the opportunity to carry out identity-relevant performances. In order to clarify this issue, a second experiment was conducted, in which subjects' self-symbolizing entailed actually solving identity-relevant problems (Gollwitzer, 1986a, Study 2). Subjects were medical students committed to becoming physicians.

They were instructed to suggest solutions for a number of problems frequently confronted by physicians (e.g., "A diabetic refuses to abide by the diet the physician prescribed. What should the physician tell the patient?"). Subjects were told that they could quit working on these problems whenever they desired, that is, they were not required to complete the entire set of 45 problems. Shortly after subjects had begun to work on the problem set, a confederate appeared. For half of the subjects, she skimmed through the solutions to the first three problems, and then addressed the subjects as physicians. For the other half of the subjects, however, the confederate did not take notice of task performance, nor did she address subjects as physicians. The subjects' subsequent persistence at task performance was measured by recording how long they continued to work on the assigned tasks after the confederate departed.

Taking notice of subjects' solutions and addressing them as physicians resulted in less task persistence than not taking notice of task performance. Thus, self-symbolizing that was noticed by others evidently provided a stronger sense of attainment of the intended identity than self-symbolizing that remained unnoticed. Since taking notice of identity striving proved efficacious for feelings of identity attainment, subjects apparently conceived of their identity goal of physician as being located on the plane of social reality.

The results of both studies suggest that one can effectively strive for identity goals not only by making identity-related verbal statements (Study 1), but also by executing identity-related tasks (Study 2). The key issue with respect to identity attainment, however, is not whether identity-related efforts take the form of verbal claims or actual performances, but whether these efforts, irrespective of their form, are *noticed* by others, and thus become a social fact.

Self-initiative in turning self-symbolizing into a social fact. Whether identity goals are conceived of as being located on the plane of social reality can also be approached by examining self-initiative in calling self-symbolizing efforts to the attention of others. Since self-symbolizing that is noticed by others appears to be more effective in providing a sense of possessing the intended identity than self-symbolizing that remains unnoticed by others, individuals oriented toward achieving a particular identity should be especially concerned with finding an audience for their identity-related striving. In order to explore this issue, people's readiness to engage in identity-related goal striving was first manipulated, and subsequent efforts to make self-symbolizing public were observed.

Whenever people are confronted with identity-related weaknesses, a heightened readiness to exert self-symbolizing efforts is elicited, as has been repeatedly demonstrated by Wicklund and Gollwitzer (1982). This principle was employed in the following two experiments in order to vary people's readiness to strive for intended identities. In the first study (Gollwitzer, 1986a, Study 3), medical students with the expressed intention of becoming physicians were told that they either possessed or did not possess the personal qualities that characterize successful physicians, thus subjecting them to either positive or negative feedback with respect to their prospects as physicians. Delivering negative feedback was meant to generate a heightened readiness to engage in self-symbolizing. In a subsequent, presumedly independent experiment, subjects were provided with an opportunity to engage in self-symbolizing through finding solutions to medical tasks. Subjects were instructed to solve a set of 15 medical problems placed in front of them. In addition, subjects were told that they could submit completed sections of the assignment to the experimenter whenever desired, that is, before having completed the entire set of 15 tasks.

More than 50% of the subjects who had received negative identity-related feedback, as opposed to only 8% of the subjects who had received positive feedback, attempted to bring completed tasks to the experimenter's notice before finishing the entire sequence of tasks. These results clearly demonstrate that individuals whose readiness to strive for an intended identity is heightened are anxious to convert identity-related goal striving into a social fact. Apparently, effective striving for an identity goal necessitates that identity-related efforts are noticed by others. That is, people feel that they need to make self-symbolizing public in order to move toward attainment of their identity goals.

The propensity toward making one's self-symbolizing efforts known to others was investigated further in an additional study (Gollwitzer, 1986a, Study 4). Female undergraduates with a commitment to the identity of dancer were requested to write a lengthy essay. Half of the subjects were instructed to describe the worst dancing instructor they had ever had, the other half their best dancing instructor ever. Thus, half of the subjects were compelled to recall a negative aspect, and the other half a positive aspect of their educational dancing background, so as to induce in the former a comparatively greater readiness to step up self-symbolizing efforts (Wicklund & Gollwitzer, 1981).

Within a different social context, subjects were subsequently asked to participate in a public dancing session, where they would be given the opportunity to dance in front of a small audience. A sign-up sheet was handed out on which subjects were asked to indicate exactly when (i.e., in how many days) they wanted to be called back for one of these sessions. Our results revealed that those who had recalled their worst dancing instructor wanted to appear in public nearly two weeks earlier than subjects who had written about their best dancing instructor. Thus, subjects whose readiness to engage in self-symbolizing had been stimulated selected comparatively earlier dates for the public performance of a dance routine. These results strongly suggest that people are more anxious for self-symbolizing efforts to be noticed by others when identity-related striving is stimulated.

Summary. The results of these four experiments suggest that self-symbolizing that is noticed by others makes further striving for identity goals less necessary than self-symbolizing that remains unnoticed by others. In addition, people who are in the process of striving for identity goals are eager to make these efforts known to others, that is, they impatiently attempt to convert their self-symbolizing activities into a social fact. These findings imply that people conceive of identity goals as located on the plane of social reality. That is, people feel that the attainment of identity goals requires that others be aware of one's potential to enact identity-related behaviors.

The Motivational Basis of Identity-Related Striving

The way in which people attempt to display identity-related goal striving to others can take many different forms. For example, the publishing efforts of a self-symbolizing scientist could be brought to others' attention by engaging in informal discussions concerning the main themes of a book in progress, or by making short declarative statements, such as "I just signed a publication contract!" Since the potential audiences available are also numerous (e.g., family, neighbors, students, or colleagues), the self-symbolizer is in a position to be rather selective in choosing an audience for identity-related efforts. In fact, however, self-symbolizing individuals are not at all selective with respect to the people they address. Nor are they interested in engaging in meaningful interactions with the audience at their disposal (Gollwitzer, 1984; Gollwitzer & Wicklund, 1985a). Rather, self-symbolizers appear to see in audiences nothing more than passive witnesses of identity-related goal striving. In order to explicate this phenomenon, it is necessary to examine the motivational basis of self-symbolizing.

Commitment to an Identity

In an early study on self-completion (Wicklund & Gollwitzer, 1981), subjects interested in such fields as music, dance, and languages were questioned with respect to their readiness to instruct others in activities related to their respective field of interest. In the course of our investigation, a most interesting observation was made. After an identity-related shortcoming with respect to their educational background (i.e., inadequate musical, dance, or foreign language training) was pointed out, some subjects indicated a reduced interest in teaching others the skill in question. Further investigation revealed that these individuals were no longer pursuing the identity of musician, dancer, or foreign language speaker respectively, that is, they had given up striving for these identities. Other subjects, however, expressed an intensified interest in teaching, and it was found that these individuals were still actively engaged in the pursuit of the identities mentioned above. On the basis of these results, we postulated that only individuals still *committed* to identity attainment attempt to compensate for identity-related shortcomings through self-symbolizing. We referred to this variable as the *commitment to a self-definition*.

In subsequent experiments, our focus of interest was primarily on individuals strongly committed to attaining a particular identity (Wicklund & Gollwitzer, 1982). We only recruited subjects who had indicated that they were still actively pursuing a certain identity and that they would be very upset if it were necessary to terminate this pursuit. In all of these studies, making subjects face identity-related shortcomings (e.g., poor identity-related educational background or inadequate identity-related personal attributes) did not result in reduced striving for the intended identity. Instead, subjects reacted by increasing their efforts to achieve the identity in question via self-symbolizing. We observed this phenomenon for a variety of different identity goals (e.g., athlete, Catholic, businessman, mathematician, vintner), as well as for various forms of self-symbolizing (e.g., writing identity-related positive self-descriptions, influencing and teaching others, displaying identity-related status symbols, and associating with others known to possess the intended identity).

Apparently, the commitment to an identity operates as a force that propels people toward attainment of that identity. The energizing quality that emanates from making an identity commitment actually becomes most evident when hindrances (i.e., the experience of identity-related shortcomings) to attaining the intended identity are encountered. Under such conditions, committed individuals become even more determined to attain the identity in question, whereas the subsequent actions of non-committed individuals appear to reflect reduced identity-related aspirations and a sense of modesty.

Deliberation Motivation Versus Implementation Motivation

Recently, Heckhausen and Kuhl (1985) suggested that it is necessary to distinguish between two qualitatively different motivational problems. Motivational problems of choice entail deliberation on the subjective importance and likelihood of certain potential outcomes and consequences associated with taking a particular course of action. Motivational problems of implementation, however, involve addressing the question of when and how to act in order to accomplish desired ends. Experimental results (Heckhausen & Gollwitzer, 1986) suggest that people engage in deliberation on incentives and expectancies *prior* to committing themselves to a particular course of action, and focus on questions of implementation only *after* this commitment has become established. Moreover, making a decision to engage in a certain course of action apparently terminates deliberative thought and launches the individual into a fundamentally different motivational state, oriented solely toward executing the selected course of action. The transition from deliberative to executive thought appears to function somewhat like crossing the Rubicon (Heckhausen, 1985), that is, once the implementation mode of thought has been entered, one can no longer return to the preceding, deliberative motivational state.

With respect to people's identity commitments, two important implications can be derived from the proposition that individuals who are oriented toward implementation of an action are not in a position to undergo deliberation on the consequences of this action. First, people committed to a particular identity should be inclined to focus on acquiring this identity, to the exclusion of deliberative concerns. Since deliberation on the importance and likelihood of potential outcomes and their consequences comes to an end as soon as the individual makes a commitment, whether the intended identity is instrumental for attaining desired consequences or whether one is suited for the pursuit of a particular identity is no longer at issue. Committed individuals should therefore not be inclined to engage in deliberative thoughts that might challenge their choice of identity goal (e.g., "Am I suited for this identity? Do I really want to be a . . .? Should I give up trying to be a . . .?"), even when confronted with identity-related shortcomings. As our research showed (Wicklund & Gollwitzer, 1982), an awareness of identity-related shortcomings actually generates an even greater determination to attain the intended identity goal. This suggests that implementation motivation (i.e., volitional strength; Gollwitzer, 1986b) actually increases when difficulties hinder identity striving. As a result, deliberative concerns should be suppressed even more effectively, thus preventing the possibility that doubts could arise with respect to the value and expectancy of identity attainment.

Second, assuming that people conceive of identity goals as located on the plane of social reality, the implementation motivation characteristic of committed individuals should compel them to convert their self-symbolizing efforts into a social fact. Self-symbolizing individuals should also be inclined to seek audiences for their efforts in accordance with increases in implementation motivation. Thus, committed individuals who have just experienced an identity-related shortcoming should be especially concerned with making others notice identity-related striving. The results of Study 3 and Study 4 (Gollwitzer, 1986a) reported above strongly support this line of thought. More importantly, however, implementation motivation should suppress any concerns with the potential consequences of addressing others, that is, it should hinder reflection on how those addressed might feel about or potentially react to one's self-symbolizing efforts. This tendency has major social implications for the type and quality of interaction between self-symbolizing individuals and their audiences.

Social Implications of the Unique Motivational Basis of Self-Symbolizing

An analysis of the motivational basis of self-symbolizing reveals that not only self-reflective thoughts on the choice of identity goal, but also reflective thoughts on the potential reactions of the audience addressed are suppressed when a person engages in self-symbolizing. The issue of self-reflection with respect to one's personal attributes ("Am I a person who is smart, athletic, religious, . . .?") has been dealt with extensively by the school of symbolic interactionism, whereas the issue of individual concerns with audience reactions falls under the domain of social psychologists focusing on strategic self-presentation. Both of these research traditions, however, entertain a view of the way in which individuals relate to others that is opposed to what one would expect from the self-symbolizing individual. Thus, an analysis of the ideas advanced by symbolic interactionists, as well as by researchers concerned with strategic self-presentation, should prove fruitful with respect to explicating how self-symbolizing individuals relate to their audiences.

Self-Symbolizers Are Not Self-Reflective

Symbolic interactionists have advanced the idea that the origin and development of the self is ultimately rooted in relating to others, a proposition that is commonly attributed to the early work of Cooley (1902). Our "self-feeling" is presumably determined by the attitude we hold toward the assumed thoughts of another with respect to our appearance, aims, character, and needs. Cooley referred to this self-feeling as the *reflected* or *looking-glass self* in order to stress that taking the perspective of others allows for incorporation of their self-relevant judgments into one's self. Mead (1934) elaborated on Cooley's ideas by introducing the concept of the *generalized other* to refer to people's propensity to take the perspective of a particular reference group or a social community into consideration.

According to symbolic interactionism, the development of the self is dependent upon self-reflective thoughts (e.g., "What kind of person am I?"). Presumably, the attitudes of others toward one's self must be appraised in order to discover the nature of one's self. Thus, one forms self-related attitudes by using the presumed opinions of others regarding one's self as a source of information. This implies, however, that the individual must remain most sensitive to evaluation-relevant characteristics of these others, such as whether they are competent or credible judges of one's qualities.

Experimental research conducted within the tradition of symbolic interactionism focused on whether one takes the personal qualities (e.g., credibility, competence) of others into account when appraising their attitudes toward one's self. In order to explore this issue, subjects were instructed to engage in activities relevant to a personally important self-aspect (e.g., intelligence). An audience observed these activities and then approved or disapproved of the subjects' performance (see Haas & Maehr, 1965; Maehr, Mensing, & Nafzger, 1962; Videbeck, 1960). Each subject's self-rating (on this self-aspect) was recorded prior to and immediately following the evaluation by the audience, so as to determine the degree of self-change. Such experiments clearly bear resemblance to the classic persuasion paradigm (Hovland & Rosenberg, 1960), for the evaluative audience is conceived of as a communication source, the individual as the target of the audience's persuasive message, and the individual's self-aspect (e.g., intelligence) as the attitude object. In line with other research on persuasion (Tedeschi, 1974), the classic variables of the communication source were pivotal to the degree of self-change, that is, credible evaluators produced comparatively more self-change (Webster & Sobieszek, 1974).

These findings appear to imply that audience variables, such as credibility or competence, should also be of importance to the effectiveness of self-symbolizing. However, Mead's theorizing suggests that such an inference must be approached with great caution. Mead argued that a reflective orientation toward the self in which individuals relate to themselves as an object is limited to a special psychological condition which he labeled the *Me*-state. In contrasting the *Me*-state to the *I*-state, in which individuals actively engage in assertive self-expression, Mead claimed that the latter state is devoid of self-reflective thoughts, for individuals in this state do not conceive of themselves as the object of their concerns, but rather as the subject of their actions.

Since self-symbolizing individuals are engaged in the act of bringing identity-related striving to the attention of others, they clearly operate out of the *I*-state. The associated lack of self-reflection, with respect to self-assessment, creates a lack of concern with others' judgments toward oneself, as well as a state of ignorance with regard to attributes of the audience important to an adequate appraisal of their judgments. Thus, from the perspective of self-symbolizers, the audience's function entails nothing more than taking notice of their self-symbolizing efforts. Hence, the self-symbolizer's concern for the personal qualities of the audience is extremely limited in nature, such that anyone who has "eyes to see and ears to hear" qualifies as an adequate audience. In somewhat more metaphoric language, self-symbolizing individuals (ab)use their social surrounding as a checklist on which to register the possession of identity-related symbols. Making check marks implies no actual concern for the qualities of the checklist itself; rather, the focus of concern is solely on whether one succeeds or fails in placing check marks, that is, on whether one manages to turn self-symbolizing efforts into a social fact.

On occasion, however, the self-symbolizing individual may encounter difficulties in attempting to register the possession of an identity-related symbol on others. The audience may, for instance, respond to a person's self-symbolizing by overtly inferring an identity to which the person does not aspire. Such misinterpretations occur, for example, when a psychologist is addressed as a physician, as in Study 2 above. The audience may also simply refuse to take notice of one's self-symbolizing efforts, as in Study 1 above, in which the experimenter completely ignored subjects' self-symbolizing self-descriptions by discarding these descriptions. Audiences may also actually choose to refute the individual's claim of possession of the intended identity by pointing to identity-related shortcomings.

However, a cultural norm seems to prevail that compels individuals to refrain from conveying negative self-related feedback (Blumberg, 1972; Tesser & Rosen, 1975). As Goffman (1959) stated, only the socially disgruntled will question the realness of what is presented. Even when suspicions arise, people appear to give a person's self-presentations the benefit of the doubt. The general readiness of the public to take notice of self-symbolizing efforts without question or rebuff proves quite advantageous, for this means that self-symbolizing individuals can afford to be rather insensitive toward the audience's thoughts and feelings. Even when an audience is not particularly enthused about listening or is actually aware of an individual's underlying identity-related shortcomings, it will generally opt to remain silent. Thus, even addressing critical audiences does not prove detrimental to self-symbolizing efforts. Self-symbolizing individuals therefore do not need to be selective when choosing an audience; rather, they can simply address the audience that is immediately available in the interest of converting self-symbolizing into a social fact. Should audiences choose to completely ignore, blatantly misinterpret, or actively refute self-symbolizing, this still does not stimulate a more strategic approach to the selection of audiences. The results of the experiments reported, as well as the analysis of the motivational basis of self-symbolizing, suggest that self-symbolizing individuals who are confronted with audience resistance simply respond by increasing their efforts to register self-symbolizing on the next available, alternative audience.

Self-Symbolizers Are Not Strategic Self-Presenters

Under the heading of *strategic self-presentation* (or impression management), social psychologists have examined the efforts of individuals, referred to as self-presenters, to control the perceptions of themselves by others, referred to as targets of self-presentation. In general, strategic self-presentation is motivated by the attempt to impress an audience so that it will provide the positive consequences one desires. Such a motivational basis implies that the individual must remain highly sensitive and responsive to others' demands in order to achieve desired ends.

The social orientation of strategic self-presenters is diametrically opposed to the approach taken by self-symbolizing individuals. Driven by an implementation motivation, self-symbolizing individuals focus only on demonstrating to others that they are in possession of an intended identity, irrespective of others' wishes, needs, or potential responses. In order to demonstrate that the self-symbolizing individual is not inclined to relate to others in an interpersonally sensitive or responsive manner, it is necessary to show that self-symbolizing does not serve the goals of strategic self-presentation. Therefore, we must examine the extent to which various reasons for engaging in strategic self-presentation (Schneider, 1981) are applicable to self-symbolizing efforts.

Facilitating social interaction. Strategic self-presentation can serve to promote the structuring of a particular social situation, and thus facilitate social interaction. Individuals who find themselves in imprecisely defined social contexts can avoid confusion and embarrassment by projecting images that clearly define what part they choose to play during the course of the interaction (Alexander & Knight, 1971; Goffman, 1955, 1959). In this regard, self-presentations serve to save face, and become even more pronounced when further difficulties in maintaining face are encountered (Modigliani, 1968).

Is this issue of saving face also related to self-symbolizing activities? In view of the third and fourth study described above—where medical students brought their relevant test performances to the attention of the experimenter and where dancers set an early date for a public performance—subjects had good reason to feel confused and embarrassed since they had been confronted with an identity-related shortcoming (i.e., relevant negative personality feedback in Study 3; salience of one's worst dancing instructor in Study 4).

Assuming that subjects were, in fact, confused and embarrassed, this does not necessarily imply that their efforts to bring self-symbolizing to the notice of others was in effect an attempt to save face as a medical student or dancer, respectively. Since great care was taken in both of these studies to place the experience of the identity-related shortcoming and the opportunity for self-symbolizing into two different and independent social contexts, those who took notice of self-symbolizing efforts had not witnessed the individual losing face. Therefore, one can confidently rule out the possibility that self-symbolizing subjects behaved the way they did out of a concern with saving face, for this can only be accomplished by relating to others who have witnessed one's "losing face."

Acquiring social approval. Individuals may apply strategic self-presentation in the interest of acquiring social approval, or of avoiding disapproval by a particular target person (Schlenker, 1980). Accordingly, individuals tend to claim possession of personal qualities that are socially desirable (e.g., being smart, likeable, or easy to get along with), and reject qualities that are socially undesirable (e.g., being aggressive, egoistic, or unfriendly). In the interest of assuring a positive evaluation by the target person, maximal responsiveness to the target person's requests is exhibited. In the event that the targets of self-presentation actually specify the attributes they find desirable, individuals tend to describe themselves in the manner specified, even when these qualities are socially undesirable (Gergen & Wishnov, 1965; Schneider & Eustis, 1972). Failure to impress the target person is met with further self-presentational efforts aimed at the same target person and designed to counter initial disapproval (Schneider, 1969). The self-presenter aiming at social approval must, however, refrain from inconsistent self-presentations in order to avoid the possibility that the target person identifies the self-presenter as a dishonest person—an obviously undesirable personal quality (Baumeister & Jones, 1978; Schlenker, 1975).

Does self-symbolizing potentially serve the goal of winning social approval? The results of three experiments clearly demonstrate that self-symbolizing efforts actually lead to a neglect of the thoughts and feelings of others, a phenomenon certainly not conducive to gaining social approval. In the first experiment (Gollwitzer & Wicklund, 1985a; Study 1), female undergraduates committed to the identity of career women were subjected to a manipulation of their sense of possessing this identity. They were informed that their personality either did or did not predestine them to success with respect to becoming a career woman. Within a different social context, subjects were then grouped into pairs (i.e., subjects who had received negative personality feedback with partner subjects who had received positive personality feedback) and told to cooperate with each other in creating positive self-descriptions related either to the intended identity or to an identity to which they did not feel committed.

When the self-descriptions to be created were related to the identity as a career woman, subjects who had received negative personality feedback dominated the interaction by producing more positive self-descriptive statements than their partner subjects. Even though dominating the interaction meant running the risk of being considered egocentric and noncooperative by the partner subject—attributes that are not met with social approval—the negative identity-relevant personality feedback evidently compelled subjects to neglect any concerns with acquiring social approval. Apparently, an orientation toward self-symbolizing provoked by the negative personality feedback suppressed any such concerns.

In order to explore this issue further, a second study was conducted (Gollwitzer & Wicklund, 1985a, Study 2). Male undergraduates committed to various athletic identities (e.g., swimmer, tennis player) were first subjected to a personality-feedback manipulation similar to that employed in the previous study. In an allegedly independent second experiment, subjects were then instructed to describe their present identity-related status to an attractive female target person, this after having been informed about the female's preference for either self-deprecating or self-aggrandizing self-descriptions.

Our results revealed that both positive and negative personality feedback subjects followed the self-presentational cues set by the target person. However, negative feedback subjects showed significantly less readiness to follow the cue to be self-deprecating than did positive feedback subjects. Obviously, a strong orientation toward self-symbolizing, resulting from identity-relevant negative personality feedback, compelled these subjects to disregard the cue to be self-deprecating, even though responding to this cue would actually have provided them with approval from the target person.

Finally, in a third study on this issue (Gollwitzer, 1984), subjects committed to various academic identities (e.g., mathematician, biologist) were confronted with a situation in which they expected to get to know a partner subject through an informal conversation. Each subject was told that the partner subject had already indicated topic preferences in preparation for the upcoming conversation. These preferences expressed a definite disinterest in mathematics or biology, respectively, in favor of other conversational topics. As in the previous experiment, the subjects' sense of possessing the intended academic identity was then manipulated (in this case via a salience of worst teacher manipulation, as in the study with dancers reported above). Thereafter, the subjects' propensity to suggest an academic conversational topic related to their intended identity was measured. Consistent with the results of the two preceding studies, subjects whose sense of possessing the intended identity had been undermined consistently proposed topics related to their academic commitment. Apparently, an orientation toward self-symbolizing compelled subjects to disregard the expressed topic preferences of the partner subject, even though this meant risking being disliked by the partner subject.

The results of these three studies thus strongly suggest that self-symbolizing activities do not serve the goal of winning social approval, but rather appear to suppress such concerns.

Controlling others' actions. Strategic self-presentation can serve the goal of winning control over another person's actions. By projecting a certain image, self-presenters can attempt to compel the target person to behave in a manner that serves their interests (Jones, 1964; Jones & Pittman, 1982). The choice of image (e.g., likable, dangerous, competent, moral, or helpless) depends on the instrumentality of that image for bringing about desired ends. In order to gain admission to a prestigious college, for example, one should fare better by projecting an image of competence rather than helplessness. However, if one seeks to be treated supportively by one's fellow colleagues, it could prove more advantageous to present an image of helplessness rather than competence. In any event, the images employed are not determined by the simple desire or need to be perceived as likable, competent, and so forth, but rather by the instrumentality of those images, that is, by their suitability for bringing about desired ends.

Do self-symbolizing individuals take the instrumentality of their efforts into consideration, with respect to controlling an audience's actions? In view of the finding that self-symbolizing individuals did not capitalize on the self-deprecating self-presentational cues set by an attractive female (Gollwitzer & Wicklund, 1985a), it seems unlikely that an interest in acquiring influence over the female's actions was a motivating force. The same holds true for the results of the experiment in which the partner subject's conversational topic preference was disregarded by the self-symbolizing individual (Gollwitzer, 1984). If the self-symbolizing individuals had actually been concerned with encouraging the partner subject to converse productively with them, they would have surely taken the partner subject's topic preference into consideration. Thus, it seems justified to assume that, in both studies, self-symbolizing individuals did not take the instrumentality of their actions into account, with respect to bringing about such ends as getting along with an attractive female or with a conversation partner.

Summary. The preceding discussion suggests that self-symbolizing does not serve the kinds of goals that guide strategic self-presentation. Apparently, self-symbolizing individuals relate to others in a manner that is strikingly *nonstrategic*. With few exceptions, modern day social psychology has completely ignored such *non*strategic self-presentation, in favor of the strategic aspects relevant to presenting one's self to others. Baumeister (1982), however, points out that one may turn to others in the interest of projecting an image that incorporates one's own personal goals and ideals (self-constructive self-presentation). Since these goals can be assumed to remain relatively *stable* over time and across social contexts, constructive self-presentation is said to be frequently in conflict with *strategic* self-presentational concerns, aimed at either pleasing an immediate audience or controlling an audience's short-term or long-term actions. Clearly, self-symbolizing is self-constructive self-presentation, since it not only furnishes people with a feeling of possessing an intended identity, but also reveals a lack of strategic concerns with respect to the way in which one relates to others.

Conclusion

Individual conceptions of identity goals are found to be located on the plane of social reality. This implies that people striving for identity goals need to make their self-symbolizing efforts known to others in order to achieve a sense of goal attainment. An analysis of the motivational basis of self-symbolizing reveals that once people have committed themselves to the attainment of a certain identity, an orientation toward social implementation of that identity prevails. Fundamentally different from strategic approaches to addressing others that focus on either pleasing others or controlling their actions, the social implementation of identity goals represents a markedly nonstrategic way of relating to others. Self-symbolizing is nevertheless self-constructive for it facilitates the development of a sense of possessing the intended identity.

Acknowledgments. I would like to thank Jürgen Beckmann, Martina Eckert, Heinz Heckhausen, Stefan Hormuth, Robert A. Wicklund, and in particular Ronald F. Kinney for their insightful comments.

References

Alexander, C.N., & Knight, G. (1971). Situated identities and social psychological experimentation. *Sociometry, 34,* 65–82.

Baumeister, R.F. (1982). A self-presentational view of social phenomena. *Psychological Bulletin, 91,* 3–26.

Baumeister, R.F., & Jones, E.E. (1978). When self-presentation is constrained by the target's knowledge: Consistency and compensation. *Journal of Personality and Social Psychology, 36,* 608–618.

Blumberg, H.H. (1972). Communication of interpersonal evaluations. *Journal of Personality and Social Psychology, 23,* 157–162.

Cooley, C.H. (1902). *Human nature and the social order.* New York: Scribner.

Gergen, K.J., & Wishnov, B. (1965). Others' self-evaluations and interaction anticipation as determinants of self-presentation. *Journal of Personality and Social Psychology, 2,* 348–358.

Goffman, E. (1955). On facework. *Psychiatry, 18,* 213–231.

Goffman, E. (1959). *The presentation of self in everyday life.* Garden City, NJ: Doubleday.

Gollwitzer, P.M. (1984, April). *Striving for social recognition as a consequence of self-definitional concerns.* Paper presented at the annual meeting of the Eastern Psychological Association, Baltimore, MD.

Gollwitzer, P.M. (1986a). *Public vs. private self-symbolizing.* Unpublished manuscript, Max-Planck-Institute for Psychological Research, Munich, FRG.

Gollwitzer, P.M. (1986b). The vices and virtues of identity commitments. In F. Halisch & J. Kuhl (Eds.), *Motivation, intention, and volition.* New York: Springer.

Gollwitzer, P.M., & Wicklund, R.A. (1985a). Self-symbolizing and the neglect of other's perspectives. *Journal of Personality and Social Psychology, 48,* 702–715.

Gollwitzer, P.M., & Wicklund, R.A. (1985b). The pursuit of self-defining goals. In J. Kuhl & J. Beckmann (Eds.), *Action control: From cognitions to behavior* (pp. 61–85). New York: Springer.

Gollwitzer, P.M., Wicklund, R.A., & Hilton, J.L. (1982). Admission of failure and symbolic self-completion: Extending Lewinian theory. *Journal of Personality and Social Psychology, 43,* 358–371.

Haas, H.I., & Maehr, M.L. (1965). Two experiments on the concept of self and the reactions of others. *Journal of Personality and Social Psychology, 1,* 100–105.

Heckhausen, H. (1985, June). *Why some time-out might benefit achievement motivation research.* Invited address to a symposium entitled "Achievement and Task Motivation," Nijmegen, The Netherlands.

Heckhausen, H., & Gollwitzer, P.M. (1986). Information processing before and after the formation of an intent. In F. Klix & H. Hagendorf (Eds.), *In memoriam Hermann Ebbinghaus: Symposium on structure and function of human memory.* Amsterdam: Elsevier/North Holland.

Heckhausen, H., & Kuhl, J. (1985). From wishes to action: The dead ends and short-cuts on the long way to action. In M. Frese & J. Sabini (Eds.), *Goal-directed behavior: Psychological theory and research on action.* Hillsdale, NJ: Erlbaum.

Hovland, C.I., & Rosenberg, M.J. (1960). *Attitude organization and change.* New Haven, CT: Yale University Press.

Inkeles, A. (1968). Society, social structure, and child socialization. In J.A. Clausen (Ed.), *Socialization and society.* Boston: Little, Brown.

Jones, E.E. (1964). *Ingratiation.* New York: Irvington Publishers, Inc.

Jones, E.E., & Pittman, T.S. (1982). Toward a general theory of strategic self-presentation. In J. Suls (Ed.), *Psychological perspectives on the self.* Hillsdale, NJ: Erlbaum.

Lewin, K. (1926). Vorsatz, Wille und Bedürfnis. [Intention, will, and need.] *Psychologische Forschung, 7,* 330–385.

Lissner, K. (1933). Die Entspannung von Bedürfnissen durch Ersatzhandlungen. [The satisfaction of needs by means of substitute actions.] *Psychologische Forschung, 18,* 218–250.

Maehr, M.L., Mensing, J., & Nafzger, S. (1962). Concept of self and the reaction of others. *Sociometry, 25*, 353–357.

Mahler, W. (1933). Ersatzhandlungen verschiedenen Realitätsgrades. [Substitute actions at various levels of reality.] *Psychologische Forschung, 18*, 27–89.

Mead, G.H. (1934). *Mind, self, and society.* Chicago: University of Chicago Press.

Modigliani, A. (1968). Embarrassment and embarrassability. *Sociometry, 31*, 313–326.

Ovsiankina, M. (1928). Die Wiederaufnahme unterbrochener Handlungen. [The resumption of interrupted activities.] *Psychologische Forschung, 11*, 302–379.

Schlenker, B.R. (1975). Self-presentation: Managing the impression of consistency when reality interferes with self-enhancement. *Journal of Personality and Social Psychology, 32*, 1030–1037.

Schlenker, B.R. (1980). *Impression management: The self-concept, social identity, and interpersonal relations.* Monterey, CA: Brooks/Cole.

Schneider, D.J. (1969). Tactical self-presentation after success and failure. *Journal of Personality and Social Psychology, 13*, 262–268.

Schneider, D.J. (1981). Tactical self-presentations: Toward a broader conception. In J.T. Tedeschi (Ed.), *Impression management theory and social psychological research.* New York: Academic Press.

Schneider, D.J., & Eustis, A.C. (1972). Effects of ingratiation motivation, target positiveness, and revealingness on self-presentation. *Journal of Personality and Social Psychology, 22*, 149–155.

Tedeschi, J.T. (1974). *Perspectives on social power.* Chicago: Aldine.

Tesser, A., & Rosen, S. (1975). The reluctance to transmit bad news. In L. Berkowitz (ed.), *Advances in experimental social psychology* (Vol. 8). New York: Academic Press.

Videbeck, R. (1960). Self-conceptions and the reactions of others. *Sociometry, 23*, 351–359.

Webster, M.J., & Sobieszek, B. (1974). *Sources of self-evaluation.* New York: Wiley.

Wicklund, R.A., & Gollwitzer, P.M. (1981). Symbolic self-completion, attempted influence, and self-deprecation. *Basic and Applied Social Psychology, 2*, 89–114.

Wicklund, R.A., & Gollwitzer, P.M. (1982). *Symbolic self-completion.* Hillsdale, NJ: Erlbaum.

Wicklund, R.A., & Gollwitzer, P.M. (1983). A motivational factor in self-report validity. In J. Suls & A.G. Greenwald (Eds.), *Psychological perspectives on the self* (Vol. 2). Hillsdale, NJ: Erlbaum.

Chapter 8
Competence and Excuse-Making as Self-Presentational Strategies

George I. Whitehead, III and Stephanie H. Smith

Self-presentation is a communicative act in which people convey a particular image of themselves to others, verbally or nonverbally. Research on self-presentation generally manipulates the public or private nature of responses such that a public response is one that people anticipate presenting to others, and a private response is one that people do not anticipate presenting to anyone connected with the experiment. If the responses differ, it is presumed that public responses are affected by self-presentational concerns (Baumeister, 1982). Although there are other methodologies employed in research on self-presentation (see Tetlock & Manstead, 1985), this is the methodology employed in the research presented here.

Regardless of the public or private nature of responses, people attempt to present a desirable image and disclaim an undesirable image (Schlenker, 1980). In private, people are concerned with intrapersonal self-image management. That is, they want to have a positive image of themselves. In public, however, people are concerned with social impression management. That is, they want others to have a positive impression of them (Greenwald, 1982). To be sure, there are individual differences in personality characteristics such as social anxiety and self-esteem that can influence people to choose to project self-deprecating images rather than self-enhancing ones (Cheek & Hogan, 1983). Furthermore, there are the undesirable traits of intimidation and supplication that people may present publicly (Jones & Pittman, 1982). However, most research on self-presentation has examined people's desire to present themselves in a favorable manner.

In this chapter we examine the role of self-presentation in the maintenance of positive self-images. First, we present strategies people employ to maintain positive self-images in public and in private. Then, we present research that tests the use of these strategies in people's judgments of similarity and social comparison, beneffectance, and self- and other evaluations. Finally, we examine gender differences in the utilization of these self-presentational strategies.

Self-Image-Maintaining Strategies
in Public and Private

One strategy people employ to maintain a favorable self-image both privately and publicly is to claim competency (or to claim similarity to competent others). In private, this strategy primarily serves self-esteem needs. In public, however, additional self-presentational motives may serve to enhance the use of this strategy. Thus, people in public may claim greater competency and/or greater similarity to competent others than may people in private.

When people are faced with unfavorable feedback about performance, their positive self-images are threatened. Self-presentational concerns determine how threats to self-image are handled. In private, people are primarily motivated to restore their positive self-images. One strategy they employ is to make excuses for their poor performances. If they can excuse poor performances, they can feel better in the face of unfavorable feedback. In public, however, self-presentational concerns may inhibit excuse making for poor performances. Publicly, people are concerned with maintaining an impression of competence to others, and may feel that they are not maintaining an image of competence if they engage in public excuse making.

Research on beneffectance and self-and other evaluations has demonstrated that people use consensus-raising excuses to account for poor performances in private, whereas in public they do not. Consensus-raising excuses consist of claims that everyone would perform as poorly as they did—for example, attributions to task difficulty ("this task is so difficult, everyone would have failed") or projection ("everyone scores low on this particular trait"). Such excuses do not contribute to a public image of competence, and people may not use these types of excuses in public for fear that the audience may know that everyone else did not perform as poorly as they did. On the other hand, in private, where self-presentational concerns are absent, these consensus-raising excuses allow people to feel better about negative outcomes (restore their positive self-images) by claiming that others also received negative outcomes.

One question that arises about the utilization of these self-image maintaining strategies is the generality of their usage by both genders. That is, are men and women equally motivated to present themselves as more competent publicly than they do privately? Some research demonstrating a more modest self-presentation by women than by men suggests that they are not (Gould & Slone, 1982). Also, do men and women both excuse poor performances in private, but not in public? Another consideration is the conditions under which gender differences are manifested.

A final question concerns the conditions in which other motives take precedence over self-presentational ones. For example, when people are faced with ambiguous feedback about their performances, and thus are uncertain about the interpretation, might not information-seeking motives take precedence over self-presentational ones? Research demonstrating that under these circumstances people are more motivated by information-seeking than self-presentational concerns is presented throughout the chapter.

Maintaining Self-Image Through Judgments
of Similarity and Social Comparison

The proposition that people present themselves as more competent in public than in private has implications for research that asks subjects to indicate the person to whom their performance on a task is most similar. Thus, we (Whitehead & Smith, 1985) conducted an investigation to determine the impact of self-presentational concerns on judgment of similarity. Specifically, we predicted that if self-presentational concerns do enhance people's desire to present themselves as competent then more people should judge their performance to be similar to that of a more competent person in public than in private.

This prediction concerning people's judgments of similarity raises a question about the scores subjects choose for comparison. Festinger's (1954) social comparison theory proposes a positive relationship between judgments of similarity and comparison choices. According to Festinger, people have a need to know the correctness of their opinions and abilities. Consequently, people seek objective nonsocial means for self-evaluation. If this information is not available, people will seek social means for comparison. According to Festinger, people compare their abilities with those of similar others, and particularly, more competent others. This tendency to compare with more competent others is referred to as the "unidirectional drive upward."

A self-presentational approach would also suggest a positive relationship between judgments of similarity and comparison choices, but for a different reason. If people want to demonstrate competence to others, they should compare upward. In that way, they are giving the impression that they believe their performances to be not too different from the performance of a more competent person. A choice downward would not provide an impression of competence. Instead, downward comparison may serve functions unrelated to self-presentational concerns, such as enhancing subjective well-being (Wills, 1981) or protecting the self against threat (Taylor, 1983).

The seminal experiment demonstrating the unidirectional drive upward in social comparison was conducted by Wheeler (1966). In his study, Wheeler found that a majority of people evidenced a unidirectional drive upward: They chose a higher ranked person's score for comparison, and judged their own score to be similar to that of a higher ranked other.

In order to ascertain the impact of self-presentational concerns on judgments of similarity and comparison choices, Whitehead and Smith (1985) replicated Wheeler's (1966) study with the additional manipulation of the expected public or private nature of subjects' responses. We predicted that both privately and publicly people employ the strategy of appearing competent in order to maintain a favorable self-image. However, in private the appearance of competence primarily helps people maintain a positive self-image, whereas in public people are additionally concerned with presenting a positive image to others. Thus, self-presentational concerns enhance people's desire to appear competent. This logic leads to two hypotheses. First, more subjects should judge their performances to be similar to that of a more competent person in public than in private. Second, subjects should choose to compare their performances with that of a more competent person more often in public than in private.

In our study, subjects in groups of 7 took a bogus social sensitivity test (Social Perceptiveness Scale; SPS) that was adapted from one used by Wortman, Costanzo, and Witt (1973). Subjects were told that the SPS is a well-established test that has been administered to well over 100,000 people in various walks of life, and that high scores on the SPS are positively correlated with other characteristics such as intelligence. After taking the test, subjects received bogus feedback indicating that their score ranked 4th in the group. They were told that the scores of the people ranked just above and below them were similar to theirs, and were given a range of possible values for the extreme scores. Subjects were then asked to indicate the rank of the person whose score they thought to be the most similar to their own, and the rank of the person whose score they would like to see first and second. The expected public or private nature of responses was manipulated in the following manner. Subjects in private conditions were told to take their responses to someone in another room who knew nothing about the study, and that person would give them the scores they wanted to see. Subjects in public conditions were told that they would have to announce their responses to the group.

As predicted, subjects' judgments of similarity were affected by self-presentational concerns. When subjects expected their responses to become public, 85% indicated that their performances were similar to that of a higher ranked person. When subjects expected their responses to remain private, 71% indicated that their performances were similar to that of a higher ranked person. As predicted, then, more subjects judged their performances to be similar to that of a higher ranked person when they expected their judgments to become public than when they expected them to remain private. In private, where self-presentational concerns are absent, fewer subjects judged their performances to be similar to that of a higher ranked person. This finding confirms the proposition that (public) self-presentational concerns enhance people's use of the self-image-maintaining strategy of presenting themselves as competent.

Whether subjects expected their responses to remain private or to be made public affected similarity judgments but not comparison choices. Thus, comparison choices were not affected by self-presentational concerns. Instead, they seem to have been influenced by information-seeking motives. Most of the subjects engaged in range seeking; that is, they first chose to see the score of the person ranked first, and second chose to see the score of the person ranked last. This range seeking is consistent with previous research using the rank-order paradigm (see Wheeler et al., 1969).

The results of our investigation raise two questions. First, why did we find the predicted impact of the public/private variable on judgments of similarity but not comparison choices? The answer may be that the former are more sensitive to self-presentational concerns than are the latter. That is, the choices of a person to whose performance subjects judge their performances similar may reveal more about subjects' perceptions of their standing on a trait than would the choice of a person's score they would like to see. As a self-presentational strategy, then, subjects may have focused more on presenting themselves favorably in their judgments of similarity to a higher ranked person than in their comparison choices.

The second question is: Why did we find such strong evidence for range seeking in comparison choices? In our study, subjects used their choices of a comparison other as an information-seeking strategy rather than a self-presentational one. The reason for this may have been a function of subjects' certainty of scores at various ranks. To understand the importance of subjects' certainty of scores, let us examine the manipulations employed in various studies using this rank-order paradigm. Wheeler et al. (1969) found greater range seeking when subjects were not presented with the range than when they were presented with the range of scores. In the latter situation, when subjects were more certain of the range of scores, they chose to compare their performances with those of similar others. Furthermore, research by Wheeler, Koestner, and Driver (1982) suggested that range seeking is reduced when the exact scores of the extreme ranks are given to subjects.

In the present study, subjects were given a range of possible values for the extreme scores, rather than the exact scores. In addition, subjects were told that the scores of the people ranked just above and below them were similar to theirs. Thus, subjects may have been more certain of the scores of people holding similar rather than extreme ranks, and were therefore motivated to range seek. This interpretation is consistent with research by Gruder, Korth, Dichtel, and Glos (1975) showing that people choose extreme scores for comparison when they are less certain of them. It appears that comparison choices serve information-seeking functions when people are uncertain about the range of scores, whereas judgments of similarity serve self-presentational functions. Whether comparison choices might serve self-presentational functions when people are certain about the range of scores remains to be tested.

In general, then, our investigation supports the proposition that people more often present themselves as competent in public than in private. Specifically, more people judged their performances as similar to that of a higher ranked person when they expected their responses to be made public than to remain private. This pattern of self-enhancement was demonstrated on judgments of similarity but not comparison choices. Thus, judgments of similarity were related to self-presentational concerns, whereas comparison choices were related to informational concerns.

Expectations of Future Interaction

Other research has identified certain conditions in which comparison choices are affected by self-presentational concerns. For example, Wheeler et al. (1969) found that, when people expect to engage in future interaction, they are motivated to behave in a more modest way because their failure on the future task is possible. Thus, Wheeler et al. told subjects either that they would have a future interaction on a different task with the person with whom they chose to compare their performance (public manipulation), or that they could only look at the score of the person they chose (private manipulation). In a reanalysis of Wheeler et al.'s data, Arrowood and Friend (1969) reported that subjects chose the best score for comparison more often in private than in public conditions. When people expect future interaction, then, the unidirectional drive upward may be tempered because people do not want to risk presenting themselves as competent only to have this favorable self-appraisal invalidated. Thus, public self-presentations of competence depend on whether people expect to engage in future interaction. When they do not expect future interaction, people present themselves as competent. When they expect future interaction, however, and thus face potential failure on a future task, they present themselves modestly. It stands to reason that as people's confidence in their performance on a future task increases, their motivation to present themselves modestly would lessen.

Maintaining Self-Image Through Beneffectance

A substantial body of literature demonstrates that people tend to make greater self-attributions for their positive than negative behavioral outcomes (e.g., Bradley, 1978; Miller, 1976; Smith & Whitehead, 1984; Snyder, Stephan, & Rosenfield, 1978; Whitehead & Smith, 1984). People tend to attribute their successes to internal factors (ability and effort), and their failures to external factors (task difficulty and luck). In one such study, Smith and Whitehead (1984) administered a social sensitivity test to black and white college students, and gave them bogus feedback indicating that they had either succeeded or failed on the test. Subjects subsequently indicated to what degree they believed their successes or failures were due to ability, effort, task difficulty, and luck. Both races attributed their successes to internal factors, and their failures to external factors. This effect is not limited to college students. Frieze and Bar-Tal (1976) found that fourth through 12th graders were more likely to attribute their successes to ability and effort, whereas they attributed their failures to task difficulty.

This general pattern of results is prevalent in research on self-attributions, and has been referred to as the self-serving attributional bias by some researchers (e.g., Weary & Arkin, 1981), and beneffectance by others (Greenwald, 1982). Although the phenomenon is well established, the reasons for it are not (see Tetlock & Levi, 1982).

One explanation for beneffectance involves the need for self-esteem. According to this position, people need to protect and enhance their feelings of personal worth and competence. Thus, to the extent that feedback about outcomes is important to people's self-evaluations, they will attribute favorable outcomes to internal factors and unfavorable outcomes to external factors.

Tetlock and Levi (1982) pointed out that, although superficially there is overwhelming support for this self-esteem hypothesis, most of the studies are open to a cognitive explanation involving information processing (see Miller & Ross, 1975). Although the cognitive explanation proposed by Miller and Ross prompted attempts to find stronger evidence for the self-esteem position, no studies have decisively established a self-esteem-motivated bias (Tetlock & Levi, 1982). This failure has led some to conclude that the cognitive and self-esteem explanations are indistinguishable. However, it may be that both are important and that we have not yet specified the conditions under which each process operates.

A third explanation for beneffectance maintains that people often communicate attributions that are designed to gain public approval and to avoid embarrassment (see Arkin, Appelman, & Burger, 1980; Bradley, 1978; Tetlock, 1980). This self-presentation position leads to the prediction that concern for social approval is a more potent determinant of public than of private attributions (see Bradley, 1978). It is difficult to predict, however, exactly how the need for social approval affects attributions.

Weary and Arkin (1981) argued that beneffectance may be greater in private than in public because people in public become concerned that (a) they will have to defend their unrealistically positive self-presentations and/or (b) their attributions could be invalidated by others' present or future assessments of their behaviors. At least two experiments do demonstrate greater beneffectance in private than in public (Greenberg, Pyszczynski, & Solomon, 1982; Weary et al., 1982), although the effect is not necessarily because of the reason offered by Weary and Arkin. In this regard, Riess, Rosenfield, Melburg, and Tedeschi (1981) found that beneffectance is a real perceptual distortion that is open to self-presentational concerns.

In examining how self-presentational concerns may contribute to the greater beneffectance usually found in private than public, it is important to note that this finding is stronger for unfavorable than favorable outcomes (Greenberg et al., 1982; Weary et al., 1982). Work by Snyder, Higgins, and Stucky (1983) on excuse making and self-deception sheds light on the underlying processes. According to their analysis, people are motivated to make excuses when they feel high personal responsibility for their negative performances because such outcomes shake their positive image of themselves. One way people can lessen personal responsibility for negative performances, and thus maintain a positive self-image, is to make external attributions to task difficulty or luck.

According to our self-presentational analysis, this process of excuse making for unfavorable outcomes is exactly what people do in private, where self-presentational concerns are absent. People in private are not concerned with maintaining a public image of competence. Rather, they are concerned with maintaining a positive self-image. When faced with negative performance outcomes in private, then, people's positive self-images are threatened. They are therefore motivated to maintain their self-esteem and employ a strategy of making consensus-raising excuses for their poor performances. People typically do this by attributing their performances to external factors ("This task is so difficult, everyone would have failed").

When responses are to become public, however, self-presentational concerns are salient. People are concerned with maintaining a public image of competence. When faced with negative performance outcomes in public, people do not want to give the impression that they are less than competent. They refrain from using consensus-raising excuses because of the possibility that the audience has knowledge of others' performances ("We know everyone didn't fail this test"). To preclude the possibility of refutation, then, people temper their use of consensus-raising excuses in public.

This strategy helps them maintain a public image of competence in the face of unfavorable feedback.

The above analysis deals with how people cope with unfavorable feedback when their responses are public and private. Recall that the strongest self-presentational effects are found when people receive unfavorable rather than favorable feedback (Greenberg et al., 1982; Weary et al., 1982). One reason for this effect may be that people are more motivated to explain unfavorable than favorable feedback. Perhaps people place more weight on negative than on positive information in forming impressions of themselves, just as they do in forming impressions of others (Fiske, 1980). Thus, people receiving negative performance feedback are motivated in private to restore their positive self-images by making excuses for poor performances, and in public to restore their public images of competence by not making excuses. One of the reasons why favorable feedback may not produce strong self-presentational effects, then, is because people are not as motivated to explain it as they are to explain unfavorable feedback.

Another reason why reactions to favorable performance feedback are less affected by the public or private nature of responses may be because there are two competing self-presentational motives in public. On the one hand, people are motivated to present themselves as competent in public, and might therefore be expected to take personal credit for success. On the other hand, it is not considered socially desirable to claim too much credit for success in public. Therefore, people might want to make more modest attributions for success. This desire to take credit for successes in public may be countered by the tendency to appear modest in public, thereby resulting in the lack of differences between public and private responses to favorable performance feedback.

An Investigation of the Impact of Self-Presentational Concerns on Beneffectance

To test our self-presentational analysis, we (Whitehead & Smith, 1984) conducted an experiment with a methodology similar to the one employed by Greenberg et al. Thus, subjects received bogus favorable or unfavorable performance feedback. We predicted that, in private, people receiving unfavorable feedback would be more motivated to restore their positive self-images by making consensus-raising excuses for poor performance than would people receiving favorable feedback. We predicted that publicly, however, people concerned with maintaining a public image of competence would temper their use of consensus-raising excuses in the face of unfavorable feedback when compared to people receiving favorable feedback. Furthermore, because of the stronger motivation to explain unfavorable feedback and because of the competing self-presentational motives that operate with favorable feedback in public, the publicness of subjects' responses should have the strongest effect with unfavorable feedback.

Subjects took a test supposedly measuring their social sensitivity, and received bogus feedback indicating that they scored in the 80th percentile (favorable feedback), or the 20th percentile (unfavorable feedback). On the dependent measures, subjects made attributions for their performances to ability, effort, task difficulty, and luck. They also indicated how socially perceptive they thought they were. In private conditions, subjects sealed their responses in envelopes they were told would be sent to a professor at another university. In public conditions, subjects were led to believe that they would be going over their responses with the experimenter.

Our predictions were supported on subjects' attributions to task difficulty. In private, subjects receiving unfavorable feedback rated the test as more difficult than did subjects receiving favorable feedback. This finding supports our proposition that when people receive unfavorable feedback in private they are motivated to restore their self-images by making consensus-raising excuses for poor performances. In this case they used the consensus-raising excuse of task difficulty ("This test is so difficult, everyone does poorly on it"). In public, however, subjects' attributions to task difficulty were unaffected by the favorability of the feedback. This finding supports our proposition that people in public do not engage in consensus-raising excuse making for poor performances. Finally, subjects receiving unfavorable feedback in private rated the test as more difficult than did those receiving unfavorable feedback in public. That is, subjects engaged in consensus-raising excuse making for poor performances in private but not in public. As predicted, subjects' attributions to task difficulty were not affected by the public or private nature of responses when they received favorable feedback.

Significant results were also found on the measure assessing subjects' ratings of their social perceptiveness. In private, subjects receiving unfavorable feedback indicated that they were less socially perceptive than did subjects receiving favorable feedback. In public, subjects' ratings of their social perceptiveness were unaffected by the favorability of the feedback. Subjects receiving unfavorable feedback also evaluated their social perceptiveness as lower in private than in public. Subjects receiving favorable feedback showed no difference between public and private responding. These findings suggest the possibility that subjects publicly engaged in a type of excuse making in which they reframed their performance. According to Snyder et al. (1983), this excuse involves claiming not to comprehend the negativity of the performance ("My performance didn't appear so bad to me").

The only other significant effects were on the measure assessing ratings of the accuracy of the test. On this measure, we found a main effect for the favorability of the outcome, such that subjects receiving unfavorable outcomes rated the test as less accurate than did subjects receiving favorable outcomes. There were no effects of the publicness manipulation on this measure. This measure assessed perceptions of the validity of the test. Both publicly and privately, subjects receiving unfavorable feedback derogated the test. Snyder et al. (1983) term this excuse another way of reframing performance.

Publicly, then, people utilize excuses involving reframing performance (claiming not to comprehend the negativity of the performance, and derogating the source of the feedback) and do not utilize consensus-raising excuses ("The task was so difficult, everyone would have failed"). The former involve claims about subjective feelings, and the latter involve claims about others. Since people's subjective feelings are less likely to be refuted by an audience than are their claims about others, performance-reframing excuses are utilized in public to maintain an image of competence, whereas consensus-raising excuses are reserved for use in private, where people are not concerned with the possibility of refutation.

On the whole, our beneffectance study supports our self-presentational analysis. As predicted, self-presentational effects were strongest with unfavorable rather than favorable feedback. Our findings are consistent with our analysis that, in private, people strive to maintain positive self-images by making consensus-raising excuses for poor performances. In public, on the other hand, people strive to maintain an image of competence before others. They do so by inhibiting their use of consensus-raising excuses involving claims about others. Instead, they make excuses involving claims about their own subjective feelings, such as reframing performance ("I don't feel that my performance was bad").

Maintaining Self-Image Through Projection

Projection can be viewed as a consensus-raising excuse for poor performance (Snyder et al., 1983). That is, one way people can deny personal responsibility for a poor rating (and feel better about themselves) is to project their rating onto others ("Everyone scores low on this trait"). Thus, people may excuse poor performances on personality tests by claiming that everyone scores low on that particular trait. We argue that projection as a consensus-raising excuse for poor performances is used more in private than in public. In public, people are less likely to use this type of excuse because an audience might have information about how others scored.

One area of research that has investigated the use of projection is self- and other-evaluations. In research on self-evaluations (e.g., Eagly & Whitehead, 1972; Steiner, 1968), subjects typically take a test that purportedly measures some aspect of their personality. They then receive bogus favorable or unfavorable feedback that includes their supposed score on the test, as well as a written evaluation of that aspect of their personality. In these studies, the feedback is pretested to ensure that the favorable and unfavorable messages are equally discrepant from the subjects' self-concepts. This procedure negates Snyder and Clair's (1977) argument that people may accept favorable more than unfavorable feedback because the former is less discrepant from people's self-concepts than is the latter. After receiving feedback, subjects rate themselves and others on the aspect of their personality evaluated by the feedback. Findings on these measures tend to demonstrate that both self- and other-evaluations are ways of dealing with negative performance feedback (Eagly & Whitehead, 1972; Steiner, 1968).

Steiner (1968) conducted an investigation in which subjects changed their self-evaluations more toward the favorable than the unfavorable feedback. Steiner assessed both subjects' self-evaluations on general aspects of personality and their other evaluations (projection). On this measure of projection, subjects indicated the rating they believed the average student in the experiment would receive on each of these general aspects of personality Although subjects receiving negative feedback did not change their self-evaluations, they did project the negative evaluation onto others by lowering their ratings of the average student's standing on the trait. Steiner explains this finding in terms of the unidirectional drive upward. According to this argument, not only will people be more accepting of favorable than unfavorable feedback, but they will project unfavorable feedback onto others so that, vis-à-vis others, they can maintain the belief that they are comparatively better off. This use of projection then, can be viewed as a coping mechanism by which people can feel better about themselves in relation to others.

We argue that people receiving unfavorable feedback use projection as a consensus-raising excuse only in private. In private, claiming that others performed poorly is a strategy people use to feel better about their own performance. In public, people are less likely to use projection as a consensus-raising excuse because the audience may know that others did not perform poorly. Thus, people receiving unfavorable feedback in public will temper their use of projection.

An Investigation of the Impact of Self-Presentational Concerns on Evaluations of Self and Others

We wanted to investigate the impact of self-presentational concerns on evaluations of self and others (projection) following favorable or unfavorable feedback. To this end, we (Smith & Whitehead, 1986) conducted a replication of the Eagly and Whitehead (1972) study, with the additional manipulation of the expected public or private nature of responses. In this study, groups of 3 to 6 subjects took a series of personality tests. The first two tests purportedly assessed social sensitivity. While subjects filled out long questionnaires containing several other personality tests, the experimenter scored the subjects' first two tests and prepared bogus written feedback. Subjects were then given either favorable, unfavorable, or no feedback concerning their social sensitivity. The feedback messages had been pretested to ensure that the favorable and unfavorable messages were equally discrepant from subjects' self-concepts.

After receiving the feedback, subjects were given questionnaires containing the dependent measures. On one item, subjects rated their own social sensitivity as compared to that of other students (self-evaluation measure). On another, subjects rated the social sensitivity of the typical student at the university (projection measure). Subjects in private conditions were told that this questionnaire would be mailed to a professor at another university and would not be seen by anyone on their own campus. They were instructed to place the completed questionnaire in a mailing envelope addressed to that professor, and seal it. Subjects in public conditions, in contrast, were told that, when they finished, each of them would be discussing his or her responses with the experimenter and the rest of the group.

Recall that, according to our self-presentational analysis, people receiving unfavorable feedback make consensus-raising excuses in private, where self-presentational concerns are absent. On the other hand, in public where self-presentational concerns are salient, people receiving unfavorable feedback refrain from using consensus-raising excuses. Applying this analysis to the present study, we predicted that subjects in private, concerned with protecting their self-images, would use the consensus-raising excuse of projecting negative feedback onto others. In this way, they would excuse their low rating on social sensitivity by claiming that everyone is low on social sensitivity. In contrast, we predicted that subjects in public, concerned with maintaining a public image of competence, would not use the consensus-raising excuse of projecting negative feedback onto others.

We had conflicting predictions for the self-evaluation measure. In our beneffectance research, we found evidence of subjects publicly using the excuse of reframing performance. That is, subjects receiving unfavorable feedback publicly claimed not to comprehend the negativity of the performance by not lowering their rating of their social sensitivity. If subjects publicly reframe performance in the present study, they should change their self-evaluations toward the negative feedback less than subjects do in private. On the other hand, in the present study subjects were given much more feedback than they were given in the beneffectance study. That is, not only were they given their percentile on the test, they were also given a paragraph depicting just what the feedback meant. It may be that, in the face of such detailed feedback, subjects publicly are blocked from distorting the negativity of the performance. It would be difficult publicly to claim not to comprehend the negativity of such feedback. If this is the case then there should be no differences in self-evaluation change toward the unfavorable feedback between subjects in public and in private.

The results on the projection measure supported our predictions. In private conditions, subjects receiving unfavorable feedback rated the typical student's social sensitivity significantly lower than did subjects receiving no feedback, whereas subjects receiving favorable feedback did not rate the typical student's social sensitivity significantly higher than did subjects receiving no feedback. Also as predicted, there were no effects for the favorability of the feedback when subjects expected their responses to be made public. Thus, the results on the projection measure support our analysis that people in private use the consensus-raising excuse of projection, whereas people in public do not, presumably because they are mainly concerned with maintaining a public image of competence.

The analysis on the self-evaluation measure revealed a main effect of the favorability of the outcome: Subjects accepted the unfavorable feedback more than the favorable feedback. Thus, subjects receiving unfavorable feedback rated their social sensitivity lower than did subjects receiving no feedback, whereas subjects receiving favorable feedback did not rate their social sensitivity significantly higher than did subjects receiving no feedback.

This finding of greater change toward unfavorable than favorable feedback regardless of the public or private nature of responses is evidence that subjects in public were blocked from distorting the negativity of the feedback. Thus, people publicly refrain from claiming not to comprehend the negativity of their performance when they are given enough feedback to make such a claim ludicrous. Providing people with detailed negative feedback, then, prevents them from reframing performance.

On the whole, the results of our study show that people in public strive to maintain a public image of competence. Making consensus-raising excuses for poor performance does not fit with such an image, and therefore, people do not make them in public. In private, where self-presentational concerns are absent, people do make consensus-raising excuses for poor performance. These excuses help people to maintain a positive self-image by feeling better about poor performance. In this study, people employed the consensus-raising excuse of projecting poor performance onto others ("Everyone scores low on this trait").

Gender

So far, we have made two points. First, people claim greater competency in public than in private. Second, people in public refrain from using consensus-raising excuses for poor performances, whereas people in private do not. The next question we address is the generality of these effects. The impact of the subject's gender needs to be examined because of Lenney's (1977) argument that women are less self-confident than men and Gould and Slone's (1982) finding suggesting that this difference is a result of self-presentation.

Lenney argues that women demonstrate lower self-confidence than men when the task is masculine, when there are social cues present, and when feedback about task performance is not clear-cut. In all of our studies the task was gender neutral and cues about how the subject performed relative to others were present. One of the ways in which our studies differed was in terms of the positivity or negativity of the feedback. In our study on judgments of similarity and social comparison (Whitehead & Smith, 1985) subjects received feedback indicating that they scored at the median, whereas in our studies on beneffectance (Whitehead & Smith, 1984) and projection (Smith & Whitehead, 1986), subjects received more extreme positive or negative feedback.

Consequently, we might have anticipated differences between men and women in their self-presentation of competence because the positivity or negativity of the feedback was not extreme. We would not expect differences between men and women in the use of consensus-raising excuses because the positivity or negativity of the feedback was extreme. This statement does not mean that men and women may not sometimes make different kinds of excuses (Snyder, Ford, & Hunt, 1985). It means only that in our experiments on beneffectance and projection differences were less likely because the feedback was extreme. It may be the case that, when feedback is not extreme, men may publicly present themselves as more competent than do women, and therefore will be less likely to use consensus-raising excuses and more likely to reframe their performances than women. The latter prediction is consistent with data presented by Snyder et al. (1985).

An analysis of subjects' gender in each of our experiments revealed no gender differences. Our failure to find differences between men and women in their judgments of similarity to more competent others led us to reconsider Lenney's argument about social cues. She claims that one way to heighten social cues is to make people feel that they are working under the careful supervision of the experimenter. In our study on judgments of similarity and social comparison, subjects were tested in groups of seven. In a group this size people may not feel that the experimenter is carefully supervising them. Therefore, we replicated our study on judgments of similarity and social comparison, but tested subjects individually. Under these circumstances we hypothesized that men would present themselves as more competent than women. In light of our finding that self-presentational differences occur on a measure of similarity and not comparison choices, we predicted that men more than women would judge themselves to be similar to a more competent other.

In our study (Smith & Whitehead, 1986), males and females individually took the Social Perceptiveness Scale that purportedly assessed their social sensitivity. Subjects were then given bogus feedback about their performance indicating that their score ranked fourth out of the last seven people taking the test. They were told that the scores of the people ranked just above and below them were similar to theirs, and were given a range of possible values for the extreme scores. The experimenter then asked subjects to write the rank of the person whose score they most wanted to see, and to indicate whether they thought that their score (Rank 4) was closer to the score of the person at Rank 3 or Rank 5. The experimenter left the room while the subjects made their responses, and then collected the information upon return.

We found support for our hypothesis of gender differences on judgments of similarity. A large majority of the males judged their performances to be similar to that of a more competent other, whereas females showed no consistent preference in their judgments. Specifically, 87.5% of the males indicated that they thought that their performances were more similar to that of the third- than to the fifth-ranked person. In contrast, only 41.2% of the females indicated that they thought that their performances were more similar to that of the third-ranked than to the fifth-ranked person. Thus, when social cues are heightened and feedback is not extreme, men present themselves as more competent than do women.

Subjects' comparison choices were not as strongly affected by gender as were their judgments of similarity. In fact, subjects' comparison choices evidence range seeking, as they did in the Whitehead and Smith (1985) study. This was probably due to subjects' greater certainty of the similar rather than the extreme scores, as previously discussed. This supports our proposition that information seeking is the primary purpose of subjects' comparison choices.

Conclusion

Our research has shown that people want to appear competent in public more than they do in private. In private people want to have a positive self-image of themselves, whereas in public people also want others to have a positive impression of them. They are concerned with self-presentation so long as information seeking is not salient.

This difference between people publicly wanting others to have a positive impression of them and privately wanting to have a positive impression of themselves affects the kinds of excuses people make when they receive unfavorable feedback. People in private make consensus-raising excuses more than do people in public. Although these excuses protect people's self-images, people publicly refrain from making these excuses because the audience may know that others did not perform poorly or that others do not have the undesirable trait. Under these circumstances the audience could refute their claim, making them look incompetent.

In addition, our research suggests that people in public do not refrain from all excuse making. We found that, when feasible, people reframe their performance by claiming it was not too bad. They may feel that claims about the self are harder for the audience to refute than are claims about others. The former are more subjective than the latter, and hence less likely to be refuted.

In sum, we have demonstrated that people employ a number of self-image-maintaining strategies. Our focus has been exclusively on how self-presentational concerns affect the utilization of these strategies. Throughout the chapter, we have identified a number of issues that need to be addressed by future research. For example, we argue that the refutability of an excuse by the audience is a crucial determinant of its use. If this is the case, when there is little likelihood of refutation in public people may be more likely to use consensus-raising excuses. This and other investigations are necessary to determine the impact of self-presentational concerns on excuse-making strategies.

Acknowledgments. The authors would like to thank Frank Dane, Alice Eagly, Mark Leary, and Marc Riess for their comments on an earlier version of this paper, and Rebecca Maxwell for her assistance in collecting portions of the data.

References

Arkin, R.M., Appelman, A.J., & Burger, J.M. (1980). Social anxiety, self-presentation, and the self-serving bias in causal attribution. *Journal of Personality and Social Psychology, 38*, 23–35.

Arrowood, A.J., & Friend, R. (1969). Other factors determining the choice of a comparison other. *Journal of Experimental Social Psychology, 5*, 233–239.

Baumeister, R.F. (1982). A self-presentational view of social phenomena. *Psychological Bulletin, 91*, 3–26.

Bradley, G. (1978). Self-serving biases in the attribution process: A reexamination of the fact or fiction question. *Journal of Personality and Social Psychology, 36*, 56–71.

Cheek, J.M., & Hogan, R. (1983). Self-concepts, self-presentations, and moral judgments. In J. Suls & A.G. Greenwald (Eds.), *Psychological perspectives on the self* (Vol. 2, pp. 249–273). Hillsdale, NJ: Erlbaum.

Eagly, A.H., & Whitehead, G.I., III. (1972). Effect of choice on receptivity to favorable and unfavorable evaluations of oneself. *Journal of Personality and Social Psychology, 22*, 223–230.

Festinger, L. (1954). A theory of social comparison processes. *Human Relations, 7*, 117–140.

Fiske, S.T. (1980). Attention and weight in person perception: The impact of negative and extreme behavior. *Journal of Personality and Social Psychology, 38*, 889–906.

Frieze, I.H., & Bar-Tal, D. (1976, April). *Developmental trends in information utilization for making causal attributions*. Paper presented at the meeting of the Eastern Psychological Association, New York, NY.

Gould, R.J., & Slone, C.G. (1982). The "feminine modesty" effect: A self-presentational interpretation of sex differences in causal attribution. *Personality and Social Psychology Bulletin, 8*, 477–485.

Greenberg, J., Pyszcznski, T., & Solomon, S. (1982). The self-serving attributional bias: Beyond self-presentation. *Journal of Experimental Social Psychology, 18*, 56–67.

Greenwald, A.G. (1982). Ego task analysis: An integration of research on ego-involvement and self-awareness. In A.H. Hastorf & A.M. Isen (Eds.), *Cognitive social psychology* (pp. 109–147). New York: Elsevier North Holland.

Gruder, C.L., Korth, B., Dichtel, M., & Glos, B. (1975). Uncertainty and social comparison. *Journal of Research in Personality, 9*, 85–95.

Jones, E.E., & Pittman, T.S. (1982). Toward a general theory of strategic self-presentation. In J. Suls (Ed.), *Psychological perspectives on the self* (Vol. 1, pp. 231–262). Hillsdale, NJ: Erlbaum.

Lenney, E. (1977). Women's self-confidence in achievement settings. *Psychological Bulletin, 84*, 1–13.

Miller, D.T. (1976). Ego involvement and attributions for success and failure. *Journal of Personality and Social Psychology, 34*, 901–906.

Miller, D.T., & Ross, M. (1975). Self-serving biases in the attribution of causality: Fact or fiction? *Psychological Bulletin, 82*, 213–225.

Riess, M., Rosenfield, P., Melburg, V., & Tedeschi, J.T. (1981). Self-serving attributions: Biased private perceptions and distorted public descriptions. *Journal of Personality and Social Psychology, 41*, 224–231.

Schlenker, B.R. (1980). *Impression management: The self-concept, social identity, and interpersonal relations.* Monterey, CA: Brooks/Cole.

Smith, S.H., & Whitehead, G.I., III. (1984, April). *The effect of subject's race on judgments of causality for own success and failure.* Paper presented at the meeting of the Southwestern Psychological Association, New Orleans, LA.

Smith, S.H., & Whitehead, G.I., III. (1986, April). *The public and private use of projection.* Paper presented at the meeting of the Eastern Psychological Association, New York, NY.

Smith, S.H., & Whitehead, G.I., III. (1986). The effect of subject's gender on judgments of similarity and choice of a comparison other. *Sex Roles, 14*, 513–518.

Snyder, C.R., & Clair, M.S. (1977). Does insecurity breed acceptance? Effects of trait and situational insecurity on acceptance of positive and negative diagnostic feedback. *Journal of Consulting and Clinical Psychology, 45*, 843–850.

Snyder, C.R., Ford, C.E., & Hunt, H.A. (1985, August). *Excuse-making: A look at sex differences.* Paper presented at the meeting of the American Psychological Association, Los Angeles, CA.

Snyder, C.R., Higgins, R.L., & Stucky, R.J. (1983). *Excuses: Masquerades in search of grace.* New York: John Wiley & Sons.

Snyder, M.L., Stephan, W.G., & Rosenfield, D. (1978). Attributional egotism. In J.H. Harvey, W. Ickes, & R.F. Kidd (Eds.), *New directions in attribution research* (Vol. 2, pp. 91–117). Hillsdale, NJ: Erlbaum.

Steiner, I.D. (1968). Reaction to adverse and favorable evaluations of one's self. *Journal of Personality, 36*, 553–563.

Taylor, S.E. (1983). Adjustment to threatening events: A theory of cognitive adaptation. *American Psychologist, 38*, 1161–1173.

Tetlock, P.E. (1980). Explaining teacher explanations for pupil performance: A test of the self-presentation position. *Social Psychology Quarterly, 43*, 283–290.

Tetlock, P.E., & Levi, A. (1982). Attribution bias: On the inconclusiveness of the cognition-motivation debate. *Journal of Experimental Social Psychology, 18*, 68–88.

Tetlock, P.E., & Manstead, A.S.R. (1985). Impression management versus intrapsychic explanations in social psychology: A useful dichotomy? *Psychological Review, 92*, 59–77.

Weary, G., & Arkin, R.M. (1981). Attributional self-presentation. In J.H. Harvey, W. Ickes, & R.F. Kidd (Eds.), *New directions in attribution research* (Vol. 3, pp. 225–246). Hillsdale, NJ: Erlbaum.

Weary, G., Harvey, J.H., Schwieger, P., Olson, C.T., Perloff, R., & Pritchard, S. (1982). Self-serving presentation of the modification of the self-serving attributional biases. *Social Cognition, 1*, 140–159.

Wheeler, L. (1966). Motivation as a determinant of upward comparison. *Journal of Experimental Social Psychology, 2* (Suppl. 1), 27–31.

Wheeler, L., Koestner, R., & Driver, R.E. (1982). Related attributes in the choice of a comparison other: It's there, but it isn't all there is. *Journal of Experimental Social Psychology, 18,* 489–500.

Wheeler, L., Shaver, K.G., Jones, R.W., Goethals, G.R., Cooper, J., Robinson, J.E., Gruder, C.L., & Butzine, K.W. (1969). Factors determining choice of a comparison other. *Journal of Experimental Social Psychology, 5,* 219–232.

Whitehead, G.I., III, & Smith, S.H. (1984, April). *Self-presentation and the self-serving attribution bias.* Paper presented at the meeting of the Eastern Psychological Association, Baltimore, MD.

Whitehead, G.I., III, & Smith, S.H. (1985, March). *Judgments of similarity as a self-presentational strategy.* Paper presented at the meeting of the Eastern Psychological Association, Boston, MA.

Wills, T.A. (1981). Downward comparison principles in social psychology. *Psychological Bulletin, 90,* 245–271.

Wortman, C.B., Costanzo, P.B., & Witt, T.R. (1973). Effect of anticipated performance on the attribution of causality to self and others. *Journal of Personality and Social Psychology, 27,* 372–381.

Chapter 9
A Socioanalytic Interpretation of the Public and the Private Selves

Robert Hogan and Stephen R. Briggs

This chapter concerns the relationship between the public self and the private self as seen through the lens of a particular perspective on personality theory—socioanalytic theory (Hogan, 1983). The chapter is organized in three sections. The first offers a perspective on the relationship between the public and the private self. In the second, we describe a set of research problems that emerge from the analysis presented in the first section. Finally, we suggest some caveats regarding the entire enterprise.

Before proceeding, however, we think it is important to indicate how we are using the terms "public self" and "private self." With regard to the public self, there are, unfortunately, two meanings to the term and they need to be distinguished with some care. On the one hand, the public self refers to a person's view of how he or she is perceived by others—a private view of the public self. On the other hand, the public self refers to how a person is in fact perceived by others—a public view of the public self. For the purposes of this discussion we call the first term the public self-image or public self, and we call the second term a person's reputation.

The private self refers to the image that a person has of himself or herself. The image is different from its evaluation—which is self-esteem. The image is not necessarily unified either. There may be as many self-images as there are significant activities in which a person is engaged. Nonetheless, Mead (1934) suggested that experiences in a wide range of social encounters, each of which generates a specific self-image, also generalize over time to produce a kind of amorphous and very general self-image. This very general self-image, then, *in some way* serves to integrate and coordinate the specific self-images. As a matter of historical interest, personality psychologists typically equate a unifying self-image with a person's long-term goals and aspirations (see Allport, 1961; Maslow, 1954; McDougall, 1908). To the degree that life goals and aspirations form a part of a person's identity, we agree with these earlier analyses.

Both of these definitions of the private self—the sociological and the personological—beg the question of what the processes are through which the self-images arise.

Socioanalytic Theory

Hogan (1983; see also Cheek & Hogan, 1983; Hogan, Jones, & Cheek, 1985) has attempted to integrate insights from George Herbert Mead with a biological and evolutionary approach to human nature. From this perspective, the unique evolutionary history of *Homo sapiens* suggests that people are preprogrammed to seek social acceptance and status in consort with their fellow humans. The bottom line in evolutionary theory is fitness, defined in terms of the number of viable progeny produced by an individual. Fitness requires reproduction, which is a relatively straightforward process for cats and peacocks. In humans, however, it is a rather complicated matter typically preceded by elaborate negotiations. Three interrelated concepts mediate reproductive success in human groups: social acceptance, status, and social identity.

In normal circumstances a person must have a productive role to play in his or her group, he or she must be able to make some kind of contribution to the group's livelihood, before that person will be permitted to reproduce. In short, reproduction is normally predicated on negotiating an acceptable identity in one's living group. Identities can be scaled along the dimensions of status and social acceptance; status and social acceptance materially influence a person's opportunities for reproductive success. This—according to socioanalytic theory—is the deep structure or biogrammar underlying the infinite variety of human affairs as we know them.

At an unconscious level, most people are motivated to seek status and popularity in their living groups—because status and acceptance confer preferential opportunities for reproductive success. Status cannot be pursued directly; it is negotiated indirectly and the vehicle for negotiation (and for most intentional interaction) is a person's identity. But even that is an indirect process. Identity exists as a normally not very well articulated set of fantasies that a person harbors in the privacy of his or her imagination. Conscious or intentional social behavior often is designed to instruct others as to how one would like to be regarded—i.e., what one's identity claims are. Watch a group of psychologists at a convention cocktail party and notice how self-conscious they are as they instruct one another regarding their individual identities—as defined by their views on this, that, or the other issues of the day. Precisely the same processes are at work during any social gathering; the differences from one occasion to another reside primarily in the degree to which the actors are self-conscious (interactions with strangers and competitors tends to heighten self-consciousness).

In everyday terms, this means that, when a person approaches a potentially consequential social interaction (a job interview, a professional evaluation, a contract negotiation, a blind date), his or her behavior is guided, controlled, caused, or interpretable in terms of the identity with which he or she would like to be credited. Overt social behavior during these encounters can be seen in terms of self-presentation. These self-presentations, at least among skillful players, will be moderated by the expectations of the audience, as the actors attempt to negotiate and maintain favorable identities. In the current parlance, their behavior (self-presentations) will reflect situational influences, but it originates in an internal or private self-concept.

This is a very brief overview of socioanalytic theory. We close it with four observations that are offered with no support. First, the theory is intended to explain individual differences in status and popularity in an actor's social group—because in biological terms status and acceptance have implications for fitness. Second, self-presentation is not a trivial party game; it culminates in a person's reputation, and this has profound implications for the outcome of a person's life and career. Third, as Buss and Briggs (1984) pointed out, one serious problem with self-presentational theories is specifying when a person is and is not concerned with self-presentation. In the absence of such specification, the analysis risks becoming tautologous. Finally, self-presentation is not a thoroughly conscious and rational process; this is the reason so many of us find it so difficult to "clean up our acts." Our self-presentational styles and methods are largely nonconscious, habitual, and sometimes surprisingly self-defeating.

What, then, is the relationship between the private and the public self? The best generalization, in our view, is that it is problematic. But in very simple terms, during consequential interactions people are disposed to negotiate the most favorable image that they can. Negotiations proceed in terms of self-presentations. The identity that a person endeavors to promote, maintain, or recover is a covert aspiration—a private self-concept. His or her view of the success of these negotiations is the public self-concept. Between the two, however, lies a lifetime of potential heartbreak, disappointment, and despair.

Research Problems

Imagine a young woman who has just received an unattractive gift. She turns to the gift giver, thanks him warmly for the delightful present, and asks how he knew that this was her favorite color. The woman realizes that her reaction to the gift will be evaluated and that the gift-giver is observing her response. For reasons that we are rarely privy to—the nature of the relationship, her need for approval, her self-image—she attempts to create an impression that is appropriate to the occasion; in particular, she attempts to show that she "really" likes the gift. The attempt, however, may or may not be successful. She may or may not feign sincerity well, and he may or may not find her performance credible.

There are a number of factors operating in this scenario. First, there is the woman's reaction to the gift, which is internal and covert. Second, the woman attempts to react in a way that may be congruent with her self-image, with the way she wants to be perceived, and with the definition of the situation, but not with her private reaction. Third, the woman's actual response to the gift-giver may not be consistent with the image she is attempting to project. Finally, the impression formed by the observer will not always correspond to the actor's desired image nor to the actor's actual behavior. Indeed, the impression he forms may tell us as much about him as it does about her. These considerations are quite distinct and they would apply even if the woman in our example actually like the gift, and especially if she wanted to be sure that she conveyed this impression to the gift-giver.

The fact that we must pursue individual fitness through social interaction leaves each person caught between desires for self-enhancement and needs for social approval. Our intended social identities reflect the best compromise we can negotiate. Between a person's privately desired identity and public reputation lies a variety of opportunities for confusion, error, and unnecessary aggravation. We describe some of these, each of which is a potential area for research.

The Freddie Problem

A few years ago we had a research assistant named Freddie. Freddie is a bright, hardworking, and ambitious young man who is presently enjoying a fine career as a graduate student in a highly reputable department. Freddie has his idiosyncracies, but compared to many graduate students in psychology he is a model of normalcy—in fact, he is barely distinguishable from any other East Coast Yuppie. We were working on the HPI (Hogan, 1986) and Freddie obligingly completed the inventory. He received an appallingly low score on the Adjustment scale—this scale correlates about .90 with the first factor of the MMPI—suggesting that Freddie was a prime candidate for the emergency room at a psychiatric hospital.

The reader may believe that all Yuppies are closet neurotics and that Freddie had finally been found out, but in fact there was a serious mismatch between his score and psychological reality. Freddie is *not* neurotic but the Adjustment scale *is* well validated. The answer to the puzzle concerns an issue in item response theory. What are people doing when they respond to items on questionnaires? Do they disclose veridical information about their behavior and feelings or are they attempting to negotiate an identity with an anonymous interlocutor? In the case of Freddie, the first option is ruled out; he is neither deeply neurotic nor marginally psychotic, as the scale score would suggest. This, then, raises a second, empirical question: Why was Freddie proposing such a self-defeating identity for himself? And this is a perfectly general question—why *do* some talented, interesting, competent people present themselves in a nerdlike, creepy, off-putting manner? Here on this question, the rational and strategic view of self-presentation is falsified. But the prior question remains to be answered.

Identity Versus Self-Presentation

In the pursuit of everyday goals, some people are more successful than others (Ronald Reagan versus Walter Mondale). In terms of the model presented here, does the difference lie in the identity that a person aspires to or in the manner in which the identity is proposed? The question brings to mind an old Charles Schulz cartoon in which Charlie Brown asks his crestfallen teammates, "How can we lose when we are so sincere?" Rather than prejudge the issue, we submit that this is a question that can be resolved empirically. It is the old question of style versus substance. The technical problem will be to separate the effects of a positive self-image from the effects of well-developed social skills.

Good Scout or Good Soldier

Gordon Allport (1961) remarked that everything of importance in personality is correlated with social class. This means that personality is correlated with social status. More precisely, those aspects of personality that are associated with social performance (e.g., sociability and self-confidence) are also associated with status (see Hogan, 1985). But this generalization has yet to be analyzed in detail. Self-presentational skill breaks down logically into social acuity (skill at reading the expectations of an audience) and acting ability (skill at public self-expression). It is of some importance for a self-presentational theory to understand which of these skills carries more variance in predicting status. Because there are some reasonably well-validated measures of social acuity (Hogan, 1969) and acting (Lennox & Wolfe, 1984; Snyder, 1974) now available, it should be a relatively simple matter to determine the contributions of both to status attainment.

When Actors and Observers Disagree

At the outset of this chapter we distinguished the public self (an actor's view of how he or she is perceived by others) from reputation. Because actors differ in terms of their ability to construct a public identity and because observers differ in terms of their sensitivity to the image actors are trying to portray, there will always be a *discrepancy* between a person's public self and his or her reputation. Moreover, there will be individual differences in this discrepancy; it will be small for some people and large for others. To our knowledge there has been little research in the last 20 years evaluating the interpersonal consequences of discrepancy scores, defined in terms of the difference between self-image and reputation. It is tempting to believe that in normal or nondepressed populations small discrepancies are associated with greater interpersonal competence, and larger discrepancies are associated with interpersonal awkwardness and even failure (e.g., Jones & Briggs, 1984), but no one really knows.

Changing the Discrepancy Score

Once we understand the significance of discrepancy scores (that is, measurements of the discrepancy between how one thinks one is perceived by others and how one is actually perceived by others) in normal populations, then other questions come quickly to mind. For example, can these scores be changed; specifically, can large discrepancy scores be reduced? What would one do to reduce these scores? And what would be the consequences to an individual of reducing large discrepancy scores—assuming it can be done? This is a very different question from the problem studied in the 1950s: the consequences of discrepancies between the real and the ideal self-image. The consequences of changes in the discrepancy between public self-concept and reputation is an interesting research topic.

Person Perception

Personality psychology has always been interested in individual differences in the ability to judge others—in the language of this chapter, individual differences in the ability to read the image an actor is projecting (and possibly the image an actor wants to project or even to hide). Allport's (1937) book, for example, contains a detailed treatment of the various processes that affect how we form impressions of others and a review of research regarding the characteristics of accurate judges.

Taft (Sarbin, Taft, & Bailey, 1960, Chapter 2) provided an especially thoughtful review of the history of this topic. He noted that the formal study of epistemology is as old as philosophy itself, but the self-conscious study of how we perceive other people (as opposed to the physical world) begins with Darwin's (1872) book, *The Perception of Emotions in Animals and Men*. Taft pointed out that person perception research was initially stimulated by applied problems in vocational guidance and personnel selection, and it remains a problem in research on performance appraisal (Borman, 1979) and the employment interview (Arvey & Campion, 1982).

Taft argued that all perception depends on the prior existence of a perceptual model or postulate system. This is consistent with the tradition of epistemological analysis, from Kant through Hering, Stumpf, and the Gestalt psychologists, which maintained that some categories or types of perception are more appropriate to *Homo sapiens* than others. Specifically, said Taft, the analysis of social perception requires that we identify the distinctive cues and categories of inference used by humans. In our view, trait terms are the crucial categories into which observers sort the behaviors of actors.

This very interesting research topic has been almost completely ignored for 20 years. We believe this reflects the influence of two critical trends. On the one hand, Cronbach's (1955) definitive critique of the methodology of early person perception research seems to have fostered the notion that there are no reliable individual differences in social acuity—or perhaps that, should they exist, they cannot be reliably assessed. On the other hand, the more extreme versions of attribution theory maintain that there is no stable core to personality. If there is nothing within actors that is stable and enduring, then there is nothing for observers to perceive. And, indeed, we are told that personality exists more in the minds of observers than in the psyches of actors. In any case, one of the more interesting topics in personality psychology has been ignored for some time, and it is a topic that is central to a self-presentational analysis of social behavior. We are interested first in the characteristics of "good judges," but, more importantly, it would be useful to know about the implications of accuracy for the process of identity negotiation, and for the pursuit of status and social acceptance.

Caveats

This volume assumes that the public and the private self are distinct, and the purpose of the book is to explore the relationship between these separate selves. Although we are generally sympathetic with the undertaking, we wish to point out that the analysis is by no means straightforward. Consider, for instance, the following three issues: What exactly do we mean by the terms "public" and "private" self?; What is it that we are trying to explain when we distinguish between them?; and For what reasons do we invoke the concept of self in the first place?

What Are the Private and Public Selves?

At the beginning of this chapter we noted that the term public self has at least two different meanings. We distinguished between how an individual is perceived by others (a person's public reputation) and how an individual thinks he or she is perceived by others (the public self-image). Thus, one can adopt either a private or a public view of the public self. Neither image, however, corresponds precisely with an individual's actual behavior; both are subject to perceptual biases of various kinds.

The term "private self" can also assume at least two meanings. On the one hand, it can refer to a person's self-concept, to the manner in which a person thinks about himself or herself. On the other hand, the private self refers to the full range of talents and tendencies latent in an individual. It includes aspects of the self of which one may not be aware—deep-seated emotions, unarticulated attitudes and beliefs, and unconscious motives—but that may nonetheless influence one's actions. This is the part of the self to which people may refer when they try to "find themselves" or "get in touch with their true feelings." Although this is sometimes called the "true self," we prefer a more neutral term such as the "latent self."

Therefore, to say that the public self and private self are distinct is to mean several things. I may mean that one's private self-image differs from one's public self-image; that is, I see myself differently from the way I think you see me. Presumably it may also mean that one's ideal public self-image differs from one's ideal private self-image; that is, the way I would like to see myself differs from the way I would like you to see me. It may mean that the private self-image (or the ideal private self-image) differs from one's public reputation, or it may mean that one's latent self differs from that public reputation. Obviously, the terms are imprecise.

What Are We Trying to Explain?

One way to sort through this maze of meanings is to ask what it is that we are trying to explain. Making distinctions is not an end in itself; one must also show why the distinctions are important. We suspect that the relation between the private self-concept and the public self-concept is probably not as important as the relation between either self-concept and one's social reputation. How one is perceived by others is important by definition because status and popularity are socially negotiated and bestowed. Thus, the distinction between the public self and the private self is worth making when we want to explain the relationship between an individual's social reputation and his or her self-image (whether that be the public or private self-image, and whether it be actual or ideal).

Why Do We Need a Self-Concept?

Most self-presentational theorists distinguish between self-presentation as a short-term adaptive strategy and self-interpretation or self-construction as a long-term identity statement. Self-presentation refers to self-conscious attempts to create a desired impression in response to the expectations of a specific external audience, whereas self-interpretation involves attempts to communicate an enduring self-image, where both the attempt and the image may be largely nonconscious; here the self-image guides one's behavior in social interactions and that behavior is typically habitual and situationally noncontingent.

Most self-presentational theorists also use images as explanatory concepts. For instance, Snyder (1979) emphasized the causal role of images in his elaboration of the construct of self-monitoring:

> The high self-monitoring individual reads the character of the situation to identify the type of person called for by that type of situation, constructs a mental image or representation of a person who best exemplifies that type of person, and uses that pro-totypic person's self-presentation and expressive behavior as a set of guidelines for monitoring his or her own verbal and nonverbal actions. . . . the low self-monitoring individual draws upon an enduring self-image or self-conception that represents knowledge of her or his characteristic actions in the behavioral domains most relevant to this situation. This self-image then serves as the low self-monitoring individual's operating guidelines. (pp. 102–103)

In this view, social performances are shaped, guided, and constrained either by situationally induced images or enduring self-images. Behavior follows from one type of mental image or the other, but only the enduring image involves the self-concept.

But to invoke self-images as causes begs an important question: What exactly is a self-image? For the average person the term "self-image" probably refers to a consciously apprehended mental picture or visual image. Snyder's use of the term has this flavor. The term "self-interpretation" (Cheek & Hogan, 1983), however, refers to processes that are largely unconscious or habitual. Thus, for Snyder and others the self-image is something that is consciously accessed, whereas we believe that the self-image, because it was formed during development, guides behavior in ways that may not be consciously accessible.

Our usage here has important implications. If we use the term to refer to a consciously apprehended image, then we have greatly limited the scope of our investigation because much of our social behavior unfolds without any conscious or deliberate reference to an enduring self-image. Conversely, if we define self-images as largely nonconscious and enduring cognitive structures that guide behavior in a variety of situations, then we have simply rediscovered Allport's (1937, 1961, 1966) notion of traits. We may prefer the term self-image because it seems cognitively oriented, but, like Allportian traits, self-images imply little more than processes or structures in the brain (or mind) that guide, direct, and initiate behaviors and cause regularities in our actions.

Summary

In summary, we believe there are two important items to be resolved before we are fully ready to analyze the relations between the public self and private self. First, we must be clear about what it is we are trying to explain. Why is it important to distinguish between the public and the private self? What is the phenomenon that this distinction explains? Second, we need to be clear about what we mean by the term self-image. In recent years a bewildering number of "self-" terms have been coined (e.g., self-perception, self-consciousness, self-verification, self-monitoring, self-presentation, self-construction, self-interpretation). To the extent that these "self-" concepts refer to nonconscious and habitual processes, they strongly resemble the concept of personality traits, as Brissett and Edgley (1975) warned in their study of dramaturgy:

> Most social psychologists . . . have preferred the concept of 'self' in order to avoid certain assumptions inherent in personality theory. This semantic preference for the self avoids construing (1) individuality as an internal psychobiological entity consisting of conscious and unconscious elements; (2) individuality as a structure of attitudes, values, traits, and needs; and (3) individuality as the mainspring for or motivation of a person's consistent behavior. (p. 55)

This, however, may be good news. By rediscovering traits in the form of self-images, social psychology may now be open to some of the original insights and research problems of personality psychology. Both disciplines would profit from a detente, from a cessation to the hostilities triggered by the early excesses of attribution theory.

References

Allport, G.W. (1937). *Personality: A psychological interpretation*. New York: Holt.
Allport, G.W. (1961). *Pattern and growth in personality*. New York: Holt, Rinehart & Winston.
Allport, G.W. (1966). Traits revisited. *American Psychologist, 21*, 1–10.
Arvey, R.D., & Campion, J.E. (1982). The employment interviews: A summary and review of recent research. *Personnel Psychology, 35*, 281–322.
Borman, W.C. (1979). Individual differences correlates of accuracy in evaluating others' performance effectiveness. *Applied Psychological Measurement, 3*, 103–115.
Brissett, D., & Edgley, C. (Eds.). (1975). *Life as theater*. Chicago: Aldine.
Buss, A.H., & Briggs, S.R. (1984). Drama and the self in social interaction. *Journal of Personality and Social Psychology, 47*, 1310–1324.
Cheek, J.M., & Hogan, R. (1983). Self-concepts, self-presentation, and moral judgments. In J. Suls & A.G. Greenwald (Eds.), *Psychological perspectives on the self* (Vol. 2). Hillsdale, NJ: Erlbaum.
Cronbach, L.J. (1955). Processes affecting scores on "understanding of others" and "assumed similarity". *Psychological Bulletin, 52*, 177–193.
Darwin, C.R. (1872). *The expression of emotions in man and animals* (6th ed.). London: Murray.
Hogan, R. (1969). Development of an empathy scale. *Journal of Consulting and Clinical Psychology, 33*, 307–316.

Hogan, R. (1983). A socioanalytic theory of personality. In M. Page (Ed.), *Nebraska symposium on motivation* (pp. 55–89). Lincoln: University of Nebraska Press.

Hogan, R. (1986). *Manual for the Hogan Personality Inventory.* Minneapolis: National Computer Systems.

Hogan, R., Jones, W.H., & Cheek, J.M. (1985). Socioanalytic theory: An alternative to armadillo psychology. In B.R. Schlenker (Ed.), *The self and social life* (pp. 175–198). New York: McGraw-Hill.

Jones, W.H., & Briggs, S.R. (1984). The self-other discrepancy in social shyness. In R. Schwarzer (Ed.), *The self in anxiety, stress, and depression* (pp. 93–107). Amsterdam: North Holland.

Lennox, R.D., & Wolfe, R.N. (1984). Revision of the self-monitoring scale. *Journal of Personality and Social Psychology, 46,* 1349–1364.

Maslow, A.H. (1954). *Motivation and personality.* New York: Harper.

McDougall, W. (1908). *An introduction to social psychology.* London: Methuen.

Mead, G.H. (1934). *Mind, self, and society.* Chicago: University of Chicago Press.

Sarbin, T.R., Taft, R., & Bailey, D.E. (1960). *Clinical inference and cognitive theory.* New York: Holt, Rinehart & Winston.

Snyder, M. (1974). The self-monitoring of expressive behavior. *Journal of Personality and Social Psychology, 30,* 526–537.

Snyder, M. (1979). Self-monitoring processes. In L. Berkowitz (Ed.), *Advances in experimental social psychology* (Vol. 1, pp. 185–207). Hillsdale, NJ: Erlbaum.

Chapter 10
The Causes and Consequences of a Need for Self-Esteem: A Terror Management Theory

Jeff Greenberg, Tom Pyszczynski, and Sheldon Solomon

> *True dignity abides with him alone*
> *Who, in the silent hour of inward thought,*
> *Can still suspect, and still revere himself,*
> *In lowliness of heart.*
> William Wordsworth

Throughout the past few thousand years, historical accounts, philosophical treatises, and works of fiction and poetry have often depicted humans as having a need to perceive themselves as good, and their actions as moral and justified. Within the last hundred years, a number of important figures in the development of modern psychology have also embraced this notion that people need self-esteem (e.g., Adler, 1930; Allport, 1937; Horney, 1937; James, 1890; Maslow, 1970; Murphy, 1947; Rank, 1959; Rogers, 1959; Sullivan, 1953). Of these, Karen Horney most thoroughly discussed the ways people try to attain and maintain a favorable self-image. The clinical writings of Horney, and other psychotherapists as well, document the ways in which people attempt to defend and enhance self-esteem; they also suggest that difficulty maintaining self-esteem, and maladaptive efforts to do so, may be central to a variety of mental health problems. In this chapter, we will first review the research supporting the existence of a need for self-esteem. Then we will present a theory that accounts for this need and specifies the role it plays in a variety of phenomena including self-presentation.

Empirical Support for a Need for Self-Esteem

It was not until the early 1950s that researchers began to obtain quantitative evidence concerning the need for self-esteem. Since then, research on psychopathology has shown low self-esteem to be associated with a variety of psychological problems, including alcoholism, anxiety, depression, neuroticism, and schizophrenia (see Wylie, 1979, for a review). Such findings suggest that people do need self-esteem for healthy psychological functioning; however, this research is correlational and therefore subject to a number of alternative explanations. For example, it may be that psychological difficulties lead to low self-esteem, or that whatever factors contribute to such difficulties also cause low self-esteem.

The Self-Serving Bias in Causal Attribution

Clearer support for the existence of a self-esteem need has been found in experimental research, beginning with studies demonstrating a self-serving bias in individuals' causal attributions for their own successes and failures. These studies typically entail randomly assigning subjects to experience either a favorable or unfavorable outcome on a test and then obtaining their estimates of the extent to which potential causal factors such as ability, effort, luck, and task difficulty were responsible for their particular outcomes. The one highly consistent finding has been that individuals who experience success assign greater responsibility to factors within themselves (e.g., internal factors, such as ability) and less responsibility to factors outside themselves (e.g., external factors, such as luck) than do individuals who experience failure (e.g., Johnson, Feigenbaum, & Welby, 1964; Miller, 1976; Stephan, Rosenfield, & Stephan, 1976; also see Bradley, 1978, and Zuckerman, 1979, for reviews). Thus, as would be expected if people do indeed have a need for self-esteem, individuals seem to take credit for success but deny responsibility for failure.

Eliminating cognitive alternative explanations. In the last 10 years, however, a set of alternative explanations for this self-serving bias has received considerable attention. Miller and Ross (1975) proposed a number of cognitive mechanisms that could lead to a self-serving attributional bias in the absence of a self-esteem motive. Despite the fact that the notion of a need for self-esteem was the basis for all of the research on the self-serving bias up to that point in time, it was argued that such cognitive explanations are preferable because they rely only on the widely accepted information-processing framework for understanding human behavior (see also Nisbett & Ross, 1980). The most compelling of these cognitive explanations is that if individuals believe they are generally competent, they are likely to infer that when they perform competently it is because of their abilities, and when they perform poorly it is because of external factors.

However, since 1975, a number of studies have provided support for the self-esteem explanation of the self-serving bias. McFarland and Ross (1982) conducted a study in which subjects were led to attribute success or failure to either their level of ability or the characteristics of the test. Success-internal subjects reported more positive affect, less negative affect, and higher self-esteem than did success-external subjects; failure-internals, on the other hand, reported less positive affect, more negative affect, and lower self-esteem than did failure-external subjects. Correlational research (e.g., Arkin & Maryuma, 1979; Feather, 1969) and research using hypothetical outcomes (e.g., Nicholls, 1976; Weiner, Russell, & Lerman, 1978, 1979) have found similar effects. These studies show that the self-serving pattern of attributions does indeed increase the favorability of the consequences of outcomes for affective experience and self-esteem. If people are motivated to maximize positive affect and minimize negative affect, a motivational influence on attributions for performance outcomes is likely. Furthermore, self-serving attributions do seem to help the individual maintain self-esteem.

Other research provides more direct support for the self-esteem explanation by demonstrating that the intensity of the affective consequences of an outcome alters the extent to which people's attributions are self-serving. Stephan and Gollwitzer (1981) found that subjects led to believe a placebo pill they had taken would produce autonomic arousal were less prone to make self-serving attributions for a prior success or failure than were no placebo subjects. In a similar vein, Fries and Frey (1980) found that subjects were less likely to derogate a test after failure if they could attribute arousal caused by the failure to a nonthreatening source.

In another study, Stephan and Gollwitzer (1981) provided subjects with false feedback concerning their level of physiological arousal after a success or failure experience. Subjects led to believe they were highly aroused were more self-serving in their performance attributions than were low-arousal feedback subjects. Finally, Gollwitzer, Earle, and Stephan (1982) demonstrated that unlabeled residual arousal from physical exercise also increased the self-serving nature of subjects' attributions. Presumably, this residual arousal intensified subjects' perceptions of outcome-related affect, thus motivating them to become more self-serving in their attributions. To the extent that such affective consequences are attributed to the implications of the outcome for self-esteem, these studies show that the self-serving bias is mediated by self-esteem concerns.

Other Self-Esteem Maintenance Strategies

The resolution in favor of a motivational explanation for the self-serving bias is quite similar to the resolution of the earlier dissonance versus self-perception controversy. A number of studies have clearly shown that negative affect does play a role in attitude change after individuals feel responsible for engaging in behavior that has foreseeable negative consequences (see Fazio & Cooper, 1983, for a review). Interestingly, the findings of attitude change that have been attributed to a dissonance reduction process can be interpreted as resulting from a need to defend self-esteem (see Wicklund & Brehm, 1976, for a review of the dissonance literature). In virtually all these studies, the attitude change can be viewed as a way for the individual to deny that he or she has done something that is either immoral or stupid (see Aronson, 1968; Bowerman, 1978; Schlenker, Forsyth, Leary, & Miller, 1980; Steele & Liu, 1983).

In recent years, a substantial number of other studies have also yielded findings supportive of the existence of a need for self-esteem. Phares and Lamiell (1974) and Berglas and Jones (1978) reasoned that if individuals try to protect self-esteem by attributing failures to external factors, when failures are anticipated, they may set up plausible external attributions by engaging in performance-inhibiting behavior prior to and during performance. Evidence for the use of this strategy, which Berglas and Jones (1978) have aptly labeled self-handicapping, has been obtained in a number of studies (Berglas & Jones, 1978; Frankel & Snyder, 1978; Kolditz & Arkin, 1982; Phares & Lamiell, 1974; Snyder, Smoller, Strenta, & Frankel, 1981; Tucker, Vuchinish, & Sobell, 1981). Such findings attest to the strength of self-esteem needs, because they show that people will actually undermine their own chances for success to be sure that they have justification for a self-esteem-protecting external attribution should they subsequently fail.

Research has also demonstrated other types of efforts to establish self-esteem-protective attributions, by showing that individuals will report a variety of states and traits when they believe these factors could serve as excuses for subsequent failure (Greenberg, Pyszczynski, & Paisley, 1984; Pyszczynski & Greenberg, 1983; Smith, Snyder, & Handelsman, 1982; Smith, Snyder, & Perkins, 1983; Snyder, Smith, Angelli, & Ingram, in press). For example, Smith et al. (1982) and Greenberg et al. (1984) have shown that, for individuals who are highly concerned about possible failure on an upcoming test, reports of test anxiety are reduced if they are told that test anxiety does not affect performance on the particular test. Thus, individuals report more test anxiety when it can serve as an excuse for subsequent failure than when it cannot.

Studies have also shown that, under certain conditions, once a shortcoming on a specific dimension becomes salient, individuals compensate by overevaluating themselves on unrelated dimensions (e.g., Baumeister & Jones, 1978; Greenberg & Pyszczynski, 1985; Pyszczynski, Greenberg, & Beck, 1986) or, if the dimension is very important to the individual, by engaging in positive self-descriptions regarding the threatened dimension (e.g., Gollwitzer & Wicklund, 1985; Gollwitzer, Wicklund, & Hilton, 1982; Wicklund & Gollwitzer, 1981). Thus, people alter their self-perceptions to maintain self-esteem when it is threatened.

Individuals also alter their perceptions of and comparisons with others to maintain self-esteem. Research on self-serving attributive projection has shown that people overestimate consensus for their poor performances and underestimate consensus for their good performances, especially when the performance is on an ability dimension of personal importance (Campbell, in press). In other words, when people perform poorly on an ego-involving task, they overestimate how many others would also perform poorly; when people perform well on an ego-involving task they underestimate how many others would also perform well. In addition to a self-serving bias in perceived consensus, Pyszczynski, Greenberg, and LaPrelle (1985) have found a self-serving bias in information search such that, after receiving a performance outcome, individuals search more extensively for social comparison information if they expect to find that others performed poorly than if they expect to find that others performed well. It has also been found that when individuals are exposed to social comparison information, they prefer to compare themselves with others who have performed worse on a salient dimension than with others who have performed better (see Wills, 1981, for a review). Perhaps as a consequence of this downward comparison process, people believe they are better than average on a wide variety of dimensions (Felson, 1981).

Guided by a self-evaluation maintenance model (Tesser, 1980; Tesser & Campbell, 1983; Tesser & Moore, in this volume), Tesser and his colleagues have demonstrated a number of other ways in which individuals seem to adjust the nature of their social comparisons to protect self-esteem. This line of research has yielded some compelling support for the operation of self-esteem maintenance processes in social behavior (see Tesser and Moore, Chapter 5, this volume, for a more complete account). Tesser and Campbell (1980) had subjects perform two different tasks with a confederate posing as another subject; on one of the tasks they performed equally but on the other task the confederate outperformed the subject. Subjects reduced the personal importance (i.e., relevance) of the dimension on which the confederate outperformed them, especially when the confederate had been described as similar to the subjects; thus, they minimized the threat to self-esteem of being outperformed by a similar other. Similarly, in a correlational study of high school students, Tesser and Campbell (1982) found that low performance in school relative to similar but not dissimilar classmates is associated with low ratings of the personal relevance of school performance. Further evidence that individuals deny the personal relevance of threatened attributes has been obtained by Greenberg, Pyszczynski and Solomon (1982), Greenberg and Pyszcynski (1985) and Tesser and Paulhus (1983).

Tesser (1980) obtained evidence of a related process in male sibling relations. For males whose siblings were generally more competent than themselves, the closer the sibling was in age (and therefore the more appropriate for social comparison), the less the males perceived themselves as similar to their siblings. This inverse relationship was not found for males who were not less competent than their siblings. Presumably, males with superior siblings close in age attempted to deny the appropriateness of a threatening social comparison; consistent with this reasoning, these individuals also reported more friction in their relationships with their siblings than any of the other subjects in the study.

A laboratory study by Pleban and Tesser (1981) obtained further support for this process. They found that, when the performance dimension was low in relevance, the more a confederate outperformed a subject, the more the subject perceived the confederate as similar to himself or herself. This finding can be viewed as an attempt to bask in reflected glory, just as identification with a football team increases with success of the team (Cialdini et al., 1976). However, when the performance was high in relevance and, therefore, similarity would imply that a potentially threatening social comparison would be appropriate, the more the confederate outperformed a subject, the less the subject perceived the confederate as similar to himself or herself. As in the sibling study, when threatened with a self-esteem-damaging social comparison, individuals deny similarity to the potential comparison other.

Evidence for Self-Esteem Maintenance or Public Impression Management?

To summarize, a substantial body of evidence has accumulated suggesting that, in order to maintain self-esteem, we alter our self-referent causal attributions, our self-reports of states and traits, our performance-related behavior, our attitudes and beliefs, and our social perceptions and comparisons. Despite this impressive array of support for a need for self-esteem, an alternative explanation based on impression management warrants consideration. Indeed, much of the aforementioned evidence can be explained by a need to protect public image rather than private self-image. Instead of needing self-esteem, perhaps individuals simply need to maintain a positive image in the eyes of others. This reasoning has been used to explain the evidence for the self-serving bias (Bradley, 1978), dissonance reduction (e.g., Schlenker et al., 1980; Tedeschi, Schlenker, & Bonoma, 1971; Tedeschi & Rosenfeld, 1981), compensation effects (Baumeister & Jones, 1978), and self-handicapping (Kolditz & Arkin, 1982). Research has shown that individuals do engage in a variety of behaviors to manage impressions for others (see Baumeister, 1982; Jones & Pittman, 1982; Schlenker, 1980; and Tedeschi, 1981 for reviews). Therefore, given the public nature of most laboratory research, it is possible that many of the findings attributed to a need for self-esteem actually resulted from self-presentational concerns about public image.

However, a number of recent studies have demonstrated the self-serving attributional bias under conditions in which attributions were unlikely to be influenced by such self-presentational concerns (Greenberg et al., 1982; House, 1980; Ries, Rosenfeld, Melburg, & Tedeschi, 1981; Weary et al., 1982). For example, Greenberg et al. (1982) created private success and failure by giving groups of subjects an intelligence test they could score themselves, and instructing them to conceal their scored answer sheets and keep them when they left the study. Subjects were then asked on an anonymous questionnaire to attribute causal responsibility to potential factors. In this way their attributions would have no clear implications for public image unless others knew whether they had succeeded or failed. Under these private conditions, a strong self-serving bias was found. There were also some indications that under public conditions the bias was weaker. Along with a private self-serving attributional bias, this study, and a study by Frey (1978) as well, found a self-serving tendency for subjects to privately evaluate a test as more valid if they had succeeded than if they had failed.

These studies suggest that a need for self-esteem, apart from a desire for public esteem, seems to underlie the self-serving bias. Recent research has shown that a number of other self-esteem maintenance strategies also function to protect one's private self-image. With regard to anticipatory attributional defenses, Greenberg et al. (1984) found that self-reports of test anxiety to set up an excuse for possible future failure occurred under anonymous conditions and, furthermore, did not occur when the incentive for success was high. The latter finding suggests that the self-reports of test anxiety were privately believed because they did not occur when subjects did not want their chances for success hindered; if the self-reports of test anxiety were simply to serve as potential public excuses, they would have been used even when subjects were primarily concerned with succeeding on the test.

It has also been shown that a general increase in the favorability of self-evaluations in response to a specific threat to self-esteem occurs even under conditions in which such compensatory self-inflation could serve no public impression management function (Greenberg & Pyszczynski, 1985). Similarly, research has recently found attitude change after counterattitudinal behavior under bogus pipeline conditions and under private conditions, thereby supporting an intrapsychic explanation of dissonance phenomena over a public impression management explanation (Baumeister & Tice, 1984; Stults, Messe, & Kerr, 1984). Finally, Tesser and Paulhus (1983) have shown that individuals deny the ego relevance of a test they have failed even when they are led to believe that only they know they failed *and* that the experimenter believes they succeeded.

The findings of these studies cannot be accounted for by public impression management explanations such as those posited by Bradley (1978), Tedeschi et al. (1971) and others. Clearly, individuals do engage in a variety of strategies to maintain self-esteem even when public image is not at stake. However, this point is compatible with a number of self-presentation theories that propose that individuals have a need to present a positive image to themselves as well as to others (e.g., Baumeister, 1982; Goffman, 1955; Schlenker, 1980). In fact, such a proposition is indistinguishable from the notion that people need self-esteem. These theorists simply conceptualize self-esteem maintenance as analogous to, and perhaps a special case of, maintaining a positive image for an audience. In contrast, we describe below a theory that conceptualizes public image maintenance as a component of self-esteem maintenance.

Threats to Public Image Threaten Private Self-Esteem

The evidence reviewed above suggests that, even when public image is not at stake, individuals use a number of strategies to protect self-esteem when it is threatened. However, it has also been found that, when an outcome *does* threaten public image, *private* efforts to protect self-esteem are especially vigorous (Apsler, 1975; Frey, 1978; Greenberg & Pyszczynski, 1985). Apsler (1975) found that, after females were embarrassed by engaging in a series of silly behaviors in the presence of an audience, they were especially likely to engage in a helpful act, even if no witnesses to their silly behavior would know of their helpfulness. Apparently, after damage to their public image, people need to engage in positive, socially desirable behavior—not to restore a positive image for those others, but to restore a positive image for themselves (self-esteem). Similarly, Gollwitzer and Wicklund (1985) have found that individuals threatened by undesirable personality feedback will describe themselves especially positively to someone unaware of the negative feedback, even if the subject believes the other person prefers people who are self-deprecating. Clearly, in this study, the subjects were not acting to gain public esteem but to restore self-esteem.

In addition, Frey (1978) demonstrated that the self-serving tendency to *privately* evaluate a test as more valid after success than after failure was stronger if the performance outcomes were public than if they were private. Similarly, Greenberg and Pyszczynski (1985) found that individuals greatly inflated the favorability of their self-images on a private measure of self-esteem after public failure but not after private failure. Finally, Tesser and Paulhus (1983) found that subjects who thought the experimenter believed they had performed poorly on a certain ability dimension *privately* reduced the personal relevance of the dimension, even if they knew they had actually performed well and the experimenter's belief was erroneous. Thus, even when *only* public image is threatened, individuals privately engage in self-esteem defense.

To summarize, the empirical research on self-esteem maintenance shows that individuals do engage in a variety of strategies to privately defend self-esteem when it is privately threatened. On the other hand, it has also been shown that, when public esteem is threatened, individuals are particularly likely to engage in private self-esteem maintenance strategies. To explain these phenomena, as well as other evidence concerning self-esteem maintenance, and the evidence of the deleterious concomitants of low self-esteem, we require a theory that explains: (a) what self-esteem is; (b) why we need it; (c) how self-esteem is affected by public esteem; and (d) how the need for self-esteem affects social behavior.

A Terror Management Theory of the Need for Self-Esteem

Now that we have established the existence of a need for self-esteem and have reviewed a variety of its manifestations, we outline such a theory. Our theory is based largely on the writings of Ernest Becker, especially *The Birth and Death of Meaning* (1962), *The Denial of Death* (1973), and *Escape from Evil* (1975). Becker attempted to synthesize the ideas of a very diverse array of theorists in order to understand the dynamics of human social behavior. In doing so, he found that Alfred Adler, Norman Brown, Peter Berger and Thomas Luckmann, Charles Horton Cooley, Sigmund Freud, Erving Goffman, Karen Horney, Soren Kierkegaarde, George Herbert Mead, Friedrich Nietzsche, Otto Rank, and Harry Stack Sullivan had all arrived at certain very compatible insights concerning the role of self-esteem in social behavior. Becker built upon these insights in constructing his own theoretical conception of the human animal; consequently, the current theory has benefited from them as well.

The Cultural Animal

Becker (1962) proposed that the need for self-esteem is uniquely human, and exists because of our capacities for symbolic, temporal, and self-reflective thought. Although these attributes have greatly enhanced our ability to survive in a wide variety of environments, they have also led to some uniquely human problems (see M. B. Smith, 1978). Specifically, we have the capacity to wonder why we exist and to consider the possibility that the universe is an uncontrollable, absurd setting in which the only inevitability is our own ongoing decay toward absolute annihilation, which, to make matters worse, could occur at any moment because of any one of a variety of chance events.

Becker (1973, 1975) argued that we would be paralyzed with terror if we could not deny such a conception; therefore, over time, as our cognitive capacities increased, we developed cultural world views that imbued the universe with order, predictability, meaning, and permanence. As Becker noted, all cultures provide a description of how the world was created, a prescription for leading a good, meaningful life, and some hope of immortality (see Rank, 1950). Thus, each culture provides the individual with a relatively benign world view that allows for the denial of his or her ultimate vulnerability and mortality.

From this perspective, humans are not unique because they are social animals, but because they are *cultural animals*. Humans live within a shared symbolic conception of the universe that is ultimately determined by culture, and yet is believed to be an absolutely accurate representation of reality by individuals within the culture. As the source of meaning and value, the culture provides the individual with a basis for valuing himself or herself. The individual can have a sense of worth to the extent that she or he satisfies the cultural criteria for being good (valuable). Thus, self-esteem consists of viewing oneself as valuable within the context of the universal drama conveyed by the culture.

Self-Esteem as a Cultural Anxiety-Buffer

I have seen the moment of my greatness flicker,
And I have seen the eternal Footman hold my coat, and snicker,
And in short, I was afraid.

T. S. Eliot

But why do humans seem to have such a desperate and pervasive need to view themselves as valuable (i.e., to have self-esteem)? From birth through early childhood, the only basis of safety and security is the care from the parents. They satisfy needs and minimize anxiety. Indeed, human infants are completely dependent on their parents for survival. As infants develop into children, they begin to acquire self-consciousness; along with this, the warmth and care of the parents becomes increasingly conditional. Therefore, they develop an understanding that as long as they are good boys or good girls, they will receive good outcomes and be protected from bad outcomes by their apparently omnipotent parents; they also learn that if they are bad boys or bad girls, they risk loss of the ultimate care and protection of the parents and, perhaps, annihilation by them. Consistent with this reasoning, Rochlin (1965) has observed a transformation in children from dread of being abandoned to dread of being worthless. As a consequence of this perceived contingency, a positive self-concept becomes associated with feelings of warmth and security, and a negative self-concept becomes associated with terror (Becker, 1962, 1973; Sullivan, 1953). From this point on, in order to avoid feelings of terror, individuals must believe they are good (i.e., valuable); therefore, individuals need self-esteem to function with minimal anxiety.

For the child, this sense of equanimity consists of believing that he or she is of primary value to the parents. However, as the child's cognitive capacities increase, he or she begins to realize that there are outcomes from which the parents cannot protect him or her. The child may also begin to realize that his or her parents are vulnerable creatures who will eventually die and cannot protect the child from a variety of aversive experiences, including their own death. Thus, the child's basis for equanimity is undermined and new means of dealing with the terror of annihilation must be developed. At this point, it is not sufficient to be loved by the mortal parents; to restore equanimity, a superior basis of value and protection must be found. Fortunately, the culture provides such a basis by providing values, standards and roles, conceptions of the world as just (Lerner, 1980), and the possibility of immortality.

Essentially, once the task of imparting a sense of absolute value and, consequently, immortality, becomes too great for the parents, it is transferred to the religious and secular concepts, symbols, and authorities of the culture. Of course the parents greatly facilitate this transformation by virtue of their intentional and unintentional conveyance of the world view espoused by their culture. The child learns that, to minimize terror, he or she must believe he or she is valuable and deserving within the context of the culture to which he or she subscribes; thus, for the adult human, self-esteem is a cultural-anxiety buffer.

Consistent with this conceptualization of self-esteem as an anxiety-buffer, a number of researchers have found that individuals who are chronically low in self-esteem are especially prone to anxiety (e.g., Bledsoe, 1964; French, 1968; Lipsitt, 1958; Rosenberg, 1965; Rosenberg & Simmons, 1972; Truax, Schuldt, & Wargo, 1968; Winkler & Myers, 1963). The research reviewed earlier, showing that a state of arousal labeled as negative affect mediates self-serving attributions and test evaluations following failure and attitude change following counterattitudinal behavior, also supports this idea (for self-serving beliefs, see Fries & Frey, 1980; Gollwitzer, Earle, & Stephan, 1982; Stephan & Gollwitzer, 1981; for dissonance phenomena, see Fazio & Cooper, 1983, for a review). From the present perspective, these findings occurred because, by threatening self-esteem, failures and counterattitudinal behaviors weakened individuals' cultural anxiety-buffers and thereby engendered anxiety. We are suggesting, then, that the psychological significance of such events goes far beyond their implications for the specific domain in which the threats occur. This point is supported by the research demonstrating that under certain conditions individuals compensate for failures by generally inflating the favorability of their self-images (e.g., Greenberg & Pyszczynski, 1985).

The Two Components of Self-Esteem

To summarize, because we can conceive of our ultimate vulnerability and mortality and can anticipate a variety of horrifying experiences, we have the potential to be paralyzed by terror at any moment in our lives. By elevating us above the rest of the living world, and providing a view of the world as orderly, predictable, meaningful, and permanent, culture allows for the possibility of minimizing our terror by denying our essential creatureliness (i.e., our impotence, vulnerability, and mortality). This possibility is realized to the extent that we can feel we are valuable members of the culture.

From this perspective, self-esteem is an anxiety-buffering sense of personal value (or heroism, as Becker refers to it) that consists of two components: first, faith in a particular cultural drama that portrays human life as meaningful, important, and enduring; and second, belief that one plays a significant part in that drama. Each component is essential for self-esteem and, thus, for adequate terror management.

It is fairly obvious that events that suggest we have shortcomings can threaten our self-esteem; however, events that suggest that our cultural drama is not absolutely valid threaten self-esteem as well. If the standards by which we imbue ourselves with value are questioned, our personal claims of value are questioned as well. Therefore, we propose that a substantial portion of our social behavior is directed toward either or both of the following two goals: sustaining faith in a cultural drama that provides the basis for self-esteem and maintaining a sense of value within that cultural world view. It may be fruitful, then, to consider the possible role of each of these two goals in social behavior. In considering these issues we find it useful to distinguish between general maintenance processes and defenses against threat. In order to keep the anxiety-buffer provided by self-esteem, one must continually reaffirm one's value and one's faith in the absolute validity of one's world view. This facilitates one's ability to cope with specific threats when they arise. When threats do occur, the urgency of maintaining one's anxiety-buffer is greatly enhanced and a wide range of defensive strategies aimed at defusing the threat or repairing the damage it produced may be used.

Sustaining faith in the cultural drama. General maintenance. Volumes have been, and still could be written on the innumerable ways in which faith in a given culture is developed and maintained. We will not even attempt here to do this topic justice, except to mention a few basic modes of cultural affirmation. Most socialization and education of children serves to instill the values and world view of the culture. Formal and informal historical and religious teachings may be particularly directed toward conveying a cultural conception of reality that provides order, meaning, and the possibilities of significance and immortality.

Cultural symbols (e.g., in the United States, government officials, churches, monuments, flags, currency, religious and historical artifacts) and cultural rituals (e.g., in the United States, singing the national anthem, going to church, visiting historical locations and theme parks, following news and sports events, fashion, and entertainment) also play major roles in maintaining our faith in the reality, significance, and permanence of the cultural drama, because they objectify it and demonstrate social consensus.

Defenses against threat. This theory implies that any experience that suggests that our cultural drama is wrong, or that other versions of reality are equally valid, threatens self-esteem and is therefore a source of anxiety. Consequently, such experiences motivate us to eliminate the threat; by so doing, we can sustain faith in the basis of our self-esteem.

Such threats can result from environmental events; for example, when one's culture predicts the world should end on a certain day but it does not. As Festinger, Riecken, and Schachter (1956) have observed, such dramatic disconfirmations of a central aspect of one's cultural world view often lead to renewed efforts to convince oneself of the validity of the threatened belief. Threats to one's cultural drama more commonly result, however, from the knowledge that others do not subscribe to the same cultural drama. For example, outgroups often have very different beliefs and values from the cultural mainstream. We suggest that the pervasive tendency of ingroup members to display negative attitudes, beliefs, and behaviors toward outgroup members is an attempt to defuse the threat to one's own beliefs implied by the existence of the outgroup.

Quite consistent with our theory, a substantial body of research has shown that this bias against outgroup members results largely from the belief that they have different cultural values and beliefs (e.g., Byrne & Wong, 1962; Goldstein & Davis, 1972; Moe, Nacoste, & Insko, 1981; Rokeach, 1968; Rokeach & Mezei, 1966; Silverman, 1974; Stein, Hardyck, & Smith, 1965). It has even been found that, with the possible exception of intimate contacts, outgroupers who seem to share the ingroup's values may be liked just as much as ingroupers (e.g., McKirnan, Smith, & Hamayan, 1983). It is when individuals are confronted with others who view the world quite differently that they are threatened and consequently react negatively.

Our theory suggests that such negative reactions are increasingly likely the more compelling the alternative conception of reality appears to be and the more committed the outgroupers are to their views. The awareness of such people is threatening because they call into question the absolute validity of one's own cultural drama; the individual cannot maintain a sense of absolute personal value if the basis of such a judgment is merely one of a wide variety of subjective world views, none any more correct than the others. History is replete with examples of cultural efforts to eradicate such threats, ranging from derogating to proselytizing to annihilating. In fact, most, if not all wars can be viewed as battles to determine whose cultural terror-shield is the right one (e.g., the Crusades, the wars between Moslems and Jews, Hindus and Moslems, Protestants and Catholics, and the United States and the Soviet Union). Consistent with this position, we suggest that, although political and economic considerations have certainly played a role in many armed conflicts, it is the *ideological* threat upon which leaders focus to motivate masses of people into battle.

Although threats to the cultural drama at the intergroup level may be particularly dramatic, such threats may be significant at the interpersonal level, as well. Even within a given culture, particularly a large heterogeneous culture with highly differentiated roles, value discrepancies among its members are likely. Although, for simplicity's sake, we have referred to the cultural drama upon which self-esteem is based as if it were the same for everyone who is technically a member of a particular culture, clearly this is not the case. For example, for a professional football player, performance on the field is highly valued; the world of football is a substantial part of the basis of his possibilities for self-esteem. In contrast, the ability to read Latin may seem to be a completely worthless skill to him. On the other hand, for a philosophy professor, understanding Latin may be a source of self-esteem; he or she may believe that football is a completely inane and absurd activity. Both individuals may share certain cultural values, such as dedication and integrity, yet their respective views regarding what is important may undermine each other's basis of self-esteem.

Consequently, it is rather unlikely that these two people would like each other, unless they altered their views. In general, then, our theory implies that, even within the context of the overall culture, others whose views are dissimilar may threaten our basis of self-esteem and therefore engender negative reactions. Consistent with this idea, a large body of research has shown that the more dissimilar another person is, in terms of important attitudes, beliefs, and values, the less an individual will like and help the person and the more willing an individual will be to hurt the person (for reviews, see Byrne, 1971; Rokeach, 1968).

It also has been shown that people try to convert persons with deviant opinions and, if that fails, they reject such persons (Schachter, 1951). Reactions of this type to those who do not display uniformity, conformity, or obedience follow directly from our theory. Rejection of deviants occurs even when their deviance seems to be innocuous. One of the most common examples in U.S. culture is rejection of those who do not maintain their appearance in accord with cultural prescriptions for a particular role or situation. If one is working for an accounting firm, one is required to wear the right type of clothing, and it must be unwrinkled and in good condition. Official dress requirements are much more lax for some occupations, such as college professors. However, if a new faculty member should be seen conducting his duties wearing shorts and unmatched socks, his or her colleagues are likely to be bothered by this, and may even request that the person wear more "dignified" apparel.

Such deviant behavior poses no direct, concrete threat to the well-being of the individuals disturbed by it. The threat exists at a symbolic level. Such behaviors (as well as less and more extreme acts of deviance) threaten the values underlying the cultural prescriptions that have been violated. If individuals derive self-esteem from viewing their occupation as a highly valued cultural role, then someone with the same occupation who has the appearance of a transient or a "common laborer" poses a threat to their cultural anxiety-buffer. The threat may also be more general in that someone who does not maintain an appropriate appearance is, in a small way, challenging the absolute rightness of the cultural way of life (the hippies, as a group, seemed to be viewed as such a threat in the United States in the 1960s). Minor threats of this nature can usually be defused through derogation (e.g., the person can be labeled oddball, nerd, geek, eccentric, neurotic, etc.). Unfortunately, more serious threats may engender such behaviors as ridicule, efforts at conversion, brainwashing, ostracism, beatings, and killings.

Maintaining a sense of personal value within the cultural drama. General maintenance. We are proposing that self-esteem is entirely a cultural creation. People cannot have a sense of self-worth without meeting the requirements of value prescribed by the cultural drama to which they subscribe. Such prescriptions consist of both general standards and more specific role expectations (for both occupational and social positions). The general standards specify certain competencies and moral attitudes that all members of a given culture need to demonstrate. Other requirements for value, however, differ among members of the culture, depending on their ascribed and chosen roles. Similarly, Wicklund and Gollwitzer (1982) have proposed and found support for the notion that individuals vary in their requirements for self-completion (i.e., self-definitional needs) as a function of their chosen self-defining goals (e.g., to be a musician). From the present perspective, these self-defining goals are ways to attain and maintain cultural value; in other words, they are roles from which individuals attempt to secure their self-esteem.

To the extent that self-esteem derives from living up to shared cultural standards and role expectations, approval from others signifies that we have met these standards and thus are indeed valuable. As Festinger (1954) suggested, such reliance on social reality is especially likely to occur when objective sources of information about one's value are unavailable, as is the case with most culturally valued attributes. Therefore, the affection, attention, and approval that people receive from others within their culture are very important sources of a sense of personal value. Thus we suggest that much self-presentational behavior is motivated by a desire to maximize the favorability of our own self-evaluations; the more approval and the less disapproval that we receive from others, the easier it is for us to privately believe that we are valuable individuals.

The human propensities for conformity, uniformity, and obedience, which have been demonstrated in a variety of contexts, are consistent with this idea, especially given the negative reactions to deviance discussed earlier (e.g., Asch, 1958; Gergen & Wishnov, 1965; Jones, Gergen, & Jones, 1963; Milgram, 1974; Stires & Jones, 1969). Other research has shown that individuals respond positively to those who praise and like them and negatively to those who disapprove of them (e.g., Berscheid & Walster, 1978; S. C. Jones, 1973; Kenny & Nasby, 1980; Shrauger, 1975).

Perhaps the most potent form of approval occurs when one is loved; therefore, mutual love relationships may be primary sources of self-esteem. In such cases, individual A imbues individual B with great value; if B wants and needs A, then A can perceive himself or herself as valuable as well. In other words, the more a person loves his or her partner, the more his or her partner's love adds to his or her sense of personal value. This may account for the intensity of familial and romantic love in most, if not all cultures. Interestingly, in Western culture, love is often lauded as magical, transcendent, and eternal (see Rubin, 1973), thus making it a particularly suitable basis for minimizing existential terror. As Becker (1973) noted, the one problem is that one's sense of equanimity then becomes dependent on the romantic partner. Perhaps this is why people will do almost anything to preserve good relationships; from this perspective, the negative feeling when such a relationship is threatened, which we call jealousy, is anxiety engendered by the threat of loss of an important source of self-esteem.

Children also play a major role in maintaining a sense of personal value. As many theorists have suggested (e.g., Becker, 1962; Rogers, 1959; Sullivan, 1953), the child's sense of value is derived from the parent's (or parents') love; but offspring provide parents with a tremendous sense of value as well. Parents can take credit for the existence of these creatures; therefore any value they perceive in their children and their behaviors (from being cute to saving the world) imparts value to the parent(s). In addition, parents know they are needed by their children and are almost constantly reminded of this. Finally, parents can derive a sense of permanent value and immortality to the extent that they view their children as extension of themselves who can eventually have their own children, ad infinitum. These ideas can help explain the intensity of parental concern for their children's well-being, prosperity, and adherence to the parents' cultural drama.

In general, then, individuals can feel valuable to the extent that they feel needed. Therefore, a person can build and maintain self-esteem by being helpful to others, particularly others who have been deemed by the culture to be particularly worthy of help. Helping imparts a sense of value both because of the approval it generates from others and because of one's private sense of living up to cultural standards of goodness.

There are also more tangible bases of value in most cultures. For example, in the United States a wide variety of material symbols of value exist, most of which indicate one's financial status (e.g., jewelry, clothes, automobiles). For most members of American culture, material wealth is a prime indicator of success in the cultural drama. Such a basis of self-esteem may be particularly appealing because it allows for visible, tangible, and enduring symbols of one's worth. In small and large ways, Americans may build their own pyramids.

Perhaps individuals can also establish a sense of worth vicariously through identification with real and fictional cultural heroes. By identifying with someone special and important, especially someone who has defied death, one can attain a feeling of being significant and immortal, even if only momentarily. This may be particularly likely to occur when a culture is having difficulty providing self-esteem for its people. Under such circumstances, people may flock to an individual with heroic qualities and a clear alternative world view to establish or restore a sense of their own value. This may help explain why certain historical figures gained so many dedicated followers (e.g., Gandhi, Hitler, Jesus).

Similarly, it may be that the appeal of much entertainment derives from the portrayal of heroism (see Bettelheim, 1977; Campbell, 1968). Heroes in literature, film, television, and sports also allow us to share the glory. Perhaps one of the clearest examples of this is the Spanish bullfight, in which the heroic matador, as the representative of the culture, defies death by "vanquishing" the terrifying bull; however, this analysis applies equally well to a variety of spectator sports, films, and works of fiction. Such portrayals of heroism may also help individuals frame their own lives within a heroic context (e.g., in the United States, one could be the Bob Hope or Richard Pryor of teachers, the Dr. J. of shortorder cooks, the John Wayne of computer troubleshooters, or the Clint Eastwood of politics).

Similarly, participatory forms of entertainment, such as gambling, video games, board games ("Dungeons and Dragons" may be a rather extreme example of this), theater groups, and participatory sports provide individuals with contexts in which they may attain a temporary sense of heroism (i.e., self-esteem). Thus, leisure activities may be enjoyable primarily because they allow individuals to bolster their cultural anxiety-buffers.

Each of these modes of attaining self-esteem probably varies with regard to the strength and durability of the sense of personal value that it confers. An inspiring movie may provide a couple of hours' worth, bringing one's partner to orgasm a couple of days' worth, and saving someone's life a couple of months' worth. However, the effects are always transitory, making self-esteem maintenance a complex and taxing problem. People adapt quickly to whatever they have already attained; therefore, a sense of personal value is a tenuous, day-to-day proposition (see Brickman & Campbell, 1971). Consequently, people have a virtually constant need for reminders or new indicators of achievement and being loved. The athlete needs to come through in the next pressure situation, the millionaire businessman needs to keep accumulating money, the Don Juan needs new romantic conquests, and the parents need continual affection from their offspring.

Defenses against threat. Our theory implies a number of conditions that may threaten self-esteem and consequently require some form of defense to minimize anxiety. Clearly, self-esteem will be threatened whenever individuals become aware that some aspect of themselves may undermine their efforts to fulfill a valued role, be desired by others, gain social approval, avoid disapproval, or accumulate symbols of worth. A particular activity will therefore be ego-involving to the extent that it has potential for providing information concerning attributes relevant to the individual's ability to be a valued participant in his or her particular cultural drama. Our previous discussion has shown that, when individuals are anticipating, or have experienced, failures on tasks, they alter their beliefs, attitudes, and behaviors in a variety of ways to protect self-esteem.

Aside from specific failures, events that generally heighten self-awareness may also make potentially threatening shortcomings salient. Recall that Becker proposed that the capacity for self-awareness is largely responsible for the human potential for existential terror; it is when we are self-aware that our creatureliness and our isolated existence is salient. Therefore, it is when we are most self-aware that we should be most concerned with being valued participants in the ongoing cultural drama. Consistent with this reasoning, a substantial body of research has shown that, under conditions of heightened self-awareness, individuals are much more likely to act in accord with salient internalized cultural standards (see Buss, 1980; Carver & Scheier, 1981; and Wicklund, 1975, for reviews) and also to defend self-esteem from the threat of failure (Hull & Levy, 1979; Kernis, Zuckerman, Cohen, & Sparafora, 1982).

Our analysis so far implies that, although the basis of self-esteem threat consists of its implications for *cultural* value, the threat can consist of *private* awareness of a culturally relevant shortcoming; therefore private failures can threaten self-esteem and private ways to minimize the threatening implications of such failures can protect self-esteem. Thus, our theory is consistent with the previously discussed research demonstrating private efforts to defend self-esteem. However, the theory can also account for research showing heightened private self-esteem defense when a shortcoming is known to others; the opinion of others provides a link to the shared cultural drama from which self-esteem is derived. Being of value means living up to shared cultural standards; if others who are fellow participants in, and validators of the cultural drama do not believe we are meeting those standards, our own beliefs that we are doing so are threatened. Self-esteem is therefore threatened whenever individuals become aware that some component of their value as perceived by others within the culture falls short of their own perception of that component. This explains why public awareness of a shortcoming leads to especially vigorous private attempts to defend self-esteem, even if, as in the Tesser and Paulhus (1983) study, the individual knows that such public awareness is based on erroneous information.

It follows, then, that self-esteem concerns are aroused not only in achievement settings, but in virtually any social situation. Theorists have often noted that individuals try to establish and maintain a particular positive social identity in the public arena (e.g., McCall & Simmons, 1978). Along the same lines, Goffman (1955) has discussed the need to protect the "sacred self" by maintaining face in all social encounters. More recently, Wicklund and Gollwitzer (1982) have argued that public acknowledgment is necessary to anchor one's self-definition in social reality. Quite similarly, Baumeister (1982) has proposed that one of the two major functions of self-presentation is to establish and maintain a preferred self-concept (self-construction). All of these ideas are quite compatible with our proposition that self-esteem is a sense of value that is culturally created and maintained. Whereas each of these approaches is unique in some ways, they all explicitly or implicitly acknowledge that the favorability of social image will directly influence the favorability of private self-image; from our perspective, this is because self-esteem is a function of perceived cultural esteem, which, in turn, is reflected largely in the appraisals of others. Thus, self-presentational behavior is not only designed to garner specific rewards and avoid specific punishments from a particular present audience—it is also designed to maintain and bolster self-esteem.

This idea is highly consistent with the research on interpersonal attraction and self-presentation mentioned in the above discussion of general maintenance. It can also help explain a wide variety of everyday experiences. When a teacher addresses his or her first class, the teacher's concerns about doing well and the associated anxiety are far greater than would be expected if outcomes from the particular audience were all that is at stake—clearly a potential threat to self-esteem is involved. When a lonely man, alone in a bar, refuses to approach attractive women because he is "afraid of rejection," clearly what he is avoiding is not merely negative outcomes from the particular denizens of the bar, but a threat to self-esteem.

In fact, a wide variety of social behaviors, some trivial, some very serious, are influenced by our needs to protect self-esteem. Toward the trivial end, concerns about self-esteem may keep people from buying porno magazines or from dancing in public. Toward the serious end, they may keep someone in dire need of counseling from seeking such nelp. Finally, an extreme example can be seen in Japanese culture, where a traditional response when one's public image has been severely undermined is suicide; an honorable death, which is deemed worthy by the culture, may be preferable to life without the cultural anxiety-buffer.

In each of these instances, and innumerable others, we can see the powerful influence self-esteem needs exert on social behavior. Phenomenologically, people in these situations modify their behaviors to minimize negative feelings that are described variously as anxiety, embarrassment, guilt, humiliation, nervousness, and shame. Although a variety of theorists have assumed these reactions occur (e.g., Goffman, 1967), and a few have briefly addressed their source (e.g., Berger & Luckmann, 1967), theories directed toward explaining these phenomena are rare. Following Becker (1962, 1973), our theory posits that these feelings are a leakage of the basic existential terror from which self-esteem protects us. Threats to public image threaten one's value in the cultural drama, thereby undermining one's basis of equanimity.

Conclusion

Summary

We have reviewed the research supporting the existence of a need for self-esteem and have attempted to account for these findings with a theory that explains what self-esteem is, why we need it, and how the need for self-esteem affects social behavior. Briefly, we propose that culture reduces the terror engendered by awareness of our vulnerability and mortality by providing a shared symbolic conception of reality that imputes order, predictability, significance, and permanence to our lives. This cultural drama provides the possibility of leading a meaningful and enduring existence; equanimity is attained only when a person believes that she or he is a valued participant in such a cultural drama. This attitude, which is referred to as self-esteem, serves the essentially defensive anxiety-buffering function of imbedding the individual within a transcendent cultural drama. Stated simply, self-esteem gives people a basic sense of security that is needed very badly.

Strengths of the Theory

We have attempted to show how this theory can provide a powerful explanatory framework for a wide variety of social psychological findings. We also believe that, because the theory focuses on the relationship between the individual and culture, it can account for a broad range of phenomena that have not been, or cannot be addressed by other social psychological conceptions of human behavior. It has been noted that social psychology has traditionally been an ahistorical and acultural discipline (see Gergen, 1973; McGuire, 1973; Sampson, 1978). Therefore, many issues concerning past and ongoing human events have been ignored or dismissed as beyond the bounds of legitimate psychological discourse and, thus, have been left to historians, sociologists, anthropologists, political scientists, and economists. In contrast, by exploring the psychological functions of culture, the terror management theory suggests that historical, cultural, and economic behaviors cannot be understood without considering the psychological needs of the individual. By doing so, perhaps the theory can aid the slow process of integration of the social sciences toward a full understanding of human behavior.

Research implications. We also believe that the theory has considerable potential for generating empirical research. We are currently examining the proposed anxiety-buffering property of self-esteem by bolstering or threatening self-esteem in a variety of ways and assessing subsequent affect and behavior in potentially anxiety-provoking situations. Another direction we are taking is assessment of the effects of heightened salience of creatureliness and mortality on propensities to protect self-esteem and adhere to cultural values. Interestingly, Paulhus and Levitt (in press) have recently found that subtle exposure to affect-laden words, such as death, coffin, guts, and blood, led individuals to evaluate themselves in an especially favorable manner.

We also hope to assess how direct threats to self-esteem may lead people to bolster such things as cultural values, group identification, and the tendency to like similar others and reject dissimilar others. Conversely, we are also considering the possibility that heightened group identification decreases the threat to self-esteem of a particular task outcome, and that threats to group identification or other aspects of one's cultural drama intensify the need to bolster self-esteem.

Another direction we hope to take is to assess the role of public knowledge in self-esteem threat. For example, our theory implies that performance on a task that is initially viewed by the individual as trivial may become ego-involving if others seem to value good performance, especially if the others are similar to or valued by the individual. Similarly, when individuals perform potentially embarrassing acts, the extent of embarrassment should covary directly with the perceived similarity and value of the audience. We are also studying the effects of entertainment activities on self-esteem. We could go on, but the main point is that the theory can generate a variety of testable hypotheses, and therefore, judgments of its validity will ultimately depend on the outcome of ongoing and future empirical work.

Final Thoughts

One general implication from this theory is that a variety of mental health problems may result from the individual's inability to maintain a cultural anxiety-buffer, because of loss of faith either in one's ability to maintain a valued role within one's cultural drama or in the cultural drama itself. Thus cultures can be evaluated by examining how well they fulfill the responsibility of providing a compelling conception of reality that allows the greatest number of individuals within the culture to derive self-esteem, with the least expense to others inside and outside the culture. If this idea could be kept in mind, along with acknowledgment of the ubiquitous need for a sense of personal heroism (Becker, 1973), perhaps societies could evolve more effective and benign ways for all of us to manage our basic terror.[1]

Acknowledgments. Thanks to Jack Brehm, Nancy Hobbs, Donna Morganstern, Abram Rosenblatt, John Thibaut, Challenger Vought, and Catherine Wylie for their contributions to this work.

References

Adler, A. (1930). *Understanding human nature.* New York: Greenberg.
Allport, G.W. (1937). *Personality: A psychological interpretation.* New York: Holt.
Apsler, R. (1975). Effects of embarrassment on behavior toward others. *Journal of Personality and Social Psychology, 32,* 145–153.

---

[1]We would like to reemphasize that we derived our theoretical analysis largely from the writings of Ernest Becker. However, in adapting and applying Becker's ideas to serve our purposes, we have probably neglected and oversimplified many of his insights. Therefore, we strongly urge individuals unfamiliar with Becker to read his books, especially *The Birth and Death of Meaning* (1962), *The Denial of Death* (1973), and *Escape from Evil* (1975).

Arkin, R.M., & Maryuma, G.M. (1979). Attribution, affect, and college exam performance. *Journal of Educational Psychology, 21*, 85–93.

Aronson, E. (1968). Dissonance theory: Progress and problems. In R.P. Abelson, E. Aronson, W.J. McGuire, T.M. Newcomb, M.J. Rosenberg, & P.H. Tannenbaum (Eds.), *Theories of cognitive consistency: A source-book*. Chicago: Rand McNally.

Asch, S.E. (1958). Effects of group pressure upon modification and distortion of judgments. In E.E. Maccoby, T.M. Newcomb, & E.L. Hartley (Eds.), *Readings in social psychology* (3rd ed.). New York: Holt, Rinehart, & Winston.

Baumeister, R.F. (1982). A self-presentational view of social phenomena. *Psychological Bulletin, 91*, 3–26.

Baumeister, R.F., & Jones, E.E. (1978). When self-presentation is constrained by the target's knowledge: Consistency and compensation. *Journal of Personality and Social Psychology, 36*, 608–618.

Baumeister, R.F., & Tice, D.M. (1984). Role of self-presentation and choice in cognitive dissonance under forced compliance: Necessary or sufficient causes? *Journal of Personality and Social Psychology, 46*, 5–13.

Becker, E. (1962). *The birth and death of meaning*. New York: Free Press.

Becker, E. (1973). *The denial of death*. New York: Free Press.

Becker, E. (1975). *Escape from evil*. New York: Free Press.

Berger, P.L., & Luckmann, T. (1967). *The social construction of reality: A treatise in the sociology of knowledge*. Garden City, NY: Anchor Books.

Berglas, S., & Jones, E.E. (1978). Drug choice as a self-handicapping strategy in response to a non-contingent success. *Journal of Personality and Social Psychology, 36*, 405–417.

Bersheid, E., & Walster, E. (1978). *Interpersonal attraction*. Reading, MA: Addison-Wesley.

Bettelheim, B. (1977). *The uses of enchantment*. New York: Vantage Books.

Bledsoe, J. (1964). Self concepts of children and their intelligence, achievement, interests and anxiety. *Journal of Individual Psychology, 20*, 55–58.

Bowerman, W. (1978). Subjective competence: The structure, process, and function of self-referent causal attributions. *Journal for the Theory of Social Behavior, 8*, 45–75.

Bradley, G.W. (1978). Self-serving biases in the attribution process: A reexamination of the fact or fiction question. *Journal of Personality and Social Psychology, 36*, 56–71.

Brickman, P., & Campbell, D.T. (1971). Hedonic relativism and planning the good society. In M.H. Appley (Ed.), *Adaptation-level theory*. New York: Academic Press.

Buss, A.H. (1980). *Self-consciousness and social anxiety*. San Francisco: W.H. Freeman.

Byrne, D. (1971). *The attraction paradigm*. New York: Academic Press.

Byrne, D., & Wong, T.J. (1962). Racial prejudice, interpersonal attraction, and assumed dissimilarity of attitudes. *Journal of Abnormal and Social Psychology, 65*, 246–253.

Campbell, J. (1968). *The hero with a thousand faces*. Princeton, NJ: Princeton University Press.

Campbell, J. (in press). Accuracy in projection: The effects of attribute type, relevance, and individual differences in self-esteem and depression. *Journal of Personality and Social Psychology*.

Carver, C., & Scheier, M. (1981). *Attention and self-regulation*. New York: Springer-Verlag.

Cialdini, R.B., Borden, R.J., Thorne, A., Walker, M.R., Freeman, S., & Sloan, L.R. (1976). Basking in reflected glory: Three (football) field studies. *Journal of Personality and Social Psychology, 34*, 366–375.

Fazio, R.H., & Cooper, J. (1983). Arousal in the dissonance process. In J.T. Cacioppo & R.E. Petty (Eds.), *Social psychophysiology*. New York: Guilford Press.

Feather, N.T. (1969). Attribution of responsibility and valence of outcome in relation to initial confidence and success and failure of self and other. *Journal of Personality and Social Psychology, 18*, 173–188.

Felson, R.B. (1981). Ambiguity and bias in the self-concept. *Social Psychology Quarterly, 44*, 64–69.

Festinger, L. (1954). A theory of social comparison processes. *Human Relations, 7*, 117–140.

Festinger, L., Riecken, H.W., & Schachter, S. (1956). *When prophecy fails*. Minneapolis: University of Minneapolis Press.

Frankel, A., & Snyder, M.L. (1978). Poor performance following unsolvable problems: Learned helplessness or egotism? *Journal of Personality and Social Psychology, 36,* 1415–1423.

French, J.R.P. (1968). The conceptualization and measurement of mental health in terms of self-identity theory. In S.B. Bells (Ed.), *The definition and measurement of mental health*. Washington, DC: U.S. Department of Health, Education, and Welfare.

Frey, D. (1978). Reactions to success and failure in public and private conditions. *Journal of Experimental Social Psychology, 14,* 172–179.

Fries, A., & Frey D. (1980). Misattribution of arousal and the effects of self-threatening information. *Journal of Experimental Social Psychology, 16,* 405–416.

Gergen, K.J. (1973). Social psychology as history. *Journal of Personality and Social Psychology, 26,* 309–320.

Gergen, K.J., & Wishnov, B. (1965). Others' self-evaluation and interactions anticipation as determinants of self-presentation. *Journal of Personality and Social Psychology, 2,* 348–358.

Goffman, E. (1955). On face-work: An analysis of ritual elements in social interaction. *Psychiatry, 18,* 213–231.

Goffman, E. (1967). *Interaction on ritual: Essays on face-to-face behavior*. Garden City, NY: Doubleday.

Goldstein, M., & Davis, E.E. (1972). Race and beliefs: A further analysis of the social determinants of behavioral intentions. *Journal of Personality and Social Psychology, 22,* 346–355.

Gollwitzer, P.M., Earle, W.B., & Stephan, W.G. (1982). Affect as a determinant of egotism: Residual excitation and performance attributions. *Journal of Personality and Social Psychology, 43,* 702–709.

Gollwitzer, P.M., & Wicklund, R.A. (1985). Self-symbolizing and the neglect of others' perspectives. *Journal of Personality and Social Psychology, 48,* 702–715.

Gollwitzer, P.M., Wicklund, R.A., & Hilton, J.L. (1982). Admission of failure and symbolic self-completion: Extending Lewinian theory. *Journal of Personality and Social Psychology, 43,* 358–371.

Greenberg, J., & Pyszczynski, T. (1985). Compensatory self-inflation: A response to the threat to self-regard of public failure. *Journal of Personality and Social Psychology, 49,* 273–280.

Greenberg, J., Pyszczynski, T., & Paisley, C. (1984). The effect of extrinsic incentives on the use of test anxiety as an anticipatory attributional defense: Playing it cool when the stakes are high. *Journal of Personality and Social Psychology, 47,* 1136–1145.

Greenberg, J., Pyszczynski, T., & Solomon, S. (1982). The self-serving attributional bias: Beyond self-presentation. *Journal of Experimental Social Psychology, 18,* 56–67.

Horney, K. (1937). *The neurotic personality of our time*. New York: Norton.

House, W.C. (1980). Effects of knowledge that attributions will be observed by others. *Journal of Research in Personality, 14,* 528–545.

Hull, J.G., & Levy, A.S. (1979). The organizational functioning of the self: An alternative to the Duval and Wicklund model of self-awareness. *Journal of Personality and Social Psychology, 37,* 756–768.

James, W. (1890). *The principles of psychology*. New York: Dover.

Johnson, T.J., Feigenbaum, R., & Welby, M. (1964). Some determinants and consequences of teachers' perceptions of causation. *Journal of Educational Psychology, 55,* 237–246.

Jones, E.E., Gergen, K.J., & Jones, R.G. (1963). Tactics of ingratiation among leaders and subordinates in a status hierarchy. *Psychological Monographs, 77*(Whole No. 521).

Jones, E.E., & Pittman, T.S. (1982). Toward a general theory of strategic self-presentation. In J. Suls (Ed.), *Psychological perspectives on the self* (Vol. 1, pp. 231–262). Hillsdale, NJ: Erlbaum.

210   Jeff Greenberg, Tom Pyszczynski, and Sheldon Solomon

Jones, S.C. (1973). Self and interpersonal evaluations: Esteem theories versus consistency theories. *Psychological Bulletin*, *79*, 185–199.

Kenny, D.A., & Nasby, W. (1980). Splitting the reciprocity correlation. *Journal of Personality and Social Psychology*, *38*, 249–256.

Kernis, M.H., Zuckerman, M., Cohen, A., & Sparafora, S. (1982). Persistence following failure: The interactive role of self-awareness and the attributional basis for negative expectancies. *Journal of Personality and Social Psychology*, *43*, 1184–1191.

Kolditz, T.A., & Arkin, R.M. (1982). An impression management interpretation of self-handicapping. *Journal of Personality and Social Psychology*, *43*, 492–502.

Lerner, M.J. (1980). *The belief in a just world: A fundamental delusion*. New York: Plenum.

Lipsitt, L.P. (1958). A self-concept scale for children and its relationship to the childrens' form of the Manifest Anxiety Scale. *Child Development*, *29*, 463–472.

Maslow, A.H. (1970). *Motivation and personality*. New York: Harper.

McCall, G.J., & Simmons, J.L. (1978). *Identities and interactions*. New York: Free Press.

McFarland, C., & Ross, M. (1982). Impact of causal attributions on affective reactions to success and failure. *Journal of Personality and Social Psychology*, *43*, 937–946.

McGuire, W.J. (1973). The yin and yang of progress in social psychology: Seven koan. *Journal of Personality and Social Psychology*, *26*, 446–456.

McKirnan, D.J., Smith, C.E., & Hamayan, E.V. (1983). A sociolinguistic approach to the belief-similarity model of racial attitudes. *Journal of Experimental Social Psychology*, *19*, 434–447.

Milgram, S. (1974). *Obedience to authority*. New York: Harper.

Miller (1976). Ego involvement and attributions for success and failure. *Journal of Personality and Social Psychology*, *34*, 901–906.

Miller, D.T., & Ross, M. (1975). Self-serving biases in the attribution of causality: Fact or fiction? *Psychological Bulletin*, *82*, 213–225.

Moe, J.L., Nacoste, R.W., & Insko, C.A. (1981). Belief versus race as determinants of discrimination: A study of Southern adolescents in 1966 and 1979. *Journal of Personality and Social Psychology*, *41*, 1031–1050.

Murphy, G. (1947). *Personality*. New York: Harper.

Nicholls J.G. (1976). Effort is virtuous but it's better to have ability: Evaluative responses to perceptions of effort and ability. *Journal of Research in Personality*, *10*, 306–315.

Nisbett, R.E., & Ross, L. (1980). *Human inference: Strategies and shortcomings of social judgment*. Englewood Cliffs, NJ: Prentice-Hall.

Paulhus, D.L., & Levitt, K. (in press). Automatic self-enhancement: Some evidence for fast-rising arousal. *Journal of Personality and Social Psychology*.

Phares, E.J., & Lamiell, J.T. (1974). Relationship of internal–external control to defensive preferences. *Journal of Consulting and Clinical Psychology*, *42*, 872–878.

Pleban, R., & Tesser, A. (1981). The effects of relevance and quality of another's performance on interpersonal closeness. *Social Psychology Quarterly*, *44*, 278–285.

Pyszczynski, T., & Greenberg, J. (1983). Determinants of reduction in intended effort as a strategy for coping with anticipated failure. *Journal of Research in Personality*, *17*, 412–422.

Pyszczynski, T., Greenberg, J., & Beck, G. (1986). *Compensatory self-inflation following self-focus after failure*. Unpublished manuscript, University of North Carolina, Chapel Hill.

Pyszczynski, T., Greenberg, J., & LaPrelle, J. (1985). Social comparison after success and failure: Biased search for information consistent with a self-serving conclusion. *Journal of Experimental Social Psychology*, *21*, 195–211.

Rank, O. (1950). *Psychology and the soul*. New York: A.S. Barnes & Co.

Rank, O. (1959). *The myth of the birth of the hero, and other writings*. New York: Vintage Books.

Riess, M., Rosenfield, R., Melburg, V., & Tedeschi, J.T. (1981). Self-serving attributions: Biased private perceptions and distorted public descriptions. *Journal of Personality and Social Psychology*, *41*, 224–231.

Rochlin, G. (1965). *Griefs and discontents: The forces of change*. Boston: Little, Brown.

Rogers, C.R. (1959). A theory of therapy, personality, and interpersonal relationships, as developed in the client-centered framework. In S. Koch (Ed.), *Psychology: A study of a science* (Vol. 3). New York: McGraw-Hill.

Rokeach, M. (1968). *Beliefs, attitudes, and values*. San Francisco: Jossey-Bass.

Rokeach, M., & Mezei, L. (1966). Race and shared beliefs as factors in social choice. *Science, 151*, 167–172.

Rosenberg, M. (1965). *Society and the adolescent self-image*. Princeton: Princeton University Press.

Rosenberg, M., & Simmons, R.G. (1972). *Black and white self-esteem: The urban school child*. Washington, DC: American Sociological Association.

Rubin, Z. (1973). *Liking and loving*. New York: Holt, Rinehart, & Winston.

Sampson, E.E. (1978). Scientific paradigms and social values: Wanted—A scientific revolution. *Journal of Personality and Social Psychology, 36*, 1332–1343.

Schachter, S. (1951). Deviation, rejection and communication. *Journal of Abnormal and Social Psychology, 46*, 190–207.

Schlenker, B.R. (1980). *Impression management*. Monterey: Brooks/Cole.

Schlenker, B.R., Forsyth, D.R., Leary, M.R., & Miller, R.S. (1980). Self-presentational analysis of the effects of incentives on attitude change following counterattitudinal behavior. *Journal of Personality and Social Psychology, 39*, 553–577.

Shrauger, J.S. (1975). Responses to evaluation as a function of initial self-perceptions. *Psychological Bulletin, 82*, 581–596.

Silverman, B.I. (1974). Consequences, racial discrimination, and the principle of belief congruence. *Journal of Personality and Social Psychology, 29*, 497–508.

Smith, M.B. (1978). Perspectives on selfhood. *American Psychologist, 33*, 1053–1063.

Smith, T.W., Snyder, C.R., & Handelsman, M.M. (1982). On the self-serving function of an academic wooden leg: Test anxiety as a self-handicapping strategy. *Journal of Personality and Social Psychology, 42*, 314–321.

Smith, T.W., Snyder, C.R., & Perkins, S.C. (1983). On the self-serving function of hypochondriacal complaints: Physical symptoms as self-handicapping strategies. *Journal of Personality and Social Psychology, 44*, 787–797.

Snyder, C.R., Smith, T.W., Angelli, R., & Ingram, R.E. (in press). Shyness as a self-handicapping strategy. *Journal of Personality and Social Psychology*.

Snyder, M.L., Smoller, B., Strenta, A., & Frankel, A. (1981). A comparison of egotism, negativity, and learned helplessness and explanations for poor performance after unsolvable problems. *Journal of Personality and Social Psychology, 40*, 24–30.

Steele, C.M., & Liu, T.J. (1983). Dissonance processes as self-affirmation. *Journal of Personality and Social Psychology, 45*, 5–19.

Stein, D.D., Hardyck, J.A., & Smith, M.B. (1965). Race and belief: An open and shut case. *Journal of Personality and Social Psychology, 1*, 281–289.

Stephan, W.G., & Gollwitzer, P.M. (1981). Affect as a mediator of attributional egotism. *Journal of Experimental Social Psychology, 17*, 443–458.

Stephan, W.G., Rosenfield, D., & Stephan, C. (1976). Egotism in males and females. *Journal of Personality and Social Psychology, 34*, 1161–1167.

Stires, L.K., & Jones, E.E. (1969). Modesty vs. self-enhancement as alternative forms of ingratiation. *Journal of Experimental Social Psychology, 5*, 172–188.

Stults, D.M., Messe, L.A., & Kerr, N.L. (1984). Belief discrepant behavior and the bogus pipeline: Impression management or arousal attribution. *Journal of Experimental Social Psychology, 20*, 47–54.

Sullivan, H.S. (1953). *The interpersonal theory of psychiatry*. New York: Norton.

Tedeschi, J.T. (1981). *Impression management theory and social psychological research*. New York: Academic Press.

Tedeschi, J.T., & Rosenfeld, P. (1981). Impression management theory and the forced compliance situation. In J.T. Tedeschi (Ed.), *Impression management theory and social psychological research* (pp. 147–180). New York: Academic Press.

Tedeschi, J.T., Schlenker, B.R., & Bonoma, T.V. (1971). Cognitive dissonance: Private ratiocination or public spectacle? *American Psychologist*, *26*, 685–695.

Tesser, A. (1980). Self-esteem maintenance in family dynamics. *Journal of Personality and Social Psychology*, *39*, 77–91.

Tesser, A., & Campbell, J. (1980). Self-definition: The impact of the relative performance and similarity of others. *Social Psychology Quarterly*, *43*, 341–347.

Tesser, A., & Campbell, J. (1982). A self-evaluation maintenance approach to school motivation. *Educational Psychologist*, *17*, 1–12.

Tesser, A., & Campbell, J. (1983). Self-definition and self-evaluation maintenance. In J. Suls & A.G. Greenwald (Eds.), *Social psychological perspectives on the self* (Vol. 2). Hillsdale, NJ: Erlbaum.

Tesser, A., & Paulhus, D. (1983). The definition of self: Private and public self-evaluation maintenance strategies. *Journal of Personality and Social Psychology*, *44*, 672–682.

Truax, C.B., Schuldt, W.J., & Wargo, D.G. (1968). Self-ideal concept congruence and improvement in group psychotherapy. *Journal of Consulting and Clinical Psychology*, *32*, 47–53.

Tucker, A., Vuchinish, R.E., & Sobell, M.B. (1981). Alcohol consumption as a self-handicapping strategy. *Journal of Abnormal Psychology*, *90*, 220–230.

Weary, G., Harvey, J., Schwieger, P., Olson, C., Perloff, S., & Pritchard, S. (1982). Self-presentation and the moderation of self-serving attributional biases. *Social Cognition*, *1*, 140–159.

Weiner, B., Russell, D., & Lerman, D. (1978). Affective consequences of causal attribution. In J.H. Harvey, W.J. Ickes, & R.F. Kidd (Eds), *New directions in attribution research* (Vol. 2). Hillsdale, NJ: Erlbaum.

Weiner, B., Russell, D., & Lerman, D. (1979). The cognition–emotion process in achievement-related contexts. *Journal of Personality and Social Psychology*, *37*, 1211–1220.

Wicklund, R.A. (1975). Objective self-awareness. In L. Berkowitz (Ed.), *Advances in experimental social psychology* (Vol. 8). New York: Academic Press.

Wicklund, R.A., & Brehm, J. (1976). *Perspectives on cognitive dissonance*. Hillsdale, NJ: Erlbaum.

Wicklund, R.A., & Gollwitzer, P.M. (1981). Symbolic self-completion, attempted influence, and self-deprecation. *Basic and Applied Social Psychology*, *2*, 89–114.

Wicklund, R.A., & Gollwitzer, P.M. (1982). *Symbolic self-completion*. Hillsdale, NJ: Erlbaum.

Wills, T. (1981). Downward comparison principles in social psychology. *Psychological Bulletin*, *90*, 245–271.

Winkler, R.C., & Myers, R.A. (1963). Some concomitants of self-ideal discrepancy measures of self-acceptance. *Journal of Counseling Psychology*, *10*, 83–86.

Wylie, R.C. (1979). *The self-concept, Vol. 2: Theory and research on selected topics*. Lincoln: University of Nebraska Press.

Zuckerman, M. (1979). Attribution of success and failure revisited, or: The motivational bias is alive and well in attribution theory. *Journal of Personality*, *47*, 245–287.

Chapter 11
Depression: A Self-Presentation Formulation

Martha G. Hill, Gifford Weary, and Joan Williams

The manifestations of depression—dejected mood, passivity, feelings of guilt—are easily recognizable. Perhaps Freud's (1957) description of "melancholia" best expresses the distinguishing features of depression:

> profoundly painful dejection, cessation of interest in the outside world, loss of the capacity to love, inhibition of all activity, and a lowering of the self-regarding feelings to a degree that finds utterance in self-reproaches and self-revilings, and culminates in a delusional expectation of punishment. (p. 244)

Many theorists have offered explanations for the source or cause of the profound suffering characteristic of human depression. Freud (1957) argued that it was the result of aggression turned inward, of an imbalance between aggressive drives and libidinal impulses. Theorists in the medical model tradition have emphasized the role of biochemical factors (se Akiskal & McKinney, 1975). More recently, depression has been described as the consequence of dysfunctional cognitive processes (Beck, 1967) and as "learned helplessness" (Seligman, 1975a, 1975b). Some attention also has been given to the social and interpersonal factors (Coates & Wortman, 1980; Coyne, 1976b; Lewinsohn, 1974) that may influence the development and expression of depressive symptoms.

Whatever the presumed cause of depression, a number of theorists long have recognized the manipulative nature of depressive symptoms. For example, Cohen (1954) suggested that depressed individuals view others as "objects to be manipulated for the purpose of receiving sympathy and reassurance." Bonime (1960, 1966) considered depression to be a way of relating to others in order to achieve pathological satisfactions. Fenichel (1945) described depressed individuals as blackmailing others for attention. Despite this theoretical recognition of the depressed person's use of his or her symptoms to manipulate others, researchers have given little attention in their studies to the possibly strategic nature of depressive symptoms (Coyne & Gotlib, 1983). This is particularly surprising since self-presentation motives have been implicated in a variety of social psychological processes (Baumeister, 1982), including causal inference processes (Weary & Arkin, 1981), and in various forms of mental illness (Braginsky, Braginsky, & Ring, 1969).

In this chapter, we examine the role of self-presentational processes in depression. More specifically, we argue that, regardless of the cause of a depressive episode, depressive symptoms may represent individuals' attempts to manage or control interpersonal relationships. While we by no means suggest that all depressive symptoms are rooted in conscious or unconscious attempts to control others, we do suggest that symptoms that ultimately obtain sympathy and permit the avoidance of performance demands may be strategically employed. Specifically, we propose that the depressed individual's self-doubt and shaky self-confidence may lead him or her to adopt a protective self-presentational style across a variety of interaction settings. The particular manifestation of that style may vary depending upon particular social contextual variables; however, the underlying motive is likely to be avoidance of future performance demands and potential further losses in esteem. Indeed, we argue that the depressive may accept or even engender short-term disapproval in an attempt to terminate or withdraw from current and avoid future performance obligations. Finally, we suggest that the responses elicited from others by such a depressive self-presentation style may have the unintended effect of maintaining the depression.

While there are many theoretical formulations of the psychology of depression (see Blaney, 1977; Eastman, 1976), the models proposed by Beck (1967), Seligman (1975a, 1975b), Lewinsohn (1974), and Coyne (1976b) have influenced to a great extent the conceptualizations of depression that have guided researchers' and clinicians' efforts to understand and treat depressed individuals. Accordingly, we present an overview of each of these models[1] and then discuss the notion of depressive self-presentation. This provides a context within which the classic or frequently cited studies relevant to Beck's (1967) and Seligman's (1975a, 1975b; Abramson, Seligman, & Teasdale, 1978) cognitive and Lewinsohn's (1974) interpersonal models of depression may be reviewed. Included in our review are the few studies that have included an explicit manipulation of the "public" and "private" nature of the experimental setting. This manipulation is the most common method of testing for the arousal of self-presentation motives and presumably is a manipulation of evaluation apprehension (Rosenberg, 1969). Cognitive and interpersonal theorists generally have not considered self-presentation motives to be important influences of depressives' behaviors; however, much of the empirical evidence for the cognitive (Beck, 1967; Seligman, 1975a, 1975b) and interpersonal (Lewinsohn, 1974) models has been derived from experiments that essentially were "public" in nature. When reexamined, evidence frequently cited as supportive of these models may provide indirect support for a self-presentational interpretation of depression. Studies

---

[1] A complete review of the literature in support of these models is beyond the scope of this paper. Although each model has strengths and limitations, no attempt is made to evaluate the relative merits of the different models in order to conclude or determine which one is superior. The models are presented in order to provide a context within which to discuss depressive self-presentation.

stimulated by Coyne's interpersonal formulation of depression are directly relevant to the self-presentation view presented in this chapter and are discussed within the context of reactions of others to depressive self-presentations.

Overview of Contemporary Cognitive and Interpersonal Models of Depression

Cognitive Models of Depression

Depressive cognition. The cognitive model of depression proposed by Beck (1967, 1974) characterizes the thinking of depressives as illogical and distorted. According to Beck's model, the depressive cognitive triad—a negative and distorted view of the world, the self, and the future—precipitates the emotional and motivational changes that are recognized generally as components of depression. The thoughts of the depressed center on a theme of loss; the depressed dwells on "hypothetical losses" and "pseudo-losses." Beck described the depressed person's pessimism as absolute and global. Depressed persons, according to Beck, tend to overinterpret daily events in terms of loss while remaining oblivious to more positive interpretations:

> he is hypersensitive to stimuli suggestive of loss and is blind to stimuli representing gain. . . . He is facile in recalling unpleasant experiences but 'draws a blank' when questioned about positive experiences. (Beck, 1974, p. 14)

Beck's model emphasizes that it is individuals' appraisal of life events rather than the events themselves that are precipitants of depression. The negative affect associated with depression is, then, secondary to negative cognitions. The emotional manifestations include dejected mood, self-reproach, and self-criticisms; the depressed individual seems preoccupied with his or her deficiencies. Negative expectations are manifested in motivational changes; the depressed individuals may engage in less demanding activities, exert less effort, or avoid activity altogether.

Learned helplessness. A second model of depression in which individuals' cognitions are presumed to precede and cause depressive affect and related symptoms is the learned helplessness model (Seligman, 1975a, 1975b). Originally drawn from laboratory experiments with dogs, this theory suggests that, through exposure to uncontrollable stress or trauma, individuals learn that responses and outcomes are independent, or noncontingent: "The depressed patient has learned or believes that he cannot control these elements of his life that relieve suffering or bring him gratification" (Seligman, 1975a, p. 98).

Helpless individuals come to believe that active coping efforts are futile. Learned helplessness is manifested in motivational, cognitive, and emotional changes. Motivational changes are inferred from the depressed individual's general passivity and from slow response initiation in experimental settings. Negative expectations are presumed to reflect cognitive changes. The emotional consequence of learned helplessness is a depressed mood.

The helplessness model of depression has been reformulated and elaborated (Abramson et al., 1978) as a model for a subset of depression, "hopelessness depression." According to this model, individuals' expectations of hopelessness accompanied by lowered self-esteem have been identified as sufficient causes of depressive symptoms. Although the reformulated model allows for a variety of causes of "hopelessness," it focuses on individuals' causal attributions for negative events as important contributory causes of hopelessness and the subsequent depression. That is, experiencing an uncontrollable negative event may not result in depression; the depressed response is mediated by individuals' attributions regarding the experience.

Individuals who experience negative events presumably attempt to evaluate and understand the causes of their experience. Three attributional dimensions are especially relevant to the reformulated learned helplessness model of depression—internality, stability, and globality. The internality dimension determines the impact of an event on self-esteem. For example, an attribution to a personal characteristic (internal) is more likely to have an impact on self-esteem than an attribution to an environmental cause (external). The stability dimension presumably relates to an individual's ability to predict future experiences; a stable cause (e.g., ability) is likely to remain unchanged and is, therefore, a better predictor of future experiences than an unstable cause (e.g., luck). The globality dimension is important in determining the generalizability of the experience. That is, a global cause is one that is likely to affect many areas of experience. According to the reformulated learned helplessness model, depression is most likely to occur with an internal, stable, global attribution for a negative event and least likely to occur with an external, unstable, specific attribution for the event. The depressogenic attributional style (internal-stable-global) presumably leads to a generalized expectation of hopelessness, and, consequently, to depression.

Interpersonal Models of Depression

Social skill deficit. Lewinsohn (1974, 1975) proposed a behavioral model of depression in which the onset of depression is preceded by a reduction of "response-contingent positive reinforcement." Although the model is described in behavioral language, it can be interpreted as an interpersonal model in a very general sense. That is, the difficulties postulated to lead to depression occur in relationship to the social environment. More specifically, social skills deficits are presumed to be an important antecedent condition for depression.

According to Lewinsohn's model, a low rate of contingent positive reinforcement provides sufficient explanation for the onset of depressive symptoms. That is, Lewinsohn proposed that depression could be explained in terms of learning theory without reference to cognitions (e.g., Beck, 1967). The model proposed that the cognitive aspects of depression are "secondary elaborations of the feeling of dysphoria, which in turn is presumed to be the consequence of a low rate of response-contingent positive reinforcement" (Lewinsohn, 1974, p. 169). Lewinsohn argued that there exists a qualitative and quantitative difference between depressed and nondepressed individuals in terms of the number of types of events that are potentially reinforcing. He suggested that depressives' low rate of response-contingent positive reinforcement is a function of three variables: the environment may have few available positive reinforcers; the person may lack the skills necessary to obtain available positive reinforcers; and the positive reinforcement potency of events may be reduced. In addition, Lewinsohn suggested that depressed individuals might be more sensitive to aversive stimuli (Lewinsohn, Lobitz, & Wilson, 1973) and would therefore exhibit greater avoidance behavior. This avoidance initially could lead to greater social isolation of the depressed person and, consequently, result in less skill acquisition. The cognitive changes associated with depression (pessimism, guilt, low self-esteem) are considered, in this model, to be a consequence of the low rate of response-contingent positive reinforcement, rather than a primary cause of depression.

Coyne's interactional model of depression. The model of depression proposed by Coyne (1976b) focuses on the importance of the interaction of the depressed individual with the social environment. Coyne described depression as a self-perpetuating interpersonal system in which social responses to the depressed person contribute to the maintenance of depression by validating the depressive's negative feelings about himself or herself.

According to Coyne, initial expression of depression may be precipitated by social stress (e.g., loss of a significant relationship) or by changes in an individual's social structure. Symptoms (e.g., expression of helplessness and hopelessness) are exhibited in order to elicit social support: "Depressive symptomatology is seen as a set of messages demanding reassurance of the person's place in the interactions he is still able to maintain, and further action by others to alter or restore his loss" (p. 33).

The initial response of others to the depressed person generally is supportive and reassuring, presumably guided by a social norm dictating that people be helpful to needy others (Goffman, 1963; Schwartz, 1972). The depressed person faces an attributional dilemma in evaluating the positive reactions of others (Coates & Wortman, 1981). In his or her attempt to determine if others' supportive responses are sincere or merely normative, the depressed person continues to elicit feedback by emitting symptomatic behaviors:

> The symptoms of depressed persons are aversive yet powerful in the ability to arouse guilt in others and to inhibit any direct expression of annoyance and hostility from others. Members of the social environment attempt to reduce the aversive behavior of depressed persons and alleviate guilt by manipulating them with nongenuine reassurance and support. At the same time, these same persons reject and avoid the depressed persons. (Coyne, 1976a, p. 187)

The ambivalent or discrepant responses of others contribute to the depressed individual's feelings of uncertainty and doubt. These feelings stimulate symptomatic behaviors. What follows is

> a series of interactive stalemates. . . . Members of the social environment become increasingly annoyed, and their angry outbursts and hostile retaliations against the

depressed become more frequent. The depressed person becomes more aware that others dislike him. (Coates & Wortman, 1980, p. 162)

The responses of others, then, confirm the depressive's negative feelings and contribute to the maintenance and exacerbation of depressive symptoms. Depressives' negative cognitions regarding the social environment appear to be, in the context of this model, perceptions that are congruent with the experience of the depressed person (i.e., a hostile, rejecting social environment) rather than "distortions" and "misperceptions" as described by Beck (1967). In addition, the "social skills deficits" often attributed to depressed persons (Lewinsohn, 1974) are understandable within the social context described by Coyne (1976b): "The person facing this situation is dealing with a changing environment, and . . . the skills needed to deal with it are likely to be different from those required by a more stable normal environment" (p. 37).

By emphasizing the important impact of the social context, Coyne's model presents depression as more than an intrapersonal, cognitive-affective phenomenon; it is a social or interpersonal process. This theoretical model of depression, more than those models discussed previously, suggests the importance of self-presentation in the context of depression.

Depressive Self-Presentation

The process of strategic self-presentation can be defined as "the more or less intentional control of appearances in order to guide and control the responses made by others to us" (Weary & Arkin, 1981, p. 225). The desired appearance or impression is created by purposive nonverbal behaviors, verbal descriptions of attributes and behaviors, and verbal descriptions of reasons for particular behaviors (Schlenker, 1980; Weary & Arkin, 1981). Although theorists have emphasized social approval seeking as the primary goal of strategic self-presentation, there may be other goals (Jones & Pittman, 1982).

We suggest that depressive symptoms may be strategic self-presentations designed to control interpersonal interactions. Moreover, we believe that clarification of the self-presentational goals and strategies of depressed individuals may lead to a better understanding of depression since those goals may be quite different than the goals characteristic of nondepressed individuals. In this section, we discuss the form depressive self-presentation may take.

Protective Self-Presentation

Arkin (1981) has argued that there exists a protective self-presentation style that can be differentiated from the generally recognized "acquisitive" (to acquire social approval) self-presentation style. The protective self-presentation motivation can be considered as a conservative orientation toward interaction that leads individuals to act "like a very conservative investor in a risky, volatile economic market. Expectation of what might be gained is out-weighed by anticipation of what could be lost by getting involved" (Zimbardo, 1977, p. 40).

The arousal of the protective motivation may be situation specific, as in the presence of an unpredictable audience (e.g., an experimenter) or it may be chronic as a consequence of self-doubt and "shaky" self-confidence (Arkin, 1981).[2] Individuals may seek to avoid disapproval by creating impressions that are completely defensible or entirely innocuous. Expressions of the protective self-presentation can be seen in compliant and conforming behaviors, and in highly modest presentations of personal characteristics and accomplishments. Social avoidance and withdrawal may represent extreme examples of protective self-presentation.

Depressive Self-Protection

It seems reasonable to argue that self-protection may be the major goal of depressive self-presentation. Specifically, the depressive characteristics of self-doubt, shaky self-confidence, and social anxiety (Sacco & Hokanson, 1978) may increase the likelihood that the depressed individual, in the context of social interaction, will experience heightened concern over social evaluations. Such evaluation apprehension, in turn, may lead him or her to adopt a protective self-presentation style across a variety of social interaction settings. As suggested above, this style may be expressed in highly modest descriptions of accomplishments (e.g., underestimates of positive outcomes), in social reticence (e.g., low levels of social interaction), or in extreme cases, social avoidance and withdrawal).

Whatever the particular manifestation of depressive self-protection, it is important to consider what it is that the depressed person may be trying to avoid. In his description of the protective self-presentation style, Arkin (1981) emphasized the avoidance of social disapproval. However, in the case of depression, it seems likely that the avoidance of performance demands and obligations may be at least as important as, if not more important than, the avoidance of disapproval. Indeed, Coyne has argued that the depressed individual's messages of distress and suffering implicitly demand

> "a suspension of the rules; a moratorium on the web of obligations under which a person lives, such as admission to the sick role." (McPartland & Hornstra, 1964, p. 256)

By emphasizing his or her weakness or illness, the depressive, then, may risk short-term disapproval and may even deprecate his or her present accomplishments in order to avoid altogether future demands to perform, or at least to avoid the embarrassment that may result from unanticipated future negative performance out-

---

[2] A discussion regarding the source of these findings is beyond the scope of this paper; however, analyses have been offered elsewhere (e.g., Jones & Berglas, 1978; Sullivan, 1953; Teevan & McGhee, 1972; Weinstein, 1968).

comes (i.e., the depressive may risk a short-term loss of esteem in order to avoid any further losses). Unfortunately, the avoidance of future performance likely serves only to maintain the depressive's self-doubts and shaky self-confidence.

Empirical Evidence for Self-Presentation in Depression

As previously noted, the strategic nature of depressive behaviors has received relatively little attention from researchers. Much of the research stimulated by the cognitive and interpersonal theories of depression has been conducted in relatively "public" settings, i.e., with the experimenter present. Such settings are likely to increase subjects' concerns regarding evaluation of their performance and, consequently, to arouse self-presentational concerns. It is quite possible that depressed and nondepressed subjects adopt different strategies in response to evaluation apprehension (Sacco & Hokanson, 1978). For example, nondepressed subjects may be characteristically self-enhancing while depressed subjects may adopt self-protective strategies. The following sections of this chapter examine studies stimulated by Beck's (1967) and Seligman's (1975a, 1975b; Abramson et al., 1978) cognitive and Lewinsohn's (1974) interpersonal theories of depression. Reinterpretation of experimental results in terms of self-presentational motivations may yield quite different conclusions regarding depressives' responding and may provide empirical support for the notion that depressive behaviors represent individuals' attempts to manage interpersonal processes.

Empirical Evidence: Cognitive Theories

Distorted recall. One way in which researchers have evaluated cognitive distortion in depression has been to provide depressed and nondepressed subjects with varying rates of positive, negative, and neutral feedback and to measure subsequently subjects' recall of the feedback. Differences between depressed and nondepressed subjects' recall have been interpreted as evidence of depressive cognitive distortion. Presumably a depressed individual overestimates the rate of negative feedback, and distorts the rate of positive and neutral feedback in a negative way. Such cognitive processing would make environmental feedback consistent with the depressed individual's negative view and serve to maintain depression.

Two studies (DeMonbreun & Craighead, 1977; Nelson & Craighead, 1977) in this area of research might be considered "classics" as they frequently are cited as supportive of the notion of depressive cognitive distortion. These studies are reviewed in detail in this section to familiarize the reader with the methodology and in order to illustrate how the "cognitive distortions" found in these studies may reflect self-presentational concerns.

Nelson and Craighead (1977) experimentally controlled the rates of positive and negative feedback received by depressed and nondepressed subjects while they were performing an ambiguous laboratory task and subsequently measured subjects' recall of feedback. These authors reasoned that high levels of positive feedback and low levels of negative feedback would be most inconsistent with the depressed subjects' expectations and, therefore, differences in attributions between depressed and nondepressed subjects would be greater at a relatively high rate of reinforcement and at a relatively low rate of punishment.

Subjects in the study were college students selected on the basis of their scores on the Beck Depression Inventory (BDI) (depressed, BDI > 10; nondepressed, BDI < 5). Subjects were assigned to one of four experimental conditions such that they were reinforced 30% or 70% on 40 trials or were punished 30% or 70% on 40 trials of identifying nonsense syllables. After the 40 trials, the subjects verbally estimated the number of times they had been reinforced or punished. This estimate was reported to the experimenter and recorded on the subjects' data sheets.

The results were consistent with the experimental hypotheses. In the low-rate-of-reinforcement condition, depressed and nondepressed subjects did not differ in their recall; both groups underestimated the rate of reinforcement. In the high-rate-of-reinforcement condition, the actual rate of reinforcement was significantly underestimated by depressed but not by nondepressed subjects. In the punishment conditions, the groups did not differ in their recall of punishment when it was administered at a high rate. When a low rate of punishment was administered, depressed subjects recalled a significantly greater number of punishments received than did nondepressed subjects. It is important to note, however, that depressed subjects' estimates were similar to the actual rate of punishment while nondepressed subjects actually underestimated the amount of negative feedback received. Nelson and Craighead argued that their results provided evidence of "selective recall" associated with depression. The selective recall of negative versus positive events illustrated by this study presumably provided evidence that depressed individuals distorted environmental information in a way that was consistent with their negative cognitive structure (Beck, 1967).

DeMonbreun and Craighead (1977) investigated distorted perception and recall of positive and neutral feedback among clinically depressed subjects, psychopathic controls, and normal controls. Consistent with previous research, DeMonbreun and Craighead anticipated that depressed subjects, compared to controls, would underestimate high rates of positive feedback. In addition, the researchers hypothesized that depressed subjects would distort neutral feedback in a negative direction.

Subjects were required to identify nonsense syllables and then received feedback slides indicating whether responses were acceptable or unacceptable.[3] During the first 40 trials, all subjects received 16 positive, 16 negative, and 8 neutral feedback slides. During the second 40 trials, subjects in the "high" condition received 22 positive, 10 negative, and 8 neutral slides. Subjects in the "low" condition received 10 positive, 22 negative, and 8 neutral slides. Following each phase of 40 trials, subjects were asked to recall the number of trials for which they had received positive feedback.

---

[3]The feedback slide was one of a set of five that ranged from light gray to black and that indicated that responses were 100% acceptable, 75% acceptable, 75% unacceptable, or 100% unacceptable. The fifth slide was neutral and subjects were not informed of its existence.

Results indicated that, during both phases of the study, depressed and non-depressed subjects accurately perceived, when measured on a trial-by-trial basis, the type of feedback (positive, negative, and neutral) that they had received. On the recall measure, however, depressed subjects significantly underestimated the number of positive feedback slides they had received while the nondepressed groups did not. The authors concluded that their results provided evidence of depressive cognitive distortion of environmental feedback. Presumably the high rate of positive feedback was inconsistent with the depressed subjects' negative self-view and was distorted. Since no differences were found between groups in the perception of positive feedback when measured on a trial-by-trial basis, yet differences were found on the recall measure, the authors concluded that "distortion does not occur at the point of stimulus perception but that there is a cognitive transformation of the environmental input subsequent to the immediate perception of the feedback stimulus" (p. 377).

The results of these studies provide evidence of depressed-nondepressed differences in recall of positive and negative feedback following performances on experimental tasks. Those differences have been interpreted as evidence of cognitive distortion associated with depression. That is, high rates of positive feedback and low rates of negative feedback are presumed to be inconsistent with depressives' negative self-views and therefore are distorted. This "cognitive transformation" of performance feedback (DeMonbreun & Craighead, 1977) would be consistent with Beck's (1967) cognitive theory of depression.

Distorted recall and self-presentation. The depressed-nondepressed differences in recall found in these studies may reflect response bias rather than cognitive distortion. Such an explanation is plausible for two reasons. First, the reader will recall that in the Nelson and Craighead (1977) study depressed subjects were able to recall low rates of punishment accurately. That feedback was presumably inconsistent with their expectations and, consequently, should have been distorted. Second, in both studies estimates were communicated to the same experimenter who had given the original feedback and who easily could confirm or disconfirm the accuracy of the reports. An important implicit assumption in each of these studies was that the experimenter's presence either did not influence subject responses or influenced depressed and nondepressed subjects in an equal and similar manner. But, as we have argued, depressed individuals are likely to adopt a conservative or protective self-presentation style when concerns for avoiding future performance demands are aroused. If avoidance of such demands is one's primary goal, perhaps it would be most prudent to claim that one simply is not capable (i.e., emphasize negative and deemphasize positive performance feedback) of satisfactory performance. Depressed-nondepressed differences in recall, then, may reflect different self-presentation styles (e.g., self-protective versus self-enhancing) rather than depressive cognitive distortion.

Self-reward and self-punishment. Self-reward and self-punishment have been considered to be analogue measures of individuals' tendencies to evaluate their behavior positively or negatively in a variety of settings. A common research strategy has been to ask subjects to reward or punish their performance on a laboratory task of ambiguous outcome. Depressed subjects' tendencies to exhibit lower levels of self-reward and higher levels of self-punishment relative to nondepressed subjects generally has been interpreted as indicative of the depressives' negative self-view and, therefore, consistent with the cognitive theories of depression (Abramson et al., 1978; Beck, 1967).[4]

Rozensky, Rehm, Pry, and Roth (1977) evaluated the relationship between depression and self-reinforcement behavior in hospitalized medical patients. Subjects participated in a verbal recognition memory task and were instructed to self-reward when they believed their word selection was correct and to self-punish when they believed that their word selection was incorrect. Self-reward consisted of a button press that lit a lamp; self-punishment was a button press that sounded a shrill tone. No external feedback regarding word choice correctness was given.

Rozensky et al. found that, although groups did not differ on actual performance, the depressed subjects self-rewarded less and self-punished more than did control subjects. In addition, depressed subjects gave "no response" more frequently than did control subjects, indicating they were more uncertain about the accuracy of their word selection.

Lobitz and Post (1979) investigated the relationship among self-expectation, self-evaluation, and level of self-reward for depressed and nondepressed psychiatric patients. Subjects performed three tasks—a word association task, WAIS Digit Symbol, and a "ward assistance task"—for which they could earn tokens that were exchangeable for small prizes. The experimenter did not observe subjects' responses to the experimental tasks, but did observe the self-rewarding behaviors.

Results from the study indicated that depressed subjects demonstrated a significantly lower level of self-expectation, self-evaluation, and self-reward than did nondepressed subjects. Additional analyses showed no significant differences between groups in levels of self-reward beyond those predictable from level of self-expectation and self-evaluation. Moreover, there was no difference between groups in self-evaluation beyond that predictable from self-expectation. Lobitz and Post proposed that depressed subjects brought negative cognitions (i.e., negative self-expectations) about themselves to the experiment, and behaved in a way that was

---

[4]Nelson and Craighead (1977) also investigated self-reinforcement and self-punishment of depressed and nondepressed subjects. The results of that study are frequently cited as supportive of the hypothesis that depressed individuals self-reinforce less and self-punish more than do nondepressed individuals (e.g., Lobitz & Post, 1979). Because self-rewarding and self-punishing behaviors were measured during the second phase of the study (see section on "Distorted Recall"), and because subjects had received feedback on their performance during the first phase (see section on "Distorted Recall"), rates of self-reward and self-punishment were seriously confounded with the previous rate of feedback. Consequently, the study has not been reviewed here. To consider the results as evidence of how subjects (depressed and nondepressed) self-reward or self-punish "in the absence of external feedback" seems questionable.

consistent with those cognitions (Festinger, 1957). Lobitz and Post also suggested that the experimenter's presence may have inadvertently affected the depressed subjects' responses. That is, depressed subjects' low levels of self-expectation and self-reward might have been intended to elicit sympathy from the experimenter.

Self-reward and self-presentation. The studies reviewed in this section provide evidence that in some situations depressed subjects self-reward less and self-punish more than do nondepressed subjects. These results have been interpreted as consistent with the cognitive theories of depression. However, self-rewarding and self-punishing involve an implicit evaluation of the quality of one's performance. When that evaluation consists of a public statement or act, it may well be influenced by self-presentational concerns. Depressives' lower levels of self-reward may reflect the protective self-presentation of individuals who are uncertain about the quality of their performance (Rozensky et al., 1977). An interpretation of the self-rewarding and self-punishing behavior of depressives as strategic self-presentation is plausible and is supported by the results of two studies (Forrest & Hokanson, 1975; Sacco & Hokanson, 1982).

Self-reward in public and private. Sacco and Hokanson (1982) compared self-reinforcement of depressed, nondepressed, and nondepressed-helpless subjects during a 22-trial skill task. Sacco and Hokanson reasoned that if depressed individuals use symptoms strategically to control interpersonal processes then the symptomatic behaviors would be more likely to occur in a public (interpersonal) situation than in a private one. Sacco and Hokanson predicted that depressed subjects would exhibit lower levels of self-reinforcement, relative to nondepressed subjects, in public but not in private. In addition, they argued that nondepressed subjects pretreated with failure (nondepressed-helpless) should respond similarly to depressed subjects in both the public and private conditions (see Sacco & Hokanson, 1978). Subjects were assigned to a "public" performance and reinforcement condition or a "private" performance and reinforcement condition. Sacco and Hokanson noted that "neither of the cognitive theories imply that the presence or absence of another person should alter the dysfunctional cognitive processes said to characterize the depressed person" (p. 378).

The experimental task, which presumably measured "perceptual and attentive abilities," required subjects to estimate how many colored lights flashed during each of 22 trials. "After the subjects indicated their answer, either the experimenter (public condition) or a light (private condition) signalled whether the answer was correct or incorrect" (p. 383). Success rate (number of correct trials) was experimentally controlled. Subjects' self-reinforcement was measured after each trial (self-credit) and after each 11 trials (satisfaction level) by verbal report (public) or by pushing a button (private).

Sacco and Hokanson found that in the public condition the level of self-credit for nondepressed subjects was numerically higher (albeit not significantly) than that of the depressed and the depressed-helpless groups. In addition, they found that in the private condition the self-credit level of the depressed and nondepressed-helpless groups was numerically higher (not significantly) than the public self-credit measures for the depressed and nondepressed-helpless subjects, respectively. Sacco and Hokanson concluded that the pattern of the depressed groups' cell means in public and private conformed to predictions of the interpersonal view of depression.

The results of the Sacco and Hokanson study, then, suggest that the presence of the experimenter differentially affected self-reinforcement in depressed, nondepressed, and nondepressed-helpless subjects. That influence is not accounted for by the cognitive theories. Moreover, in the public condition, subjects in all groups expressed greater evaluation apprehension and efforts at impression management tactics than did subjects in the private condition.[5] Sacco and Hokanson concluded that "a major difference between depressed and nondepressed individuals is not their sensitivity to public evaluation but, rather, in the way they respond to evaluation apprehension" (p. 383).

The findings of this study provide direct evidence of the influence of self-presentational motivations on depressive self-rewarding behaviors. Further investigation is needed since the effects found in this study were interesting but relatively weak.

Self-punishment. While many researchers have interpreted self-punishment as indicative of depressives' negative self-view (e.g., Beck, 1967; Nelson & Craighead, 1977; Rozensky et al., 1977), Forrest and Hokanson (1975) proposed that depressive self-punishment may have instrumental value in controlling aversiveness and threat from others.

Forrest and Hokanson compared the responses of depressed and nondepressed subjects in a two-person interaction situation. Subjects received periodic shocks from a partner and had the option of responding aggressively (shock the partner), in a friendly manner, or in a self-punishing manner (self-shock). The experimental situation was designed to foster the development of self-punishment responses; subjects could avoid a painful shock from the partner by administering a mild self-shock.

Forrest and Hokanson found that, when aggressed against (shocked), depressed subjects responded with a higher frequency of self-punitive behavior than did nondepressed subjects. In addition, depressed subjects were more responsive to the contingencies that favored self-punishment. The authors interpreted their results as suggesting that "depressed patients have learned to cope with environmental and interpersonal stresses with self-punitive and/or nonassertive behaviors and these behaviors have been successful in dealing with their day to day existence" (p. 356).

Summary. Taken together, the results of these studies (Forrest & Hokanson, 1975; Sacco & Hokanson, 1982) support a self-presentational interpretation of the self-

---

[5]Subjects in the public condition reported that they had tried to present "a certain impression or image of themselves" to a greater extent than did subjects in the private condition (Sacco & Hokanson, 1978, p. 380).

rewarding and self-punishing behaviors of depressives. Those behaviors have been interpreted most frequently in terms of cognitive distortion. However, in the context of these studies, depressives' self-rewarding and self-punishing appear to have served an interpersonal function such as self-protection.

Expectancy change. Measures of "expectation for success" have been used in a variety of studies as indicators of depressive cognitive dysfunction. Differences found between depressed and nondepressed subjects in initial levels of expectation for success have been interpreted as reflecting the negative cognitive set brought by depressives to the experimental setting (Lobitz & Post, 1978; Loeb, Beck, & Diggory, 1971). In addition, smaller expectancy changes expressed by depressed as compared to nondepressed subjects following success or failure on experimental tasks have been accepted as evidence of depressives' generalized expectation that responses and outcomes are noncontingent (e.g., learned helplessness). Changes in expectancies usually are measured as subjects perform skill and chance tasks. Depressed subjects presumably perceive responses and outcomes as more independent than do nondepressed subjects in skill situations, whereas both depressed and nondepressed subjects perceive responses and outcomes as independent in chance situations.

Garber and Hollon (1980) investigated expectancy changes for depressed and nondepressed subjects in a study that was focused primarily upon the distinction between universal and personal helplessness. That study is reviewed here because the methodology provides an example of the measurement of changes in expectations and because the results of the study may provide indirect evidence of the influence of self-presentational motivations on statements of expectancy.

The study was designed to assess whether depressives' cognitive distortions (as indicated by expectancy changes) were "specific to their belief about their own skilled action (personal helplessness), or a result of a general belief in uncontrollability in the world (universal helplessness)" (p. 58). Depressed and nondepressed subjects were asked to generate expectancies for success on a skill task and a chance task for themselves (actor condition) or for another (observer condition). The chance task required the subject (or confederate) to guess which of two slides (X or O) would appear next. The skill task required the subject (or confederate) to raise a platform by pulling a string without letting a ball fall off the platform. There were 10 trials of each task. Success and failure were manipulated by the experimenter; the same 50% reinforcement schedule was used throughout. Subjects indicated to the experimenter how certain they were that they (or the confederate) would be successful on the next trial.

The results, using a measure of "total expectancy change,"[6] were summarized by Garber and Hollon:

---

[6]The total expectancy change score was computed by taking the sum of the absolute value of the expectancy changes from one trial to the next for trials in which the subject increased his or her expectancy following a success or decreased his or her expectancy following a failure, for trial 1 through trial 10 inclusive (Garber & Hollon, 1980; Sacco & Hokanson, 1978).

In a skill task, depressed subjects showed significantly smaller changes in expectancy than nondepressed when estimating their own probability of success, whereas both depressed and nondepressed observers showed similarly large changes in expectancy when estimating the probability of another person's success. Further, nondepressed actors showed more change in skill than in chance, while depressed actors showed similarly small amount of expectancy change in both skill and chance. (p. 61)

Garber and Hollon interpreted their results as providing evidence that depressed individuals viewed themselves as "helpless" in the skilled situation but did not view the situation as uncontrollable (as indicated by their expectancy changes for the confederate). They concluded that the results supported the reformulation of the learned helplessness model of depression that differentiates between personal and universal helplessness.

Measurement of expectancy for success. As exemplified in this study, the standard method of measuring expectancy change has been to request subjects to state their certainty of success prior to each trial of an experimental task. This method of eliciting expectancy statements, however, may alter the expectancies (Dweck & Gilliard, 1975). That is, subjective probability estimates and confidence in the accuracy of those statements is confounded (Wollert, 1977). The confounding of those factors may be an especially important source of distortion for depressed subjects, who have been demonstrated to be less confident on a variety of judgments (Rizley, 1978; Rozensky et al., 1977).

A public statement of expectancy prior to each trial is likely to make salient the potential for public disconfirmation and subsequent embarrassment. It has been argued in this chapter that depressed subjects respond more cautiously than nondepressed subjects when confronted with self-presentational risks. Although depressed and nondepressed subjects in these studies may have had similar estimates of probability for their success, depressed subjects, who may be less confident of their estimates and who may experience heightened concerns over future performance demands, may have expressed more cautious (i.e., lower) expectations for their success. Such a self-protective strategy, while it may not permit avoidance of future performance trials, would serve to lower others' expectations for depressed subjects' performance and would decrease the likelihood of engendering disapproval as a consequence of failure to perform at levels consistent with optimistic expectations. Moreover, self-presentational concerns would be expected to exert a relatively stronger influence on what subjects say about their own outcomes as compared to statements regarding others' outcomes. For example, in the Garber and Hollon (1980) study, the depressed subjects showed small amounts of expectancy change for their own but not for the confederate's probability of success. That is, they were more cautious in estimating their own as compared to another's outcome.

Expectancy change in public and private. The results of a recent study (Sacco & Hokanson, 1978) provide direct evidence of the influence of self-presentational motivations on statements of expectancies. Sacco and Hokanson examined changes in expectancies for success on a perceptual task in public and private with depressed, nondepressed, and "helpless" subjects. Subjects completed a perceptual task in which they were asked to estimate the number of colored lights that flashed during each of 15 trials. The task was described as a measure of perceptual and attentive abilities; subjects were told their performance would be determined by skill. Actually, all subjects received the same (randomly determined) 50% pattern of success and failure. Prior to each trial, subjects indicated either verbally (public) or by pushing a button (private) their estimated probability of success ("expectancy for success").

Evaluation of the total expectancy change yielded a significant Depression × Publicity interaction. In the public condition, depressed and "helpless" subjects tended to show less expectancy change than did nondepressed subjects. In the private conditions depressed subjects showed significantly greater expectancy changes than did nondepressed subjects. Sacco and Hokanson (1978) interpreted these results as supportive of a self-presentational formulation of depression. More specifically, these authors proposed that "depressed persons . . . exhibit a relatively constricted range of expectancies concerning task performance in order to avoid negative social evaluations and further loss of esteem" (p. 123). The support for a self-presentational formulation of depression, however, must be considered tentative as few of the differences actually reached statistical significance.

Expectancy and self-presentation. Taken together, the results of these studies (Garber & Hollon, 1980; Sacco & Hokanson, 1978) suggest that interpretation of differences between depressed and nondepressed subjects' expectations of success in terms of cognitive distortion without consideration of self-presentational motivations may be misleading. Small expectancy changes characteristic of depressed subjects may reflect individuals' generalized expectations of helplessness as well as strategic attempts to avoid further or potential losses of esteem. Statements of expectancies may be valid indicators of cognitive processes only in situations where self-presentational concerns are aroused minimally or not at all.

Causal attribution. The cognitive models of depression implicate causal attributions in the etiology of depression. Beck's (1967) model suggests that depressed individuals exaggerate their causal responsibility for negative events and underestimate or deny causal responsibility for positive events. The reformulated learned helplessness model (Abramson et al., 1978) proposes that a depressogenic attributional style is an important antecedent of depression. Depressives presumably make internal, stable, global attributions for failure and make external, unstable, specific attributions for success. This style indicates that depressives blame themselves for negative outcomes and do not accept credit for positive outcomes. The depressogenic attributional style has been contrasted with the "self-serving" bias in attribution characteristic of nondepressed individuals. That is, nondepressed individuals tend to make external attributions for failure (e.g., Miller & Ross, 1975; Weary Bradley, 1978). By making such attributions, individuals presumably enhance or protect their self-esteem (e.g., Kelley & Michela, 1980; Snyder, Stephan, & Rosenfield, 1978; Weary Bradley, 1978; Zuckerman, 1979).

Differences in causal attributions found between depressed and nondepressed individuals for outcomes on skill and chance tasks (e.g., Kuiper, 1978; Rizley, 1978; Seligman, Abramson, Semmel, & Von Baeyer, 1979), interpersonal tasks (e.g., Rizley, 1978), and life events (e.g., Gong-Guy & Hammen, 1980; Janoff-Bulman, 1979)[7] have been interpreted as evidence of the depressogenic attributional style. Whether the depressed-nondepressed attributional differences precede, follow, or occur concomitantly with depression remains a controversial question that is not discussed here. What is of importance to this discussion is the possibility that self-presentational motivations rather than "dysfunctional cognitive processes" may account for depressed-nondepressed attributional differences. Indeed, Hammen and Mayol (1982) have argued that "much of the inadequacy of current attributional reformulations of depression could be seen to stem from disregard of situational factors and contextual parameters that may themselves affect a person's causal analyses" (p. 166).

Social contextual variables, such as publicity, may be important when the methodology of studies of depressives' causal attribution is examined. In the following sections, three studies are reviewed that provide indirect evidence for the influence of self-presentational concerns on depressives' causal attributions.

Skill-chance task performance. Kuiper (1978) examined the types of attributions made by depressives and nondepressives (female university students) on a bogus word association task. The performance outcome was controlled by the experimenter in such a way that subjects either failed (20% correct), succeeded (80% correct), or obtained an intermediate score (55% correct). Following the word association task, subjects indicated how much each of four possible causal factors (ability, effort, task difficulty, luck) had determined their performance outcome. Results indicated that depressed and nondepressed subjects made similar attributions for success. Both groups attributed their success to internal (ability, effort) factors. However, nondepressives attributed their poor performance outcomes to external factors (task difficulty, luck) while depressives made internal attributions for their poor performance outcomes. Kuiper interpreted these results as partially supportive of the learned helplessness model of depression.

Rizley (1978) examined the causal ascriptions for success and failure on a number-guessing task for depressed and nondepressed college students. Students were told that their performance outcome would be determined by skill. However the list

---

[7]Janoff-Bulman (1979) and Peterson, Schwartz, and Seligman (1981) have argued for an important distinction between characterological and behavioral self-blame for life events. They have argued that it is the characterological attribution for negative events that is compatible with depression. The distinction between characterological and behavioral self-blame is conceptually similar to the attributional dimensions discussed by other theorists, e.g., internal–stable–global versus internal–unstable–specific. The importance of this distinction is most relevant to a discussion of perceived control rather than self-presentation. Consequently, studies of attributions for life events are excluded from this discussion.

of numbers was randomly constructed so that individuals' scores were determined by chance.

Results indicated that depressed subjects rated internal factors (ability, effort) as more important determinants of failure but not of success than did nondepressed subjects. In addition, depressed subjects rated effort (internal–unstable) as a significantly more important cause of failure and rated ability (internal–stable) as a less important causal factor of success than did nondepressed subjects. The results also indicated that depressed subjects provided similar (internal) attributions for their successes and failures while nondepressed subjects exhibited a "self-serving bias" in their causal ascriptions. Rizley interpreted his results as consistent with Beck's (1967) cognitive model of depression, which would predict that depressed subjects would attribute failure to internal factors to a greater extent than would nondepressed subjects.

Interpersonal influence. In a second study, Rizley (1978) examined attributions of causality in an interpersonal influence situation. Based upon the work of Schopler and Layton (1972, 1973), Rizley reasoned that

> the self-attribution of interpersonal influence is a direct function of the degree to which the target person's behavior following an intervention is inconsistent with his or her behavior prior to the intervention. Self-attributed influence is high when behavior following the intervention is not expected or predicted from behavior prior to the intervention. (p. 41)

Subjects were told they would be an "adviser" to another student, John (a confederate), while he took a Social Perceptiveness test. They were asked to keep track of the confederate's "right" or "wrong" answers as communicated by the experimenter via intercom. Subjects gave their advice (via intercom) to the confederate during the second half of the test only. They were told "You will only hear whether John was right or wrong on each question. You won't be able to hear what his answers actually are or whether he took your advice" (p. 42). Subjects were led to believe that the confederate's performance improved or deteriorated after the subject's intervention. This manipulation of feedback presumably would elicit differential self-attributions of interpersonal influence. Consistent with previous research (Schopler & Layton, 1972, 1973), perceived influence was predicted to be greater for an evaluatively positive outcome (i.e., improving performance) than for an evaluatively negative outcome (i.e., deteriorating performance).

Results indicated that both depressed and nondepressed subjects attended to the confederate's changing performance. Depressed subjects rated their advice as a significantly more important factor in John's performance than did nondepressed subjects. In addition, depressed subjects rated themselves as having had greater interpersonal influence than did nondepressed subjects, irrespective of the direction of John's behavior change (improving or deteriorating). Rizley concluded that the findings were consistent with "Beck's (1967) contention that depressed individuals exhibit an 'egocentric' and 'primitive' notion of causality, believing themselves 'to blame for everything that goes wrong around them' " (Rizley, 1978, p. 45).

Summary. The three studies reviewed above provide evidence suggesting that depressed subjects tended to make similar attributions for evaluatively positive and negative outcomes on different laboratory tasks, while nondepressives' attributions reflected a "self-serving bias." One conclusion that can be drawn from such data is that nondepressed individuals are motivated to maintain or protect their self-esteem but depressed individuals are not (Alloy & Abramson, 1981, 1982). Such an interpretation is consistent with cognitive theories of depression (Abramson et al., 1978; Beck, 1967), which suggest that depressed compared to nondepressed individuals blame themselves for negative outcomes but fail to accept credit for positive outcomes.

An alternative explanation is that self-presentational concerns influenced subjects' causal attributions for their outcomes. Because subjects' performances and attributional activities were public in each of these studies (Kuiper, 1978; Rizley, 1978), it is likely that subjects experienced increased evaluation apprehension. There is some evidence that depressives and nondepressives respond to evaluation apprehension with different self-presentations (Sacco & Hokanson, 1978). For example, nondepressives may be characteristically self-enhancing. By taking credit for positive outcomes and denying responsibility for negative outcomes, nondepressives may maximize public esteem (Weary Bradley, 1978).

Depressed subjects, however, may experience heightened concern over social evaluations and future performance demands because of their greater self-doubt and lack of confidence. Consequently, depressives may adopt a protective self-presentation style in response to evaluation apprehension. By making similarly internal attributions for their positive and negative outcomes, depressed individuals presumably avoid any further loss in esteem that could result from others publicly challenging a too-positive interpretation of their outcomes (see Arkin, Appleman, & Burger, 1980). It is possible, then, that both depressed and nondepressed subjects were motivated to protect their esteem, but they adopted different strategies toward that end.

Cognitive Processes in Depression—Summary

The cognitive theories of depression (Abramson et al., 1978; Beck, 1967) have postulated that dysfunctional cognitive processes are important antecedents of depressive affect. Researchers have used a variety of indicators of the cognitive processes of the depressed; however, little attention has been given to the interpersonal context in which those indicators have been measured. It was argued and evidence was presented consistent with the notion that measures of cognitive processes may be influenced by social contextual variables within the experimental setting. Moreover, these indicators of dysfunctional cognitive processes may be viewed as interpersonal behaviors under the control of the depressed individual. As such, they may represent strategic self-presentations.

The results of the studies reviewed were consistent with the notion of depressive protective self-presentation. The responses of depressed subjects were characterized as more cautious, more modest, and less self-enhancing than the responses of nondepressed objects. It was argued that depressed subjects, especially in the unusual situation of a laboratory experiment, may experience heightened concerns over social evaluations. Their responses, then, may reflect a strategic trade-off—the risk of short-term disapproval in order to avoid future performance demands and potential future losses in esteem.

Empirical Evidence: Lewinsohn's Interpersonal Model

Lewinsohn (1974) proposed that depression is a consequence of a low rate of response-contingent positive reinforcement. Research activities have focused primarily on two areas: determination of the relationship between mood and pleasant activities (e.g., Hammen & Glass, 1975; Lewinsohn & Libet, 1972; Mac-Phillamy & Lewinsohn, 1974), and the relationship between social competence and depression (e.g., Libet & Lewinsohn, 1973). Research regarding the number and kinds of potentially reinforcing events is less relevant to the present discussion of depressive self-presentation than is research regarding social competencies. In this section, consequently, two studies that evaluated depressives' social skills are reviewed.

Social skill deficits. Lewinsohn's model of depression proposes that social skill deficits are important antecedents of depression. He defined social skill as the ability to maximize the rate of positive reinforcement and to minimize the rate of punishment elicited from others. Lewinsohn (1974) has argued and provided evidence consistent with the notion that depressed individuals, as a group, are less socially skillful than nondepressed individuals.

Libet and Lewinsohn (1973) compared the interpersonal behaviors of depressed subjects, psychiatric controls, and nondepressed controls in small self-study groups that met for 8 weeks. These researchers predicted and found that depressed subjects interacted with fewer individuals, were slower to respond to others, and gave fewer positive responses to others than did nondepressed subjects. It is important to note that these group differences were attenuated during the later sessions. Libet and Lewinsohn concluded that these results were consistent with the hypothesis that depressed individuals lack social skills, and that the social skills deficit is maximized by conditions of strangeness and ambiguity.

Youngren and Lewinsohn (1980) provided a multitrait, multimethod assessment of the functional relation of depression and interpersonal behaviors uniquely associated with depression. The study included observations of dyadic and group interactions, measures of verbal and nonverbal behaviors, self-report, peer ratings, and observers' coding of behaviors. Depressed subjects were compared to two non-depressed control groups—normal controls and psychiatric controls (based upon elevated MMPI profiles).

The results of the study suggested that differences between depressed subjects and nondepressed controls occurred primarily on the level of self-report, especially for self-reported frequency and comfort in "social initiation" activities (e.g., talking with a stranger). On ratings of interpersonal style in groups, depressed subjects rated themselves more negatively and received more negative ratings from peers and observers. In dyads, depressed subjects were rated as less socially skillful by nondepressed peers; however, observer ratings indicated no significant between-group differences. Measurements of verbal and nonverbal behaviors identified no deficits uniquely associated with depression. However, depressives' scores were "in the more problematic direction relative to normals" (p. 339).

Depressive self-presentation and social skill. The results of these studies generally are cited as support for Lewinsohn's theory that depressed individuals are less socially skillful or less adept at eliciting positive social reinforcement. Indeed, depression is presumed to be a consequence of the postulated social skill deficit. Both studies actually show, however, that depressives are capable of behaviors comparable to those of nondepressives, suggesting that the differences between groups are differences in performance rather than competence. Further, these differences are accentuated in group interaction and by conditions of "strangeness and ambiguity" (Libet & Lewinsohn, 1973).

The depressed subjects' lower levels of social behaviors and self-reported infrequency and discomfort in "social initiation" activities may reflect depressed individuals' social anxiety. Indeed, Sacco and Hokanson (1978) found that depressed subjects scored higher on measures of social anxiety than did nondepressed subjects. Individuals high in social anxiety tend to be sensitive to public scrutiny (e.g., Watson & Friend, 1976) and may adopt a protective self-presentation style (Arkin, 1981). Once involved in interaction,

> individuals high in social anxiety appear unwilling to initiate and structure conversation; they speak a smaller percentage of the time, contribute more to conversational dysfluencies, and tend not to interpret. . . . This reticence syndrome seems somewhat less prominent in highly structured situations, however, suggesting that anxious individuals who are more certain about what is expected of them are more inclined to be interactive in some manner. (Arkin, p. 327)

The procedure used by the researchers (Libet & Lewinsohn, 1973; Youngren & Lewinsohn, 1980), group and dyadic interaction in a lab, may have increased depressed subjects' social anxiety by emphasizing explicitly that social behaviors were of primary interest. Lower levels of social interaction would reduce the risk of further performance demands and negative social evaluations. The depressives' social reticence, then, may be one manifestation of their protective self-presentation style. The depressives' possibly strategic social reticence may also serve as a stalling technique, allowing the depressed individual to gain more information (including criteria of evaluation) about the social interaction. As the depressive becomes more certain of what is expected, behavior becomes less tentative. Although this description of depressives' social interaction is speculative, it is consistent with the results of the Libet and Lewinsohn (1973) study in which social skill deficits, which are identified in early sessions of the self-study groups, were attenuated in later groups.

Depressive Self-Presentation and the Reactions of Others

One purpose of the present chapter has been to elaborate the role of interpersonal processes in depression. We have argued and reviewed evidence consistent with the notion that depressive behaviors and symptom displays may represent strategic attempts to control the responses of those with whom the depressed interact. Specifically, the depressed individual has been characterized in this chapter as having a conservative orientation toward interaction. It has been argued that the depressive's self-doubt and shaky self-confidence may lead him or her to adopt a protective self-presentation style across a variety of interaction settings. The particular manifestation of that style may vary depending upon particular social contextual variables; however, the underlying motive is likely to be avoidance of future performance demands and potential further losses in esteem. Indeed, we have argued that the depressive may accept or even engender short-term disapproval in an attempt to terminate or withdraw from current and avoid future performance obligations.

This self-presentational model of depression, while consistent with the data, is admittedly post hoc. Direct tests of it must, of course, await further research. However, it may be useful at this point to examine how others respond to the depressive. Do they respond in a way that would be consistent with the proposed depressive self-presentation style? In this section, studies that have evaluated the reactions of others to depressed individuals are reviewed. Much of this research was stimulated by Coyne's (1976b) interpersonal model of depression.

In a study (Coyne, 1976a) presumably concerned with the process of acquaintanceship, college student subjects engaged in 20-minute telephone conversations with a depressed patient, a nondepressed patient, or a normal control. The behavioral and content analyses of the conversations did not differentiate among three target groups. The results indicated, however, that the college student subjects were more depressed, anxious, and hostile following interactions with depressed patients than following interactions with nondepressed patients or normal controls. In addition, subjects were more rejecting of depressed patients.

Hammen and Peters (1978) also evaluated the interpersonal consequences of depressed behaviors. These investigators asked college students to enact a depressed or nondepressed role during a telephone conversation with a nondepressed peer. Hammen and Peters found that interaction with "depressed" persons elicited more feelings of depression in the listener than did interactions with nondepressed persons. In addition, "depressed" subjects were more strongly rejected than were "nondepressed" subjects.

Howes and Hokanson (1979) evaluated the conversational content of a social encounter between college student subjects and a confederate enacting the role of a normal, a physically ill, or a depressed person. Results indicated that subjects responded to the "depressed" confederate with a distinct conversational pattern. Subjects gave direct support equivalent to that given to the "physically ill" confederate, but they also made more direct negative comments and exhibited higher levels of silence.

The results of the studies reviewed above provide consistent evidence that the responses of others to depressed individuals' social behaviors are negative and rejecting. These findings are in accord with the notion that the depressive self-presentation style may result in short-term disapproval. The critical question, however, is whether the presumably strategic behaviors of depressed individuals are effective in achieving the longer term goals of release from current and/or future performance demands. A recent study by Strack and Coyne (1983) is pertinent. These investigators asked pairs of college students (depressed-nondepressed, nondepressed-nondepressed) to engage in 15-minute conversations in order to become acquainted. Following the interaction, subject mood and willingness to interact under varying conditions were measured. Subjects also completed a questionnaire indicating their perception of the other person that they were told would be either "confidential" or "shared" with the other participant.

The results indicated that subjects who interacted with a depressed partner were more depressed, anxious, and hostile, and less willing to interact further. In the shared feedback condition, both depressed and nondepressed subjects indicated that they were less honest on the perceptions questionnaire than were subjects in the confidential condition. These results provide further evidence that social behaviors associated with depression elicit negative social responses from others. More importantly, they also provide some evidence for the notion that such behaviors may be effective in avoiding future performance demands. Clearly more research regarding the possible long-term effectiveness of the proposed depressive self-presentation style is needed.

Summary and Conclusions

The purpose of the present paper was to examine the empirical support for the cognitive (Abramson et al., 1978; Beck, 1967) and interpersonal (Lewinsohn, 1974) models of depression with particular emphasis on the evidence for depressive self-presentation. It has been argued that depressed individuals attempt to control the responses of others by the strategic display of symptoms. More specifically, evidence was presented that depressive "cognitive distortions" (e.g., recall of positive reinforcement, expectations for success) are influenced by the presence of others. Such influence is not accounted for by the cognitive theories but is consistent with a self-presentational formulation of depression.

It has been argued with some supporting data that depressive self-presentation may be generally self-protective rather than self-enhancing, motivated primarily by concerns for avoiding long-term performance demands. Consequently, depressive behaviors often may reflect modesty, caution, and even self-deprecation when nondepressive behaviors may reflect self-enhancement.

Depressed individuals have been described as perceiving the environment in a distorted way and as being ineffective in interacting with the environment. The research reviewed in this paper suggests that depressives may be quite active in directing and controlling the environment and individuals with whom they interact. Moreover, their efforts appear to be effective. While the social behaviors of depressives often engender short-term disapproval, there is some evidence to suggest that they may allow depressives to escape from further performance demands.

It has been argued in this paper that depressives exhibit a protective self-presentational style. However, it is difficult to determine to what extent such self-presentation is related to depression, anxiety, or psychopathology in general, since these variables are conceptually and empirically linked. Indeed, the notion of a protective self-presentation style originally was proposed as an explanation for the "cost oriented" social behaviors of high socially anxious individuals (Arkin et al., 1980). We have argued, however, that, while the antecedents of a protective self-presentation style (e.g., shaky self-confidence and self-doubts) may be similar for depressed and socially anxious individuals, their presentational goals may differ. That is, depressives may be more interested in the avoidance of future performance demands even if to do so means that they must accept or even engender short-term disapproval. Socially anxious individuals presumably have as their goal the avoidance of disapproval (Arkin, 1981). Clearly, further research is needed to clarify how depressive self-presentation differs from the self-presentation of other anxious or psychologically disturbed individuals.

The empirical evidence reviewed in this paper was taken from studies involving individuals classified as depressed by a wide variety of standards. Intuitively, one would expect there to be some fundamental differences between an experimental confederate's role enactment of depression, the mild depression of a college student, and the depression exhibited by the clinically depressed individual. For example, a confederate's role enactment may reflect depressive behaviors that have been salient and perhaps troublesome to the confederate or the experimenter. However, research results have shown that actual behavioral differences, when obtained at all, are quite subtle (Youngren & Lewinsohn, 1980). Future research will be necessary to identify in what ways, if any, the self-presentations of mildly and clinically depressed individuals differ. The issue of whether normal sadness and clinically depressed aspect differ qualitatively and quantitatively is a matter of dispute (Beck, 1967; Buchwald, Coyne, & Cole, 1978). Given the diversity of populations of depressive studies, it is remarkable that experimental results provide consistent results regarding depressive cognitions, social behaviors, and elicited reactions.

Conclusion

It is the thesis of this paper that any theoretical model of depression may be incomplete if it excludes consideration of self-presentation. That is not to say that depression and depressive symptoms are simply manipulative, artifactual displays. Such a position would suggest that depression is little more than malingering, an assertion that would be indefensible. However, recognition of the important role of social contextual variables in depression allows us to interpret depressive symptoms as strategic communications. The behavioral changes associated with depression—crying, sadness, reporting and showing anergia—are shared cultural meaning and, consequently, may be interpreted as a form of symbolic communication. To the extent that depressives use these symbolic behaviors to control and direct interpersonal processes, the symptoms represent strategic self-presentations.

References

Abramson, L.Y., Seligman, M.E.P., & Teasdale, J.D. (1978). Learned helplessness in humans: Critique and reformulation. *Journal of Abnormal Psychology, 87*, 49–74.

Akiskal, H.S., & McKinney, W.T. (1975). Overview of recent research in depression. *Archives of General Psychiatry, 32*, 285–305.

Alloy, L.B., & Abramson, L.Y. (1981). Induced mood and the illusion of control. *Journal of Personality and Social Psychology, 41*, 1129–1140.

Alloy, L.B., & Abramson, L.Y. (1982). Learned helplessness, depression, and the illusion of control *Journal of Personality and Social Psychology, 42*(6), 1114–1126.

Arkin, R.M. (1981). Self-presentation styles. In J.T. Tedeschi (Ed.), *Impression management theory and social psychological research*. New York: Academic Press.

Arkin, R.M., Appelman, A.J., & Burger J.M. (1980). Social anxiety, self-presentation, and the self-serving bias in causal attribution. *Journal of Personality and Social Psychology, 38*(1), 23–35.

Baumeister, R.F. (1982). A self-presentational view of social phenomena. *Psychological Bulletin, 91*(1), 3–26.

Beck, A.T. (1967). *Depression: Clinical, experimental and theoretical aspects*. New York: Hoeber.

Beck, A.T. (1974). The development of depression: A cognitive model. In R.J. Friedman & M.M. Katz (Ed.), *The psychology of depression*. Washington, DC: V.H. Winston.

Beck, A.T., & Greenberg, R.L. (1974). Cognitive therapy with depressed women. In V. Franks & V. Burtle (Eds.), *Women in therapy*. New York: Basic Books.

Blaney, P.H. (1977). Contemporary theories of depression: Critique and comparison. *Journal of Abnormal Psychology, 86*, 203–223.

Bonime, W. (1960). Depression as a practice. *Comprehensive Psychiatry, 1*, 194–201.

Bonime, W. (1966). The psychodynamics of neurotic depression. In S. Arieti (Ed.), *American handbook of psychiatry* (Vol. 3). New York: Basic Books.

Braginsky, B., Braginsky, D., & Ring, K. (1969). *Methods of madness: The mental hospital as a last resort*. New York: Holt, Rinehart & Winston.

Buchwald, A.M., Coyne, J.C., & Cole, C.S. (1978). A critical evaluation of the learned help-lessness model of depression. *Journal of Abnormal Psychology, 87*, 180–193.

Coates, D., & Wortman, C. (1980). Depression maintenance and interpersonal control. In A. Baum & J. Singer (Eds.), *Advances in environmental psychology* (Vol. 2). Hillsdale, NJ: Erlbaum.

Cohen, M.B. (1954). An intensive study of twelve cases of manic-depressive psychosis. *Psychiatry, 17*, 103–137.

Coyne, J.C. (1976a). Depression and the response of others. *Journal of Abnormal Psychology, 85*, 186–193.

Coyne, J.C. (1976b). Toward an interactional description of depression. *Psychiatry, 39*, 28–40.

Coyne, J.C., & Gotlib, I.H. (1983). The role of cognition in depression: A critical appraisal. *Journal of Personality and Social Psychology, 94*, 472–505.

DeMonbreun, B.G., & Craighead, W.E. (1977). Distortion of perception and recall of positive and neutral feedback in depression. *Cognitive Therapy and Research, 1*(4), 311–329.

Dweck, C.S., & Gilliard, D. (1975). Expectancy statements as determinants of reactions to failure. *Journal of Personality and Social Psychology, 32*, 1077–1084.

Eastman, C. (1976). Behavioral formulations of depression. *Psychological Review, 83*, 277–281.

Fenichel, O. (1945). *The psychoanalytic theory of neurosis*. London: Norton.

Festinger, L.A. (1957). *A theory of cognitive dissonance.* Stanford, CA: Stanford University Press.

Forrest, M.S., & Hokanson, J.E. (1975). Depression and autonomic arousal reduction accompanying self-punitive behavior. *Journal of Abnormal Psychology, 84,* 346–357.

Freud, S. (1957). Mourning and melancholia. In J. Strachey (Ed.), *The standard edition of the complete psychological works of Sigmund Freud* (Vol. 14). London: Hogarth Press. (Original work published 1923).

Garber, J., & Hollon, S.D. (1980). Universal vs. personal helplessness. *Journal of Abnormal Psychology, 89*(1), 56–66.

Goffman, E. (1963). *Stigma: Notes on the management of spoiled identity.* Englewood Cliffs, NJ: Prentice-Hall.

Gong-Guy, E., & Hammen, C. (1980). Causal perceptions of stressful events in depressed and nondepressed outpatients. *Journal of Abnormal Psychology, 89*(5), 662–669.

Hammen, C., & Glass, D.R. (1975). Depression, activity and evaluation of reinforcement. *Journal of Abnormal Psychology, 84*(6), 718–721.

Hammen, C. & Mayol, A. (1982). Depression and cognitive characteristics of stressful life-events types. *Journal of Abnormal Psychology, 91*(3), 165–174.

Hammen, C., & Peters, S. (1978). Interpersonal consequences of depression: Response to men and women enacting a depressed role. *Journal of Abnormal Psychology, 87*(1), 322–332.

Howes, M.J., & Hokanson, J.E. (1978). Conversational and social responses to depressive interpersonal behavior. *Journal of Abnormal Psychology, 88*(6), 625–634.

Janoff-Bulman, R. (1979). Characterological versus behavioral self-blame. *Journal of Personality and Social Psychology, 37*(10), 1798–1809.

Jones, E.E., & Berglas, S. (1978). Control of attributions about the self through self-handicapping strategies: The appeal of alcohol and the role of underachievement. *Personality and Social Psychology Bulletin, 4,* 200–206.

Jones, E.E., & Pittman, T.S. (1982). Toward a general theory of strategic self-presentation. In J. Suls (Ed.), *Psychological perspectives on the self* (Vol. 1). Hillsdale, NJ: Erlbaum.

Kelley, H.H., & Michela, J.L. (1980). Attribution theory and research. *Annual Review of Psychology, 31,* 457–501.

Kuiper, N.A. (1978). Depression and causal attributions for success and failure. *Journal of Personality and Social Psychology, 36,* 236–246.

Lewinsohn, P.M. (1974). A behavioral approach to depression. In R.C. Friedman & M.M. Katz (Eds.), *The psychology of depression.* Washington, DC: V.H. Winston.

Lewinsohn, P.M. (1975). Engagement in pleasant activities and depression level. *Journal of Abnormal Psychology, 84,* 729–731.

Lewinsohn, P.M. & Libet, J.M. (1972). Pleasant events, activity schedules, and depression. Journal of Abnormal Psychology, *79,* 291–295.

Lewinsohn, P.M., Lobitz, W.C. & Wilson, S. (1973). Sensitivity of depressed individuals to aversive stimuli. *Journal of Abnormal Psychology, 81*(3), 259–263.

Libet, J.M., & Lewinsohn, P.M. (1973). Concept of social skill with special reference to the behavior of depressed persons. *Journal of Consulting and Clinical Psychology, 40*(2), 304–312.

Lobitz, W.C., & Post, R.D. (1979). Parameters of self-reinforcement in depression. *Journal of Abnormal Psychology, 88,* 33–41.

Loeb, A., Beck, A.T., & Diggory, J. (1971). Differential effects of success and failure on depressed and nondepressed patients. *Journal of Nervous and Mental Disorders, 152,* 106–114.

MacPhillamy, D.J., & Lewinsohn, P.M. (1974). Depression as a function of levels of desired and obtained pleasure. *Journal of Abnormal Psychology, 83*(6), 651–657.

McPartland, T.S., & Hornstra, R.K. (1964). The depressive datum. *Comprehensive Psychiatry, 5,* 253–261.

Miller, D.T., & Ross, M. (1975). Self-serving biases in the attribution of causality: Fact or fiction? *Psychological Bulletin, 82,* 213–225.

Nelson, R.E., & Craighead, W.E. (1977). Selective recall of positive and negative feedback, self-control behaviors, and depression. *Journal of Abnormal Psychology, 86*, 379–388.

Peterson, C., Schwartz, S.M., & Seligman, M.E.P. (1981). Self-blame and depressive symptoms. *Journal of Personality and Social Psychology, 41*(2), 253–259.

Rizley, R.C. (1978). Depression and distortion in the attribution of causality. *Journal of Abnormal Psychology, 87*, 32–48.

Rosenberg, M.J. (1969). The conditions and consequences of evaluation apprehension. In R. Rosenthal & R.L. Rosnow (Eds.), *Artifiact in behavior research*. New York: Academic Press.

Rozensky, R.H., Rehm, L.P., Pry, G., & Roth, D. (1977). Depression and self-reinforcement behavior in hospitalized patients. *Journal of Behavior Therapy and Experimental Psychiatry, 8*, 31–34.

Sacco, W.P., & Hokanson, J.E. (1978). Expectations of success and anagram performance of depressives in a public and private setting. *Journal of Personality and Abnormal Psychology, 87*, 122–130.

Sacco, W.P., & Hokanson, J.E. (1982). Depression and self-reinforcement in a public and private setting. *Journal of Personality and Social Psychology, 42*(2), 377–385.

Schlenker, B.R. (1980). *Impression management: The self-concept, social identity, and interpersonal relations*. Belmont, CA: Brooks/Cole.

Schopler, J., & Layton, B. (1972). Determinants of the self-attribution of having influenced another person. *Journal of Personality and Social Psychology, 22*, 326–332.

Schopler, J., & Layton, B. (1973). *Attributions of interpersonal power and influence*. New York: General Learning Press.

Schwartz, S.H. (1972). Normative influences on altruism. In L. Berkowitz (Ed.), *Advances in experimental social psychology* (Vol. 6). New York: Academic Press.

Seligman, M.E.P. (1975a). Depression and learned helplessness. In R.J. Friedman & M.M. Katz (Eds.), *The psychology of depression*. New York: Wiley.

Seligman, M.E.P. (1975b). *Helplessness: On depression, development, and death*. San Francisco: Freeman.

Seligman, M. E. P., Abramson, L. Y., Semmel, A., & Von Baeyer, C. (1979). Depressive attributional style. *Journal of Abnormal Psychology, 88*, 242–247.

Snyder, M. L., Stephan, W. G., & Rosenfield, D. (1978). Attributional egotism. In J. H. Harvey, W. Ickes, & R. F. Kidd (Eds.), *New directions in attribution research* (Vol. 2). Hillsdale, NJ: Erlbaum.

Strack, S., & Coyne, J. C. (1983). Social confirmation of dysphoria: Shared and private reactions to depression. *Journal of Personality and Social Psychology, 44*(4), 798–806.

Sullivan, H. S. (1953). *The interpersonal theory of psychiatry*. New York: Norton.

Teevan & McGhee (1972). Childhood development of fear of failure motivation. *Journal of Personality and Social Psychology, 21*, 345–348.

Watson, D., & Friend, R. (1969). Measurement of social evaluation anxiety. *Journal of Clinical and Counseling Psychology, 33*, 448–457.

Weary Bradley, G. (1978). Self-serving biases in the attribution process: A reexamination of the fact or fiction question. *Journal of Personality and Social Psychology, 36*(1), 36–71.

Weary, G., & Arkin, R. M. (1981). Attributional self-presentation. In J. H. Harvey, W. J. Ickes, & R. F. Kidd (Eds.), *New directions in attribution research*. Hillsdale, NJ: Erlbaum.

Weinstein, E. (1968). The development of interpersonal competence. In D. Goslin (Ed.), *Handbook of Socialization Theory and Research*. Chicago: Rand McNally.

Wollert, R. W. (1977). *The expectancy confidence hypothesis*. Unpublished doctoral dissertation, Indiana University.

Youngren, M. A., & Lewinsohn, P. M. (1980). The functional relation between depression and problematic interpersonal behavior. *Journal of Abnormal Psychology, 89*(3), 333–341.

Zimbardo, P. G. (1977). *Shyness: What it is, what to do about it*. New York: Jove.

Zuckerman, M. (1979). Attribution of success and failure revisited or: The motivational bias is alive and well in attribution theory. *Journal of Personality, 47*, 245–287.

Chapter 12
Epilogue: The Next Decade of Self-Presentation Research

Roy F. Baumeister

I began this book by calling for more ideas. Now it is time to call for more data. The contributors to this book have done their job. After reading these chapters, one cannot dismiss self-presentation as a minor or trivial matter of just trying to look good now and then. Self-presentation emerges from these pages as a pervasive, fundamental, and important part of modern life, and no aspect or view of the self can remain unaffected by self-presentation. These chapters have explored the various relations of self-presentation to self-concepts, to personal fulfillment and achievement, to personality traits and interpersonal styles, to cognitive styles and patterns, to self-protection, to self-completion, to self-regulation, to self-deception, and more. The ideas are here. To conclude, then, it is worth taking a moment to ask: What are some of the pressing issues and questions for empirical research?

Each of the chapters here has offered several testable ideas, and I do not intend to list them all. My intent is to list the major themes in research directions that were suggested by several chapters, for it is likely that these will be the dominant issues in self-presentation research in the next decade or two.

Effects of Self-Presentation on the Inner Self

Expressive, public behavior can have strong residual effects on the inner selves (both self-concept and actual self), but there is much that we do not know about these effects. When and how is self-presentational behavior internalized? Many of the chapters in this volume commented on the article by Jones, Rhodewalt, Berglas, and Skelton[1] showing effects of induced self-presentation on private self-esteem. This article was clearly a landmark event in the history of self-presentation research. But

---

[1]Jones, E. E., Rhodewalt, F., Berglas, S., & Skelton, J. A. (1981). Effects of strategic self-presentation on subsequent self-esteem. *Journal of Personality and Social Psychology, 41,* 407–421.

although it was undeniably an important and intriguing paper, it was hardly the final word. It reported three experiments, none of which turned out as predicted; its theory was heavily post hoc, with some peculiar twists and turns; its measure of self-esteem was an idiosyncratic, unknown one rather than a standard, validated one, so there is even room for doubt about what was being measured. That an article with so many loose ends should generate such interest attests to the importance of the topic and the urgent need for more studies like it.

Several directions are clearly indicated for further study of how public behavior affects the private self. Rhodewalt lists a series of personality traits that should affect the "carry-over" (internalization) effect, and these promise to shed light on the processes and factors involved in internalization. What kinds of people, in other words, internalize their self-presentational behavior more, and what traits make someone immune to that effect? Schlenker proposes that a crucial mediator of internalization is perceived representativeness. That is, the person makes some judgment about how well each act of self-presentation represents his or her true nature, and these judgments determine the course of internalization.

Even more provocative is the suggestion by Arkin and Baumgardner that internalization can proceed by different routes (personal and social). Thus, there may be multiple processes by which self-presentation can alter the private self. Finally, Tedeschi proposes that emotional arousal and self-perceived responsibility play important roles in determining whether internalization occurs. Are these indeed powerful causes and, if so, are they necessary or sufficient ones?

Audiences and Relationships

Most past research has studied how people present themselves to people they are meeting for the first time. Theories of self-presentation are typically vague about who exactly the audience is. Does it make a difference? How much does self-presentation vary according to the type of audience and self-presenter's relationship to that audience?

Tedeschi argues forcefully that there are major differences between intimate and impersonal audiences, even suggesting that our use of the terms "public" and "private" should be revised in light of that distinction. Given social psychology's growing interest in intimate interactions within long-term relationships, it seems natural and useful to explore different patterns and strategies of self-presentation in such contexts. Do people use the same self-presentational ploys with intimates as they do with strangers? Are their motives similar? And, assuming there are major differences, how are these reflected in behavior?

Consideration of inner audiences and reference groups is another issue that has received little empirical attention. Schlenker proposes that self-presentations can be geared toward such audiences. Arkin and Baumgardner discuss private rehearsal for public interactions and performances. Greenberg, Pyszczynski, and Solomon go even further, suggesting that many public interactions are aimed at the private or inner audience despite the presence of a living, breathing, external audience. We need a methodology to study inner or internalized audiences. Probably the idea of inner audiences should replace the uncertain concept of "self-presentation to oneself," some of the fallacies of which have been described here by Hogan and Briggs and by Tedeschi.

Before devoting too much energy to the study of the effects of different audiences however, it is valuable to recall the evidence from Gollwitzer's chapter. He has studied self-presentation aimed at claiming identities to which the individual aspires and is committed. In such cases, the audience seems to make surprisingly little difference. When claiming a desired identity, it is vitally important that *someone* witness, but it does not matter much who that is. This interchangeability of audiences is counterintuitive. How much of self-presentation is that way (i.e., willing to accept audiences interchangeably)?

Cognition and Self-Presentation

I observed in the Preface to this book that self-presentation has been primarily a motivational idea. But that does not mean that cognition is irrelevant. Nowadays we know so much more about cognition than social psychology knew a decade ago—it would be a waste not to apply some of this knowledge to self-presentation.

Whitehead and Smith report evidence that different cognitive processes operate in public versus private situations. People may simply think differently when alone versus when in the presence of others. Putting self-presentation in that perspective opens up a vast realm of research possibilities. Many of the patterns and processes demonstrated in recent research on social cognition deserve to be checked for responsiveness to self-presentational factors. The goal is not to provide alternative explanations for social cognition effects, but rather to see how self-presentation changes the individual's thought processes. The cognitive impact of self-presentation affects more than how the self thinks about the self; self-presentation may alter how the self perceives and understands the social world.

Once we know more about differences in information processing in public versus private settings, this knowledge can be applied to other problems. To what extent do such differences account for the cognitive effects of depression, as reinterpreted by Hill, Weary, and Williams? And do they explain the seeming paradox cited by Greenberg, Pyszczynski, and Solomon that the private self is more heavily involved in public situations than in private ones?

Consistency between public and private selves may also be mediated by cognitive processes. Tesser and Moore suggest that public self and private self will tend to converge due to the pressures of cognitive convenience. Are honesty and integrity heuristic strategies for simplifying the mind's job? Baumeister and Tice, on the other hand, suggest that inconsistencies and contradictions spread from the ideal self to the public and private selves. People may choose their personal ideals and goals without requiring strict logical consistency or even compatibility. They may only discover latent contradictions when attempting to be (or to appear to be) what they want to be.

Convergence of Public and Private Selves

All the effort that has gone into distinguishing between the public and private selves should not blind us to their similarities. Once source of convergence between public and private selves is the internalization of self-presentation (such as the carry-over effect), which I have already discussed. Another is the involvement of the private self in public events, as described by Greenberg, Pyszczynski, and Solomon (and in a different way by Whitehead and Smith).

Above and beyond those factors, however, there may be powerful additional reasons for the similarities between public and private selves. Tesser and Moore show how the public self and private self often have the same goals, the same motives, and hence essentially the same processes. Baumeister and Tice go a step further and argue that even when the processes differ, the results may be the same—hence the capacity of the public self to substitute for the private self.

Control

One of the oldest ideas in self-presentation is that it is rooted in efforts to gain control. In this book, we have seen self-presentation portrayed as a vital part of a program to control one's existential terror (Greenberg, Pyszczynski, and Solomon), to control one's status and popularity in one's social group (Hogan and Briggs), to control one's symbolically complete attainment of identity (Gollwitzer), and more.

Several chapters, however, were centrally concerned with issues of control, and these take self-presentation beyond the mere fact of desiring and exerting control. Foremost among these is Arkin and Baumgardner's analysis of self-presentation according to the theory of primary and secondary control. In other words, different patterns of control can guide self-presentation in different contexts. Baumeister and Tice proposed that self-presentation should be considered as a form of behavioral self-control or self-regulation. Hill, Weary, and Williams suggest that self-presentational patterns that characterize depression are based on certain strategies for controlling and manipulating others—in a sense, depressive self-presentation is a means of exerting a rational but ultimately self-destructive control over one's interactions.

Thus, the idea that self-presentation is related to control may be old, but there are new implications and distinctions to be studied. Perhaps it is time to look at self-presentation in the context of power relationships, as a way of learning about its multiple functions in interpersonal control.

Multiple Forms of Self-Presentation

Even the most casual perusal of this book is sufficient to convince the reader that there are multiple varieties of self-presentation. The patterns and the effects of self-presentation are not homogeneous, uniform, or ubiquitous. Therefore, a last, broad question is this: What factors determine which of the various approaches, strategies, and aftereffects of self-presentation will prevail?

One approach to answering this last question was provided in Schlenker's chapter, in which he described the trade-off between accuracy and enhancement (positivity) of self-presentation. In his view, self-presentation is mainly guided and constrained by the two motives of beneficiality and believability. Another approach to the multiplicity of self-presentational patterns is to consider individual differences, such as Rhodewalt's discussion of traits that bear on the carry-over effect, or Hogan and Briggs' discussion of multiple self-images. A vitally important issue is to understand the slippery relationship(s) between self-presentation and self-esteem, including depression. Indeed, over half the chapters in this book addressed that relationship in one way or another.

To some extent, the multiplicity of self-presentation is an issue implicit in several of the themes already discussed, such as those of different audiences or different forms of control. Rather than reiterating these, I shall offer only the general observation implied in all this. Until now, researchers have tended to think of self-presentation as one factor that was either present in a given situation or absent from it. In the future, however, it is necessary to think carefully in terms of the multiple varieties of self-presentation.

Conclusion

If we have data answering all these questions a decade from now, it will have been a remarkable decade! It does seem likely, however, that the immediate future of self-presentation research will include collecting some data on each issue. These are the issues that the contributors to this volume have identified as the most pressing and promising ones. To work, then . . .

Author Index

Subject Index

Springer Series in Social Psychology

Attention and Self-Regulation: A Control-Theory Approach to Human Behavior
Charles S. Carver/Michael F. Scheier

Gender and Nonverbal Behavior
Clara Mayo/Nancy M. Henley (Editors)

Personality, Roles, and Social Behavior
William Ickes/Eric S. Knowles (Editors)

Toward Transformation in Social Knowledge
Kenneth J. Gergen

The Ethics of Social Research: Surveys and Experiments
Joan E. Sieber (Editor)

The Ethics of Social Research: Fieldwork, Regulation, and Publication
Joan E. Sieber (Editor)

Anger and Aggression: An Essay on Emotion
James R. Averill

The Social Psychology of Creativity
Teresa M. Amabile

Sports Violence
Jeffrey H. Goldstein (Editor)

Nonverbal Behavior: A Functional Perspective
Miles L. Patterson

Basic Group Processes
Paul B. Paulus (Editor)

Attitudinal Judgment
J. Richard Eiser (Editor)

Social Psychology of Aggression: From Individual Behavior to Social Interaction
Amélie Mummendey (Editor)

Directions in Soviet Social Psychology
Lloyd H. Strickland (Editor)

Sociophysiology
William M. Waid (Editor)

Compatible and Incompatible Relationships
William Ickes (Editor)

Facet Theory: Approaches to Social Research
David Canter (Editor)

Action Control: From Cognition to Behavior
Julius Kuhl/Jürgen Beckmann (Editors)

Springer Series in Social Psychology